CLASSICS IN URBAN HISTORY

Michael H. Ebner, Editor

THE FRAGMENTED METROPOLIS

Books by Robert M. Fogelson

America's Armories: Architecture, Society, and Public Order (1989)
Pensions: The Hidden Costs of Public Safety (1984)
Big-City Police (1977)
Violence as Protest: A Study of Riots and Ghettos (1971)
The Fragmented Metropolis: Los Angeles, 1850-1930 (1967)

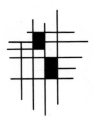

THE FRAGMENTED METROPOLIS

LOS ANGELES, 1850–1930

by Robert M. Fogelson

Foreword by Robert Fishman

UNIVERSITY OF CALIFORNIA PRESS

BERKELEY · LOS ANGELES · LONDON

University of California Press
Berkeley and Los Angeles, California

University of California Press, Ltd.
London, England
First Paperback Printing 1993

Library of Congress Cataloging-in-Publication Data

Fogelson, Robert M.
   The fragmented metropolis : Los Angeles, 1850-1930 / by
Robert M. Fogelson.
     p.   cm. — (Classics in urban history)
   Originally published: Cambridge : Harvard University Press,
1967. With new introd.
   Includes bibliographical references and index.
   ISBN 0-520-08230-3 (alk. paper)
   1. Los Angeles (Calif.)—History.   I. Title.   II. Series.
F869.L857F64   1993
979.4'94—dc20   92-29078
                                     CIP

To my mother and my father

CONTENTS

CONTENTS

ILLUSTRATIONS AND CREDITS

MAPS AND CREDITS

TABLES

CHARTS

FOREWORD

More than twenty-five years after its original publication, this book remains the definitive account of what is perhaps the most fascinating single story in American urban history: the rise of Los Angeles.

Like every other major American city, Los Angeles rose from humble origins to the scale and status of a metropolis; but, as the British traveler Morris Markey observed in 1932 in a quotation that Robert M. Fogelson uses as the epigraph for Part One of this book: in Los Angeles alone, "there is no plausible answer to the question, 'Why did a town spring up here and why has it grown so big?'" Fogelson's achievement is precisely that he answers this uniquely difficult question.

The other great American cities all possessed some crucial locational advantage, usually a natural port with extensive river connections that immediately made the city the focus of a vast region. New York, for example, rose in the midst of one of the world's best harbors and possessed in the Hudson River a great natural highway into a fertile hinterland.

By contrast, Los Angeles was founded by the Spanish in 1781 in the middle of the empty, semi-arid coastal plain; the isolated pueblo depended on an unnavigable river whose irregular flow meant an alternation of droughts and floods; the Pacific shoreline some fifteen miles away offered no suitable harbor sites, certainly nothing comparable to San Diego's fine harbor. Even after California had been annexed by the United States in 1848, Los Angeles remained a quiet agricultural town whose most important product was half-starved cattle from the surrounding ranches driven north for sale to the booming gold-rush city of San Francisco.

Yet from these unpromising beginnings there arose a city that would dominate first southern California and then the American Southwest.

The nineteenth-century city is now lost in the midst of a massive metropolitan region of more than fourteen million people that is surpassed in population in the United States only by the New York region. The Los Angeles region is also a close second to New York in manufacturing output, and its port ranks first in the nation.[1]

Just as importantly, Los Angeles has come to define a lifestyle and an ideal of prosperity which has profoundly shaped not only the American imagination but that of the whole world. Michael Arlen has recounted visiting a remote village in Armenia where he was told, "Here all the young people want to go to Los Angeles. They call it 'Los.' 'When I get to Los,' they say, 'I will have a house and a red BMW.' "[2] Indeed, in the 1980s Los Angeles was the leading destination for immigrants to the United States, 25 percent of whom settled there, more than double the number who headed for New York.[3] In David Rieff's provocative account, Los Angeles is now the "capital of the Third World."[4]

Although *The Fragmented Metropolis* stops in 1930, well before Los Angeles's present eminence, the book identifies the crucial forces that took Los Angeles from a forgotten pueblo to a global city. As in the biography of an individual, an "urban biography" tends to be most interesting when dealing with the early years, the years when identity is established and strategies for ultimate success are first attempted. Among American urban biographies, this is the ultimate "rags-to-riches" story.

Fogelson's answer to the question "Why Los Angeles?" takes the form of a detailed and meticulously researched narrative that is alert to all the unexpected twists and turns in the history of the city. Nevertheless, two major themes emerge. In his introduction Fogelson calls the first theme "the emergence of a populous, urbanized, and industrialized settlement." The key to this theme, I believe, lies in the title to Chapter 2: "Private Enterprise, Public Authority, and Urban Expansion."

Precisely because Los Angeles lacked natural advantages and a dominant industry, its leaders realized that they would have to create these attributes themselves. Where other municipalities provided facilities in response to population growth and industrial expansion, the Los Angeles elite very early realized that their real business was growth itself. That is, they must invest to provide the essential infrastructure that the city lacked—water, power, a port, transportation—and then use this infrastructure to lure the new population and businesses which alone could justify the investments.

Such investments were too large and too risky to be accomplished by private enterprise alone. The Los Angeles elite thus became experts in the use of public authority—especially the city's borrowing power—to fund urban expansion. Moreover, they formed key alliances at the federal level to gain the facilities (rail links, an artificial port) they could not create for themselves. The result was a strange policy schizophrenia. The Los Angeles elite was absolutely dedicated to free enterprise— it abhorred trade unions and anything "socialistic"—yet it was surprisingly flexible and creative in using big government or even municipal ownership in the pursuit of an urban environment that maximized growth and private profit.

Fogelson is very much aware of these contradictions, and he patiently unravels the tangled links of public and private entrepreneurship. His tone, however, is detached and scholarly—the opposite of that of the muckrakers who have seen conspiracies and power elites as central to the growth of the city. This is especially evident in Fogelson's brief and unsensational treatment of perhaps the most legendary use of public authority for growth and private profit, the Owens Valley Aqueduct project (completed 1913).

The more critical elements of Fogelson's interpretation enter the book through his second theme: fragmentation. Fogelson means many things by this controlling metaphor that gives the book its title, but all revolve around an essential paradox of the city. Although its growth required the intensive and highly effective use of public power, the metropolis that emerged was strangely bereft of any unifying civic life. Los Angeles was fragmented politically, socially, and culturally. The resulting tension between the theme of growth and the theme of fragmentation gives Fogelson's narrative its drive and complexity.

Fragmentation means first the fact that the metropolis never evolved into a single political unit; instead, it split between city and suburbs, and between city and county. More importantly, the city divided between its dominant white majority—"native Americans" as Fogelson calls them—and its minorities.

The treatment of minorities is perhaps the most original aspect of the book. Los Angeles never received the tide of European immigrants that settled in Eastern and Midwestern cities; hence the perception that it was an "Anglo-Saxon" city largely populated by affluent migrants from the Midwest. But, as Fogelson shows, Los Angeles had a significant percentage of blacks, Hispanics, and Asians by 1930. These groups, however, confronted a white majority that regarded itself as homogeneously "American." Thus, unlike Eastern cities with their complex mosaic of ethnic politics, Los Angeles offered a far sharper divide between the white majority and an excluded and segregated minority population.

Published only two years after the Watts riots of 1965, *The Fragmented Metropolis* emphasizes that the slums and racial conflicts of the 1960s were not, as many conservative Angelenos believed, new problems in an essentially harmonious city. Fogelson argues that segregation of minorities had been built into the structure of the city for almost a century. Moreover, even the "minorities" were fragmented in Los Angeles, with black, Hispanic, Chinese, and Japanese communities isolated from and suspicious of each other. "Exploited economically, separated residentially, isolated socially, and ignored politically," Fogelson concludes, "these people remained entirely outside the Los Angeles community between 1885 and 1930."

Los Angeles fragmented not only socially and politically; it also fragmented spatially. Fogelson is concerned to answer not only the question "Why did Los Angeles grow?" but also the question "Why did its growth take a more dispersed form than in any other American city?" The answers to the second question are scattered through the book, but they provide the main theme of Fogelson's illuminating discussion of the failure of the electric railways. This is perhaps the book's central episode, for it brings together the growth and fragmentation themes.

As Los Angeles in the 1990s strives at tremendous expense to construct a comprehensive rail-based transit system, we would do well to recall that the city in the first quarter of the twentieth century built (and then slowly destroyed) the nation's most extensive electric railway system. Dominated by the "traction magnate" Henry E. Huntington, the Los Angeles Railway and Pacific Electric Railway systems at their height in the 1920s operated rapid and efficient service along a thousand miles of track. The electric railways spurred the growth of Los Angeles, as Huntington and other members of the Los Angeles elite constantly extended the tracks to serve their speculative real estate developments on the city's periphery. But the rail system also controlled fragmentation by limiting growth to developments adjacent to its lines and by focusing all the system's lines on a single center—the still-lively downtown that functioned as a true regional hub.

As Fogelson emphasizes, the 1920s saw a crisis in the electric railways system. To maintain efficient operations the system needed a massive overhaul and reorganization which entailed buying out the private investors and creating a single consolidated public rapid transit system that could borrow at low rates to construct elevated lines and other improvements. But nothing was done, and by the 1930s the only thing rapid about the street railways was their deterioration.

The problem was not fear of public ownership or of large expenditures; as we have seen, this strategy of massive public investment for growth was already the preferred strategy of the Los Angeles elite. The real explanation was that both the elite and the general population had switched their allegiance from mass transit to the automobile. The major transportation expenditures of the 1920s were devoted to constructing the wide boulevards proposed in the Major Traffic Street Plan (1924)—those "surface" roads which are still the basic roadways for the city. This massive road grid opened the whole Los Angeles basin to development—not simply the areas adjacent to streetcar lines. Since automobile traffic could now avoid the congested downtown streets for more convenient shopping areas like the "Miracle Mile" on Wilshire Boulevard, the shift from rail to automobile also meant the decline of the downtown. Already fragmented socially and politically, Los Angeles now entered an era of radical spatial fragmentation.

The theme of division, privatism, and fragmentation finds an apt conclusion in Fogelson's description of the ambitious plans to construct a Civic Center for Los Angeles. Located on the edge of a downtown that was itself dying because of the reductions in mass transit, this would-be architectural and political focus for the region endured successive cutbacks until it was finally built on a cramped site divided by heavily traveled roads. The Civic Center thus became an all-too-perfect symbol for a fragmented metropolis that had no real civic life and no real center.

Throughout this book, Fogelson displays the intensive mastery of detail and local sources that is usually the prerogative of a scholar who grew up in the city that is his subject and who has already published extensively on its history. But *The Fragmented Metropolis* is in fact the first book—indeed, originally the Ph.D. thesis—of a young historian who grew up in New York City and received his bachelor's degree from Columbia University and his Ph.D. from Harvard University. Fogelson was one of a remarkable group of doctoral students who studied with Oscar Handlin in he late 1950s and early 1960s, a group that included Stephen Thernstrom and Sam Bass Warner, Jr. While Thernstrom and Warner chose to analyze cities close to Cambridge, Fogelson was motivated by the challenge of chronicling a major city whose history was then virtually unexplored by professional historians.

Writing this book thus meant going directly to the masses of primary documentation that were still scattered among a score of Los Angeles city agencies. Fogelson obtained a series of traveling fellowships that gave him the opportunity to undertake archival research in the arduous era before the photocopier and the microfiche. He was also fortunate enough to find Robert Ingman, an official in the Los Angeles City Administrator's office who "literally open[ed] every door in city hall" for him.

Fogelson had essentially completed the book before the Watts riots of 1965, an event which would mark a key turning point in his scholarly career. Affronted by the official McCone Commission report that attributed the riots to local "riffraff" and outside agitators, he set out to give a truer account that would reflect the history of black exclusion and exploitation he had presented in *Fragmented Metropolis*. The result was a remarkable series of publications on the urban riots of the 1960s culminating in a major work, *Violence As Protest: A Study of Riots and Ghettos* (1971).[5]

As a professor of history and urban planning at MIT since 1968, Fogelson has gone on to produce a series of books that address the theme of civic order in the fragmented modern metropolis: *Big-City Police* (1977), *Pensions: The Hidden Cost of Public Safety* (1984), and *America's Armories* (1989).[6] All but the last deal extensively with the Los Angeles experience in the years since 1930.

Nevertheless, Fogelson has never returned to the "urban biography" format of *Fragmented Metropolis*, nor has he attempted to update or extend that book into the present. The continuing influence of *Fragmented Metropolis* since 1967 testifies not only to the depth of the book's archival research but also to the unusual balance and complexity of its narrative and point of view. In his widely read *City of Quartz*, Mike Davis remarks that Los Angeles historians tend to split into two camps: "sunshine or *noir*."[7] (Davis himself is decidedly among the latter). *Fragmented Metropolis*, however, escapes this dichotomy, and it has proved a remarkably seminal book for a whole range of analyses.

Indeed, many of the most important studies of Los Angeles history published since 1967 can be read as book-length expansions of topics or themes first introduced to the scholarly literature in *Fragmented Metropolis*. This includes such "sunshine" scholars as Reyner Banham, whose enthusiastic and insightful *Los Angeles: The Architecture of the Four Ecologies* (1971)[8] owes much to Fogelson's chapter entitled "The Urban Landscape"; and Kevin Starr, whose California trilogy—*Americans and the California Dream, 1850–1915, Inventing the Dream: California through the Progressive Era*, and *Material Dreams: Southern California through the 1920s*[9]—expands upon themes Fogelson emphasized in his chapters

"The Quest for Community" and "The Politics of Progressivism." *The Fragmented Metropolis* can also be seen as the starting point for such important academic studies as Scott Bottles's *Los Angeles and the Automobile* (1987)[10], largely about the transition from streetcar to automobile; William L. Kahrl's, *Water and Power* (1982)[11], the definitive account of the Owens Valley aqueduct; and Marc Weiss's, *The Rise of the Community Builders* (1987)[12], which takes up issues raised in Fogelson's chapter "City and Regional Planning."

Moreover, Fogelson has been an important source for many of the *"noir"* critics of Los Angeles—not least Mike Davis himself—and Fogelson's metaphor of fragmentation has even found its way into the fashionable discourse of neo-Marxist cultural critics and the "Los Angeles School" of social geographers. When cultural critic Fredric Jameson refers to the "postmodern hyperspace" of Los Angeles and geographer Edward Soja remarks that "there may be no other comparable urban region which presents so vividly such a composite assemblage and articulation of urban restructuring processes," they are repeating in the language of French post-structuralism the crucial insight that Fogelson presents in this book.[13] Finally, Fogelson's careful treatment of the Spanish origins of the city and his pioneering treatment of the city's Latino, black, and Asian minorities makes his book the starting point for a history of urban diversity that is only beginning.

If *The Fragmented Metropolis* has been a seminal book, it has also been a prophetic book in a deeper and darker sense than Fogelson could have realized in the mid-1960s The forces of disintegration that Fogelson analyzes for early twentieth-century Los Angeles have taken on a new intensity in the late twentieth century. Even as a global city and Pacific Rim capital, Los Angeles remains recognizably the place Fogelson chronicles in this book: a city hooked on growth, deeply divided socially, and perhaps too fragmented to generate the kind of public life that could override the destructive consequences of maximizing private profit.

If we consider Los Angeles since 1930 (when *Fragmented Metropolis* ends) and especially Los Angeles since 1967 (when the book was published), we can see a steadily diminishing hope that Los Angeles would prove to be a new kind of city where the great masses would share in a prosperity heretofore available only to the few. By the 1990s this Los Angeles ideal seems lost, the victim of the very forces of unrestrained growth that formed the city. As Mike Davis observes with well-justified pessimism, the "postwar virtuous circle of good jobs, rising incomes, cheap land, and quality public services" has degenerated into "the present vicious circle of social polarization, expensive land, and a declining public sector."[14]

Moreover, this radically fragmented society is now facing unprecedented challenges stemming directly from explosive growth, and these challenges seem to demand a strong unified public response which, as Fogelson shows, has never been part of the Los Angeles tradition. A society that has never coped gracefully with diversity must now strive to assimilate an unprecedented tide of immigration; a region whose symbol is the freeway and which is almost totally dependent on automobile transportation must now deal with intractable roadway gridlock; and a city that boasted to the world its mild climate and leisure opportunities must now scramble to secure minimally healthy air and adequate water supplies for its population.

In one sense, Los Angeles today is the inevitable culmination of the growth obsession that Fogelson chronicles throughout this book. Indeed, the success of the region as a manufacturing and financial center goes beyond the most fervent dreams of its early boosters. Fogelson observes that by the 1920s the Los Angeles elite was eager to match the city's success in attracting new residents by attracting new industry to create an independent manufacturing base for the region. Their wishes have been abundantly fulfilled. Once again, success rested on a shrewd alliance between private profit and public resources.

First, Los Angeles used its publicly subsidized port and transportation network to attract the West Coast branch plants of national corporations. More importantly, the movement of the aircraft industry from the Midwest to Los Angeles before and during World War II gave the region a vital base in advanced engineering and made it a favored locale for postwar Cold War federal defense expenditures. These expenditures in turn financed a massive high-tech economy with strengths in aerospace, computers, and biotechnology which has also transformed Orange and San Diego counties to the south.

Los Angeles was also the beneficiary of a series of federal programs during the Great Depression to help the homebuilding industry. When population boomed after 1945, homebuyers benefited from an industry that had been restructured to provide efficiently constructed houses built on a seemingly inexhaustible supply of cheap land and long-term mortgages at low rates. The entertainment industry added recording and television production to motion pictures, as popular culture became America's most reliable export industry. The wave of immigration described below provided labor and entrepreneurship for a low-tech manufacturing sector based on the garment industry. Finally, the rise of Japan and other Asian nations made the Los Angeles/Long Beach port the most important in the nation, and made Los Angeles a Pacific Rim financial capital and rival to New York. Japanese capital was particularly prominent in reviving the long-dormant Los Angeles downtown as a high-rise center for international finance.

But this explosive economic growth has unleashed in the late twentieth century a series of chain reactions that threaten to undermine the very viability of the city. For example, prosperity and population growth combined with inflationary factors in the national economy in the 1970s set off a two-decade-long land boom, driving up home prices in the most desirable areas to as much as ten times their original value and making Los Angeles among the most expensive housing markets in the nation. As land values shot up, homebuyers moved outward into the cheaper arid lands at the periphery of the region. And this dispersion meant greater water consumption, longer commutes, and intolerable strains on the region's road network (and commuters' psyches).

Moreover, physical dispersion has meant increased social fragmentation. Fogelson shows that by 1925 the city of Los Angeles had abandoned hopes of annexing all of Los Angeles County. In the years after 1945 many emerging middle-class districts located outside the city of Los Angeles but within the county incorporated themselves as independent cities, using their new powers to zone out poor people and tailor their services to the needs of the middle class. Moreover, civic fragmentation has been written into law in the so-called taxpayers' revolt. With property tax receipts limited by Proposition 13 (passed 1978), the public sphere has begun to unravel, a crisis that has struck first at vital social service institutions like schools and hospitals and now threatens the very infrastructure that the Los Angeles elite strove so hard to develop.

There are now 128 incorporated municipalities within Los Angeles County, ranging from the City of Los Angeles (1990 census population 3,485,000; 37% Anglo (a term used to designate non-Latino whites); 41% Latino; 13% black; 9% Asian) to such upper class enclaves as Rolling Hills, a "gated city" on the Palos Verdes peninsula where only residents and guests may enter (pop. 1,871; 85% Anglo; 4% Latino, 1% black; 10% Asian.)[15]

The contrasting ethnic mix of the city of Los Angeles and its affluent suburbs points up what is surely the most important social and spatial transformation in the region since 1930. Once the most "Anglo" of American cities, Los Angeles is now a place where the "minorities" comprise a clear majority. For Los Angeles County as a whole in 1990, 41% are Anglo; 38% Latino; 11% black; and 10% Asian.[16] Nearly 40%

of the city's residents are foreign-born; half speak a language other than English at home; and students in the Los Angeles school system speak more than eighty languages.[17] This contrasts with Los Angeles in 1930, where, as Fogelson shows, 88% of the population was Anglo (including the 3% born in Southern and Eastern Europe); 8% Latino; 2% black; and 2% Asian.

Yet this profound transformation has not made Los Angeles today a truly multicultural city. Instead, new patterns of social and spatial discrimination have emerged, some more subtle than those of an earlier era and some even more vicious. Although Los Angeles never knew the crowded tenements and teeming masses of turn-of-the-century Eastern cities, it has evolved its own dispersed version of central-city slums and sheltered peripheral affluent suburbs.

As late as the 1960s, patterns of segregation in the city were relatively stark and simple. With blacks concentrated in the South-Central district centered around Watts, Los Angeles vied with Chicago for the dubious title of the most segregated city in the nation.[18] But the wave of Latino and Asian immigration in the 1970s and 1980s inevitably produced sprawling mixed-race poverty districts. Blacks are now a minority in South-Central Los Angeles, with 35% of the population compared to 60% Latino.[19] In districts where Latinos, blacks, and Asians make up nearly equal thirds, one can find immigrant Cambodian grocers who stock soul foods, Mexican and South American specialties, and a range of Asian staples from anywhere from Taiwan to Pakistan.

But this diversity exists in a complex setting that juxtaposes an almost Third World economy with the prosperity of a global capital, and creates as many occasions for conflicts among the poor as for solidarity. Asians have found work (and sometimes prosperity) in a network of sweatshop enterprises and family-run stores; Latinos have been largely confined to poorly paid service jobs. As for black Los Angeles, Fogelson had written in 1968 that the urban riots of the 1960s were "an indicator of the necessity for fundamental changes in American society." But for many residents of South-Central Los Angeles, these changes either never came or were changes for the worse.

Black Los Angeles has suffered especially from the economic restructuring of the last twenty years, as national manufacturing plants once located in the district either moved to the periphery or left the region. Unemployment brought with it social disorganization, drug use and gang violence. As in 1965, anger and despair produced riots. On April 29, 1992, after a jury in Simi Valley, a predominantly Anglo suburban enclave, acquitted Los Angeles police officers who had been videotaped beating black motorist Rodney King, South-Central Los Angeles erupted into the most serious American urban disturbance since the 1863 New York Draft riots. More than 50 lives were lost, 500 buildings burnt, and $750 million worth of property destroyed.[20]

In 1967 when *The Fragmented Metropolis* was first published the Watts riots could not wholly displace the image of Los Angeles as an endless, egalitarian expanse of detached middle-class homes. This new edition comes in the wake of more somber and disturbing images: racial hatreds as complicated and profound as the city's newfound diversity (Korean-owned stores were the favorite targets of black and Latino looters); extremes of wealth and poverty; and an urban environment out of control. Los Angeles once owed its rapid growth to people fleeing the East and Midwest. Now many areas in the Southwest and the Pacific Northwest owe their expansion to people fleeing Los Angeles.

The Fragmented Metropolis might be read as the urban biography of a brilliant failure: the formative years of a city that had the ambition and the promise to be great and succeeded only in growing very big. But cities, even more than individuals, are made up of complex and contradictory elements. It is no coincidence that so many of the most progressive projects for the Los Angeles of the 1990s are among the rejected or discarded policies described in *The Fragmented Metropolis*. For this book also reminds us of the forgotten alternatives to destructive growth: the "other Los Angeles" of a balanced mass transit system; a vital downtown; a commitment to municipal ownership and progressive planning; a concern for a balanced environment between city and countryside; and a commitment to creating a city without slums or tenements.

These possibilities have been shunted aside by the dominant forces in Los Angeles history, but the recent revival of a rail-based mass transit reminds us that they have not necessarily been lost forever. The elaborate plans of the Los Angeles County Transportation Commission to give the region a balanced transportation system based on a 400-mile rail network can be seen as the first of many revivals of the "other Los Angeles." The initial "Metro Blue" trolley line opened in 1990, followed in 1993 by the first link in a subway line which by 2001 will connect the downtown to the San Fernando Valley.[21] The subway and trolleys will also be linked to a revived commuter rail system. The *Wall Street Journal* might scoff at the scope of the mass transit projects—estimated to cost $184 billion by 2020[22]—but Fogelson's book teaches that the survival of Los Angeles has always depended upon the daring use of massive resources to create new opportunities in a difficult environment.

This book remains important not only because it contains the most penetrating diagnosis of the city's rise and fragmentation. It defines the basic and continuing political problem of the city: to build a strong democratic consensus in a fragmented society. It presents historic alternatives that can become crucial starting points for planning a truly great metropolis. Anyone seeking to create the Los Angeles of the future would do well to begin by reading this remarkable account of the city's past.

Robert Fishman

Philadelphia
November 1992

NOTES

1. Figures based on 1990 census and 1987 Census of Manufactures. See U.S. Bureau of the Census, *Statistical Abstract of the United States: 1991* (11th edition) (Washington,D.C.: Government Printing Office, 1991), Table 36, Metropolitan Areas—Population 1970–1990; U.S. Bureau of the Census, *Census of Manufactures (1987)*. Subject Series, General Summary (Washington, D.C.: Government Printing Office, 1991), Table 3. *Los Angeles Times Magazine*, "Home Port," February 3, 1991, p. 22.

2. Michael Arlen, "An Armenian Journal: Faucet Sales and Crash Syndrome," *The Nation* 248, no. 16 (April 24, 1989): 556.

3. U.S. Bureau of the Census, *Statistical Abstract (1991)*, Table 8.

4. David Rieff, *Los Angeles: Capital of the Third World* (New York: Simon & Schuster, 1991).

5. Robert M. Fogelson, *Violence as Protest: A Study of Riots and Ghettos* (Garden City, New York: Doubleday, 1971). See also "White on Black: A Critique of the McCone Commission Report," *Political Science Quarterly* (1967), reprinted in Robert M. Fogelson, ed., *The Los Angeles Riots* (New York: Arno Press, 1969); and "Who Riots? A Study of Participation in the 1967 Riots" (written with Robert B. Hill), *Supplemental Studies for the National Advisory Commission on Civil Disorders* (New York: Praeger, 1968), pp. 217–248.

6. Robert M. Fogelson, *Big-City Police* (Cambridge: Harvard University Press, 1977); *Pensions: The Hidden Costs of Public Safety* (New York: Columbia University Press, 1984); *America's Armories: Architecture, Society and Public Order* (Cambridge: Harvard University Press, 1989).

7. Mike Davis, *City of Quartz: Excavating the Future in Los Angeles* (London: Verso, 1990), Chapter 1.

8. Reyner Banham, *Los Angeles: The Architecture of the Four Ecologies* (Harmondsworth: Penguin, 1971).

9. Kevin Starr, *Americans and the California Dream, 1850–1915* (New York: Oxford University Press, 1973); *Inventing the Dream: California through the Progressive Era* (New York: Oxford University Press, 1986); *Material Dreams: Southern California through the 1920s* (New York: Oxford University Press, 1990).

10. Scott L. Bottles, *Los Angeles and the Automobile: The Making of the Modern City* (Berkeley and Los Angeles: The University of California Press, 1987.)

11. William L. Kahrl, *Water and Power: The Conflict over Los Angeles Water Supply in the Owens Valley* (Berkeley and Los Angeles: The University of California Press, 1982).

12. Marc A. Weiss, *The Rise of the Community Builders: The American Real Estate Industry and Urban Land Planning* (New York: Columbia University Press, 1987).

13. Fredric Jameson, "The Cultural Logic of Late Capitalism," and Edward Soja, "It All Comes Together in Los Angeles," quoted in Davis, *City of Quartz*, p. 84.

14. Davis, *City of Quartz*, p. 174.

15. Frank Clifford and Ann C. Roark, "Racial Lines in County Blur but Could Return," *Los Angeles Times*, May 6, 1992, p. A1.

16. Richard Simon, "Los Angeles County: The Census Story," *Los Angeles Times*, May 6, 1991, p. B1.

17. Barbara Vobejda, "Los Angeles Swept by a Decade of Social, Economic Change," *Washington Post*, May 11, 1992, p. A1.

18. Reynolds Farley, "Residential Segregation of Social and Economic Groups among Blacks, 1970–1980," in Christopher Jencks and Paul E. Peterson, eds., *The Urban Underclass* (Washington, D.C.: The Brookings Institution, 1992), p. 277.

19. Vobejda, *"Los Angeles Swept,"* p. A8.

20. Michelle L. Norris et al., "Victims of the Riots," *Los Angeles Times*, May 11, 1992, p. A1.

21. "Wait for Train Ends, Next Train Leaves in 1993," *New York Times*, April 22, 1992, p. A14.

22. Frederick Rose, "Transit Agency Plans $184 Billion Program (Yes, That's Billion)," *Wall Street Journal*, April 22, 1992, p. 6.

PREFACE TO THE PAPERBACK EDITION

I am delighted that the University of California Press has reprinted *The Fragmented Metropolis: Los Angeles, 1850–1930* in its new series Classics in Urban History. I am also delighted that Michael Ebner, the general editor of the series, was able to prevail upon Robert Fishman, an historian whose work I greatly admire, to write an introduction to the book. His introduction is, I think, splendid, a model of is kind.

The Fragmented Metropolis was originally published over twenty-five years ago. Yet somehow it does not seem that long. With only a little effort I can still see myself in the mid-1960s, then a graduate student in my mid-twenties, rummaging through various archives in Los Angeles, trying to account for the city's remarkable growth and distinctive character. (Although I am not sure I knew it then, I was also trying to figure out what it meant to be an historian.) Even today I am amazed at how many people went out of their way to help.

The reissue of *The Fragmented Metropolis* also reminds me how much of my later work, especially my work on riots and ghettos, on police departments, and on pensions and municipal finance, was inspired in one way or another by my early study of Los Angeles. Indeed, Los Angeles has been central to all but one of my books. And in my current research, a study of downtown from the late nineteenth century to the mid-twentieth, I find myself returning to many of the issues I first explored in Los Angeles nearly three decades ago.

As Professor Fishman points out, the past two or three decades in Los Angeles have been very eventful, to say the least, probably more eventful than many of its residents would like. Los Angeles has fully realized its goal to become a great metropolis. But as the recent riots there made painfully clear, it is still struggling, as I wrote in 1967, "to reconcile its conception of the good community with its ambitions as a great metropolis."

Except for making a few changes in the illustrations, changes which were made for technical reasons, I have resisted the temptation to revise *The Fragmented Metropolis*. (I was not tempted to bring it up to date, a task that would have required another volume, at least as long as the original one.) The book therefore stands as written, the work of a young (and energetic) historian who was just learning his craft, a work that revealed much—though, as recent historians have shown, by no means all—about the formative years of an American metropolis.

For making *The Fragmented Metropolis* available again, I want to thank Professor Ebner and Charlene Woodcock of the University of California Press.

Robert M. Fogelson

Cambridge, Massachusetts
November 1992

ACKNOWLEDGMENTS

This study was supported by fellowships from the Graduate School of Arts and Sciences and the Frederick Sheldon Fund, Harvard University, and the Joint Center for Urban Studies of the Massachusetts Institute of Technology and Harvard University. To these organizations and especially to Martin Meyerson, former director of the Joint Center, I am much indebted. My research was facilitated by the cooperation of the following libraries: the Bancroft Library of the University of California at Berkeley, the California State Library at Sacramento, the Harvard University Library, the Henry E. Huntington Library, the Junipero Serra Museum Library, the Los Angeles Municipal Reference Library, the Los Angeles Public Library, the Stanford University Library, the University of California at Los Angeles Library, and the University of Southern California Library. To their staffs, and particularly to Dr. John Pomfret, director of the Huntington Library, and Wilbur Smith, director of the Special Collections Division of the University of California at Los Angeles Library, I acknowledge my gratitude.

My work was also furthered by the assistance of the following individuals, companies, and voluntary and governmental agencies: the California Public Utilities Commission (James Gibson), Arnold Haskell, the Huntington Land Companies (John Youngken), the Los Angeles Chamber of Commerce (Harold Wright), the Los Angeles City Administrator's Office (Robert Ingman), the Los Angeles City Planning Department (Karl Ourston), the Los Angeles City Clerk's Office, the Los Angeles Department of Water and Power (Leonard Hansen and Fred Luke), the Los Angeles Harbor Department, the Los Angeles Metropolitan Transit Authority (John Curtis), the Los Angeles Public Utilities Department (Ted Hoffman), the Los Angeles Regional Planning Department (Milton Breivogel), the Santa Monica Land and Water Company (Arthur L. Loomis), the Security First National Bank (Clyde Simpson), and the Title Insurance and Trust Company (Joseph LaBarbera). To them, and above all to Mr. Ingman, for literally opening every door in city hall, Mr. Luke, for rendering countless personal and professional favors, and Mr. Loomis, for granting me access to the Robert C. Gillis Papers, I express my appreciation.

My manuscript was also improved by colleagues, friends, and relatives who gave generously of their own knowledge and time. Nelson Van Valen and Richard Weiss allowed me to read their doctoral dissertations in manuscript form. Robert D. Cross, Mrs. David Beal, Richard Hofstadter, James P. Shenton, Laurence Veysey, and Mrs. Frank Kirk all read and criticized the manuscript. Mrs. Kirk is undoubtedly responsible for the few felicitous phrases that appear in the text. Jeffrey Fogelson undertook the arduous task of proofreading the typescript, and to him as well as to the others I am indeed grateful. Oscar Handlin supervised this study as a doctoral dissertation ("Los Angeles: The Emergence of a Metropolis, 1850–1930," Harvard University, 1964) and guided me as I revised it for publication. His influence on my scholarship is immeasurable, and my debt to him is incalculable. Finally, many Californians—far too many to list—made my visits there memorable experiences; and whatever my professional impressions of Los Angeles, I regard these Californians and their region with great affection.

Robert M. Fogelson

New York City
December 1966

THE FRAGMENTED METROPOLIS

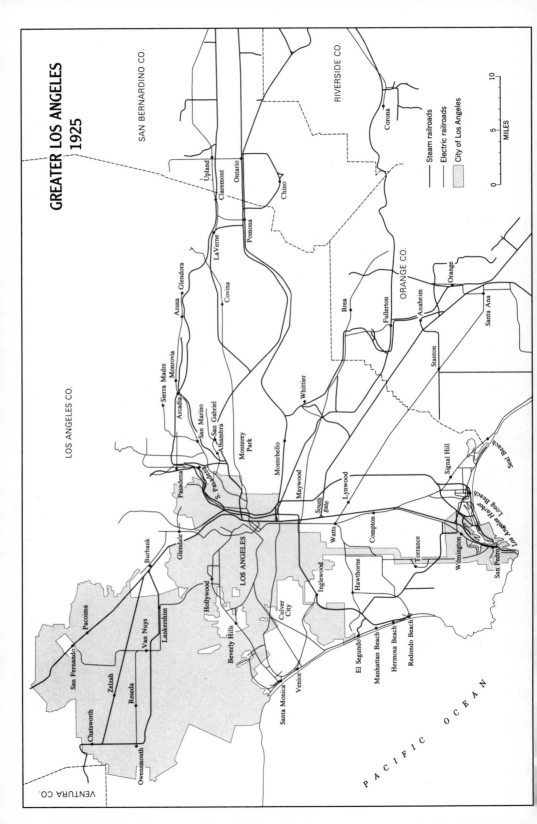

GREATER LOS ANGELES
1925

VENTURA CO.

LOS ANGELES CO.

SAN BERNARDINO CO.

RIVERSIDE CO.

ORANGE CO.

Steam railroads
Electric railroads
City of Los Angeles

0   5   10
MILES

San Fernando
Pacoima
Chatsworth
Zelzah
Reseda
Owensmouth
Van Nuys
Lankershim
Burbank
Glendale
Hollywood
Beverly Hills
Culver City
Santa Monica
Venice
El Segundo
Manhattan Beach
Hermosa Beach
Redondo Beach
Inglewood
Hawthorne
Torrance
Wilmington
San Pedro
LOS ANGELES
Pasadena
S. Pasadena
Sierra Madre
Arcadia
San Marino
San Gabriel
Alhambra
Monterey Park
Montebello
Maywood
South gate
Watts
Compton
Lynwood
Signal Hill
Long Beach
Los Angeles Harbor
Seal Beach
Whittier
Brea
Fullerton
Anaheim
Stanton
Orange
Santa Ana
Corona
Chino
Ontario
Upland
Claremont
Pomona
La Verne
Glendora
Azusa
Monrovia
Covina

PACIFIC OCEAN

INTRODUCTION

When California joined the Union in 1850, nothing about Los Angeles foreshadowed its emergence as one of America's foremost metropolises. It was simply a nondescript agricultural village with 1,610 people, no railroads, and few streets or other public improvements. It was isolated, geographically and economically, from the large population centers of the United States and western Europe. And it lacked the natural harbor and surface resources that attracted commerce and generated industry elsewhere in the country. During the next eighty years, nonetheless, Los Angeles underwent perhaps the most extraordinary expansion in American urban history. It grew into a city of 1.2 million and a metropolitan district of 2.3 million persons, by far the largest settlement on the Pacific coast. It built a vast network of railways and highways, tapped northern Sierra sources for its water supply, and subdivided the vast southern California countryside. It also developed into a flourishing commercial entrepôt, an impressive industrial producer, and the economic center of the great Southwest. Indeed, by overcoming its natural handicaps, Los Angeles in 1930 stood fourth in population, second in territory, and ninth in manufacturing among American metropolises.

Los Angeles' character was no less extraordinary. It differed markedly in its landscape, transportation, community, politics, and planning from the great American metropolis of the late nineteenth and early twentieth century. In Los Angeles, residences were more widely dispersed, and businessess more extensively decentralized. Electric railways approached bankruptcy faster, and private automobiles handled a greater share of urban transportation. Middle-class native-white Americans were a larger majority, and working-class European immigrants a smaller minority. Reformers dismantled the political

1

machine more rapidly—only to falter before conservatism, radicalism, and indifference. And city and regional planning were adopted earlier, implemented more thoroughly, and yet undermined more insidiously. More than any other American metropolis—and with remarkably few misgivings—Los Angeles succumbed to the disintegrative, though not altogether undesirable, forces of suburbanization and progressivism. And as a result it emerged by 1930 as the fragmented metropolis par excellence, the archetype, for better or worse, of the contemporary American metropolis.

Thus the history of Los Angeles revolves around two separate but related themes. The first is the emergence of a populous, urbanized, and industrialized settlement—a process which involved the transformation of the Mexican village into an American town, the establishment of a tradition of urban expansion, the triumph of Los Angeles in its rivalry with San Diego, the relentless movement of people to southern California, the provision of transport facilities, domestic water, and subdivided real estate, and the expansion of commercial and industrial enterprise. The second theme is the rejection of the metropolis in favor of its suburbs—a decision which was reflected in the dispersal and decentralization of the landscape, the failure of the electric railway industry, the quest for community by the white majority and the colored minorities, the progressive reform of local politics (including the battle for municipal ownership of public utilities), and the implementation and frustration of city and regional planning. To trace these themes—to define thereby the urbanization of greater Los Angeles—is the purpose of this book.

The quintessence of Los Angeles is the tension between these themes, the ambivalent attitude toward urbanization. Indeed, nothing is more central to Los Angeles' history than the efforts of its residents to join the spirit of the good community with the substance of the great metropolis. This problem was by no means unique to Los Angeles before 1930, though nowhere else was it quite so pressing and poignant. Nor, from the perspective of 1967, was the resolution unusual, though nowhere else did it antedate the Great Depression. Since the Second World War, in fact, most American metropolises have duplicated, to a remarkable degree, the patterns of Los Angeles' landscape, transportation, community, politics, and planning. Hence Los Angeles' efforts to reconcile its conception of the good community with its ambitions as a great metropolis are illuminating not only for what they reveal about Los Angeles' past but also for what they imply about the alternatives available to America's cities in the future.

PART ONE
LOS ANGELES, 1850–1930

As I wandered about Los Angeles, looking for the basic meaning of the place, the fundamental source of its wealth and its economic identity, I found myself quite at sea. The Chamber of Commerce people told me about the concentration of fruit, the shipping, the Western branch factories put up by concerns in the East. But none of these things seemed the cause of a city. They seemed rather the effect, rising from an inexplicable accumulation of people—just as the immense dealings in second-hand automobiles and the great turnover of real estate were an effect. It struck me as an odd thing that here, alone of all the cities in America, there was no plausible answer to the question, "Why did a town spring up here and why has it grown so big?" (Morris Markey, 1932)

Our inheritance is turned to strangers—our houses to aliens. We have drunken our water for money—our wood is sold unto us. Our necks are under persecution—we labor and have no rest. (Juan Bandini, 1855)

1   FROM PUEBLO TO TOWN

Los Angeles, far from being a new settlement, was almost seventy years old when California joined the Union. It was founded in the late eighteenth century when Spain decided to defend its empire and propagate Catholicism by colonizing California. Since the crown lacked the resources and since its subjects showed little interest, the church assumed this responsibility. Its priests, accompanied by government troops and vowing to enhance the glory of God and King, marched north from western Mexico along the Pacific Ocean into coastal California. There they encountered thousands of primitive but peaceful Indians who were intrigued by the mysteries of Christianity and impressed by the devotion of its messengers. The clerics gained the natives' confidence, converted many to Catholicism, and then persuaded or compelled them to leave their tribal villages for sacred communities known as missions.[1] Resistance was ineffective against ecclesiastical determination and military power, and between the 1780's and 1830's the Spaniards resettled the California Indians on missions extending from San Diego north to Point Reyes.

To the aborigines, conversion meant confinement and civilization equaled subjugation. While in theory the missions prepared the natives for eventual independence, in fact the priests retained complete control. As missionaries they instructed the Indians in the gospel, as overseers they supervised their work, and as judges they punished their infractions. They exactingly regimented life and labor on the missions in accord with their church's absolute authority, their estates' material advancement, and their wards' spiritual improvement. For the aborigines, slavery in this world was a prerequisite for salvation in the next. And despite the sincerity of the Spaniards, Christian civilization was disastrous for the Indians. Uprooted from cultures

5

which had accommodated tribal abilities to environmental conditions, they suffered grievously from the clerics' inflexibility and the soldiers' brutality. Thus not only did the aboriginal population decline from 130,000 to 90,000 between 1770 and 1832,[2] but, in addition, few Indians survived without irreparable physical and psychological damage that rendered them unfit for independent life.

The missions thrived nonetheless. Endowed with a mild climate and abundant land, California made only modest demands on its sparse and backward population. And the priests possessed adequate knowledge of productive techniques and ample power to force steady work from the Indians. Under clerical supervision, the aborigines planted and harvested cereals and vegetables, pastured and tended cattle and sheep, and then slaughtered and sheared them for meat and wool. They also cut the branches and dug the adobe for their simple huts and the priests' elaborate chapels, and, when finished with their labors, prayed, studied, and slept according to schedules set by the missionaries.[3] Although this training was intended to teach the natives to govern themselves and manage the estates, the priests were unwilling to relinquish their authority and property. Conceived of as a temporary means of facilitating colonization, the missions became firmly fixed as California's dominant economic and social institutions in the early nineteenth century.

For the defense of the missions, Spain founded presidios at San Diego, San Francisco, and other sheltered places along the Pacific coast. The presidios were supplied by ship from Mexico, and, to relieve the royal exchequer of this burden, the imperial authorities decided to establish pueblos (agricultural villages) in California. According to Governor Felipe de Neve, the pueblos were supposed to provide the presidios with foodstuffs, wine, and horses, furnish their garrisons with soldiers, and, beyond this, stimulate agriculture, stock raising, and related industries.[4] As few *gente de razon* (people of reason, or Europeans as opposed to Indians) resided in the province, however, the government was obliged to recruit *pobladores* (colonists) from among the Mexican people. But they displayed so little enthusiasm for the dangerous trip and precarious enterprise that the Governor, following precedents codified in Spain's Laws of the Indies, offered inducements to stimulate interest.

De Neve promised the pobladores a subsidy of money, stock, and tools, a building lot close to the plaza for residence, several tracts of outlying farmland for sustenance, adequate grazing land, and a share in the common water, pasturage, firewood, and lumber. He also exempted them from tithes or any other taxes on their produce for five years. The colonists, in return, were obliged to complete their homes, cultivate their fields, increase their cattle, and construct a dam and other public works. They were also bound to sell their surplus at a fair price to the presidios, and to reimburse the royal treasury for its initial assistance from the profits.[5] Since the pueblos were supplemental agricultural units, the authorities instructed that they be located at sites close to the presidios and suited for farming, which, in an arid country, meant near available water. Guided by the institution's rationale and the province's environment, the imperial government then designated several places as pueblos.

Among these was *el pueblo de Nuestra Señora la Reina de Los Angeles* (the village of Our Lady the Queen of the Angels) which was founded by Governor de Neve in 1781. Following his instructions to select a site in southern California's coastal plain, the pobladores first located Los Angeles near enough to the Porciuncula River to tap its waters yet high enough above it for protection against winter floods. They then took possession of the land and laid out the pueblo, setting aside a parcel two hundred by three hundred feet for the plaza and fixing its corners at the cardinal points of the compass. They also divided the surrounding territory into *solares* (building lots twenty by thirty varas) and *suertes* (sowing fields two hundred by three hundred varas) and reserved the remaining property for common use and newcomers. Finally, they held a lottery and distributed one solare, two irrigable suertes, and two dry ones to each poblador.[6] Subsequently, the settlers exploited the village's fertile soil, ample water, and warm weather so effectively that Los Angeles prospered beyond expectations, attracted more colonists, and, with about one thousand inhabitants, ranked first in size among California's settlements in the 1830's.[7]

The missions fared less well. In the 1830's, a decade after Mexico declared its independence of Spain, the republic, in response to claims that the priests were monopolizing the land and exploiting the natives, transferred the missions from the church to the state.[8] The Mexican authorities then reversed the Spanish policy of granting little property to individuals and even encouraged people to apply for parcels. Although they insisted that the petitioners be Mexican citizens, head their own households, and possess sufficient stock,[9] these requirements were moderately phrased and liberally interpreted. As a result applicants acquired more than seven hundred concessions for estates ranging from less than a hundred to more than a million acres during the following decade.[10] And by 1846 private proprietors (known as rancheros) owned nearly all of southern California's arable and pasture land and directed the region's economy and society.

Although the rancheros were less restricted than the missionaries in pursuing their material advantages, they too were severely circumscribed by the province's geography and resources. Thousands of miles of mountains, deserts, and plains separated California from the markets of the eastern United States and the central Mexican plateau, and thousands of miles of ocean isolated it from the ports of the Hawaiian Islands and the Orient. The earth's surface contained no precious metals, and the settlers lacked the capital to support a quest for mineral wealth. The abundant land and limited water discouraged intensive cultivation, and a mild climate and sparse population permitted an indolence impossible in colder and more crowded countries. Nor did the Californians endeavor to overcome these handicaps. Trained as soldiers of Spain and Mexico, they regarded work with distaste and business with contempt, equated improvement with adherence to their ancestors' arts, science, and religion, and measured progress by participation in lengthy visits, ceremonial display, and vigorous exercise. As they accomodated their inclinations to the region's character, the Californians appeared to some visitors as "the least promising colonists of a new country" and to others as "a happy people, possessing the means of physical pleasure to the full." [11]

The Californians based their economy and society on vast estates known as ranchos. The ranchos were divided into three parts: sprawling haciendas on which the rancheros and their families resided; nearby gardens, vineyards, and fields; and, by far the largest chunk, surrounding pasture for the cattle. The cattle, which were originally established in southern California by the priests and later appropriated from the secularized missions by the rancheros, were the rancho's primary source of wealth. They provided meat, clothing, candles, and ropes, among other essentials. For the rancheros, indeed, stock raising was more than a means of livelihood well suited to the region's environment; it was also a way of life consistent with their own inclinations. Given the mild weather and limited but adequate rainfall, the herds could forage the hills unsupervised; and thus freed from more mundane matters, the rancheros could live—or so they thought—in the style of Spanish grandees.[12]

The Indians, not the Californians, made up the labor force. Although many did not survive the mission experience and others returned to their villages after secularization, a substantial number who were incapable of caring for themselves stayed in the vicinity of the ranchos. The Californians promptly recruited them, offering, in return for labor and service, plain but ample fare, simple but adequate shelter, and unenlightened but patriarchic guidance. For these benefits the Indians watched the herds and slaughtered the cattle, prepared the meat and cured the hides. They planted the gardens, vineyards, and fields and then cultivated the potatoes, peppers, beans, and peas, tended the grapes, and harvested the corn, wheat, maize, and barley. They dug the adobe and erected the buildings, sawed the lumber, and constructed the furniture.[13] With their women, who cooked the food, sewed the garments, cleaned the haciendas, and served the Californians, the natives were as indispensable as the cattle to the rancho economy.

The rancheros geared production to the immediate requirements of their households, and the ranchos achieved a substantial degree of self-sufficiency. Moreover, the herds multiplied so rapidly that the excess hides and tallow were exchanged for goods unavailable in California. American and British merchantmen that plied between the United States, Europe, China, and the Pacific Islands conducted this commerce. Their owners filled them with liquor, tea, and coffee; linen, velveteen, and silk; cutlery, crockery, and tinware; and boots, shoes, and jewelry. Their supercargoes then bartered for the hides and tallow which were later sold to shoe and soap manufacturers in Massachusetts.[14] Since the trade was restricted by California's isolation and the market's limitations, however, the ranchos continued to provide all the necessities of life down through the 1840's.

The Californians and the Indians were not only owners and workers; they were also masters and servants. The rancheros, however, did not exploit the natives as intensively as, say, the southern planters did the Negro slaves; nor did they handle them as harshly. After all, the ranchos produced enough for all, and everyone there well knew his place. It was partly because no uncertainties about responsibilities and privileges unsettled the ranchos that one ranchero could claim that "We treat our servants rather as friends than as servants." [15] By virtue of this arrangement, the Californians and the Indians shared the same haciendas but not the same adobes, and they ate at the same tables but in assigned seats. Moreover, the natives worshipped and relaxed within the ranchos, and the rancheros prayed in private chapels and socialized on their estates. By thus meeting the emotional as well as the material imperatives of their households, the ranchos attained a social self-sufficiency as nearly complete as their economic autonomy.

9

Meanwhile, Los Angeles not only retained its position as California's largest settlement, but also increased its population to approximately 1,200 in 1840. The native Californians, a substantial majority, were joined by some Mexicans, pobladores who migrated to the province, and a few Americans, sailors from the Northeast who deserted their ships and pioneers from the Midwest who crossed the continent. But notwithstanding its growth, the pueblo underwent no fundamental changes in its agricultural economy or village society. Few people engaged in crafts, trade, professions, or manufacturing; most natives and newcomers alike cultivated the land or labored for farmers.[16] As they planted additional acreage and established new households, Los Angeles prospered and expanded; it thus developed through the accumulation, not the alteration, of its productive units.

Los Angeles' origins were still visible in its structure in the 1840's because of the pervasive influence of the ranchos in southern California. Their self-sufficiency inhibited opportunities for artisans, merchants, professionals, and manufacturers, and precluded urban growth in the pueblo. "I went to town only occasionally," one prominent ranchero recalled, "and then it was on some urgent business, and I returned without loss of time."[17] Even the American and British supercargoes bargained with the Californians on their estates, stored the hides and tallow in coastal warehouses, and outfitted their ships as shops. They did no business in the pueblo.[18] Thus by 1846 only a basic disruption in the region's economy and society could have altered the pattern of labor and life in Los Angeles, and from the perspective of the Californians nothing in their culture appeared capable of propelling changes of such magnitude.

After all, they had experienced rebellion without change and turbulence without disruption throughout the early nineteenth century. They had witnessed successive factions revolt against authority in the cause of liberty, and settle for new officials in the name of fraternity. They had become convinced that their economy and society, so recently created out of the desert wilderness, was impervious to political upheaval. So, when the United States commenced to wage war on Mexico in 1846, the Californians showed little anxiety as they prepared to defend the province. And indeed, they offered scant resistance. The invaders soon imposed military rule in California, then suppressed a passionate but hopeless insurrection there, and later defeated the Mexican army at Chapultepec. Incapable of protecting its empire, the Mexican government ceded New Mexico and California to the United States for $15 million.[19]

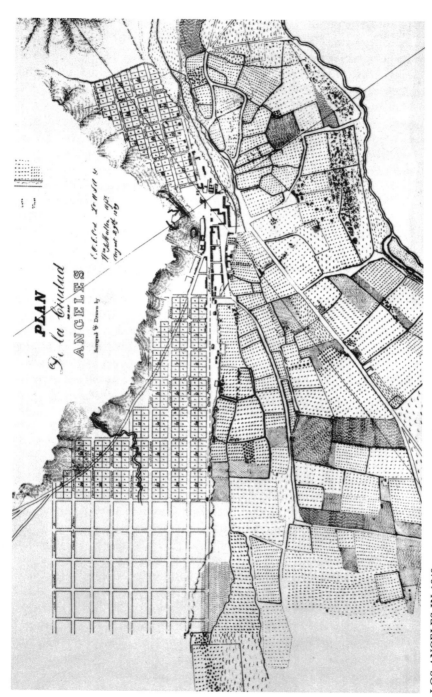

PLAN
De la Ciudad
ANGELES

Surveyed & Drawn by

LOS ANGELES IN 1849

The Californians, who were not consulted by either country, awaited a declaration of policy with trepidation. Previous contacts with the conquerors had dismayed them. "We find ourselves suddenly threatened by hordes of Yankee emigrants, who have already begun to flock into our country, and whose progress we cannot arrest," Pio Pico, a prominent Californian, lamented in 1845. "Already have the wagons of that perfidious people scaled the almost inaccessible summits of the Sierra Nevada, crossed the entire continent, and penetrated the fruitful valley of the Sacramento." "Already are those adventurous land-voyagers spreading themselves far and wide over a country which seems suited to their tastes," he added. "They are cultivating farms, establishing vineyards, erecting mills, sawing up lumber, building workshops, and doing a thousand other things which seem natural to them, but which Californians neglect or despise." [20]

To relieve this anxiety, the new governor, Richard B. Mason, issued a proclamation from Monterey in August of 1848. "From this new order of things there will result to California a new destiny," he declared. "Instead of revolutions and insurrections, there will be internal tranquility; instead of fickle and vacillating policy, there will be firm and stable government . . . The arts and sciences will flourish, and the labor of the agriculturist, guided by the lamp of learning will stimulate the earth to the most bountiful production. Commerce, freed from the absurd restrictions formerly imposed, will be greatly extended; the choked up channels of trade will be opened, and the poisoned fountains of domestic faction forever dried up." "Americans and Californians," he concluded, "will now be one and the same people, subject to the same laws, and enjoying the same rights and privileges." [21] As the Governor envisioned an American destiny and American order, however, his assurances challenged the status quo and demanded a flexibility never before required of the Californians. And for that reason the future of the region's economy and society depended on their ability to meet the novel conditions imposed upon them by the Americans.

By effectively exploiting their physical isolation, the Californians had hitherto created a sufficient if not affluent economy. Their ranchos were nevertheless grossly inefficient. Compared with farms in the United States, they produced extremely little per acre and per person. That they survived anyway was due to the sparse population, mild environment, and proliferating stock. That they also prospered was due to the absence of taxes on land and the availability of involuntary labor. During the 1830's and 1840's the provincial authorities met

12

their administrative expenses with revenues from commercial duties, punitive fines, and forced loans; they levied no taxes on property according to value.[22] Throughout the Mexican period, moreover, the number of natives was sufficiently large that the Californians were seldom forced to employ wage earners. Under such conditions the rancheros thrived merely by maintaining their herds, holding their laborers, and avoiding extravagance.

All this changed soon after the cession of California. Although the Americans guaranteed the rancheros legal recognition of their holdings, they did not exempt the estates from assessments levied everywhere in the United States. Since the expenses of the new state exceeded those of the former province, the government followed the traditional practice of raising revenue by taxing property. Unfortunately for southern California, northern California, which was principally a mining center, contained much less assessable land and many more eligible voters. Tempted by the expansive plains owned by a few rancheros, the elected officials levied taxes which fell heavily on the southern ranchos.[23] Assessments on pasture, it is true, rarely exceeded twenty-five cents an acre; but when charged against estates of 10,000 and 20,000 acres, whose proprietors had never before been compelled to market their produce, they were considered by the Californians "burdens which our people are poorly able to bear." [24]

The Americans also presumed a clarity concerning the ownership of land that was unwarranted in southern California. "There were no surveyors in the country, and fortunately no lawyers," one ranchero explained. "Judges were not professors of law; every transaction was executed in simplicity and good faith; and it should not be considered strange that . . . involuntary errors should have been committed by the grantees or others intrusted with the measurements, boundaries, maps, etc." [25] Hence a host of conflicting, and even fraudulent, claims confronted the American Congress. To adjudicate them, it created a Land Commission in 1851 with power to confirm or reject all petitions for Mexican property in California. The rancheros, who assumed that the earlier assurance implied the validity of their titles, now heard with dismay that the Land Commission would demand proof of ownership, and that unless it or, on appeal, the courts upheld their claims, the ranchos would revert to the public domain.

The commissioners reviewed the petitions impartially and ultimately confirmed the titles of most rightful proprietors. But the proceedings were often interminably prolonged, as many rancheros had difficulty finding the documents which authorized the concessions and locating the boulders, trees, and streams that defined the estates. Appeals from the Commission to the courts further delayed granting of the titles without which the rancheros were unable to manage their holdings properly.[26] Also, the Californians, as they protested to Congress, knew so little about American justice that they had to retain attorneys to present their petitions. Law being "proverbially dear," as the most prominent ranchero explained, "the sums that the Claimants are forced to pay for the defense of their titles are often disproportionate to the value of the lands." "The law creating the Land Commission," he argued, "has from the beginning operated as a direct tax upon all private owners of real estate." [27]

In addition to compelling the Californians to pay litigation fees and property taxes, the transition from Mexican to American rule permanently disrupted the labor force. The Indians, whose population stabilized between 85,000 and 90,000 under the paternalism of the Mexicans,[28] were now liberated only to suffer the indifference or hostility of the Americans. The natives "caught the idea that they are free," one sympathetic Californian wrote, but found that "American freedom does not profit them." They were unprepared for hard work, he continued, and "ashamed or afraid to go back to their old *amos* (masters)." Some moved to Los Angeles, where they were rapidly ruined by the vices of the white man, while others, who longed for "the old and kindred associations of their tribes," [29] returned to their mountain villages. There they shared poverty and mourned the dead together.

Some Americans urged the federal government to place the Indians on reservations. Their plea came too late, however, and the Indian population fell from 85,000 to 35,000 between 1852 and 1860. From the viewpoint of the rancheros it mattered little whether the Indians returned to their villages, left for the reservations, or died in Los Angeles. They lost their traditional supply of involuntary labor in any case, and had to employ many free workers for the first time. Under American sovereignty, then, the rancheros were obliged to pay salaries as well as taxes and legal fees. But the limited market for hides and tallow prevented them from meeting these obligations merely by slaughtering more cattle. Since the rancheros had to retain their estates in order to maintain their standard of living and position in society, they were left with no option other than to shift their enterprise from self-sufficient agriculture to market agriculture—from varied production for immediate consumption to specialized production for distant consumers.

After 1848, moreover, the discovery of gold in northern California generated an immense migration which created a mammoth market for cattle.[30] Although the southern California rancheros were amazed by the sudden inundation of nearly 100,000 miners from all over the world, they soon realized that the gold rush offered them an extra-ordinary opportunity to meet their new financial responsibilities. They alone could provide the prospectors with meat. To tap this mar-ket, the rancheros drove their herds half the length of the long and uncharted state to the cattle marts of the Sacramento Valley. There the growing population and dwindling supply forced prices to twenty dollars a head for mixed stock and forty-five to seventy dollars a head for prime cattle. With profits handsomely compensating for the treacherous trek, the rancheros shared fully in California's remarkable windfall.[31]

"Everybody in Los Angeles seemed rich," one early settler remem-bered, "everybody *was* rich, and money was more plentiful at that time, than in any other place of like size, I venture to say, in the world."[32] But such wealth spoiled the Californians. "They be-came too proud and too careless to milk, and so now you find no milk on the ranchos. They could buy clothing and all kinds of supplies, and so their useful and ingenious industries perished. They came to town dressed in absurd gold and silver lace, with gold stirrups and gold-mounted saddles, and wasted their money in gambling-houses; and so their business was neglected."[33] Their desire for goods unat-tainable to them as self-sufficient rancheros need not have been dis-astrous. But their infatuation with luxury and pursuit of pleasure distracted them from the fact that their monopoly of the beef trade was temporary. Indeed, it ended once the reports of high prices for cattle in California reached Texas and Missouri and inspired cross-country drives by enterprising southwestern cattlemen.[34]

At the same time the gold rush passed its peak and the population started to stabilize. Competition between California and southwestern suppliers became intense, and prices plunged to fifteen dollars and even ten dollars a head.[35] As southwestern stock was fatter and its meat more tender, few rancheros found purchasers even at these low figures. Rather than accept poor offers, most held on to their herds, "hoping that as the season advances, the prices of cattle will advance." "Vain hope!" commented the Los Angeles *Star*, "as all who have trav-elled through the mining region know."[36] Vain and also costly, for the rancheros still had to pay taxes, fees, and salaries, and, having abandoned self-sufficiency, to buy life's necessities as well. Hence several sold their land for a fraction of its value, while others saw the sheriff foreclose on their thousand-acre estates for hundred-dollar delinquencies. "Our inheritance is turned to strangers—our houses to aliens," lamented one ranchero. "We have drunken our water for money—our wood is sold unto us. Our necks are under persecution—we labor and have no rest." [37]

Other rancheros entered even more deeply into the competitive economy. To meet their obligations, improve their stock, and wait for better prices, they not only borrowed money at excessive interest rates but also mortgaged their estates for collateral. Completely dependent on California's cattle market, the rancheros anxiously listened for news of an advance. But the supply of cattle far exceeded the demand, and prices remained extremely low throughout the decade. "The cattle market has never been so depressed in California as this year," an observer wrote to a ranchero in 1859; "for the present it is completely glutted." [38] By the early 1860's some rancheros sought outlets for stock in Chile, and others slaughtered the animals and sold the tallow, hides, horns, and hoofs piecemeal.[39] That these parts were worth more than the entire animal was testimony to the appalling plight of the rancheros.

Few Californians survived this crisis with their ranchos intact. Trained as soldiers and dedicated to the ideal of the Spanish grandee, they did not understand the complexities of the market economy. Instead of fortifying their position during the boom of the early 1850's, they expanded their holdings and squandered their profits. Now, with the price of cattle depressed and the costs of operation high, they witnessed interest compounded at 2 and 4 per cent per month overwhelm their once independent and flourishing estates. They failed to meet their taxes or payments and read their names on the delinquency lists or forfeited their mortgages. "Some, who at one time had been the richest landowners," a group of rancheros wrote to the Congress in 1860, "today find themselves without a foot of ground, living as objects of charity—and right in view of the many leagues of land with many a thousand head of cattle they once called their own." [40]

American ranchers and moneylenders purchased these estates at public auctions and private sales. More capable and less sentimental than the Californians, they still faced the same problems as their predecessors. In order to acquire the ranchos, rationalize their organization, and improve their cattle, they too had to borrow heavily from Los Angeles and especially San Francisco capitalists and mortgage their lands as collateral. And in order to meet their obligations, the

Americans, like the Mexicans before them, depended on a rise in the price of beef.[41] Unfortunately for them, the abundance of cattle in California prevented any advances during the late 1850's and early 1860's. It was thus at this point—with the ranchers watching the compounding of deferred interest force them closer and closer to bankruptcy—that a series of natural catastrophes precipitated the impending collapse of southern California's rancho economy.

Late in 1861 unusually heavy winter rains flooded the region, damaged much property, and destroyed some stock.[42] Most ranchers remained calm, confident that the smaller herds and richer pasture would revive the lagging cattle market. But the normally dry summer and autumn months passed, and, to the astonishment of the ranchers, the weather remained dry in the winter. "We have had no rain as yet," an anxious overseer reported in February 1862; "there is no grass and the cattle are very poor." "The cattle will commence dying within a month," [43] he wrote five weeks later. Although thousands of head perished during the spring and summer, thousands more found sufficient feed in the once-flooded fields. So the ranchers waited hopefully, but when another dry year followed they realized that southern California was caught in a prolonged drought. Their herds did not last long: "In passing over the plains," the Los Angeles *Star* observed, "it is sad to see the number of dead cattle; while those that survive present an appearance, such as to produce sympathy for the suffering of the poor dumb animals." [44]

A few ranchers unsuccessfully attempted to drive their stock out of the region, and then, in despair, stripped the hides and tallow from carcasses strewn over the land. By the spring of 1864 everyone had lost hope for the future. "We believe the stock interests of the county, as well as the adjoining counties, to be 'played out' entirely," remarked the Los Angeles *Southern News*. "Famine has done its work, and nothing can now save what few cattle remain on the desert California ranches." [45] The ranchers now had no way to meet their outstanding debts and property taxes. Once again the moneylenders foreclosed on the mortgages, and the sheriff sold estates of nearly 10,000 and 20,000 acres for delinquencies of only thirty and sixty dollars.[46] The inability of the ranchers to pay such trifling sums revealed that California's rancho civilization was indeed incompatible with America's competitive economy.

Possession of southern California's ranches passed to a few prominent Los Angeles and San Francisco capitalists. Some chose to utilize their holdings as residential estates and paid for this luxury out of savings and investments.[47] But most, whether as individuals or in syndicates, considered the ranches economic enterprises and sought monetary returns. Burdened by substantial expenses and motivated by material considerations, they did not contemplate a reversion to self-sufficiency. From previous experience, they also realized that California's meat market did not justify operating their properties as cattle ranges. The new proprietors therefore decided to engage vigorously in competitive agriculture. And by exploiting the abundant land and mild climate and accommodating production to the distant markets and transportation costs, they often succeeded in subsequent decades.

Some ranchers concentrated on goods not susceptible to spoilage and inexpensively shipped by sea. James Irvine and the Bixby brothers, who stocked several ranches with sheep, hired Indians as shearers, and sent their wool by water to San Francisco, Boston, and New York, proved that lands which had failed as cattle ranges could be profitably operated as sheep ranches.[48] Others, impressed by the availability of farmland at low prices, resorted to large-scale production. The San Fernando Farm Association, a group of San Francisco capitalists which planted nearly 60,000 acres of wheat in the San Fernando Valley, demonstrated that extensive agriculture could increase yields, reduce expenses, and assure profits.[49] Still others cultivated crops which flourished nowhere in the United States but in southern California. J. de Barth Shorb and his San Gabriel Wine and Vineyard Company, which grew vines, produced wines, and distilled brandies, received returns that enabled the corporation to maintain the ranch at a time of rising values.[50]

Although these ranches (and others like them) covered thousands and even tens of thousands of acres, they differed as completely from the historic ranchos as the Americans did from the Mexicans. Whereas the ranchos needed only abundant herds and relied largely on involuntary labor, the ranches required substantial sums of capital and hired mainly wage earners. Whereas the ranchos produced for immediate household consumption and provided their own necessities, the ranches produced for the future demands of distant markets and depended upon outsiders for essential goods. And whereas the ranchos fostered stable personal relationships and achieved social self-sufficiency, the ranches were strictly economic enterprises in which owners and employees were tied only by money. These differences were indeed the most striking evidence of the transformation of the southern California countryside.

Other ranchers tried to escape the fate of their predecessors not by more efficient production but by subdivision and sale of their lands. This alternative had not been feasible before the 1870's when inflated values and elevated expectations inhibited potential sellers and dubious titles and heavy encumbrances discouraged prospective purchasers. Also, most rancheros considered proprietorship socially as well as economically beneficial and for that reason refused to dispose of even a fraction of their holdings. By contrast, the new owners recognized the risks inherent in these immense but inefficient estates and promised the purchasers free and clear titles. They also evaluated property not by estimating its social connotations but by measuring profits from its production against interest on its market value. "What is the good of so much land that does not pay any income?" they asked. "The best thing to be done is to sell everything and convert all into cash and then invest in something that will yield a sure income." [51]

Furthermore, the market for farmland, which was severely limited before the Civil War, improved with the increase of migration after 1865. Impressed by the thousands, even tens of thousands, of acres capable of producing one hundred bushels of corn each, the newcomers envisioned southern California as a region of unparalleled opportunity.[52] In response to their demand, many ranchers tentatively offered their land for sale. They "are beginning to see that men and women are more profitable than cattle," reported one observer; "that a small number of thoroughbred cows and sheep is better than a large stock of worthless animals; that a thousand acres of land well cultivated is more profitable than 10,000 lying waste; that 500 families on the fourth of a 40,000 acre tract more than doubles the value of the remaining 30,000." [53] The ranchers then divided their estates into farms of twenty, forty, and eighty acres, promoted them as the choicest in all California, and sold them to the immigrants. By 1877, according to the Los Angeles *Express,* there were "but a few of the old ranches that have not been cut up" in Los Angeles and vicinity.[54]

The newcomers who settled on the ranchos lived and labored much like farmers elsewhere in the United States. "I now own a farm in the El Monta of one hundred acres," one pioneer wrote from the western San Gabriel Valley, "with forty enclosed with a live fence and a good house in the middle of my field, on a gentle elevation." [55] He and others like him grew corn, wheat, grapes, and fruit for the market, not for themselves, and met the expenses of ownership and cultivation as well as bought the necessities and luxuries of life from the proceeds. They erected modest homes instead of elaborate haciendas and lived there with their wives, children, and perhaps one or two hired workers, not with assorted relatives and retainers. In sum, the American farmers, unlike the Mexican rancheros, did not have the land or the inclination to establish self-sufficient households in southern California.

The emergence of commercial ranches and small farms transformed the countryside around Los Angeles. The amount of cultivated acreage increased more than a hundredfold, and the number of existing farms in 1880 nearly equaled the number of improved acres in 1850. The value of agricultural land multiplied twenty times, and the value of buildings and equipment thirty times. The combined harvest of wheat, barley, and corn in 1850 totaled less than 3 per cent of the yield of corn alone in 1880. Of all the major products, only cattle did not record a substantial increase in value. Reflecting and measuring this material progress, Los Angeles County's population grew tenfold, from 4,000 to 34,000, and its assessed valuation multiplied nine times, from $2 million to $19 million.[56] And no less important, the ranchers and farmers who wrought these changes became dependent in ways the rancheros had never been on economic intermediaries and external institutions.

Both the ranchers and the farmers required the assistance of merchants to sell their produce in southern California and the western states or to ship it on commission to San Francisco and the eastern cities. They also relied on tradesmen for food and clothing, implements and furniture, and a variety of other necessities and luxuries which their specialized estates did not provide. They employed only enough workers to produce cash crops, and depended on local artisans and manufacturers for such crafts as carpentry and such goods as farm equipment. They often bound their properties in complicated legal arrangements, borrowed capital to survive in the competitive economy, and generated opportunities for lawyers and bankers too. And because the Americans rarely found full emotional gratification within their ranches and farms, they sought outside social, fraternal, and religious affiliations.[57]

The repercussions profoundly affected Los Angeles. So long as self-sufficient ranchos covered the countryside, it remained an agricultural village with no unique function in the region's economy or society. The failure of the ranchos, however, generated opportunities for urban enterprises and associations which transformed the Mexican pueblo into an American town. The extent of this transformation was roughly measurable by the increase in population. With only 1,200 persons in

1840, the pueblo was the largest settlement in California; yet with 1,610 inhabitants a decade later, it was surpassed by the inland towns and coastal ports of the gold country. Then in response to the region's progress, Los Angeles expanded from 4,385 residents in 1860 to 5,728 in 1870, 11,183 in 1880, and approximately 20,000 in 1885.[58] Compared with San Francisco, northern California's metropolis, Los Angeles had grown little; but from the perspective of the pueblo, as Table 1 reveals, it had advanced considerably.

The character of the transformation was revealed by the occupations of the newcomers. Unlike the Californians, the Americans worked as grocers and druggists, retail and commission merchants, painters, plumbers, carpenters, and masons, physicians and attorneys, bankers and realtors, manufacturers of brick, millers of flour, and distillers of wine.[59] Their trades, crafts, professions, and industries facilitated contact between the countryside and town, encouraged a crude interdependence within the urban economy, and fostered the separation of business activities and family households. The expectations of the Americans also differed from those of the Californians. They were not only accustomed to higher standards of personal comfort and public convenience, but, as most of them had consciously chosen to work and live in Los Angeles, self-interest and civic pride dictated that their anticipations justify their actions. "They believe their city and county to be the choicest part of the earth," a perceptive visitor observed, "and are determined that no one shall have it in his power to point out wherein it is wanting."[60]

Thus Mexican civilization all but vanished in southern California. While a few great ranchos were still intact, they were operated as commercial ranches and interspersed with small farms. Specialized agri-

TABLE 1. Population Growth in Los Angeles and San Francisco, 1850–1880

Year	Total population		Rate of growth	
	Los Angeles	San Francisco	Los Angeles	San Francisco
1850	1,610	34,776	—	—
1860	4,385	56,802	172%	63%
1870	5,728	149,473	27	163
1880	11,183	233,959	95	57

Source: U.S. Bureau of the Census, *Fifteenth Census of the United States: Volume I. Population* (Washington, 1931), pp. 18–19.

1. Los Angeles in 1857

2. Los Angeles in 1873

cultural units supplanted self-sufficient households everywhere in the countryside. Likewise, the pueblo of Los Angeles all but disappeared. While vineyards and orchards were still cultivated, their owners were principally in the wine, fruit, and real estate businesses. Merchants, artisans, professionals, and manufacturers replaced agriculturists throughout the settlement. Indeed, nowhere in southern California was the new order and new destiny promised by the conquerors in the 1840's more evident than in the emergence of Los Angeles as an American town by the 1880's.

I intend to spend money and keep on spending money in improvements and grading streets until this locality [the northwestern hill district] *meets the attention it deserves, and it will not be long I assure you. (Prudent Beaudry, 1877)*

2   PRIVATE ENTERPRISE, PUBLIC AUTHORITY, AND URBAN EXPANSION

The transformation of the Mexican pueblo into an American town profoundly altered the tradition whereby public authority rather than private enterprise guided the expansion of Los Angeles. Hitherto an *ayuntamiento* (municipal council), which was entrusted with the responsibility to transplant Spanish civilization into the pueblo, implemented this tradition. It supplied Los Angeles' services, controlled its lands, and supported its institutions so as to accommodate a modest population, household agriculture, and Latin culture. The coming of the Americans undermined this arrangement, however. Their numbers were large not small, their enterprises urban not rural, and their expectations American not Mexican. They disrupted the means by which Los Angeles distributed water and land, transported people and goods, protected against fire, disorder, and pestilence, and erected churches and schools. They then insisted that a better balance be established between the demands of the settlers and the facilities of the community.

Given southern California's arid climate, the Americans realized, a sufficient water supply was Los Angeles' cardinal requirement. Heretofore the residents of the pueblo conveyed water from the river to the fields through *zanjas* (irrigation ditches) built by the ayuntamiento.[1] They bathed themselves and cleaned their animals in these ditches, and, by filling their buckets or contracting with carriers, drew their domestic supply from them.[2] Thus the zanjas not only tapped a small portion of the river's flow and wasted much of it through seepage and evaporation, but they carried polluted water as well. For the Mexicans, who cultivated small farms and accepted indiscriminate use of water, the system was satisfactory. But for the Americans, who consumed much more water in intensive agriculture and urban enterprise and expected a separate domestic supply, the waste and pollution of Los Angeles' most precious resource was incomprehensible and intolerable.[3]

The pueblo's land system seemed little better to them. The ayuntamiento not only administered the *ejidos* and *propios* (common and municipal lands), but also regulated the solares and suertes so as to prevent speculation.[4] The Mexicans, who were not assessed for their property and considered it a livelihood, were satisfied with these arrangements. But the Americans, who paid taxes on their real estate and treated it as a commodity, objected to governmental restrictions on its exploitation. From their perspective, the thousands of acres the town inherited from the pueblo were more a liability than an asset. So long as the municipality held the land, the newcomers could not cultivate it, and the council could not derive tax revenue from it.[5] The Mexican policy whereby the community retained control over the development of its land ran counter to both the American inclinations and their traditions.

The enlarged population and its urban enterprises also strained existing transportation facilities. In the pueblo no premium was placed on rapid movement because work was confined to the houses and fields. Moreover, the buildings were grouped in compact clusters, a short walk away from the cathedral and plaza. As the streets were muddy in winter, dusty in summer, and dark at night, the ayuntamiento ordered each proprietor to sweep from the front of his house to the center of the road and to hang a lantern on his door from dusk to dawn.[6] But this did not suffice in the town where merchants, artisans, professionals, and manufacturers often worked away from their homes; their stores, offices, and shops had to be accessible, and their goods easily transported. Impassable, dangerous, too few, too narrow, and too rough, Los Angeles' streets inhibited the town's economy. More roadways—wider and smoother as well as cleaner and lighter—were imperative.[7]

Life and property were less secure in the town than in the pueblo too. Los Angeles, as one early settler recalled, was never before threatened by fire. "The adobe houses with their clay walls, earthen floors, tiled roofs and rawhide doors were as nearly fireproof as human habitation could be made. The cooking was done in detached kitchens and in beehive-shaped ovens without flues. The houses were without chimneys, so the danger of fire was reduced to a minimum." [8] Americans constructed their homes and shops of wood and brick, however. Merchants stored hay and other inflammables, and manufacturers burned petroleum and other fuels. The new buildings were more susceptible to fire than the old ones, and the town was more exposed to conflagration than the pueblo. This situation led the Los Angeles *News* to warn that "If a fire should break out at any of the leading business points, an entire block would doubtless be swept away." [9] And to the dismay of the residents, such warnings were all too often justified.

Order was maintained in the pueblo by the church and the family. Since almost everyone was Catholic and resided in a household, supervision was thorough and discipline rigid. Private violence so rarely erupted into public crime that a volunteer guard effectively patrolled the pueblo. The American conquest released the Indians from captivity, however, and opened Los Angeles to strangers who did not subscribe to any religion or admit the authority of any family.[10] Public order was strained and then sundered. "The name of this city is in Spanish the city of Angels, but with much more truth might it be called at present the city of Demons," an itinerant minister wrote in 1854. "While I have been here in Los Angeles only two weeks, there have been it is said eleven deaths, and only one of them a natural death . . . If I am to stay here," he prayed, "may the Lord be with me." [11] Under such circumstances, the townspeople, suspicious of the Mexicans and fearful of the transients, demanded better police protection.

Los Angeles' inadequate sanitation also alarmed the Americans. The little waste left in the pueblo was easily disposed of on the farms, and the few visitors to the region rarely contaminated the community. But the town's larger populace and varied industries produced far more refuse and reduced the space available for its disposal. More strangers drifted into Los Angeles, and many consumptives sought their health there. Watching the natives drink polluted water, one observer expressed more surprise at Los Angeles' prevailing health than its sporadic sickness. "Place this city as it is made up where Chicago or any other eastern city is," he prophesied, "and the month of June would decimate it." [12] Nonetheless, as one resident remembered, the "whole population was on such a friendly footing that every death made a very great impression," [13] and even occasional epidemics generated intense pressure for improved sanitation.

The newcomers despaired of Los Angeles' communal shortcomings too. The Mexicans who moved to the pueblo were assimilated by an extended family, an established church, and a paternalistic government. These traditional institutions fostered personal relationships, buttressed individual weaknesses, and promoted common interests. The Americans who arrived later not only found a less familiar settlement, but also worked in more precarious occupations. As traders, artisans, professionals, and manufacturers, they were dependent—as the Mexican farmers were not—on the marketplace. Moreover, the Americans transplanted their nuclear families, their voluntary churches, and their impoverished governments into Los Angeles. Hence they placed greater demands on the community at the same time that they undermined the institutions which formerly met these demands.

The Americans even thought Los Angeles spiritually neglect. They knew, of course, that the Californians, as Catholics, supported a cathedral—a cathedral that the Indians had been forced to build after the Spaniards decided that the church constructed when the pueblo was founded was too small. But the Americans, as Protestants, preferred to do without religion than to join the Californians. The entire situation disturbed the local press, which believed that organized religion was particularly important in a frontier settlement such as Los Angeles. A city with a large American population but without a church or even a minister, Los Angeles, the *Star* observed in 1856, "presents a case of destitution, we are certain, without precedent in the State." [14] To remedy this deficiency, the press appealed to missionary groups for assistance and at the same time urged the residents of Los Angeles to form their own religious institutions.

The newcomers considered the town educationally backward as well—and with good reason. True, the Mexicans, though not the Spaniards, encouraged the establishment of schools in Los Angeles. The ayuntamiento allocated small sums to teachers in the pueblo, and the provincial authorities sometimes offered additional subsidies. Indeed, the Mexicans were for the most part content with their educational arrangements. These schools closed during the American war, however, and their instructors quit during the gold rush. So by the time the Americans—who, as the *Star* noted in 1856, placed an extremely high priority on public education—arrived in Los Angeles, they found no school system whatsoever. And anxious lest their adopted settlement remain an unprogressive community, they wholeheartedly seconded the press's plea to "Let schools multiply." [15]

The town's legal status hampered the municipal government somewhat in its efforts to remedy these deplorable conditions. Los Angeles, which was entitled to the rights of a private corporation, was subject to the authority of the California legislature which had created and could abolish it and could expand, contract, or otherwise modify its powers.[16] In practice, however, the state seldom interfered except to limit the town's tax rate and bonded debt, and Los Angeles' government was fettered less by its legal inferiority than by its citizens' political attitudes. For while they persistently appealed for additional services and facilities, they staunchly resisted proposals that taxes be raised.[17] Since here, as in many other small western settlements, an excess of imports over exports left chronic cash shortages and rendered monetary payments difficult, their position was understandable if misguided.

Caught between pleas for expanded improvements and objections to higher taxes, the mayor and the council were deemed incompetent and corrupt by the populace. "The matter of the present City Government has been called to our notice," a grand jury reported in 1861, "and we are unanimous in our opinion that the City Government is a nuisance, kept alive only for the purpose of raising a revenue to support useless officers; and, therefore, we pray that if it can be got rid of, let it be wiped from existence." [18] Instead of annulling the charter and abolishing the municipality, however, the citizens continued to demand essential facilities and withhold necessary funds. This dilemma so distressed those persons with interests to promote, families to protect, and institutions to support that they turned to private enterprise and voluntary associations as well as to municipal authority for requisite improvements.

Municipal authority assumed partial responsibility for the general welfare by exercising its police powers in cases where the citizens preferred reasonable restrictions on personal liberties to taxation for otherwise unavoidable undertakings. The council increased the zanjas' efficiency by appointing an official to evaluate petitions for water and administer its distribution, and prevented excessive contamination by forbidding the residents to bathe, wash clothing, and clean animals in the ditches.[19] The legislature also facilitated transportation by prohibiting horses, carts, hackney carriages, and job wagons from obstructing passageways, and expedited access by limiting hitching to one hour on busy streets and outlawing merchandise displays on crowded sidewalks.[20] Nevertheless, regulatory legislation alone could not materially enlarge the quantity or improve the quality of the water supply; nor could it open and maintain additional streets or widen and surface existing ones.

The council also acted to prevent fires, eliminate vice, and preserve public health. It limited the storage of grain and oil, prohibited the manufacturing of matches and refining of petroleum in certain parts of town, and compelled builders to use brick and stone, separate the interior woodwork from the outside structure, cover the roofs with tin, and install spark catchers on chimneys.[21] It also forbade residents to gamble, carry weapons, and operate saloons during the early morning hours, and outlawed beggars, drunkards, loiterers, and prostitutes (though it ignored them as long as they kept their distance from respectable folk).[22] The legislature even ordered property owners to maintain cesspools and appointed officials to impound animals as well as to inspect dairies, slaughterhouses, groceries, and butcher shops.[23] And during plagues it vaccinated school children, quarantined infected homes, closed streets to the stricken, and placed the destitute ill in a pest house.[24] Notwithstanding this legislation, conflagrations, crime, and epidemics still occurred in Los Angeles.

Regulation failed to restore the balance upset by urban growth because implementation, however efficient, was incomplete and prevention, however imaginative, was insufficient. More positive and more expensive action was imperative. But the municipal authorities lacked the funds, and the property owners opposed tax increases. Moreover, businessmen urged the council to encourage private enterprise to undertake community services. Landholders insisted that it intervene in cases where proposed improvements provoked dissension. And the state legislature compelled Los Angeles to assume responsibility for the education of its children. These pressures directed governmental expansion toward modest activities such as supplying water for irrigation, self-sustaining ones such as improving streets and building sewers, and traditional ones such as operating public schools.

The administration of the zanjas shifted from the ayuntamiento to the common council after the conquest of California. During the next thirty-five years the municipal authorities increased the water supply by creating an elaborate network of main and supplementary ditches and reduced its seepage by replacing the zanjas with iron pipes. Although the citizens voted bond issues to finance improvements and the consumers paid moderate sums to maintain operations, the irrigation system was not profitable. Hence local entrepreneurs were not inclined to purchase the zanjas or to construct others. For this reason the diversion and distribution of water for agriculture remained the city's responsibiliy until the urbanization of Los Angeles made irrigation anachronistic early in the twentieth century.[25]

Providing transportation was far more complicated than supplying water. Opening new streets required the purchase of private property; widening and surfacing existing ones involved heavy construction. The town's financial resources were ample for any single project, but not for all the proposed improvements. Also, it was politically inexpedient for the authorities to endorse one and deny another. Hence the council undertook street work only upon requests from a majority of the frontage owners and assessed the cost against the adjacent property which was expected to appreciate as a result.[26] Although few denied the desirability of more and better thoroughfares or challenged this method of financing them, at least one landholder usually opposed each petition on the grounds that the costs exceeded the benefits. To ensure that disagreement did not render this approach inequitable or impracticable, the council compelled the recalcitrant to submit to the majority. In this way, about two hundred miles of streets were dedicated in Los Angeles by 1880.[27]

Sewers, which were as essential to the town as streets, raised even more perplexing problems. Not only were they much more expensive, but, in addition, they functioned only as parts of a larger system. Assessments on frontage, which were modest and equitable when imposed for a single street, were heavy and unfair when levied for a sewer which collected from the others and disposed of the accumulated waste. The common council, aware of this difference, tried to use zanja number nine as a main sewer, but it was not steep enough and the refuse was congested rather than removed. Action became imperative in 1876 as fetid and noxious cesspools formed at the ends of flooded sewers. Accordingly, the authorities, overriding the protests of aggrieved landowners, ordered construction of a main sewer to flush all waste to southern Los Angeles. They later extended it to the charter boundary where the South Side Irrigation Company disposed of the sewage in return for the right to sell the sewer water.[28]

This undertaking provided Los Angeles with adequate sanitation until the 1880's when population growth and economic expansion produced an unprecedented amount of waste. To handle it, the city engineer devised a plan for a comprehensive sewer system which consisted of three main interceptors and a single outfall emptying into the Pacific Ocean.[29] Sanitary experts who examined the project expressed their approval, but many citizens severely criticized the proposed outfall sewer. They objected not only to its cost—$450,000 out of the $1 million total—but also to the waste of even polluted water in a region where countless acres were not cultivated for lack of rainfall.[30]

A private concern, known as the Pacific Sewerage Company, intensified the opposition by offering to accept the town's refuse, filter out the impurities, and sell the water for irrigation.

This corporation asked the council for a $150,000 bonus, promising, in return, to connect every building in town with the system and to transfer the entire plant to the municipality in ten years. When the council dismissed this proposal and nearly approved a $350,000 bond issue for sewer construction, the company revised its proposal. It reduced the donation, added a service charge, set the maximum selling price at $250,000, and even offered to build three separate treatment centers and accept the subsidy in installments. The council's sewer committee favored the proposition, but critics—who wondered why the city should "pay a bonus . . . instead of receiving a compensation for making so profitable a grant to a private corporation" [31]—persuaded the legislators to postpone a decision. The council then met with the Board of Trade and Chamber of Commerce in January 1889, and, when all agreed that the gravity of the situation precluded experimentation, authorized a $1.3 million bond issue for the construction of intercepting sewers, storm drains, and an outfall sewer.[32]

Those citizens who accepted the city engineer's statement that sanitation and irrigation were incompatible supported the issue. Those who rejected it denounced the proposition. "The sewage," they argued, "should be used and not wasted." [33] A majority of the electorate, but not the necessary two-thirds, approved the bonds. An anti-sewer-bond committee then demanded that the council advertise for bids. The legislators agreed, but simultaneously organized a Sewer Commission. It endorsed the interior sewer and separate drainage systems, but left unsettled the critical question of disposal. Pacific Sewerage promptly affered to convey the refuse to the corporate limits and filter it for fifty years at $5,000 per annum. After considering the alternatives, the Sewer Commission decided that sewer water could be used for irrigation and recommended that this proposition should be adopted.[34]

The legislators appointed a Board of Engineers to review the report. Although it agreed that sewage treatment and utilization was theoretically the ideal solution, the board foresaw economic and legal complications which forced it to disagree with the commission. "Other things being equal," it concluded, "an outfall to the sea, which requires a minimum of care and attention on the part of the municipality is therefore to be preferred." [35] The council accepted this verdict and authorized separate bond issues for interior sewers, storm drains, and an outfall sewer. The electorate gave each a simple majority, but only the internal section the requisite two-thirds. The council, which could not construct the long overdue local sewers without also building the disposal facilities, resubmitted the outfall sewer proposition in 1892. More than two-thirds of the voters then endorsed it.[36] And henceforth the municipality assumed sole responsibility to collect and remove refuse and to maintain proper sanitation in Los Angeles.

The council committed Los Angeles to the principle of public education with far less controversy. Like the ayuntamiento, it initially subsidized individual schoolmasters, allocating a portion of the town's fines and fees and levying a ten cent tax per one hundred dollars of assessed property for this purpose. But in 1852 the state legislature authorized every incorporated town to raise "whatever amount of money shall be requisite . . . for the support of a competent number of public schools."[37] In compliance with this order, the municipality soon after erected a few elementary schools, fixed appropriate taxes, and created a Board of Education. Subsequently, the board constructed several new buildings, hired the necessary teachers, administered the system's finances, and offered at least a rudimentary education to the children of Los Angeles.

Municipal authority charged the costs of all these undertakings to the beneficiaries. Believing that regulatory legislation and public schools served the entire community, the council met these expenses principally by levying taxes on the town's assessable real estate. Convinced that zanjas promoted the welfare of Los Angeles in general and of the farmers in particular, it floated bond issues for initial expansion and exacted moderate fees for operating costs. Assuming that streets rendered limited rather than widespread advantages, the legislature opened, widened, and surfaced roadways only upon petitions from property owners willing to pay for improvements. And classifying interceptor and outfall sewers as essential to the municipality and connecting ones as beneficial to its landholders, it authorized a bonded debt for the former and levied separate assessments for the latter. In these limited ways municipal authority acted effectively to accommodate physical and educational facilities to economic and social change.

Municipal authority was supplemented in these efforts by voluntary (i.e. nonprofit and nongovernmental) associations. These associations, which were well endowed with manpower, were most active in fighting fires and preserving law and order. They were active in fighting fires primarily because the town did not inherit from the pueblo any other arrangements for doing so. In emergencies, shopkeepers and homeowners were forced to call on passers-by and neighbors who were more cooperative than competent. Down through the 1860's, however, all efforts to establish fire companies failed, as the *News* complained in 1867, for want of support.[38] Thus it was not until 1871 that several prominent merchants and wealthy landholders organized the first voluntary fire company. Other businessmen and residents followed their lead soon after, so that by the 1880's Los Angeles was well protected against fires by a host of engine, hook and ladder, and hose companies.

Voluntary associations were also active in preserving law and order, even though the town marshall and county sheriff who replaced the pueblo guard normally prevented widespread disorder. For from time to time, when Los Angeles' security was seriously threatened by internal upheaval or external invasion, the citizens banded together to defend their lives and properties. Usually they disbanded after the crisis was over, but sometimes they created permanent para-military organizations such as the Los Angeles Rangers and the Los Angeles Home Guard.[39] These associations combined social affairs with vigilante actions, and, like the fire companies, thrived because of the loneliness of their members and the opportunities for fellowship more than the perils to the community and the importance of their tasks. Indeed, few organizations took a more active part in the community life of Los Angeles than the voluntary fire and police companies.

By the 1870's and 1880's, however, the residents were more anxious about their lives and properties and less willing to rely on enthusiastic but amateur groups for protection. Busier and more pacific, they no longer found the time or felt the inclination to serve as part-time firemen and ad hoc policemen. At their insistence the municipal authorities reorganized the voluntary fire companies into an official fire department, employing its members as full-time public servants. They also created a professional police force whose employees were designated as the sole guardians of the peace in Los Angeles.[40] Here too the council adhered to the policy of charging the expenses to the beneficiaries. It levied higher taxes on landholders, who paid lower fire insurance premiums and received better police protection, and imposed higher license fees on businesses, such as saloons, which required extra supervision.[41]

Los Angeles' religious associations, unlike its fire companies and military brigades, became more not less important in time. This occurred largely because the municipal government, though it favored religion in general and Protestantism in particular, was inhibited by America's traditional separation of church and state from offering more than token assistance to either. Instead of the common council, individual congregations assumed chief responsibility to create the proper religious environment in Los Angeles—just as they did in other American cities—and, employing subscriptions, entertainments, and other similar devices, raised funds to purchase lots, erect churches, and support ministers.[42] Indeed, by the 1880's, largely as a result of their labors, Los Angeles' churches and temples offered nearly as wide a range of Protestant, as well as Catholic and Jewish, services as could be found in other small far western communities.

Other voluntary associations compensated for the absence of an extended family, an established church, and a paternalistic government in Los Angeles. Fraternal and nationality organizations founded hospitals and other charitable institutions, facilitated contacts among newcomers, and in these ways shielded their members against the insecurity and anonymity of the urban economy and society. Commercial and civic associations exerted pressures on municipal authorities and private enterprises and negotiated with governmental officials and corporate interests in an effort to make them more responsive to community sentiment. These groups assimilated the newcomers and tied them together, offered the weak protection and provided the ambitious backing, and, just as municipal authority improved Los Angeles' physical facilities, otherwise revitalized the town's communal life.[43]

Private enterprise, unlike municipal authority and voluntary associations, supplied essential services only when confident of a decent return on its investment. And as a rule it encountered least resistance in its quest for profits when the government and community organizations lacked the requisite capital and/or competence. This was the pattern revealed in the history of the Los Angeles waterworks, which had its origins in the demand for a domestic water supply separate from the zanja system. The story began late in the 1850's when the common council granted William Dryden permission to place a wheel on the main zanja, lay pipes under the streets, and sell water in Los Angeles. Dryden and his associates constructed the waterworks shortly after, but when winter floods destroyed the wheel in 1862 they refused to resume service.[44] Whereupon the residents of Los Angeles demanded that the municipal authorities assume direct responsibility to provide domestic water.

The council, instead, opened negotiations with a local businessman who offered to construct a waterworks free of charge to the municipality in return for the right to operate it for his own benefit for four

3. Los Angeles water wheel, ca. 1860

4. Los Angeles reservoir, ca. 1860

years. The legislators accepted, provided that he make additional improvements, maintain the equipment, pay an annual rental, guarantee sufficient quantity, supply free water for official use, and post substantial sureties.[45] The contractor agreed and built a waterworks consisting of a dam that blocked the main zanja, a wheel that conveyed the water to a reservoir, and wooden pipes that distributed it to shops and homes located along the main streets. Unfortunately, violent floods carried the dam away in the winter of 1867–68, leaving the new waterworks as inoperative as the old and the lessee and the council each denying responsibility for the repairs. This impasse provoked the press to protest that "a work that has cost so much money, and that is of such importance to the city, should not be permitted to go to destruction when it can be made productive of so much good." [46]

Two rival syndicates tried to exploit the situation. One, claiming to be the possessor of the franchise awarded to Dryden, requested an exclusive twenty-five-year grant to provide domestic water. The council's committee recommended refusal, arguing that the municipal system "cannot be either *given away*, or leased for the purpose of being destroyed or merged into a private work." The other, presenting itself as the successor to the current lessee, asked for a new thirty-year lease of the waterworks. It promised, in return, to cancel certain municipal liabilities, replace the wooden pipes with iron ones, build commodious storage reservoirs, spend at least $50,000 on improvements, pay an annual rental of $1,000, and post securities worth $20,000. Although the committee gave its approval, the council procrastinated and then began to erect yet another dam.[47]

The legislators received other propositions that year, but seriously considered only the one prepared by John S. Griffin, Prudent Beaudry, and Solomon Lazard, the current operators of the works. This proposition revised the original offer by extending the lease from thirty to fifty years and stipulating additional improvements, maximum rates, and future sale at an arbitrated sum. The water committee, with no warning whatever, then reversed its previous position, reasoning that it was not advisable or prudent for the city to own its waterworks. But for reasons which are not clear, a divided council passed an ordinance which, instead of leasing the waterworks, sold it outright.[48] Whereupon the mayor vetoed it on the grounds that so long as the property could be leased there was no reason to sell it.

The deadlock distressed the press. The previous winter, it warned, "there was no water in the pipes for four months . . . [and] the supply of water for domestic purposes is now dependent upon a temporary dam in the river that will be destroyed by the first fall rain . . . The only remedy for the city," it insisted, "is to build a dam which will cost more than the entire revenue of the city, without any security that it will resist the floods for even a single season, or make such arrangements as will induce private capital to furnish water for the *entire* year."[49] It was amid this uncertainty that the syndicate submitted another proposal to lease the system for thirty years under similar conditions. And by now the situation was so grave that the council quickly accepted it, the mayor happily approved it, and together they entrusted the Los Angeles Water Company with the responsibility to provide the municipality with an adequate supply of domestic water.[50]

Municipal authority also relinquished control over the land in Los Angeles to private enterprise. As early as the 1850's the common council began disposing of the pueblo holdings it inherited from the ayuntamiento. At first it donated lots to prospective farmers in order to encourage cultivation and, equally important, to raise tax revenue. Later on, when the demand for property increased, it sold parcels at auctions and credited the town treasury with the proceeds. In these ways the council disposed of tens of thousands of acres before 1885.[51] Following traditional American practices, moreover, the municipal government exerted very little authority over the use of this land. It did not impose regulations on buying, improving, and marketing property—as it did on placing pipes, laying tracks, and erecting poles. Under these circumstances a few landowners, known as subdividers, attracted by the expanding real estate market, cleared, graded, and divided their acreage, platted, promoted, and sold their lots, and thereby transformed most of central Los Angeles from rural land to urban property by 1885.[52]

Other subdividers, often owners of outlying acreage, demonstrated even more initiative and took even greater risks. They not only subdivided country holdings into town lots, but, impatient with the pace of municipal authorities and corporate utilites, also supplemented the activities of these agencies with their own capital and energy. Prudent Beaudry, a prosperous merchant and former mayor of Los Angeles, typified them. After buying a large portion of the northwestern hills in the late 1860's, he asked the Los Angeles Water Company—which he and others had recently incorporated—to serve his holdings. When it refused on the grounds that the returns would not justify the outlay, Beaudry sold his stock, secured another franchise from the council, and spent $40,000 on water distribution. Meanwhile, he opened streets to connect his district with the business center, and later he and others organized a cable railway which ran into the hills. "I intend to spend money and keep on spending money in improvements and grading streets until this locality meets the attention it deserves," he declared in 1877, "and it will not be long I assure you." [53]

Improving transportation gradually became as essential as supplying water and subdividing land. Although its population tripled in the 1850's and 1860's, Los Angeles was still small and sparsely settled in 1870. More residents worked in farming than in crafts and trades; more combined than separated their shops and homes. Also, as one of the town's pioneer merchants recalled, the tempo of Los Angeles' economy remained slow and its discipline lax. "People were also not as particular about keeping their places of business open all day. Proprietors would sometimes close their shops and go out for an hour or two for their meals, or to meet in a friendly game of billiards. During the monotonous days when but little business was being transacted, it was not uncommon for merchants to visit back and forth and to spend hours at a time in playing cards." [54] Given such conditions the sporadic and uncoordinated opening and widening of streets satisfactorily expedited movement and enlarged access in Los Angeles.

Between 1870 and 1885, however, the town's population increased almost fourfold, and most residents carried on urban enterprises in stores and shops away from their homes. At the same time the pace of business accelerated and its conduct tightened. The artisan who failed to produce his wares punctually, like the tradesman who forgot to tend his store regularly, risked losing his customers to more ambitious competitors. Also, those businessmen who felt the strain of harder work placed far more value on their leisure hours. Hence Los Angeles' growth intensified the distinction between the job and the family at the same time that its expansion enlarged the distance between the shop and the home. [55] And during the 1870's and 1880's these changes generated a modest demand for transportation facilities more rapid than walking but less costly than carriages.

Only the horse-drawn railway car, whose passengers proceeded faster than pedestrians and paid a fraction of the cost of a carriage, met these specifications. But the municipal authorities lacked the capital, the capability, and even the inclination to build and operate these facilities. So entrepreneurs who trusted their imaginations in estimating patronage and landholders who foresaw the appreciation of their realty as a result provided this service. These businessmen exerted intense pressure on the council in order to secure the municipality's permission to lay tracks along the public streets. They claimed that street railways would "enhance property values, promote prosperity, increase the convenience of locomotion and expand the populous area of the city." [56] And the council, which as a rule agreed, then granted franchises that enabled private interests to lay tracks and run railways along the streets of Los Angeles.

The franchise established the railway's route, bound the builders to improve the adjacent surface, set terminal dates for the commencement and completion of construction and the beginning of operation, and fixed maximum fares, minimum schedules, and safety standards.[57] It was not binding on the municipality unless the entrepreneur adhered to these specifications. Nor was the franchise perpetual; granted for twenty, thirty, or at most fifty years, it had to be renegotiated by the authorities and the businessmen at its expiration. The franchise was, in essence, the means whereby Los Angeles resolved the dilemma posed by the municipality's grand aspirations and its limited capacities: it ensured reasonable service for the public without discouraging private enterprise from undertaking the task.[58] Popular support and official cooperation notwithstanding, the market for transportation was too small before 1885 to stimulate construction of more than a few short horse-drawn street railways in Los Angeles.

The common council granted franchises to private enterprise for gas, electric, and telephone service as well. In the 1860's the legislators issued an exclusive twenty-year privilege for gas distribution, and obliged the entrepreneur, in return, to construct a plant worth at least $5,000.[59] Against the Los Angeles Gas Company's opposition, they awarded the Los Angeles Electric Company the right to market electricity in the town less than two decades later.[60] And at the same time they granted a ten-year franchise to the Los Angeles Telephone Company to erect poles and string wires along the public streets.[61] The council normally specified terminal dates for construction, reserved power to supervise service and set rates, and made the contract contingent upon these conditions. But it did not infringe upon the integral autonomy of these politically influential businesses which consistently pursued their own rather than the community's interests.

By the late 1880's municipal authority directed the fire, police, and sanitation departments and the public schools. Voluntary associations operated the churches and the fraternal, commercial, and civic groups. And private enterprise controlled domestic water, street railways, public utilities, and real estate. This division of responsibility had crucial implications for the expansion of Los Angeles—for the transformation of rural acreage into town property. Newcomers could and did purchase land and even erect houses without the fire, police, sanitary, and educational facilities which logically and traditionally followed settlement. But they could not and did not make such commitments without available water, transportation, utilities, and lots, services which, on the other hand, necessarily and historically preceded settlement.

As a result, the pace of expansion in the town depended not, as in the pueblo, on the policies of municipal authority, but on the willingness of private enterprise to extend domestic water mains, construct street railway lines, install public utility connections, and subdivide rural real estate. The individuals and corporations involved were, of course, influenced by regional growth, market conditions, and consumer preferences. Still, they, and not public officials, interpreted these indicators, undertook the transformation, and thereby assumed the decisive role in urban expansion. And without minimizing the importance of this tradition during these years—or implying that it was peculiar to Los Angeles, for it clearly was not—its impact on the character of Los Angeles was even more profound when the city developed into a metropolis after 1885.

Los Angeles cannot be retarded in her development. She is and must be the center of everything in Southern California for all time to come. (C. W. Smith, 1886)

3 THE RIVALRY BETWEEN LOS ANGELES AND SAN DIEGO

The emergence of Los Angeles as the metropolis of southern California was not inevitable. Located in the northwestern corner of a long and narrow coastal plain, it did not monopolize trade, crafts, services, or manufacturing there. Smaller towns—Wilmington to the south, San Bernardino to the east, and Anaheim to the southeast— all competed for the countryside's business. Each assumed that southern California was so undeveloped and its economy so fluid that each could reasonably aspire to be the regional emporium. Although they fought with the vigor typical of the American West, Los Angeles dominated the nearby ports and towns by the 1870's.[1] It then engaged in a struggle with San Diego, a more distant and formidable opponent—a struggle that marked a great turning point in the city's history. For the outcome determined that Los Angeles rather than San Diego would be the pre-eminent urban center in southern California.

The opposite was expected before the 1880's. For San Diego, just north of the Mexican border and one hundred miles south of Los Angeles, was the only southern California settlement with a deepwater harbor as splendid as San Francisco Bay. Unlike the roadstead of San Pedro, twenty miles from Los Angeles, whose shallow waters lay exposed to most winds, the Bay of San Diego was commended as commodious and safe by shippers and sailors alike.[2] Hence San Diego alone was a potential rival to San Francisco for the trade with the Orient and as the terminus of a southern transcontinental railroad. For these reasons San Diegans expected to dominate southern California as San Franciscans did northern California. Those Los Angeles residents who considered natural advantages decisive in urban rivalry agreed with them. "We are too far inland and have no reliable harbor

43

in our country," one conceded in 1869. "We must be content to be the political and social capital of south California; we must be satisfied with our genial climate, our fruitful soil, our generous wines, our golden fruit, our productive mines, our cattle upon a thousand hills . . . The great commercial city of south California must be San Diego." [3]

San Diego did not achieve this destiny in the 1850's and 1860's, however. Founded as a Spanish presidio and later used as a port for the hide and tallow trade, it gained few people and little wealth before the American conquest. Also, the rush to the gold country by-passed the town and Richard Henry Dana, Jr., who first visited San Diego in 1835, returned more than twenty years later to find "no change whatever." "It certainly has not grown," he wrote. [4] Nor did San Diego progress much during the Civil War. Arriving there in 1865, when its population numbered under 1,000, a local merchant's wife observed that "Of all the dilapidated, miserable looking places I have ever seen, this was the worst." [5] Yet San Diego attracted a few promoters who envisioned its unexcelled bay as a terminus for a southern transcontinental railroad and purchased extensive tracts of inexpensive waterfrontage for speculative purposes. [6]

Their confidence was contagious, and many easterners—some of whom later moved to Los Angeles—left for San Diego in the 1850's. [7] Together with the promoters, they organized in 1854 the San Diego and Gila Southern Pacific and Atlantic Railroad to connect San Diego Bay with a projected thirty-second parallel transcontinental —a line already recommended by the Secretary of War, himself a southerner, in preference to several more northerly routes—at the California-Arizona border. San Diego then granted the San Diego and Gila 9,000 acres of public land to cover the costs of construction. But the company lacked the capital to undertake more than preliminary surveys, [8] and, in any event, the Congress was so immobilized by sectional animosities that it refused to implement the Secretary of War's recommendation for a southern transcontinental railroad. For these reasons San Diego's hopes for a transcontinental terminus were frustrated down through the 1850's.

San Diego's interest in a southern transcontinental revived after the Civil War when the San Diego and Gila stockholders, who had not met since 1858, reorganized the company and appointed William S. Rosecrans president. A former Union general, Rosecrans had been tempted on a recent visit to San Diego by the profits awaiting anyone who could transform the dilapidated seaport into a commercial emporium. He urged General William J. Palmer, who was in charge of fixing the Kansas Pacific's route to California, to adopt the thirty-second parallel, arguing that it possessed a milder climate, required a shorter distance, and ended at a finer harbor than any of the alternatives.[9] Palmer refused, explaining that the Kansas Pacific's success depended on reaching San Francisco and that a southern line would compel it to rely on San Diego. "If the 32nd parallel were a good route to San Francisco as well as San Diego, the case might be different," he wrote. "The 35th parallel however is undoubtedly the best route to the present metropolis of this Coast."[10]

In the meantime, the expectation that a Congress that had aided a northern transcontinental during the war would assist a southern one in peacetime brought a horde of prominent railroadmen to Washington. Among them were the promoters of the Memphis, El Paso and Pacific, a company chartered to build across Texas which had laid about twenty-five miles of track before 1860 and now sought federal aid to continue the line to California. Impressed by the influence of the Memphis, El Paso directors—and especially its president, John C. Fremont— Colonel Thomas S. Sedgwick, the San Diego and Gila's Washington lobbyist, proposed that the two railroads join forces.[11] The Memphis, El Paso, heretofore unaware of the San Diego and Gila, agreed and offered to purchase its charter and subsidies for $600,000 in stock and a guarantee to construct the San Diego–Fort Yuma road as part of its southern transcontinental railroad.

Sedgwick accepted, and the Memphis, El Paso dispatched an agent to San Diego. He explained the agreement to the San Diego and Gila's directors, who subsequently transferred their franchise and properties. The Memphis, El Paso then started preliminary surveys. But, as Rosecrans, to his dismay, soon discovered, the Texas company was in a precarious financial position. "It is not certain," he reported to the San Diego and Gila, "whether it will be possible to arrange its affairs so as to command the confidence of business men and of Congress." French bondholders compounded the difficulties by claiming that Fremont had deceived them and demanding restitution by the corporation. Only immediate governmental action would have shored up the Memphis, El Paso, and when Congress refused to intervene the courts declared the railroad bankrupt in 1870.[12] Whereupon the San Diego and Gila sought to salvage its charter and subsidy from the corporate ruins.

Although San Diego's efforts to secure a transcontinental terminus were thus far disappointing, the townspeople were not discouraged. They realized, of course, that twenty years had passed since the promoters first perceived San Diego's possibilities as a railroad center and fifteen since they organized the San Diego and Gila Company. But they also knew the Secretary of War had recommended a thirty-second parallel line to San Diego, and the Memphis, El Paso had intended to terminate its tracks there. Construction had been delayed not by San Diego's location, they were confident, but by sectional animosities in the 1850's and financial mismanagement in the 1870's. Hence, notwithstanding these setbacks, San Diego's promoters remained convinced that their bay was still the natural terminus for a southern transcontinental railroad.

Revising their strategy, they now proposed to build a coast line running from San Francisco to San Diego and connecting there with a southern transcontinental. Unfortunately, these plans conflicted with the determination of the Central Pacific—the western section of the initial transcontinental, which under the management of Collis Huntington, Leland Stanford, Mark Hopkins, and Charles Crocker monopolized transportation in California—to prevent construction of competing rail or ship lines. The company, which was committed to San Francisco where it controlled access to the bay and owned considerable real estate, preferred San Diego's isolation. "I would not take a road to San Diego as a gift," Crocker once remarked. "We would blot San Diego out of existence if we could, but as we can[']t do that we shall keep it back as long as we can." [13]

The Central Pacific's antagonism was a serious obstacle because, as San Diego's leaders well knew, it had already blocked an earlier attempt to link the state's coastal points with a southern transcontinental. "If that line [the Southern Pacific] was constructed entirely independent of those who were interested in the Central Pacific," Stanford had reasoned, "it would become a dangerous rival, not only for the through business from the Atlantic Ocean, but it would enter into active competition for the local business of California. It was of paramount importance that the road should be controlled by friends of the Central Pacific." [14] His associates therefore acquired the Southern Pacific. To reinforce their monopoly, they then decided to build one line through the San Joaquin Valley to meet a thirty-fifth parallel transcontinental in Nevada and another down the coast and across the mountains to halt a thirty-second parallel road in Arizona. But lacking funds for both undertakings, they chose the inland route which by-passed San Diego.[15]

For these reasons Rosecrans appealed to Stanford for assurance that the Central Pacific would not work against his projected coast rail-

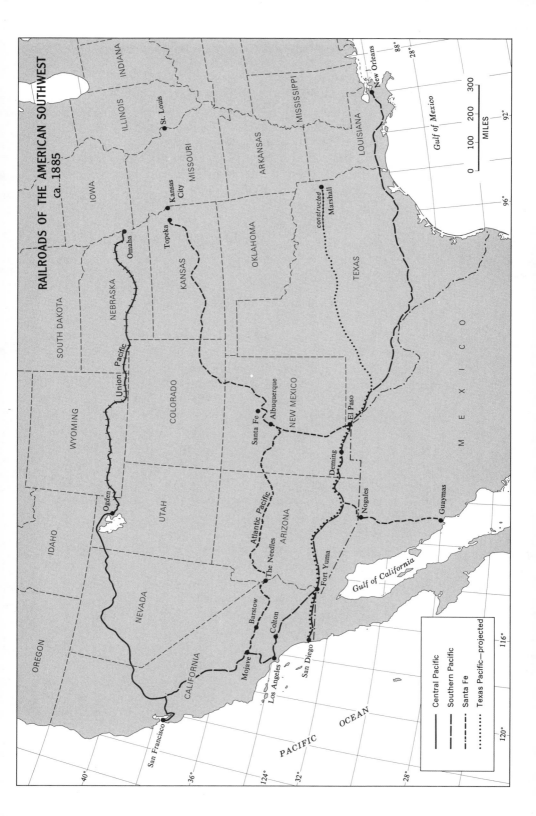

RAILROADS OF THE AMERICAN SOUTHWEST
ca. 1885

road. Stanford promised nothing, but the San Diegans and their San Francisco partners organized the California Southern Coast Railroad Company in 1871 anyway. They proposed to finance construction with county donation bonds, governmental land grants, and private stock subscriptions. The Central Pacific did oppose their efforts, however. As a result individual investors refused to risk their capital, and local and state officials rejected their requests for aid. Rosecrans therefore left for Washington, determined to join the California Southern with transcontinental interests of sufficient wealth and power to say to the Central Pacific "you gentlemen are to understand that we are all of the fishing party, and consequently you *must* fish or cut bait. Either you build the Coast line or let us do it."[16]

He arrived there to find John C. Fremont of the defunct Memphis, El Paso and Pacific, Thomas A. Scott of the Pennsylvania Central, Marshall O. Roberts of Texas, southeastern railroadmen, and New York capitalists all deadlocked in the contest for a transcontinental charter. He learned that a Southern Transcontinental Railroad had almost been authorized to build from Marshall, Texas, to San Diego at the last session, and that Collis Huntington had introduced an amendment at the present session permitting the Southern Pacific to connect with it at Fort Yuma. Fearful lest San Diego be by-passed again, Rosecrans rallied the opposition to the Central Pacific. When, to everyone's surprise, the amendment failed,[17] Huntington urged him to relent and agreed, in return, to construct the coast line. "What was to be done?" Rosecrans wondered. "Without the Huntington influence no bill could get through and no south overland would be built . . . I could only *prevent* the passage of that bill and that would be sure to *cut off present* hope of the Southern overland."[18] Hence he accepted the compromise.

Congress then chartered the Texas and Pacific from Marshall to San Diego and the Southern Pacific from San Francisco to Fort Yuma. In San Diego, where congressional procrastination had depressed the economy, confidence returned and business revived.[19] Also, the San Diegans closely followed the railroad news. From the eastern press they learned that Scott had purchased Roberts' interests and taken complete control of the Texas Pacific. From Rosecrans they found out that Scott, who originally objected to starting construction at San Diego, agreed to begin there within one year and finish twenty-five miles within two. And from pessimists they heard rumors that Scott bought the Southern Pacific and planned to by-pass San Diego.[20] Amid this uncertainty, Scott announced that he would visit San Diego

5. San Diego in the 1870's

6. San Diego in the 1880's

in 1872. "This is the most critical period in the history of San Diego," one resident observed. "A few days will decide whether we are to be one of the great cities of the United States within the next ten years or whether that time is still in the distant future." [21]

Scott arrived that summer and immediately explained his position: "We are ready to commence work here at your town," he said, "but expect you to do your share in the enterprise and help us all you can." He asked for the San Diego and Gila Company's lands and some additional waterfrontage. He refused to bargain and the town quickly accepted his terms. [22] Concerned that he might use a delay as an excuse to postpone construction, the authorities forced the local railway to sell its holdings for $58,000 in municipal bonds. They then transferred the property to the Texas Pacific, and Scott secured its release from the Memphis, El Paso and Pacific's receiver. The San Diegans were convinced that the Texas Pacific had made a firm commitment; "Scott means this place to be the actual terminus of his R. R.," one wrote, "and to make it the rival of San Francisco." One year later, however, they learned that in the wake of the Panic of 1873 Scott was unable to market Texas Pacific bonds. "What effect will all this have on San Diego?" a nervous merchant asked. "With Stanford pushing on towards the Colorado River, what will become of San Diego?" [23]

The Panic of 1873 rendered it impossible to finance construction with private capital unless extraordinary inducements were offered or entrepreneurial uncertainties reduced. A few years earlier Scott might have requested a congressional land grant as collateral for Texas Pacific securities. But the current antagonism toward these donations compelled him to eliminate all risk from the venture instead. Accordingly, he sought federal assistance on the following terms: That for a first mortgage on the properties and earnings of the Texas Pacific Railroad and on the net proceeds from the sale of its Texas real estate, Congress guarantee the *interest* on 5 per cent gold bonds valued at $30,000 a mile on the plains and $40,000 a mile in the mountains. Scott justified his appeal on the grounds that the thirty-second parallel line was a national necessity which would disperse population, form a transcontinental highway free from snow, stimulate commerce with the Orient, contribute to the Southwest's defense, and alleviate the Southeast's depression. [24]

Having weathered the panic with his empire intact, [25] Huntington now rallied the opposition to Scott. Both men well knew the prize. "It was a foregone conclusion that the [southern overland] road was going to be built," Crocker recalled later. "The only question was, who should control it, friends of the Central Pacific or enemies of the Central Pacific." [26] They argued their respective cases forcefully. Huntington denounced Scott's proposal, and then, conceding the need for another transcontinental, claimed that the Southern Pacific would construct it without governmental aid. Scott replied that Huntington had already received a substantial federal subsidy, and argued that the Texas Pacific, which would liberate California from the monopoly, requested merely a guarantee of interest. [27] When Congress postponed action, Scott asked Huntington to cooperate at the next session. "He said that he would strike out that portion that related to S[an] F[rancisco]," Huntington wrote Stanford. "I said that if he would strike out all west of the Colorado River I would help him. He said no, that he would build to San Diego . . . and then left." [28]

They resumed the contest, only to reach a virtual deadlock in 1876[29]—a situation which dismayed the San Diegans. "I think the greatest danger to San Diego now," one wrote, "is that the Central Pacific people will build out to Fort Yuma as rapidly as possible cutting us off and preventing forever a road being built into San Diego from the East." [30] The delay forced them to face certain discouraging facts. Its natural advantages notwithstanding, San Diego had grown little during the 1870's; a transcontinental terminus appeared less likely now than before; and San Pedro harbor, inadequate but accessible, handled more commerce than San Diego's superb but isolated bay. The conflict also brought the San Diegans a better understanding of the town's predicament. Neither San Diego nor southern California, they now understood, offered sufficient inducements for the transcontinentals; "To get business these roads *must connect with San Francisco* which fact we San Diegans have not sufficiently reallised." [31] But as a potential terminus for a southern transcontinental and rival to San Francisco, San Diego aroused the overwhelming opposition of the Central Pacific. Theoretically San Diego's supreme asset, the bay was actually its fatal liability.

Knowledge in this instance was not power. With the Texas Pacific bill stalled in Congress and the Southern Pacific moving towards Fort Yuma, a desperate Scott compromised with the indefatigable Huntington. For Huntington's promise to withdraw his objections to the Texas Pacific petition, Scott conceded the transcontinental's western section to the Southern Pacific. Nothing in the agreement bound Huntington to honor Scott's commitment to San Diego; everything else indicated that the Southern Pacific would by-pass the town. This entente disintegrated shortly after. But as Huntington checked Scott in Washington and the Southern Pacific crossed into Arizona, the San Diegans acknowledged that no matter who constructed the railroad's eastern section its western end was unalterably fixed at San Francisco.[32] The Central Pacific had indeed deprived San Diego of a transcontinental terminus.

The railroads had a no less important, far more beneficent, and yet equally unexpected impact on Los Angeles. Until the 1870's, the Los Angeles *Herald* admitted, "All eyes were riveted on San Diego, the asserted coming rival of San Francisco as a trade emporium. Of the immense numbers who passed South on the steamers, few stopped short of San Diego. Los Angeles was hardly deemed worthy of a visit of inspection." [33] True, San Diego numbered only 2,300 people and Los Angeles 5,728; and San Diego still awaited its first railway while Los Angeles had completed a line to the coast. Nonetheless, San Diego's population increased by 1,569 or 215 per cent and Los Angeles' by only 1,343 or 31 per cent during the 1860's; and San Diego Bay not San Pedro harbor seemed destined to be the southern transcontinental's terminus. Hence most southern Californians, who believed that "What San Diego will be with railroads is hardly possible for any man to tell," envisioned Los Angeles—which lacked coal, iron, and timber as well as a harbor—as a thriving city, but hardly a potential metropolis.[34]

Los Angeles residents were nevertheless aroused in 1872 when the *Star* warned that "Unless we have made up our minds to be satisfied to . . . remain a mere country village for an indefinite period, we must have railroads, and we must have them quickly." [35] They had followed the progress of the Southern Pacific closely enough to know that it was supposed to start from San Francisco, traverse the San Joaquin Valley, continue east of the Coast Range to Fort Yuma, and entirely by-pass Los Angeles. They were also well aware that the company would extend its tracks to Los Angeles only if persuaded that the additional traffic would be worth the extra expense or if offered a subsidy that would cover construction costs. Hence several merchants and landowners organized a Committee of Thirty in May 1872 and instructed it to discover if either the Southern Pacific or the Atlantic and Pacific—a railroad chartered in 1866 to run along the thirty-fifth parallel between St. Louis and San Francisco—could be induced to route its *trunk* line through Los Angeles.

The committee appointed Harris Newmark and John G. Downey to consult with the companies. Newmark reported that the Atlantic and Pacific planned to run forty miles east of Los Angeles and might extend a *branch* to the town. Downey revealed that the Southern Pacific would lay fifty miles of *main* track in Los Angeles County for 5 per cent of its assessed value. "I confess the conditions are pretty hard," he wrote, "but if we [are to have] communication by rail with San Francisco, and at once, I see no other way." [36] The committee, which also found the price steep, authorized three members to appeal directly to Collis Huntington in San Francisco. The magnate offered to build fifty miles of trunk line within fifteen months, added a branch to Anaheim within two years, but refused to accept a smaller subsidy. "These terms are not as good as I had hoped to get," William R. Olden admitted to the committee, "but I am certain that they are the best that will be offered us." [37]

Huntington's personal representative in Los Angeles, William B. Hyde, then complicated matters by announcing that the Southern Pacific would construct only twenty-five of the fifty miles north toward San Francisco. The committee answered that the electorate would not support a donation which did not materially shorten the distance to the northern metropolis. "We *cannot* carry this proposition without that concession," it assured him. Agent Hyde expressed profound sorrow, but replied that he was prepared to terminate the negotiations and return to San Francisco.[38] The committee reluctantly agreed, though the Southern Pacific mysteriously reversed its position and conceded this point soon after. Hyde and the committee then persuaded the county Board of Supervisors to place before the voters a proposition granting $610,000 to the Southern Pacific for fifty miles of trunk line.[39]

At first the bond issue encountered widespread hostility. Disillusionment with the railroads was so pervasive in Los Angeles that in the last election each candidate had forthrightly declared his antipathy to rail subsidies. Several ranchers from southern Los Angeles County, who feared that the donation would increase their taxes, channeled this general dissatisfaction into effective opposition. Standing against them and in favor of the proposition were Los Angeles merchants and landowners who considered a connection worth any cost and the Southern Pacific offer their only opportunity. Representative Hyde threatened and tempted the divided townspeople. If they rejected the proposition, he warned, Los Angeles could not tie into the trunk line later. But if they approved it, he promised, Los Angeles would become a financial and commercial center second only to San Francisco.[40]

Amidst this electioneering, Thomas Scott unexpectedly announced that he would back a local railroad chartered to connect Los Angeles with San Diego and the Texas Pacific.[41] And shortly after the San Diego and Los Angeles Company requested $377,000—or $233,000 less than the Southern Pacific—to aid in construction. "To say the least, the contrast between it, in its demands and promises, [and] the proposition of the Stanford Company is striking," the *News* argued. "Its petition for aid is modest. Its offers are liberal. Its promises are fair, plainly set forth and easy to understand."[42] Others disagreed. "We can better afford to give one million dollars to the Southern Pacific Company," a Los Angeles banker insisted, "than to give one dollar to the San Diego Railroad Company, a branch road . . . whose paid-in capital is a promise to pay; whose terminus is San Diego . . . ; a city from which we expect to derive no benefits; whose resources are insignificant, and whose citizens breakfast on their harbor, dine on their climate, and whose only hope of avoiding ruin is a railroad."[43]

The San Diego and Los Angeles urged the county supervisors to include its proposal on the ballot, and, after twice postponing its decision, the board approved the petition by a single vote.[44] Meanwhile, Scott elaborated on his commitment and presented a constructive alternative to the Southern Pacific offer. Provided that the local railroad raised funds to acquire a right of way, grade the roadbed, and purchase a depot, the Texas Pacific would issue $20,000 in bonds per mile to buy rails and lay track and operate the San Diego and Los Angeles as part of its system. San Diego and Los Angeles spokesmen, encouraged by this pledge, then contrasted Scott's integrity with Huntington's duplicity, and claimed that whereas the Southern Pacific's charter obliged it to run through Los Angeles, their railway would supply a competing connection. "The coming and the going of the Scott party has been made the key note for an entirely new direction of attack upon my lines," Hyde wrote to his employers, "and ever since their departure I have been under the necessity of keeping the stiffest kind of a front."[45]

Hyde responded to the challenge aggressively and even scornfully. He conceded that the Southern Pacific planned to build to Los Angeles at some time. "Mark you," he warned, "*at some time*." "It was not our intention to do so now." He also admitted that the charter bound the company to pass by way of Los Angeles. "Mark you," he repeated, "*by way of Los Angeles*." "We can come by the way of any part of Los Angeles County." "There are plenty of loopholes in the Act," he noted. "The Southern Pacific can go pretty near just where it chooses."[46] A more confident community might have replied in kind, but Los Angeles reached the conclusion that the Southern Pacific's offer was to its advantage and the Texas Pacific's to San Diego's. This argument was presented most persuasively by Judge Robert M. Widney, a prominent lawyer and landowner, in an influential pamphlet, "Los Angeles County Subsidy," published just before the election.

Assuming that Los Angeles' choice was irrevocable, Widney asked, "What do we want *any* railroad for?" To carry produce to the market, attract commerce to Los Angeles, transport residents to other cities, and promote migration to southern California, he answered. A branch line to San Diego would be valueless. San Diego already purchases its supplies from Los Angeles; the Texas Pacific would divert trade from Los Angeles to San Diego; Los Angeles people rarely travel to San Diego; and settlers seldom come by way of San Diego, he argued. But a trunk line to San Francisco would be invaluable. Northern California is Los Angeles' largest market; the Southern Pacific would attract the mountain trade to the town; its inhabitants often visit San Francisco; and newcomers usually arrive via the northern metropolis. "Stanford's Road makes this county the second railroad center on this Coast," Widney concluded, "The San Diego Road makes this county an insignificant terminus of a useless railroad . . . placing [it] *130 miles inland from San Diego,* and making our farmers and producers *pay tribute forever to San Diego* commission merchants, wharves, and warehouses." [47]

By November the pressure from the business community had eroded the antipathy to subsidies, and the resurgence of urban rivalry had overcome the distrust of Huntington. Although a small minority approved the San Diego and Los Angeles' offer, a large majority, based in the town of Los Angeles, endorsed the Southern Pacific's proposition. The railroad then began construction in Los Angeles, crossed the San Fernando Valley, tunneled beneath the Coast Range, and reached Lang's Station where, with only six strokes of a silver hammer, Charles Crocker drove in the golden spike. Los Angeles now had its connection with the trunk line to San Francisco and was indeed the southern terminus of the thirty-second parallel transcontinental. "If we mistake not, Los Angeles is only commencing her real development," the San Bernardino *Guardian* prophesied. "Her only rival is, or was, San Diego, and the fates seem 'down on' that ambitious little burgh." [48]

These "fates," embodied by Huntington, Stanford, Hopkins, and Crocker, favored Los Angeles because, unlike San Diego, it did not jeopardize the Central Pacific or San Francisco. The town's cardinal deficiency—its inadequate and unprotected port—was its saving grace. As Huntington and his associates were unwilling to connect

Los Angeles without a handsome inducement, however, the electorate's decision to make a short-term sacrifice for a long-term goal was essential. Here the ability of Los Angeles' leaders to arouse the town's latent urban rivalry was crucial. Above all, from its endorsement of the Southern Pacific's proposition Los Angeles gained an edge over San Diego that it never relinquished in the struggle to be the regional metropolis.

The Southern Pacific expanded its local facilities during the 1870's, constructing branches to Anaheim and Spadra and acquiring lines to Wilmington and Santa Monica, and centered the entire system on Los Angeles. The town, as a result, attracted so many immigrants that, as Table 2 reveals, its economy thrived and its population doubled in ten years.[49] Thus by the mid-1870's Los Angeles openly aspired to be southern California's commercial center, and its residents forcefully

TABLE 2. Population Growth and Agricultural Expansion in Los Angeles and San Diego, 1850–1880

	Population			
Year	Los Angeles City	San Diego City	Los Angeles County	San Diego County
1850	1,610	—	3,530	798
1860	4,385	733	11,333	4,324
1870	5,728	2,300	15,309	4,951
1880	11,183	2,637	33,381	6,180
	Number of acres improved		Value of farm products	
Year	Los Angeles County	San Diego County	Los Angeles County	San Diego County
1850	2,648	—	—	—
1860	20,600	4,143	—	—
1870	234,883	10,963	$201,823	$60,042
1880	303,386	69,742	1,865,056	395,683

Source: U.S. Bureau of the Census, *Fifteenth Census of the United States. Volume I. Population* (Washington, 1931), pp. 18–19; U.S. Census Office, *Statistics of the Population of the United States at the Tenth Census (June 1, 1880)* (Washington, 1883), p. 51; J. D. B. de Bow, *Statistical View of the United States . . . Being a Compendium of the Seventh Census* (Washington, 1854), p. 202; Joseph C. G. Kennedy, *Agriculture of the United States in 1860: Compiled from the Original Returns of the Eighth Census* (Washington, 1864), p. 10; Francis G. Walker, *Ninth Census—Volume III. The Statistics of the Wealth and Industry of the United States (June 1, 1870)* (Washington, 1872), p. 104; U.S. Census Office, *Report on the Production of Agriculture. Tenth Census (June 1, 1880)* (Washington, 1883), p. 106.

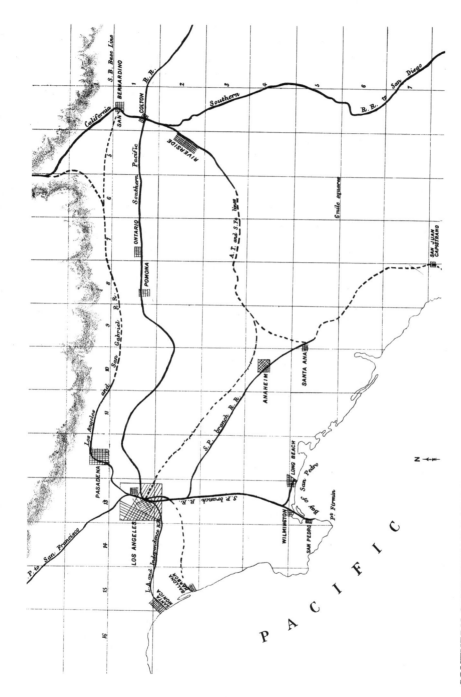

SOUTHERN CALIFORNIA'S RAILROADS, 1887

expressed their animosity toward San Diego. Previously neutral in the battle between Huntington and Scott, they now opposed the Texas Pacific on the grounds that it was not a Los Angeles road and if completed would build up San Diego instead of Los Angeles. Hitherto unconcerned about a direct connection between Fort Yuma and San Diego, they now argued that it "is emphatically not for the interest of Los Angeles that a transcontinental railway should cross the Sierras at a point further South than San Gorgonio Pass." [50]

San Diego shared little in southern California's progress. Not only did its production remain low, but, as residents departed almost as frequently as newcomers arrived, its population, as Table 2 indicates, grew little between 1870 and 1880. Its promoters still hoped to attract a transcontinental railroad to San Diego Bay, however. And to this end, they met in July 1879 and appointed Frank A. Kimball, proprietor of the vast National Ranch just south of San Diego, to renew contact with the Texas Pacific and, if necessary, to open negotiations with the Atchison, Topeka and Santa Fe—a midwestern transcontinental chartered in 1863 to build along the thirty-fifth parallel which had fallen under the control of New England capitalists after the Panic of 1873. Kimball left for Philadelphia where he conferred with the Texas Pacific directors and decided that the company lacked the ability to build a southern transcontinental.[51] He continued on to Boston, and, arriving there in the summer, arranged for an appointment with Thomas E. Nickerson, president of the Santa Fe.

Nickerson, a New Englander, had long been involved in western railroading. He had guided the Santa Fe after the Panic of 1873 when it laid the track from Kansas into Colorado and, despite the opposition of the Denver and Rio Grande, extended the line toward Albuquerque. He then persuaded Huntington, who was building the thirty-second parallel road through the Southwest, to permit the Santa Fe to connect with the Southern Pacific early in 1879. But as this connection, which was made at Deming, New Mexico, in March 1881, depended on Huntington's good will, Nickerson also encouraged a group of Boston capitalists to construct a railroad from Nogales on the American border to Guaymas on the Mexican coast. A Santa Fe branch actually met the Sonora railway in October 1882 and reached the coastal ships which steamed around Baja California to San Francisco.[52] Yet no matter how highly Nickerson valued Guaymas for bargaining purposes, he did not consider it adequate as a transcontinental terminus for the Santa Fe.

Thus Nickerson still sought an independent outlet to the Pacific coast in 1879. Just before Kimball arrived he approached the St. Louis and San Francisco, a company which had acquired the franchises and land grants of the Atlantic and Pacific after it failed during the depression of the 1870's. Since both the Santa Fe and the Frisco aspired to build another transcontinental, they decided to form a new Atlantic and Pacific railroad in which each partner would possess half interest. The Frisco would extend the Atlantic and Pacific east to St. Louis, the Santa Fe would continue it west to San Francisco, and the transcontinental would thereby receive its land grant from the federal government. As Nickerson realized that the Atlantic and Pacific directly challenged the Central Pacific, he now listened with interest as Kimball proposed that the Santa Fe proceed south to San Diego rather then north to San Francisco.[53]

Nickerson replied that the proposal was premature, but, if San Diego offered proper inducements, the company would evaluate its potential as a transcontinental terminus. "In your offer you must take into consideration that we are not Philanthropists," he advised Kimball. "Our object is primarily to get interest on our capital and this always develops a country. So your offer must be something in proportion to your prospective gains and our loss of interest by building about 200 miles of road where little trade can be expected before a through connection is made."[54] Kimball requested ten days grace, made a final (and futile) overture to the Texas Pacific, and then presented the following proposition to Nickerson: That if the Santa Fe would construct a railway from Fort Yuma to San Diego Bay, San Diego would donate 10,000 acres of the National Ranch and 5,000 acres of assorted town property. Nickerson accepted the terms and dispatched to San Diego two representatives and the company's chief engineer.

They began their investigation in October of 1879, and issued a favorable report soon after. The report released the long-restrained optimism in San Diego.[55] As in the past, though, enthusiasm was premature. In January 1880 the Santa Fe publicly announced the arrangement with the Frisco that committed it to the thirty-fifth parallel and San Francisco. "How small a figure San Diego must have cut in the great plans and consolidation they have been making during the last year," Ephraim W. Morse ruminated.[56] Kimball rushed back to Boston, only to learn that William B. Strong, formerly general manager and now president of the Santa Fe, and his associates, the investment houses of Seligman and Company, would not honor Nickerson's commitments. In despair, he proposed a partnership arrangement to

Nickerson and other New England capitalists. If they would supply funds to build a railroad between National City and San Bernardino, he would contribute real estate which could then be sold at a profit. They accepted and together incorporated the California Southern Railroad and the San Diego Land and Town Companies.

The California Southern, cheered on by jubilant San Diegans, started construction in June 1881, passed Colton in November 1882, and reached San Bernardino in September 1883. Unfortunately, the line suffered large deficits; not only did San Diego generate little traffic, but, in addition, Huntington sabotaged his competitor's business. "The Southern Pacific monopoly as completely ignores the existence of the 'California Southern R.R.' as though they had never heard of it," a San Diego merchant protested; "they refuse to receive or deliver freight to or from it in spite of the law to the contrary." The real estate venture, San Diego Land and Town, failed to prosper too; immigration to southern California remained moderate, and the Southern Pacific diverted it from San Diego. When newcomers "find out how much it costs to get *here*," the same San Diegan complained, they "*stop* at Los Angeles." Furthermore, heavy storms during the winter of 1884 destroyed thirty miles of California Southern track, leaving San Diego as isolated now as it had been in 1850.[57] And to the despair of the townspeople, the New England investors decided to abandon the railroad.

Meanwhile, as the Santa Fe commenced work on the Atlantic and Pacific, Huntington and Jay Gould, then president of the Texas Pacific, retaliated by purchasing a majority of the Frisco's outstanding stock. They forced the Santa Fe to accept a modus vivendi in 1882 whereby the Atlantic and Pacific halted at the Colorado River and the Southern Pacific extended its Mojave line to meet it. The Santa Fe thereby reached San Francisco by the middle of 1884, but Huntington diverted so much freight from the Atlantic and Pacific to the Southern Pacific that the thirty-fifth parallel road suffered heavy losses. Strong, who was more determined than ever to secure an independent connection to the coast, now threatened to build a railroad from the Needles to San Francisco that would parallel the Southern Pacific for six hundred miles. Huntington compromised. He offered to sell the Mojave branch, along with traffic rights on the San Joaquin Valley line and terminal facilities at San Francisco Bay, to the Santa Fe. Strong agreed. To secure his position, however, he also assumed control of the California Southern, and, a year after settling with Huntington, the Santa Fe repaired the track and extended the line to Barstow, California.[58]

Thus in November 1885, three decades after they organized the San Diego and Gila, the San Diegans welcomed their first transcontinental train. Proud promoters hailed their town as the Santa Fe's Pacific terminus, and the long patient and now elderly Ephraim Morse predicted that in five years San Diego would be one of the most important towns on the Pacific coast. That this attitude was at least part bravado was indicated by the San Diego *Union's* insistence that "There is no uneasiness here about our position, and not a particle of fear that Los Angeles will take away from us anything that belongs to us." [59] Indeed, the San Diegans had reason to be concerned. The Santa Fe regarded the California Southern, like the Sonora road, as a stratagem in its struggle for access to San Francisco and not as a commitment to another terminus. Once in control of the San Joaquin Valley line, it had little use for the California Southern; once connected with San Francisco harbor, it had little need of San Diego Bay. "San Diego should have anticipated from the very start that this new overland railroad would make San Francisco its ultimate objective point," the Los Angeles *Times* observed. "San Francisco is the Rome of the Pacific Coast; all roads lead to it." [60]

From this perspective San Diego was a dull town of less than 3,000 which had grown by only 10 per cent in the 1870's. Los Angeles, by contrast, was a thriving city of more than 11,000 which had gained by nearly 100 per cent during the same time. The Santa Fe made its position clear. "It doesn't stand to reason that the road can afford to put those little merchants [in San Diego], who had only two or three straight carloads of freight in a year, on the same footing with men [in Los Angeles] who have as much in a week," a company official declared. "Los Angeles is our natural and inevitable western terminus." [61] The Santa Fe acted accordingly. It leased the Southern Pacific's line from Colton to Los Angeles in September 1884, and bought the Los Angeles and San Gabriel Valley Railroad to secure an independent connection soon after. It also constructed its local lines around Los Angeles in order to compete with the Southern Pacific, and even downgraded the California Southern to a spur line. Los Angeles, a Santa Fe vice-president explained in 1886, "is and must be the center of everything in Southern California for some time to come." [62]

A year earlier, reflecting on Los Angeles' ascendancy, the *Times* conceded that "there was a possibility even five years ago . . . for San Diego to become a formidable rival by means of a transcontinental railroad." [63] A possibility, perhaps, but a remote one. Once connected with the Southern Pacific, Los Angeles far outdistanced San Diego. Business "which used to come to San Diego, goes to the railroad & then to Los Angeles," Ephraim Morse observed in 1876. "That portion of our county, which is the best of it, is now making trade connections with Los Angeles." Though San Diego Bay served a few grand ships which plied to southern California, San Pedro and Santa Monica, as Morse discovered on a visit north in 1876, were "capable of doing a larger business than will be required for many years." [64] The Santa Fe's withdrawal from San Diego signaled as well as assured the preeminence of Los Angeles.

The San Diegans now had to read San Diego's epitaphs in Los Angeles' newspapers. "The idea of a great transcontinental system making the 'harbor of San Diego' its only Pacific terminus," the *Times* sarcastically commented, "—it won't do; it won't do at all." [65] This situation, inconceivable in 1850, was irrefutable in 1885. San Diego's natural advantages notwithstanding, Los Angeles emerged as the regional metropolis, an achievement whose importance cannot be exaggerated. For as a result Los Angeles, not San Diego, was the focus of the extraordinary population movement which subsequently transformed southern California into one of the nation's foremost urban centers.

I do think farming is the slowest & poorest way in all the world to make a living. (Lucy Coit, 1890)

4   THE GREAT MIGRATION

Even before their struggle with San Diego was concluded, the people of Los Angeles measured progress in gallons of wine, feet of lumber, dollars per square foot of real estate, and, most important of all, the number of residents. Yet they realized that even if Los Angeles triumphed over San Diego, southern California was so sparsely settled and highly productive that its metropolis could grow little by natural increase and by farm to city movement. Hence they reasoned that immigration was "the one great desideratum" and that "every practicable means should be used to secure it as rapidly as possible."[1] Immigrants, the Los Angeles *Herald* stated, "know not where the best place is." "If we take the right steps to induce [immigration]," the Los Angeles *Express* added, "hither it will come."[2] The townspeople preferred "farmers and manufacturers, with the skill and means requisite for making their undertakings successful." "Of this class," one inhabitant wrote, "we cannot have too many."[3]

Proud of their fertile countryside, hospitable society, and mild climate, southern Californians tried to divert the westward movement to their section. Daniel Freeman, owner of the immense Centinela and Sausal Redondo ranches, traveled east to promote his farmlands before a Dunker congregation. The Southern California Immigration Association, founded by the Los Angeles Board of Trade and supported by prominent property owners, persistently advertised the entire region.[4] "No happier paradise for the farmer can be found than Los Angeles County," the boosters declared; its unexcelled soil assures prosperity to the industrious and frugal. Immigrants without much capital "but with strong arms and good habits," they insisted, are certain of employment at high wages and "a competency in a few years." Los Angeles lacks none of the institutions essential to "the refinement of manner or the enjoyment of life," they claimed, and its warm winters, dry summers, and clear skies create "a land of perpetual spring," and "a veritable sanitorium." [5]

Unfortunately, southern California was so isolated and unfamiliar that it attracted only a few sailors, traders, miners, and pioneers before the Civil War. Afterwards, however, the Southern Pacific connected it with San Francisco and New Orleans, and publicists depicted the Great American Desert as an irrigable southwestern garden. Los Angeles became so much more appealing and settlement there so much more practicable that landlords subdivided their vast estates into small farms. Lured by available land, adequate water, and improved transportation, eastern farmers sold their property and moved to southern California.[6] Trusting in the region's warm and dry climate, desperate consumptives sought to regain their health in the country's southwestern corner.[7] Their enterprise and demands created additional opportunities which attracted the artisans, merchants, professionals, and manufacturers who rounded out Los Angeles' population.[8]

Between 1860 and 1880, nonetheless, the population increased only from 4,385 to 11,183 in the town and from 11,333 to 33,381 in the county. Nearly three of every four inhabitants were born in the United States, and, unlike the northern Californians, many of them were native Californians. The native Americans came principally from New York, Pennsylvania, Massachusetts, and Maine, and Ohio, Indiana, Illinois, and Missouri. The European immigrants were largely English, Irish, German, and French, and whereas Chinese predominated among the foreign-born in the north, Mexicans outnumbered the Europeans in the south. As a result of the moderate pace of growth, moreover, Los Angeles was not transformed into a typical frontier settlement; the relative number of women, children, and elderly all remained higher there than in, say, San Francisco.[9] To the keen disappointment of Los Angeles' boosters, the influx of immigration was still a vision in 1880.

That only a few thousand of the many million American and European immigrants came to southern California was not surprising. After all, it had to compete for them with the Great Lakes, Prairie, Rocky Mountain, Southwest, and Pacific Northwest states. Nearly all their governments hoped to accelerate settlement and increase property values by channeling the flow of immigration to their regions. They were supported by commercial associations seeking to foster trade and encourage industry and assisted by transcontinental railroads trying to stimulate demand for their lands and traffic for their lines. These promoters agreed that, as one midwesterner put it, "We can just as well build up [a region] in five years as to be a lifetime about it." Hence they circulated pamphlets, sponsored spokesmen, subsidized advertisements, and otherwise publicized their region's advantages for prospective settlers.[10] Their success was southern California's failure.

Its boosters' laments aside, Los Angeles labored under insuperable handicaps in this competition. American immigrants traditionally moved toward the country's undeveloped districts, from the Atlantic seaboard west to the eastern Great Lakes and the southeastern frontier and also north to Maine, south to Florida, northwest to Minnesota, and southwest to Texas.[11] They normally hoped to improve their material fortunes. "If the lands in one part . . . are superior to those in another in fertility," a European visitor observed; "if they are in the neighborhood of a navigable river, or situated conveniently to a good market; if they are cheap and rising in value, thither the American will gladly emigrate, let the climate be ever so unfriendly." [12] In appealing to the restless farmers of eastern America and western Europe, therefore, the promoters stressed not the political blessings of the United States but the economic advantages of their own states—their fertile soil, inexpensive land, abundant timber, and low transportation rates.

Prospective immigrants, in turn, evaluated different regions by these criteria, and among equally desirable districts generally chose the closest one. The Arkansas farmer who secured a productive tract in Texas rarely pressed on to Arizona; the Illinois farmer who found a free homestead in Kansas seldom continued on to Oregon. Throughout the nineteenth century New Englanders relocated in western New York, Virginians in the Kentucky hills, Pennsylvanians near the Great Lakes, and midwesterners on the prairie.[13] Few undertook the long, arduous, and expensive journey to the Pacific coast. "It was an error . . . to suppose that there was a large immigrant element seeking to reach California," a Southern Pacific official remarked in 1881. "The men who landed at Castle Garden came there destined for Kansas, Nebraska and the other northwestern States." [14] And reflecting on their reluctance to depart for California, a state commissioner of immigration reported that "They say they can purchase homes [elsewhere] for what it would cost them to get here." [15]

The Far West, of course, attracted some immigrants, and southern California faced serious competition there as well. "The most energetic measures are being used to invite and secure immigration" in this region, the Los Angeles *Star* observed in 1872. Even counties "vie with each other as to who shall offer the greatest inducement to settlers."[16] Moreover, central California's San Joaquin, northern California's Sacramento, and western Oregon's Willamette valleys contained fine farmland. So did western Canada's Red River Valley, now penetrated by the Canadian Pacific, and eastern Washington's inland empire, just opened up by the Great Northern. And American immigrants—be they New York farmers who chose the forested Ohio Valley over the treeless Dakota Territory or Piedmont planters who preferred the Tennessee hills to the Louisiana lowlands—traditionally favored a countryside with a familiar climate, topography, vegetation, and agriculture.

Thus to the many midwestern immigrants, who were unaccustomed to a warm, arid climate and uneasy amid a timberless, mountainous landscape and who had never irrigated a field, pruned a vine, or grafted a citrus tree, southern California had little appeal.[17] These people cannot appreciate the region, a Central Pacific official lamented in 1884. "It seems almost impossible, by the exercise of any human powers of description, to bring them to a realization of the greater personal comfort, afforded by your equable and salubrious climate, and the additional productiveness and value that climate imparts to the soil on which it rests."[18] With varied, moist weather, timbered, flat terrains, and large, inexpensive tracts suitable for cereal cultivation and stock raising, the Pacific Northwest and northern California seemed to offer the restless farmer a better opportunity to start life anew than did southern California.

Southern California alone of these regions attracted winter visitors. But, as one resident noted, "Like birds of passage, the whole flock took wing as soon as the almanac announced that spring had come, leaving only a few to conclude to settle." By the mid-1880's, however, the region was so well promoted, the transcontinental railroads completed and the East so prosperous that "the travel in the spring of 1885," one booster observed, "instead of falling off, remained about the same as in winter, and continued so all summer."[19] As a further inducement a rate war between the Southern Pacific and the Santa Fe reduced fares from the East by two-thirds and from the Midwest by even more. "It came just at the season of largest traffic," a railway official explained, "and naturally, when rates went so low, a vast number contemplating a journey to the Pacific Coast, took advantage of the opportunity."[20] "Nowhere else in the world had such a class of settlers been seen," one witness wrote. "Emigrants coming in palace-cars instead of 'prairie schooners,' and building fine houses instead of log shanties, and planting flowers and lawn grass before they planted potatoes or corn." [21]

The influx precipitated such wild speculation in southern California that within a year real estate transfers increased from 6,000 to 14,000 and from $10 million to $28 million.[22] The turnover lured professional "boomers" who showed the Californians "how to make money out of wind." "Never were more apt scholars found," one resident remarked. The furious exchange of property accelerated in 1887. Transfers rose to 33,000 and $95 million, and prices for lots soared far beyond any rational estimates of their productivity. Admitting that most booms were transitory, the participants assumed either that southern California's was an exception or that the bust was in the future. But in 1888 confidence failed. Sellers demanded that buyers complete their payments, and, since sellers were also buyers, nearly everyone attempted to dispose of some property to save the remainder. Hence few received offers. Transactions fell sharply, prices dropped drastically, and by 1889 southern California realty lost its inflated value.[23]

The bust stunned the people of Los Angeles, depreciating the boom's significance, questioning the region's capacity for growth, and substantiating the pessimistic predictions of the 1870's. Nevertheless, the boom reinforced Los Angeles' position as southern California's metropolis. Terminus for the Southern Pacific and Santa Fe lines, it gained most of the newcomers and new business. Between 1880 and 1890 its population increased from 11,183 to 50,395, and its assessed value advanced from $7 million to $39 million.[24] Despite the bust, moreover, southern California retained its renowned productivity, mild climate, and transcontinental railroads. Thus Los Angeles' quest for immigrants was so much more promising after than before the boom that by 1890 few disagreed with the Santa Fe vice-president who prophesied in 1888 that "people will continue to come here until the whole country becomes one of the most densely populated sections of the United States." [25]

The population of Los Angeles did, in fact, double during the next decade, reaching 102,000 in the city and 170,000 in the county. True, fewer health-seekers came to southern California. Some stayed in the East now that medical theory recommended proper care instead of comfortable weather, and others recuperated in the drier and cheaper southwestern states. But other, and healthier, newcomers amply compensated for this loss. They were Americans who had accumulated fortunes in the East and Midwest and now, rejecting traditional responsibilities in favor of present pleasures, decided to retire amidst less trying surroundings. They found southern California's climate, spaciousness, and novelty especially inviting and, as their numbers increased greatly late in the nineteenth century, their migration substantially enlarged the population of Los Angeles.[26]

Emory Fiske Skinner exemplified these people. A prosperous lumberman from the Midwest, he suffered a stroke around 1900 and decided to retire in the Far West. He toured the Pacific coast's urban centers. "I went to San Diego and was much pleased with that city," he wrote, but feeling that it was too small, he continued on to Los Angeles and San Francisco. He enjoyed the southern city though not the northern metropolis. "I was prejudiced against San Francisco," he conceded, "owing to the fact that it was controlled by corrupt labor elements." He pressed on to Portland, Tacoma, and Seattle. "If I had been a younger and able-bodied man," he admitted, "I would have selected Seattle as the place to make my home." But now, attracted more by a congenial climate than entrepreneurial openings, "I selected Los Angeles as the place in which to spend most of the days left to me." [27]

The migration of newcomers such as Skinner did not satisfy Los Angeles' promoters. "We cannot have permanent prosperity merely from a few rich men coming here to build homes, without producing anything," the Board of Trade insisted. "We must make strenuous efforts to induce also that immigration of a class of farming people who will till our soil and bring forth by the sweat of their brow that which is needed for self-support."[28] But though many easterners were intensely curious about southern California, they claimed that they could not obtain reliable information about the region. Hence the boosters, seconded by the press, urged the commercial associations and governmental agencies to intensify their promotional efforts.[29] Our advertising must be appropriate, the *Examiner* warned. "General statements about a salubrious climate and fertile soil may be pleasing, but not altogether satisfactory to the majority of those who want to know the effects and products of climate and soil. Facts and figures have far more weight in influencing immigration than volumes of flowery descriptions that contain nothing more tangible than sunny skies and orange blossoms." [30]

This advice presumed that most prospective immigrants intended to remain farmers, a reasonable presumption a generation earlier. Indeed, as late as 1865 most Americans had revered agriculture, for all its drudgery,[31] as a way of life and a means of livelihood. By 1900, however, the nation's countrymen were profoundly dissatisfied with their lot. They were tired, one observer wrote; "many of them have been born tired, of tired, toil-broken parents." They yearned "to escape the toil, drudgery and drabness of their farms and shops; to free themselves from the bonds of their narrow spheres; and, most important of all, to spare their children from their own fate." [32] Holding traditional sentiments about the moral superiority of the countryside, they were increasingly reluctant to be bound indefinitely to rural America. Desiring life's amenities no less than its decencies and less arduous but more rewarding livelihoods, they were strongly attracted by the far greater comforts and better opportunities in America's cities.

Often their children detested rural America too. "We all hated it," the most eloquent of them wrote. "We saw no poetry in it." ("We hated it in the summer when the mosquitoes bit and the cows slashed us with their tails, and we hated it still more in the winter time when they stood in crowded malodorous stalls.") "I perceived beautiful youth becoming bowed and bent," he lamented. "I saw lovely girlhood wasting into thin and hopeless age . . . and I heard ambitious youth cursing the bondage of the farm." [33] The skies, clouds, fields, and trees, rather than refreshing their spirits, revealed the sordid quality and mechanical routine of the countryside. They also deprecated agriculture. "I do think farming is the slowest & poorest way in all the world to make a living," a Nebraska girl wrote her fiance in California. [34] For these youngsters the city's diverse occupations and sophisticated society were far more promising and exciting than what they perceived as the countryside's "steady drag of unremitted work" and "unvarying habits of thought." [35]

This dramatic departure from tradition generated a vast source of prospective immigrants in rural America. And to tap this source southern California's boosters called for a promotional campaign so well organized and thorough that, in the words of the Los Angeles *Examiner,* "no man in the East or Middle West contemplating either a visit or a permanent change could make that change without having been forced, as it were, to consider the claims of this city and section." [36] Before the boom individual ranchers, voluntary associations, railway companies, and governmental agencies had not fully compensated with vigor and determination for what they lacked in funds and experience. After the bust, however, a group of southern Californians formed the Los Angeles Chamber of Commerce, a high pressure outfit which operated on the assumption that "either California must take a step backward and allow other sections to push ahead or the commercial organizations and railroad men must devise ways and means for diverting travel in this direction." [37]

Between 1890 and 1920 the Chamber effectively mobilized the community's resources for promotional enterprises. It established a permanent exhibit of regional agriculture in Los Angeles, encouraged local farmers to participate in fairs and expositions, and shipped their produce to New Orleans, Omaha, Chicago, and San Francisco. More than ten million persons saw these displays of oranges, grapes, and walnuts. The Chamber of Commerce also dispatched a railroad car filled with authentic southern California fruits, vegetables, and spokesmen into rural parts of America. Another one million people walked through "California on Wheels." Moreover, the Chamber joined with local publishers to distribute Los Angeles newspapers throughout the country, worked with hotel proprietors to attract conventions to southern California, circulated innumerable pamphlets, purchased immeasurable advertising space, and replied to countless queries about the region.[38] During these years, largely as a result of the Chamber's activities, Los Angeles and environs became the best publicized part of the United States.

Nevertheless, the Chamber's efforts would have accomplished little were it not for another profound change in American values and aspirations. After all, if the dissatisfied farmers and storekeepers and their children were just seeking economic opportunity in an urban setting, they could simply have moved to eastern and midwestern metropolises. Many, as the tremendous growth of New York and Chicago in the late nineteenth and early twentieth centuries indicated, did precisely that. At the same time, however, more and more of these people were less and less willing to devote their entire lives to improving their material positions. It was not that they were economic or social radicals; actually they were quite conservative in their outlook. Nor was it that they renounced wealth, preferred poverty, opposed work, eschewed duty, or rejected progress. It was rather that they redefined these traditional American virtues in such a way that they reached conclusions about the purpose of life which differed markedly from those held by earlier generations.[39]

For these people, almost all of whom were native Americans, wealth was less a measure of achievement than a means to, in Ralph Waldo Trine's words, "the legitimate comforts of life." Poverty was objectionable not so much because it reflected character defects as because it prevented the fullest possible enjoyment of the world. Work was hon-

7. California Building at the Chicago World's Fair, 1893

8. Citrus Fair in Los Angeles, 1898

orable not as a prerequisite for spiritual or even financial salvation, but as a way to self-realization and emotional gratification. Duty was conceived of less as making the most of a poor situation than as, according to E. L. Cabot, "doing what is hard and what you love." Ambition was, at best, illusory—a well-rounded life was infinitely preferable.[40] For those rural folk who, as Stanton D. Kirkham urged, wanted to relax as well as to labor and to find personal fulfillment rather than economic opportunity, the eastern and midwestern metropolises were not much more desirable than their surrounding countrysides.

Los Angeles' promoters were not aware of these changes—the waning of the agrarian myth and the Protestant ethic—before 1900. Hence their advertising, like that of rival regions, appealed to Americans of all geographic sections and social classes, consisted of spectacular statistics of crop production, land prices, water resources, and transport facilities, and stressed the urgency of diligence and frugality.[41] After 1900 the promoters discovered that most of the immigrants came from the Midwest. *"I am satisfied that the immigration practically radiates from Chicago,"* a Chamber of Commerce president reported in 1909, "and I am equally satisfied that we will have to fight most of our battles there." [42] They also realized that, like themselves, the prospective immigrants did not intend to engage in large-scale farming, and, even more important, that, unlike previous newcomers, they were migrating for noneconomic reasons.

The focus, content, and tone of southern California's advertising changed accordingly. Not only did the promoters concentrate their efforts on the prosperous rural Midwest, but, in addition, their publicity depicted a warm, dry climate, a varied, even exotic landscape, and a familiar suburban environment. Moreover, their literature rarely referred to agriculture other than to argue—without facts and figures —that "the same amount of well-directed industry upon a small area of land will produce more return [here] than in almost any section of the United States." Even more striking, it seldom mentioned work of any kind, claiming instead that "The difference between this and many parts of our land is that [here] nature seems to work with man, and not against him" and tends to "soften the asperities . . . [and abate] the restless rush and haste of our usual life." [43] Instead of promising prospective immigrants material prosperity, southern California's promoters offered them an easier, more varied, less complicated, and well-rounded life.

The response to this appeal far exceeded the expectations of the region's boosters. Heretofore few midwestern farmers intent on engaging in agriculture in the Far West appreciated southern California. Evaluating climate in economic terms, they considered the region too hot and arid for cereal production and cattle grazing. ("I must say that I like our Spokane climate a heap better than that of southern California," one former midwesterner remarked. "A little cold gives you a lot of 'pep'.")[44] They also objected to the differences between its barren, mountainous topography and their own flat, timbered landscape. But for newcomers planning to relax rather than to work, southern California's dry warmth was particularly appealing. For them the region's mountains, deserts, and ocean were fascinating not frightening. In revolt against a way of life and a means of livelihood, these people saw southern California as a terrestrial paradise. And while their more ambitious friends departed for Chicago and other midwestern cities, they decided to resettle in Los Angeles.[45]

Often the wish to migrate long preceded the act.[46] The tight agricultural market of the late nineteenth century immobilized those farmers and storekeepers who had to dispose of their properties to secure adequate capital. Prices advanced after 1896, however, remained high in the early 1900's, and reached peaks during the First World War. Cattle rose from six to twenty cents a pound, hogs from four to eighteen a pound, and corn from twenty-five cents to two dollars a bushel. "The most prosperous people in the United States today," a Los Angeles banker remarked in 1914, "are the farmers in the Middle West from Illinois to Nebraska."[47] Many Canadian farmers too, a railway official noted in 1909, "are now in a position to retire, either wholly or partially, and enjoy life." In response to economic prosperity generally, and to the booms of 1904–1906 and 1910–1913 specifically, these farmers and traders marketed their last crops and remaining merchandise, sold their farms and shops, and sought a new life in southern California.

Their enthusiasm was contagious and, one midwesterner recalled, "spread through the quiet old street, lined with maple trees, like a panic."[48] "I'd get letters from friends that had settled here and maybe talk with someone home on a visit," another newcomer (in a novel) remarked, "and I'd hear about the orange groves and palms and figs, and the green peas and fresh vegetables the year round, and the sunny days and cool nights, and how the only snow you saw was miles off on the mountains, and—well, I was sick of prairie landscape and stoking furniture all winter and frying all summer, and first chance I got, I boarded a train to find out if this country came up to the brag."[49]

73

Deciding that it did, he settled there permanently. So, one witness wrote, did "the retired farmers, grocers, Ford agents, hardware merchants, and shoe merchants from the Middle West and other parts of these United States, thousands and tens of thousands of them." "Toil broken and bleached out," he observed, "they flock to Los Angeles, fugitives from the simple, inexorable justice of life, from hard labor and drudgery, from cold winters and blistering summers of the prairies." [50]

More and more immigrants responded to this vision during the 1920's. "We are all 'on the jump' nowadays trying to get in this big corn crop," a Nebraska woman wrote, "so that we can hit the trail for California." [51] These newcomers, like their wealthier predecessors, stimulated the urban economy and increased the available openings for younger and more ambitious immigrants. The rapidly growing population also created exceptional windfalls in real estate, and the expanding petroleum and motion picture businesses further enlarged employment opportunities. Thus for the first time since the boom of the 1880's Los Angeles attracted many immigrants motivated principally by economic aspirations. Their imaginations stirred by prodigious speculative profits, dramatic oil strikes, and the fantastic celluloid world, they sought their share of the metropolis' bounty. Once liberated by peace from the constraint of the First World War and by prosperity from the immobility of the subsequent depression, they left for Los Angeles. Thousands upon thousands, they came, one observer wrote, in "rattle-trap automobiles, their fenders tied with strings, and curtains flapping in the breeze," and arrived "with no funds and no prospects, apparently trusting that heaven would provide for them." [52]

This movement was spurred by the metropolis' pervasive publicity, the nation's intensified mobility, and the region's increased accessibility. Early in the 1920's, local promoters, responding to keen competition from Florida, formed the All Year Club of Southern California. The club, jointly supported by business interests and county governments, developed into greater Los Angeles' principal booster organization. It vigorously advertised southern California, long famous as a winter resort for the wealthy, as a summer tourist spot for the middle class.[53] It persuaded small entrepreneurs, modest farmers, and even salaried employees who no longer worked through the year to vacation there. At the same time the private automobile and the transcontinental highways markedly reduced the cost and commitment of migration. For the first time in American history immigrants could return home for little more than the price of gas and the loss of time. Hence the vacationers and their impressionable friends—some from the lower middle class and the southwestern and mountain states—left to seek their fortunes in southern California.

The appeal of Los Angeles and environs was almost irresistible during the 1920's, and, as immigration to southern California gained in momentum, it perpetuated the very conditions which attracted the newcomers. It is true, that for only a fortunate few did property appreciate by hundreds of per cent, oil wells gush forth millions of barrels, and movie studios turn unknown Americans into international celebrities. But it is also true that under the stimulus of massive migration, the metropolitan economy expanded at such an unparalleled pace that land brought high prices if not easy fortunes, and newcomers found remunerative employment if not instant fame. And the mild climate, exotic landscape, and suburban environment still so intrigued those in quest of a new life that so long as the nation and region prospered and the immigrants discounted the psychic and social costs of relocation the movement proceeded in a spiral fashion whereby response fulfilled wish and reality approximated vision.

The prospect of a more rewarding livelihood—if not a well-rounded life—appealed to immigrants of other nationalities and colors too. Down through the late nineteenth century Los Angeles' growing population consisted almost entirely of native Americans and western Europeans. Not many southeastern Europeans migrated to southern California, and hardly any Mexicans survived the rancho era. Very few Chinese preferred Los Angeles to San Francisco, and almost no Negroes left the deep South for southern California. Together these people were, as Table 3 indicates, a smaller part of Los Angeles' population in 1890 than the northern and western Europeans. Amid the native-American majority, they were an inconsequential minority.[54] Due to changing conditions in Europe, Asia, Latin America, and the United States, however, many southeastern Europeans, Japanese, Mexicans, and Negro Americans migrated to southern California early in the twentieth century.

In Europe the south and east supplanted the north and west as the primary source of immigration to the United States. These newcomers, like their precursors, usually traveled to the Atlantic seaboard and remained there; those bound for the Pacific coast normally arrived at San Francisco or Seattle and settled nearby. Once in America, however, some Italians, Russians, and Poles, among others, moved to Los Angeles and vicinity. Moreover, the inauguration of steamship service between Naples and New Orleans provided a transoceanic

TABLE 3.   Negro Population and Nativity of Foreign Born in Los Angeles, 1890–1930

Place	1890	1900	1910	1920	1930
Northern and					
Western Europe	7,900	12,245	32,041	44,391	80,272
England	1,817	3,017	7,581	11,485	22,275
Germany	2,767	4,032	9,684	10,563	18,094
Southern and					
Eastern Europe	816	1,644	13,557	29,566	60,114
Italy	447	763	3,802	7,931	12,685
Russia	73	293	4,758	9,691	19,744
Asia	1,881	2,077	5,865	11,028	18,123
Japan	40	152	3,931	8,536	11,832[a]
Other America	1,963	3,802	14,218	36,177	86,691
Mexico	493	817	5,632	21,653	53,648[a]
Other regions	192	196	452	969	1,935
American Negroes	1,250	2,131	7,599	15,579	38,894

Source: U.S. Bureau of the Census, *Thirteenth Census of the United States. 1910. Volume I. Population* (Washington, 1913), pp. 854–855; U.S. Bureau of the Census, *Fourteenth Census of the United States. 1920. Volume IV. Population* (Washington, 1922), pp. 729–731; U.S. Bureau of the Census, *Fifteenth Census of the United States: 1930. Population. Volume II* (Washington, 1932), pp. 248–250.

[a] The discrepancies between these two figures and those in the text are due to the increase of second-generation Japanese- and Mexican-Americans; unlike the children of European immigrants, they were classified Japanese and Mexicans as well as native Americans.

route which connected with the Southern Pacific's transcontinental tracks to California. From the early 1900's, through the prewar years, to the Immigration Acts of 1921 and 1924, these transportation facilities diverted thousands of newcomers to Los Angeles. As a result 60,000 southern and eastern Europeans resided in the city and 70,000 in the county in 1930—nearly as many as the number of northern and western Europeans.[55]

Patterns of migration also shifted in Asia whence, as Japan had long forbidden its subjects to leave, nearly all immigrants were Chinese before 1900. The imperial authorities later reversed this policy, and many Japanese, discouraged by the poverty of their crowded island, availed themselves of the opportunity to emigrate. They departed for America in considerable number between 1900 and 1915. Some settled in Hawaii, but most continued on to the mainland; and, unlike the Chinese, the Japanese preferred Los Angeles to San Francisco. Although the imperial government, responding to anti-Oriental hysteria on the Pacific coast, halted the emigration of laborers to the United States in 1907, 4,000 Japanese lived in the city and 8,000 in the county in 1910. Also, Congress completely prohibited Oriental immigration in 1924, but, as a result of the movement of many Japanese-Americans to Los Angeles, their population advanced to 21,000 in the city and 35,000 in the county by 1930.[56]

Latin America, and especially Mexico, generated even more immigration during these years. For those Mexicans who had borne chronic poverty and recurrent revolution for generations, the demand for agricultural labor in the American Southwest offered an exceptionally attractive opportunity to start life anew. Thousands crossed the border after 1900, tens of thousands followed them after 1910, and scores of thousands joined them in the 1920's. In all, nearly a million Mexicans immigrated to the United States. Most arrived in Texas and Arizona, but some moved west to California; most initially worked in the countryside, but a few left for the cities; most planned to stay a short time, but many settled permanently. Hence the Mexicans totaled 97,000 in the city and 167,000 in the county and were by far the largest minority group in Los Angeles in 1930.[57]

American Negroes, who faced a perplexing predicament in the late nineteenth century, made up yet another source of immigration to Los Angeles. Residents of the wealthiest of countries, they were impoverished by the South's discriminatory economy and society. Citizens of the most democratic of nations, they were silenced by that region's exclusive government and laws. By 1900 many despaired of escaping from their positions as members of a subjugated and segregated caste. Some departed for the eastern and midwestern metropolises when employment opportunities expanded during the First World War. There they obtained jobs, but seldom secured promotions; they gained civil liberty, but rarely received recognition as kindred Americans. Thus thousands of Negroes moved from the urban East, as well as the rural South, to southern California, hoping to find in that promised land rewards for their labor and evidence of their equality. By 1930 they numbered 39,000 in the city and 46,000 in the county of Los Angeles.

Altogether, immigration—native and foreign, white and colored—had such a profound impact on Los Angeles that between 1890 and 1930 the population increased from 50,000 to 1.2 million in the city and from 101,000 to 2.2 million in the county. Its southern location notwithstanding, Los Angeles, as Table 4 reveals, outdistanced its

TABLE 4. Population Growth in Selected Cities, 1890–1930
(In thousands)

City	1890	1900	1910	1920	1930	1930[a]
New York	2,507	3,437	4,767	5,620	6,930	10,901
Chicago	1,100	1,699	2,185	2,702	3,376	4,365
Philadelphia	1,047	1,204	1,549	1,824	1,951	2,847
Los Angeles	50	102	319	577	1,238	2,319
(Los Angeles County)	(101)	(170)	(504)	(936)	(2,208)	—
Boston	448	561	671	748	781	2,308
Detroit	206	286	466	994	1,569	2,105
St. Louis	452	575	687	773	822	1,294
San Francisco	299	343	417	507	634	1,290
Seattle	43	81	237	315	366	421
Portland	46	90	207	258	302	379
Denver	107	134	213	256	288	331

Source: U.S. Bureau of the Census, *Fifteenth Census of the United States: 1930. Population. Volume I* (Washington, 1931), pp. 18, 19, 131; U.S. Bureau of the Census, *Fifteenth Census of the United States: 1930. Metropolitan Districts* (Washington, 1932), pp. 10–12.
[a] Metropolitan districts.

rivals to emerge as the metropolis of the Pacific coast. Already larger than Portland and Seattle in 1890, the city outnumbered Denver in 1910 and San Francisco in 1920; and metropolitan Los Angeles exceeded the San Francisco Bay area in 1930. Only slightly smaller than these cities combined, Los Angeles in 1930 had about twice as many people as San Francisco, three times as many as Seattle, and four times as many as Portland and Denver. Ranking fifth among the nation's cities and fourth among its metropolitan areas,[58] Los Angeles was about to assume a place not among the many regional metropolises like Boston but among the few continental centers like New York.

Los Angeles' rate of growth, as Table 5 shows, was no less extraordinary. Its population quadrupled in the 1880's, doubled in the 1890's, tripled in the 1900's, and doubled in the 1910's and again in the 1920's.[59] Such spectacular progress, to be sure, was not unprecedented in the Far West. San Francisco, Denver, Portland, and Seattle all achieved comparable, and sometimes even higher, rates of growth in the late nineteenth century. But such consistent advancement was indeed unique in this region. None of these other cities matched Los Angeles' pace during the 1910's and 1920's. Hence Los Angeles grew by almost as much as all its rivals combined between 1910 and 1920

TABLE 5.   Rates of Population Growth in Selected Cities, 1890–1930

City	1880–1890	1890–1900	1900–1910	1910–1920	1920–1930	1920–1930[a]
(Los Angeles County)	(204)%	(68)%	(196)%	(86)%	(136)%	—[b]
Los Angeles	*351*	*103*	*212*	*81*	*115*	—[b]
Detroit	77	39	63	113	57	68%
San Francisco	28	15	22	22	25	34
Chicago	119	54	29	24	25	33
New York	31	37	39	18	23	28
Portland	164	95	129	25	17	—[b]
Seattle	113	88	194	33	16	20
Denver	200	25	59	20	12	18
Philadelphia	24	24	20	18	7	16
Pittsburgh	46	31	18	10	7	15
Boston	24	25	20	12	4	15

Source: U.S. Bureau of the Census, *Fifteenth Census of the United States: 1930. Population. Volume I* (Washington, 1931), pp. 18–19; U.S. Bureau of the Census, *Fifteenth Census of the United States: 1930. Metropolitan Districts* (Washington, 1932), pp. 10–12.

[a] Metropolitan districts.

[b] Comparisons cannot be made.

and by more than twice as much between 1920 and 1930.[60] From a national perspective, again, its record resembled not so much that of smaller cities such as St. Louis as that of mammoth metropolises such as Chicago.

The background of Los Angeles' population, as Table 6 indicates, was also exceptional. Before 1890, when approximately three of every four residents there were native Americans, it had a lower percentage of foreign-born than most American cities. During the next forty years the percentage of foreign-born, which declined irregularly elsewhere, remained relatively stable in Los Angeles. Unlike the typical American metropolis, Los Angeles did not have at any time in its modern history a vast group of European immigrants.[61] Among the native Americans in Los Angeles in 1890, moreover, 32 per cent were born in California, a ratio which, while extremely low for eastern cities, was not unusual for far western ones. Although this proportion increased considerably in Seattle and Denver (and slightly in Portland) afterwards, it actually decreased to 25 per cent by 1910 and then remained constant to 1930 in Los Angeles.[62] To an unparalleled degree, its population, as Table 7 reveals, consisted of people new not only to the city but to the state as well.

Down through the mid-1880's, furthermore, most of these persons—

TABLE 6. Foreign-Born White Population as Percentage of Total Population, Selected Cities, 1890–1930

City	1890	1900	1910	1920	1930
New York	39	37	40	35	33
Detroit	39	34	34	29	26
Chicago	41	35	36	30	25
San Francisco	34	30	31	28	24
Seattle	31	23	26	23	20
Philadelphia	26	23	25	22	19
Portland	28	20	21	18	16
Los Angeles	*22*	*18*	*19*	*19*	*15*[a]
St. Louis	25	19	18	13	10
Baltimore	16	13	14	11	9

Source: U.S. Bureau of the Census, *Thirteenth Census of the United States. 1910. Volume I. Population* (Washington, 1913), pp. 207–213; U.S. Bureau of the Census, *Fourteenth Census of the United States. 1920. Volume III. Population* (Washington, 1922), pp. 40–45; U.S. Bureau of the Census, *Fifteenth Census of the United States: 1930. Population. Volume II* (Washington, 1932), pp. 73–78.

[a] The Bureau of the Census reclassified the Mexicans from white to nonwhite in 1930, and the percentage of the foreign-born white in Los Angeles dropped accordingly.

TABLE 7. People Born in State of Residence as Percentage of Native American Population, Selected Cities, 1890–1930

City	1890	1900	1910	1920	1930
Boston	79%	78%	81%	83%	85%
New York	85	87	87	87	82
Baltimore	88	86	86	82	80
Philadelphia	86	85	84	82	80
Chicago	67	69	73	73	69
San Francisco	66	69	66	64	60
Denver	19	30	32	34	41
Portland	35	40	32	37	40
Seattle	12	20	23	31	39
Los Angeles	*32*	*34*	*25*	*26*	*25*

Source: U.S. Census Office, *Report on Population of the United States at the Eleventh Census: 1890. Part I* (Washington, 1895), pp. 580–583; U.S. Census Office, *Census Reports. Volume I. Twelfth Census of the United States. 1900. Population. Part I* (Washington, 1901), pp. 706–713; U.S. Bureau of the Census, *Thirteenth Census of the United States. Volume I. Population. 1910* (Washington, 1913), pp. 770–771; U.S. Bureau of the Census, *Fourteenth Census of the United States. 1920. Volume II. Population* (Washington, 1922), pp. 661–668; U.S. Bureau of the Census, *Fifteenth Census of the United States: 1930. Population. Volume II.* (Washington, 1933), pp. 204–215.

other than the Californians—came from the northeastern states. But during the late 1880's and the early 1890's the movement of wealthy residents from Ohio, Indiana, and Illinois made the east north-central section the principal source of newcomers. Then during the late 1890's and early 1900's the exodus of prosperous farmers from Iowa, Nebraska, Michigan, and Wisconsin lodged the west north-central region in second place. And during the late 1910's and the 1920's the migration of ambitious persons from Texas, Oklahoma, Utah, and Colorado increased the population from the west south-central and mountain states. Hence, unlike New York, Chicago, and even San Francisco— whose people were primarily from the Middle Atlantic, east north-central, and Pacific Coast divisions, respectively—Los Angeles contained so few residents from its own region that in 1930 of every one hundred inhabitants, as Table 8 shows, thirty-seven were midwesterners, thirteen southerners, thirteen easterners, eight westerners, and only twenty-eight far westerners.[63]

Despite the predominance of native Americans, Los Angeles was, as Table 9 indicates, racially heterogeneous in 1930—at least by the standards then prevailing, which classified Mexicans as nonwhites.

TABLE 8. Region of Birth of the Native American Population of Los Angeles, 1890–1930

Region	1890	1900	1910	1920	1930
Pacific	32.5%	35.1%	26.4%	27.1%	27.7%
East North-central	21.4	21.8	25.0	23.2	19.4
West North-central	12.6	13.7	16.2	16.8	17.8
Middle Atlantic	12.4	11.3	12.0	11.1	9.6
Mountain	1.9	2.9	3.8	5.4	8.3
West South-central	3.8	2.9	4.2	5.1	7.3
East South-central	3.6	3.0	3.8	3.6	3.3
New England	6.9	5.3	4.7	3.6	3.0
South Atlantic	2.8	2.5	3.1	2.8	2.6
Abroad or at sea	2.1	1.3	0.3	1.2	1.2

Source: U.S. Census Office, *Report on Population of the United States at the Eleventh Census: 1890. Part I* (Washington, 1895), pp. 580–583; U.S. Census Office, *Census Reports. Volume I. Twelfth Census of the United States. 1900. Population. Part I* (Washington, 1901), pp. 706–709: U.S. Bureau of the Census, *Thirteenth Census of the United States. Volume I. Population. 1910* (Washington, 1913), p. 770; U.S. Bureau of the Census, *Fourteenth Census of the United States. 1920. Volume II. Population* (Washington, 1922), p. 666; U.S. Bureau of the Census, *Fifteenth Census of the United States: 1930. Population. Volume II* (Washington, 1933), p. 212.

Note: Because of rounding, columns do not necessarily add up to 100.0%.

TABLE 9. Nonwhite Population as a Percentage of Total Population, Selected Cities, 1890–1930

City	1890	1900	1910	1920	1930
Baltimore	15.4	15.7	15.3	14.8	17.8
Los Angeles	*6.3*	*4.3*	*4.4*	*5.2*	*14.2*[a]
St. Louis	5.9	6.3	6.5	9.1	11.6
Philadelphia	3.9	4.9	5.6	7.5	11.4
Detroit	1.7	1.4	1.2	4.2	8.2
Chicago	1.3	1.9	2.1	4.3	7.6
San Francisco	9.5	5.1	4.1	3.5	6.2
New York	1.6	2.0	2.0	2.9	4.9
Seattle	1.9	4.8	4.0	4.0	4.1
Portland	10.8	10.9	4.0	2.1	1.9

Source: U.S. Bureau of the Census, *Thirteenth Census of the United States. 1910. Volume I. Population* (Washington, 1913), pp. 207–213; U.S. Bureau of the Census, *Fourteenth Census of the United States. 1920. Volume III. Population.* (Washington, 1922), pp. 40–45; U.S. Bureau of the Census, *Fifteenth Census of the United States: 1930. Population. Volume II* (Washington, 1932), pp. 73–78.

[a] The Bureau of the Census reclassified the Mexicans from white to nonwhite in 1930, a change that accounted in part for the large increase of the nonwhite percentage.

TABLE 10. Population Composition of Selected Cities, 1890–1930

	1890				1900			
	Per cent in age groups			Males to 100	Per cent in age groups			Mal to 1
City	1–19	20–54	55+	females	1–19	20–54	55+	fema
Eastern								
Chicago	41	53	6	107	40	49	10	10:
Philadelphia	37	53	9	95	37	49	14	9(
St. Louis	42	50	7	102	39	49	12	10(
Baltimore	41	50	9	90	39	47	13	9:
Los Angeles	*36*	*55*	*8*	*109*	*34*	*55*	*11*	*9*
Western								
San Francisco	33	58	8	131	31	59	10	11'
Seattle	30	65	4	167	29	66	6	17'
Portland	27	67	5	168	31	62	7	14:
Denver	32	63	5	132	35	57	8	9(

Source: U.S. Census Office, *Report on Population of the United States at the Eleventh Census: 1890. Part II* (Washington, 1897), pp. 115, 116, 118, 119, 122, 124, 127–130; U.S. Census Office, *Census Reports. Volume II. Twelfth Census of the United States. 1900. Population. Part II* (Washington, 1902), pp. 123, 126–128, 132, 133, 140, 143–145; U.S. Bureau of the Census, *Thirteenth Census of the United States. Volume I. Population. 1910*

Whereas nonwhites made up 8 per cent of the population in Detroit and 6 per cent in San Francisco, they composed 14 per cent in Los Angeles, a proportion exceeded only in Baltimore among the nation's largest metropolises.[64] Moreover, whereas the minority in Baltimore consisted entirely of long-settled Negro residents, the minority in Los Angeles included recently-arrived Mexican and Japanese as well as Negro newcomers. Unlike most eastern and midwestern metropolises, which were divided between native Americans and European immigrants, Los Angeles was divided between an overwhelming native white majority and a sizable colored minority. Nowhere on the Pacific coast, not even in cosmopolitan San Francisco, was there so diverse a mixture of racial groups, so visible a contrast and so pronounced a separation among people, as in Los Angeles.

Los Angeles' population, as Table 10 shows, differed from that of other far western cities in its balance of sexes and distribution of generations too. By contrast with eastern communities in 1890, San Francisco, Denver, Portland, Seattle, and Spokane all had far more men than women and a much heavier concentration of the middle-aged. Afterwards, these cities grew more gradually, and their populations achieved better balances between men and women and broader age

1910				1920				1930			
er cent in age groups			Males to 100 females	Per cent in age groups			Males to 100 females	Per cent in age groups			Males to 100 females
-19	20–54	55+		1–19	20–54	55+		1–19	20–54	55+	
37	51	11	106	36	51	14	103	33	52	15	103
36	49	14	96	35	49	16	99	34	49	18	99
35	52	13	102	32	52	16	97	30	51	19	97
37	48	15	92	35	49	16	97	34	48	17	97
8	*55*	*17*	*104*	*27*	*53*	*21*	*96*	*27*	*53*	*21*	*96*
27	59	14	132	26	56	17	114	23	55	20	114
27	60	12	136	29	55	16	104	28	52	20	104
27	60	14	135	30	52	18	100	28	50	21	100
32	53	15	101	29	51	18	95	30	48	22	95

(Washington, 1913), pp. 278–283, 437, 439, 447, 449, 452–455, 459, 461, 462; U.S. Bureau of the Census, *Fourteenth Census of the United States. 1920. Volume II. Population* (Washington, 1922), pp. 288, 291, 294, 301, 303, 304, 308, 315, 343, 347, 358, 359; U.S. Bureau of the Census; *Fifteenth Census of the United States: 1930. Population. Volume II* (Washington, 1933), pp. 115, 724, 726, 730, 738, 740, 754, 761, 782, 784, 793.

distributions. By comparison, Los Angeles, which was not a typical frontier settlement, had only slightly more males than females and a lighter concentration of the middle-aged in 1890. Thereafter it expanded more rapidly and its population registered a very low ratio of men to women, an extremely low proportion of young people, and, until the composition of the migration changed in the 1920's, an exceedingly high proportion of elderly.[65] The life cycle that determined the balance of sexes and distribution of generations elsewhere in the United States was not as yet operative in Los Angeles.

These characteristics aside, the immigrants were the dynamic component in the emergence of Los Angeles. Their arrival changed it from a small and little known city of fifty thousand people into the largest and most renowned of Pacific coast centers, a metropolis of two million inhabitants. Their expectations encouraged developers and authorities to convert a countryside of farms, ranches and wasteland into a conurbation of electric railways, motor highways, public utilities, and suburban subdivisions. Their demands intensified earlier pressures for improved commercial facilities and formed sizable markets first for consumer items and professional services and later for capital goods and heavy manufacturing. And—no less important—their conception of the good life so shaped the landscape, community, and government of Los Angeles as to leave an indelible imprint on the character of their adopted metropolis.

In fact, railway lines have to keep ahead of the procession [of settlement]. It would never do for an electric line to wait until the demand for it came. It must anticipate the growth of communities and be there when the homebuilders arrive—or they are very likely not to arrive at all, but to go to some section already provided with arteries of traffic. (Henry E. Huntington, 1904)

5 TRANSPORTATION, WATER, AND REAL ESTATE

The boom of the 1880's and the subsequent increase of population significantly altered the prevailing patterns of urban expansion in Los Angeles. Not that private enterprise relinquished its cardinal role. Individual businessmen and utility companies still decided whether or not to construct street railways, extend water mains, and subdivide real estate. But heretofore Los Angeles' entrepreneurs, acting according to a strict profit and loss calculus in a settlement which grew only moderately, proceeded cautiously. Territorial expansion lagged behind population growth. Now improved prospects and intense competition at once encouraged and compelled the developers to make commitments in advance of demand. Henceforth private enterprise developed Los Angeles according to these dictates. And though circumstances considerably modified its position by 1930, private enterprise exerted a profound influence on the character of the metropolis in these years.

Before 1885 Los Angeles' small population created only a modest demand for rapid transportation. Despite low construction costs and operating expenses, the few railways started earned little profit.[1] Afterwards, the immense migration generated a potentially remunerative market for improved transit, but to capitalize on it entrepreneurs were obliged to lay tracks well in advance of actual passenger requirements. "It would never do for an electric line to wait until the demand for it came," a prominent railwayman explained. "It must anticipate the growth of communities and be there when the home builders arrive—or they are very likely not to arrive at all, but to go to some other section already provided with arteries of traffic."[2] To compound this problem, the slow and inexpensive horsecars had to be replaced by more efficient and costly cable or electric trains.

The practices prevailing in large eastern cities, where transit generally followed growth, profits seemed certain, and investors accepted railway securities,[3] provided little guidance in Los Angeles, where transportation facilities preceded settlement and the lines appeared so risky that capitalists avoided their issues. For this reason Los Angeles' entrepreneurs devised alternative financial arrangements. They not only petitioned the municipality for long-term franchises that guaranteed their railways monopolies of specified routes—a common practice—but also sought to compensate for the discrepancy between original expenditures and immediate returns by sharing in the value that the railways added to adjacent property. Hence small railwaymen requested subsidies from local landowners, and large railwaymen subdivided the land themselves. In both cases the expectations of prompt profits from real estate at least as much as the hopes for eventual returns from transportation stimulated the construction of local and interurban lines throughout Los Angeles after 1885.

This pattern emerged clearly during the boom of the 1880's when several hillside landowners realized that their lots were unmarketable so long as Los Angeles relied on horse-drawn rail cars. Accordingly, they organized the Second Street and the Temple Street Cable Railways, subscribed capital and secured subsidies, and then built and operated these lines between the city and their property. Although the real estate markedly appreciated in value, the railways failed to meet expenses; and the entrepreneurs refused to subsidize them after the bust. They sold the equipment to another company, but it too failed. A group of Chicago capitalists then took possession, converted the horsecars, renovated the cable tracks, and combined them into the Pacific Railway. Its president misused company funds, however, and, though the court appointed J. F. Crank, a capable railwayman, as receiver, the corporation's net earnings fell sharply in the early 1890's.[4]

Meanwhile, the Los Angeles and Vernon Street Railway and the Electric Railway Homestead Association purchased inexpensive parcels of outlying land from which they laid tracks to the city. The lots sold well during the boom, but, as the trains attracted few passengers, the promoters stopped service, and the companies went bankrupt after the bust. Whereupon Moses H. Sherman, a shrewd banker and railwayman from Phoenix, bought these lines and merged them and several others into the Consolidated Electric Railway.[5] He also secured capital from the National Bank of California in Los Angeles and credit from the Pacific Rolling Mills of San Francisco and then applied for a franchise to compete directly with the cable railways. The council passed it over the mayor's veto, and Crank, who had lobbied against the petition, lamented that "It will be impossible for us to reduce expenses to meet such a division of the income."[6] In a last desperate effort to stimulate patronage and cut costs, he urged Pacific Railway's bondholders to electrify portions of the system, but they refused to invest any additional funds.

Competition was fatal for the Pacific Railway. It failed to meet its interest payments in 1892, and the bondholders, offered an exchange of securities by Consolidated Electric, forced the company into bankruptcy.[7] Subsequently, Sherman purchased the Pacific Railway, electrified all his remaining cable lines, and dominated the transit business in Los Angeles. Unfortunately, immigration and thus patronage lagged in these years, and a heavy indebtedness and high operating costs precluded commensurate reductions in over-all expenditures. Consolidated Electric's bondholders blamed Sherman and his nephew, Eli P. Clark, for the railway's losses and demanded their resignations. Sherman agreed—provided that the company's financial position improved within three years—and the new directors reorganized the system as the Los Angeles Railway Company. But they incurred an additional $1 million debt thereafter, and when Sherman refused to resume control,[8] sold the property to a syndicate headed by Henry E. Huntington, a nephew of the late Collis P. Huntington and a millionaire intrigued by the growth of Los Angeles.

Sherman and Clark then shifted their attention to interurban railways which extended farther into the country, crossed more sparsely-settled territory, and involved even greater risks than local lines.[9] The first interurbans were built during the boom of the 1880's by townsite developers who, pressed by competitors, were compelled to connect their holdings with Los Angeles. The Los Angeles County Railroad, for example, proposed to run a steam line from Los Angeles through Colegrove, Cahuenga, Morocco, and Sunset to Santa Monica. Aware that prospective patronage did not justify estimated expenditures, the promoters asked interested property owners for cash bonuses and land grants. They responded favorably. "I have but little confidence in its running as an *electric* road," one donor admitted, but "we need not count what we have put in as a total loss—for it will help our land in value to the amount it has cost us."[10] Their donations financed construction. Like most early interurbans, the Los Angeles County Railroad failed soon after completion, and in the 1890's Sherman and

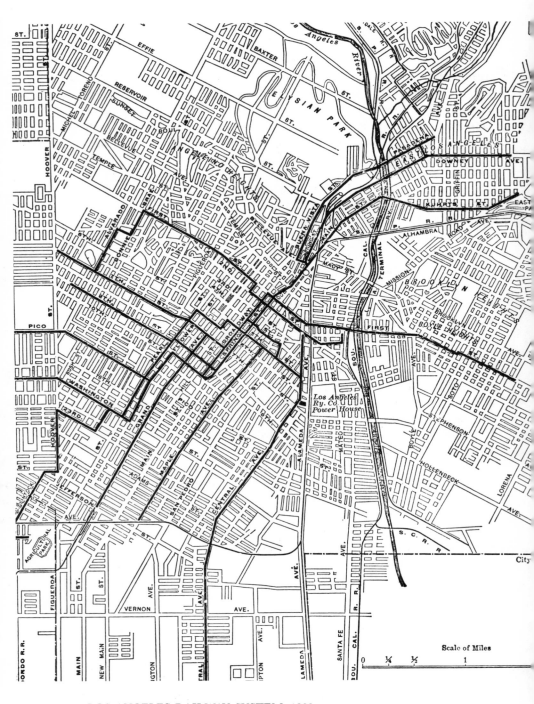

LOS ANGELES RAILWAY SYSTEM, 1898

Clark purchased it along with several others and consolidated them into the Pasadena and Pacific Railway.

Ambitious and indefatigable, Sherman and Clark planned to create an extensive, efficient, and profitable interurban network throughout greater Los Angeles. But they were not wealthy, and their project was premature. Like their predecessors, they rarely spent their own money. They did build a line connecting Westgate with Los Angeles and Santa Monica in return for services rendered them by developer Robert C. Gillis, and they also laid a track along the Pacific coast which passed through several settlements in which they owned real estate. But usually they relied on subsidies from landholders anxious to secure rail connections. When they offered to construct a road from Los Angeles through Hollywood to their Colegrove branch, for instance, a committee consisting of local property owners promptly raised a $15,000 bonus.[11] In this way Sherman and Clark covered western Los Angeles with an interurban system known as the Los Angeles Pacific railway.

Huntington, who dominated local transportation, entered Los Angeles' interurban business as well when, with a few San Francisco capitalists, he organized the Pacific Electric Railway Company in 1901. He realized that the first years of an interurban system were bound to be unprofitable, but, unlike Sherman and Clark, he possessed sufficient resources to engage extensively in real estate development. He formed the Huntington Land and Improvement Company which acquired vast tracts all over the western San Gabriel Valley—through which the Pacific Electric built its lines—and subdivided and marketed these properties whenever conditions seemed favorable.[12] Huntington not only extended the Pacific Electric throughout southern and eastern Los Angeles County, but also purchased the Los Angeles and Redondo Beach railway and its terminal townsite on the Pacific Ocean. There too returns from real estate sales compensated for the costs of railroad construction.

Although most residents approved of Huntington's activities, Edward H. Harriman, president of the Southern Pacific, regarded the Pacific Electric's expansion as a threat to his company's freight business. For this reason he decided to secure some influence over the interurban's policies. To Harriman's advantage, Huntington's partners objected to the excessive costs of the Pacific Electric. When they offered to sell their 45 per cent interest, Harriman accepted and became the minority stockholder. By 1903 he was determined to gain further control. When the Los Angeles Railway applied for a franchise along Sixth Street, and the council, following routine procedure, announced

9. Temple Street Cable Railway trains, 1889

10. Los Angeles Consolidated Electric Railway trains, 1895

11. Pacific Electric Railway line, ca. 1904

a public auction, Harriman's representative unexpectedly joined the bidding and eventually offered $110,000 for a grant worth at most $10,000. Not long after, Huntington reached an agreement with Harriman: the former retained 55 per cent of the Los Angeles Railway and 50 per cent of the Pacific Electric, and the latter gained 45 per cent of the one and 50 per cent of the other.[13]

Meanwhile, Sherman and Clark found it increasingly difficult to attract capital for the expansion, operation, and maintenance of the Los Angeles Pacific. The railway had no market for its securities, not only because it labored under heavy expenses, but also because it suffered from the competition of Huntington's Los Angeles and Redondo railway.[14] Left with so little time and no other alternative, Sherman asked Robert C. Gillis to persuade Harriman to guarantee the interest on his railway's bonds. The magnate agreed, provided that Sherman sell him controlling interest in the company. Sherman acquiesced, and, when the Los Angeles Pacific failed to prosper, he and Clark sold their remaining shares to Harriman. The Southern

Pacific thereby fortified its position in the metropolitan transit industry at the decade's end.[15]

By then Huntington had supplied his real estate with rail connections and contemplated at least partial retirement; his immense fortune notwithstanding, he preferred the less demanding and less expensive local lines. The Southern Pacific, by contrast, was principally interested in freight not passengers; as a nationwide corporation, it commanded the resources and personnel required by the costly and complicated interurban system. Hence Huntington and Harriman amicably terminated their previous agreement in 1911. Huntington took the Los Angeles Railway and organized a new Los Angeles Railway Corporation which was capitalized at $20 million, operated 350 miles of single and 170 miles of double track, and dominated local transit. The Southern Pacific acquired the Pacific Electric and formed a new Pacific Electric Railway Corporation which was capitalized at $100 million, consisted of 165 miles of single and 290 miles of double track, and monopolized interurban transportation.[16]

The Los Angeles and the Pacific Electric were crucial as a means of stimulating the subdivision of the countryside, and the expansion of the metropolis, through 1910. But the region's dispersal, prosperity, and mild climate, combined with its population's inordinate mobility and acquisitive inclinations, formed a favorable setting for the motor car too. It soon supplemented the electric train, as auto registration in Los Angeles County, less than 20,000 in 1910, exceeded 100,000 in 1920, and approached 800,000 a decade later.[17] The car did more than extend the railways' radial line of settlement. It also increased the accessibility of sections by-passed by the tracks, served places located far from the stations, opened up foothills where steep grades precluded profitable rail operations, and in these ways encouraged developers to subdivide isolated but otherwise desirable districts. As its safe and widespread use required efficient and extensive highways, however, the responsibility for transportation shifted from private enterprise to public authority.

Opening, widening, and paving roads was normally initiated by the property owners and undertaken by the common council. The costs were charged to the abutting real estate on the assumption that—in the words of one city planner—"the more a street was used the better it had to be improved and the more valuable the frontage." [18] Also, subdividers sometimes developed thoroughfares through their tracts on the expectation that these would increase the property's accessibility and enhance its desirability. Between 1904 and 1914, as a result of the

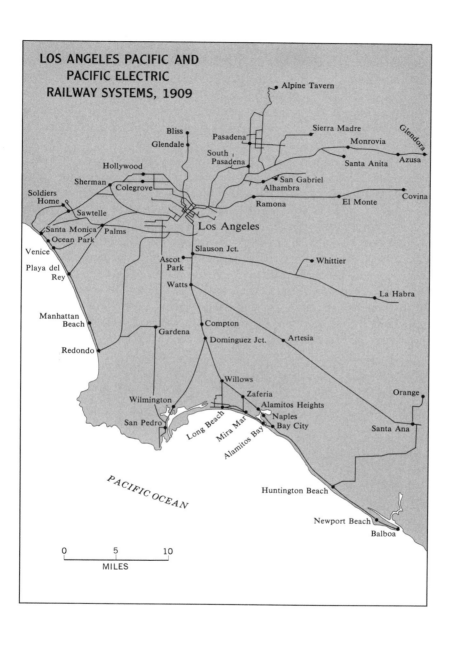

LOS ANGELES PACIFIC AND
PACIFIC ELECTRIC
RAILWAY SYSTEMS, 1909

Alpine Tavern

Bliss
Glendale
Pasadena
South
Pasadena
Sierra Madre
Monrovia
Glendora
Santa Anita
Azusa

Hollywood
Sherman
Colegrove
San Gabriel
Alhambra
Covina
Soldiers
Home
Sawtelle
Ramona
El Monte
Santa Monica
Palms
Los Angeles
Ocean Park
Venice
Slauson Jct.
Playa del
Rey
Ascot
Park
Whittier
Watts
La Habra
Manhattan
Beach
Compton
Gardena
Dominguez Jct.
Artesia
Redondo
Willows
Orange
Zaferia
Wilmington
Alamitos Heights
San Pedro
Long Beach
Naples
Bay City
Mira Mar
Santa Ana
Alamitos Bay

PACIFIC OCEAN

Huntington Beach

Newport Beach
Balboa

0   5   10
MILES

efforts of the city engineer and local developers, Los Angeles gained nearly five hundred miles of improved streets. These included not only hundreds of residential lanes, but also north and south arteries such as Central and Vermont Avenues and east and west highways such as Adams and Pico Boulevards. Few were wider than thirty to fifty feet, and most were topped with a thin, rough surface.[19] Nevertheless, as long as the vehicles weighed little and moved slowly, traffic in Los Angeles proceeded tolerably well everywhere except in the central business district.

For the thousands of heavier and faster automobiles and trucks the metropolis needed many wider, heavier, smoother, and thus more expensive thoroughfares. Wealthy developers occasionally believed that these roadways were aesthetically and materially advantageous. Hence Huntington built Huntington Drive in San Marino, and Gillis created San Vicente Boulevard in Los Angeles. Also, property owners sometimes considered arteries so essential that they formed Municipal Improvement Districts, which, by virtue of state legislation, enabled individual landholders to tax themselves in order to finance large-scale improvements. In 1923, for instance, several prominent developers organized the Hollywood Foothills Improvement Association which sponsored the establishment of a 53,000 acre Municipal Improvement District to build the twenty-one mile Mulholland Drive. Expecting the appreciation of values to compensate for the land donations and construction costs, they voted more than $1 million in bonds to finance the development of this thoroughfare.[20]

But more often the expenses exceeded the property owner's capacities, and, as these roadways were designed to move traffic past, not provide access to, adjacent real estate, their advantages were speculative for businesses and dubious for residences. For this reason many now challenged the principle of assessments for benefits. They claimed that as all the people gained from these arteries the entire populace should pay their price,[21] a rationale the authorities had already applied to the outfall sewer, the harbor, and municipal power. The voters saw no incongruity in now extending it to highways, and their willingness to accept heavier property taxes to cover construction costs resolved the apparent inconsistency in the theory underlying public improvements. This resolution, along with the popular commitment to disperse the metropolis and facilitate its transportation, encouraged the authorities to proceed with several highway projects from 1910 to 1930.

The Board of Supervisors issued $3.5 million in bonds for road construction in 1909, the California legislature, $73 million between 1910 and 1920, and the common council, $5 million in 1924.[22] Their highway departments built thoroughfares which covered the entire municipality, penetrated into the metropolis' periphery, and connected the county seats. Together with individual developers, property owners, and municipal improvement districts, they created an arterial network which extended from the San Fernando Valley to Long Beach and from Santa Monica to the San Gabriel Valley. Notwithstanding the increasing traffic congestion, the highways and the automobiles enlarged the accessibility of the countryside, spurred subdivision there, and thus contributed to the expansion of Los Angeles.

Los Angeles needed domestic water no less than street railways, and depended on its water company as much as on its transit corporations. After receiving its franchise in 1868, Los Angeles Water executed its pledges, complied with the stipulations, and began business. Subsequently, it purchased additional water-bearing lands, constructed larger storage reservoirs, and installed many miles of iron pipe. By the 1890's Los Angeles Water possessed adequate sources, capacity, and equipment to provide for a population of more than 300,000. The company also prospered; it reduced its outstanding obligations, declared regular 6 per cent dividends, and earned an estimated 10 to 35 per cent return. Thus it was hardly surprising that Los Angeles Water, its franchise due to expire in a few years, started stressing its ability to meet the city's future demand for water.[23]

Los Angeles Water provided satisfactory service. But Citizens Water, which was organized by Prudent Beaudry when Los Angeles Water refused to serve the northwestern hills in the 1870's, did not. Its operations were irregular, and its charges exorbitant. When the corporation claimed that the sparse population and rugged terrain precluded any improvement in service or reduction in rates, irate consumers insisted in 1890 that the authorities terminate Citizens Water's privilege and furnish water at the public expense.[24] The council responded by bringing suit to forfeit the franchise and ordering the city engineer to draw plans for a municipal waterworks. To this the Los Angeles *Times* objected. Questioning the efficiency and integrity of governmental enterprise, it urged the legislature to accept a recent offer by private enterprise to supply domestic water in return for a fifty-year grant. The legislators rejected this alternative, arguing that "From any point of view it seems to be desirable for the city TO OWN ITS OWN SYSTEM of water works and from the most careful observation it seems to be a safe business proposition."[25]

95

The council adopted the engineer's recommendations for a $ 3 million system, authorized a $500,000 bond issue for the headworks, conduit, and reservoir, and proposed the purchase of Los Angeles Water as well as Citizens Water. Belatedly realizing that Citizens Water's incompetence jeopardized its own prosperity, Los Angeles Water announced its intention to acquire that company and supply its customers as regularly and cheaply as its own. Although Los Angeles Water vigorously opposed the proposition, contending that additional facilities were unnecessary, an overwhelming majority of the electorate endorsed the plans for a municipally owned and operated waterworks.[26] But the courts discovered a technical error that voided the results, and in 1893 the city opened negotiations with the company for its plant. Unfortunately, the directors refused to reduce their price below $3.3 million, and the authorities declined to raise their offer above $1.5 million. Separated by so substantial a sum, the participants terminated the discussions.

Intermittent efforts brought them no closer to agreement,[27] and in 1898 the mayor warned the council that "If the city does not assume an aggressive policy the water controversy will continue indefinitely."[28] The legislators therefore instructed the engineer to draft new plans for an independent waterworks. The council and the company also started arbitration proceedings. Each appointed one representative, they selected a third, and together they held hearings to fix a fair price for Los Angeles Water's properties. But the public and the neutral arbiters agreed on a value so far below that of the company arbiter that Los Angeles Water rejected the decision. The authorities then seized the waterworks, but the courts returned it to the company and ordered the municipality to make payment before taking possession.[29] This deadlock so distressed both the council, which did not want to build another system, and the corporation, which did not relish additional litigation, that they compromised on a price of $2 million. And after the voters approved a bond issue the municipality assumed ownership in 1902.[30]

The council established a Board of Water Commissioners to manage the enterprise, and the board subsequently started to acquire Los Angeles' other water companies. Developers whose property was located outside the municipal boundaries or whose projects were blocked by Los Angeles Water's conservatism organized these firms. They regarded them—as Cornelius Cole did Colegrove Water and Los Angeles Suburban Homes did Van Nuys, Marion, and Owensmouth Water—as adjuncts to their tracts.[31] Most of these companies lost money, though a few large ones such as Huntington's San Gabriel Valley Water and Gillis' Santa Monica Water kept the deficits down. But for their owners, as for the railwaymen, remuneration from real estate activities was ample compensation for serving outlying parts of Los Angeles.[32] Hence they rarely rejected a reasonable offer by the Board of Water Commissioners, and, as the municipality acquired nearly all these concerns within the city, it assumed sole responsibility to supply water in Los Angeles.[33]

In the meantime the board realized that the differential between the waterworks' capacity and the city's consumption was dangerously inadequate. For though the river contained enough water for a settlement of 300,000, much of its flow was wasted and per capita use was excessive. The commissioners first tried to enlarge supply by improving distributing facilities and to decrease demand by installing water meters. These measures cut per capita consumption from 306 to 140 gallons daily so that whereas 85,000 people used twenty-six million gallons in 1902, 285,000 used only forty million in 1911.[34] Beyond a point, however, savings could not be attained and consumption could not be curtailed. Also, with population expanding, demand was increasing. Thus while continuing its campaign to eliminate waste, the board decided in 1904 to secure another source of water.

It authorized Superintendent William Mulholland and Lippincott and Parker Consulting Engineers to examine the city's present and future needs, the current supply and its capacity, and the feasibility of alternative sources. They projected Los Angeles' growth, calculated its requirements, estimated local resources, emphasized their deficiencies, and in conclusion recommended that the municipality search elsewhere for additional water.[35] Former Mayor Fred Eaton, who had also been a water company employee and the city engineer, had already anticipated this problem and envisioned the Owens River, located more than two hundred miles north in the California Sierras, as the solution. He even acquired options on water-bearing lands in the Owens Valley, planned a combined private and public corporation to transport and distribute the water, and afterwards informed the board of his intentions. It refused to join him, but agreed to consider the Owens River, and instructed Mulholland to make a preliminary survey. Favorably impressed, he returned with Mayor Arthur Harper who subsequently purchased Eaton's options and persuaded the council to submit a $1.5 million bond issue as payment.[36]

Harper then disclosed these proceedings. Although he was supported by Mulholland, who announced that an aqueduct was technically feasible, and by banker J. M. Elliott, who declared that the bonds were marketable, allegations of irregularities involving a water commissioner and a San Fernando Valley realty syndicate provoked so much criticism that the board had to promise to authorize impartial experts to re-examine its plans. On this basis the Chamber of Commerce, Merchants and Manufacturers Association, Realty Board, the Municipal League, the politicians, and the newspapers all endorsed the bonds. And the issue passed by a majority of fourteen to one.[37] The board next persuaded President Theodore Roosevelt to withdraw the public lands along the aqueduct route, and, honoring its pledge, appointed outside engineers to reconsider the entire Owens River project. They reported in 1907 that a 225-mile aqueduct, consisting of conduits, tunnels, and ditches connecting the Owens and San Fernando valleys, could be constructed for $24.5 million and would provide 410 second feet* of pure water[38]—or four times the current supply.

The council then authorized a $23 million bond issue, and the commercial and civic associations, supported by the press and pulpit, organized a campaign committee to convince the electorate that Los Angeles' progress required an affirmative decision. The diverse opposition of local socialists and power companies was unavailing against this phalanx. "Never before in the history of Los Angeles," the *Examiner* observed, "has there been such a unanimity of public effort in favor of a great public improvement." [39] The citizens approved the proposition in June 1907 by a ten to one vote. The investors, who deemed the $24 million debt too large and its 4 per cent interest too low, initially refused the issue, but the municipality marketed a small portion in California and placed the remainder with two New York banking houses. Construction proceeded according to schedule, and when Mulholland and the Department of Public Works completed the enormous aqueduct six years later Los Angeles secured enough water for the one million people its boosters expected by 1920.[40]

The board then had to arrange to distribute the water. But with so many people and so much territory to serve, it could not construct facilities fast enough to meet the demands of the residents and developers. Initially, the board had ordered extensions when one consumer existed for each two hundred feet of pipe, and allowed subdividers to lay mains that it repurchased when revenues equaled 10 per cent of costs. Later it ran pipes to property within two hundred feet of its

*A second foot is a unit of flow equal to one cubic foot per second.

facilities for eighty cents a front foot and to realty further away for $1.60 a lineal foot (refundable on collection of frontage charges).[41] In each case it adhered to the principle that the landholders or subdividers, and not the customers or authorities, should supply the capital for extensions. Now, rather than raise rates or incur a deficit, it obliged property owners to form improvement districts and issue bonds to cover the costs of trunk facilities.[42] So whereas the city and the users furnished the funds to acquire Los Angeles Water and build the Owens Valley Aqueduct, the landholders and the developers financed the additions to the distribution system.

The board (now the Board of Public Service Commissioners) considered the Owens Valley Aqueduct's 410 second feet and the Los Angeles River's 100 second feet adequate for another generation. But in the early 1920's a prolonged drought in the Sierras compelled it to revise its estimates. To its dismay, it learned that the city would exceed its supply by 1940, and that the metropolitan area would exhaust its resources even sooner.[43] The board therefore selected Mono Basin, a watershed located north of Owens Valley, as one abundant and feasible source of additional water. Its flow would provide a minimum of 140 second feet and an average of 195 second feet. Its tapping would involve complex but not insurmountable engineering tasks, and its supply could be transported through the existing aqueduct. The board (by now the Board of Water and Power Commissioners) persuaded the council to submit a $38 million bond issue for the development of Mono Basin. The electorate overwhelmingly endorsed it in 1930, and the water arrived at Los Angeles in 1940.[44]

Among the other sources the Colorado River, which as the Southwest's principal stream contained far more water than the Owens Valley and Mono Basin combined, was the obvious choice. But the Colorado posed extraordinary problems because competing interests had other plans for its future. Early in the twentieth century farmers from the Imperial Valley, a low-lying, prodigiously fertile plain in southeastern California, had attempted to protect their lands from the Colorado. Notwithstanding their cooperative efforts, the river rampaged the country and disrupted its economy so often during the early 1900's that the Imperial Irrigation District appealed to the federal government for flood-control assistance. Whereupon the United States Reclamation Service undertook an investigation in 1914, and reported in 1919 that the Colorado could be transformed from a reckless river into a providential stream.[45]

The governor of Utah then invited the other six states through

12. Construction of Los Angeles aqueduct, 1908–1912

13. Arrival of aqueduct water in the San Fernando Valley, 1913

which the Colorado passed to discuss the implications of this report. The Upper Basin states had little need for the water at the time, but they feared that the Lower Basin states would pre-empt the source and secure prior rights. Together they organized a League of the Southwest which, on behalf of the region, urged the states and Congress to devise an equitable apportionment. The respective legislatures and President Harding responded by appointing delegates to a Colorado River Commission. Negotiating long and hard through 1922, they divided the water between the two drainage basins and incorporated their recommendations in the Colorado River Compact.[46] Since Arizona refused to ratify it, the compact had no legal status. Nonetheless, the Los Angeles Board of Water and Power, advised by Superintendent Mulholland that an aqueduct could be built from the river to the city, applied for 1,500 second feet of the Colorado's flow.

Despite Arizona's intransigence, Congress instructed the Reclamation Service to prepare necessary plans. It recommended that the federal government construct a massive dam at or near Boulder Canyon on the Arizona-Nevada border and liquidate the debt by generating and marketing hydroelectricity. This proposal provoked a bitter battle between private and public power and in particular between the Southern California Edison Company and the Los Angeles Department of Water and Power.[47] It was only after years of contention involving not only utilities and municipalities but also landowners, farmers, utilities, and the southwestern state governments that Congress reached a settlement. Embodied in the Boulder Canyon Project Act of 1928, the settlement authorized the creation of Boulder Dam, the All-American Canal, and a power plant, the sale of electricity to cover the costs of the undertaking, and the ratification of the Colorado River Compact by only six states.

Meanwhile, at the request of Los Angeles, which needed allies in Washington, and the adjacent cities, which wanted a share of the Colorado's water, the California legislature established the Metropolitan Water District of Southern California in 1927. The metropolis and its satellites joined a year later. The district appointed a chief engineer to design an aqueduct, negotiated the prices of pumping and storage with the Secretary of the Interior, divided the available supply with southern California's irrigation interests, and signed contracts to purchase and distribute the water and power. The district then submitted a $220 million bond issue for Parker Dam and the Colorado River Aqueduct, and the electorate endorsed it by a five to one majority. The Reconstruction Finance Corporation accepted the bonds, and the district started work in 1934 and finished four years later. The Metropolitan Water District of Southern California, which supplied 1,500 second feet or enough water to meet estimated requirements in 1980,[48] was as instrumental as the Los Angeles Department of Water and Power in stimulating the region's urban expansion thereafter.

Real estate subdivision, which, as a rule, followed the provision of water and thereby completed the transformation of the countryside, changed considerably after 1885. Hitherto Los Angeles' population grew gradually, and its real estate market expanded slowly; subdivision returned only moderate profits and spurred little rivalry. As the immigrants expected modest facilities and lacked the funds for elaborate tracts, subdividers provided a bare minimum of residential conveniences and converted acreage only slightly, if at all, in advance of demand. After 1885 migration increased enormously and property appreciated commensurately; development brought very high returns and became increasingly competitive. As the prosperous newcomers also demanded better streets and more utilities, the developers now offered a full complement of residential improvements and subdivided land well ahead of actual requirements.

Some had adequate capital or credit, but most pooled their resources through syndications, paid for the real estate in installments, sold lots before completing the improvements, and even deferred payment to creditors.[49] In either case, once certain of transportation, water, and preliminary funds, Los Angeles' developers subdivided their holdings. Employing professional contractors or hiring individual engineers, surveyors, draftsmen, and laborers, they leveled the land, graded the roadways, built the sidewalks, and marked the lots. When they attempted to secure electric, gas, and telephone connections, however, they found that utility companies extended service only when anticipated revenues justified estimated expenditures.[50] But few subdivisions met this criterion. And their developers, unlike their predecessors who, under similar circumstances, had entered the water business, did not have the capital or the competence to engage in the electric, gas, and telephone industries.

Nor did the state and the city possess power to compel utility extensions that had insufficient earnings capacity. Subdividers thus had the right to service, the Board of Public Utilities explained in 1902, only if "a tender of money sufficient to defray the cost be made to the company." [51] Since this unfairly burdened the developers who financed the extensions and unduly benefited the corporations that owned them, the California Railroad Commission and the Los Angeles Department of Water and Power devised a more equitable procedure whereby the subdividers provided the capital for construction and then received refunds for connections. In the case of electricity, for example, the commission required a deposit whenever expenses exceeded eighty dollars per consumer, or three times estimated annual revenues, whereas the department, which operated its own plant, demanded an amount equal to its outlay for additional lines which was refunded according to each lighting customer, electrical appliance, and horsepower load.[52] This "contingent refund" system thereby obliged the utilities to serve the community and yet protected them against speculators.

Large tracts located far from existing facilities involved more complicated arrangements, as was revealed when a San Fernando Valley syndicate requested electric, gas, and telephone service for its tract in 1911. "You will understand that the building of lines through this territory will entail a considerable expense upon us," Southern California Edison replied, "and that for some time to come, at least, the business will be scattered and consequently not profitable."[53] It insisted on a monopoly of the electricity business, a guaranteed minimum power consumption, and a contribution toward construction costs. Southern California Gas demanded an advance of $100,000, the bulk of which was refundable on the formation of a municipal improvement district and the remainder on the basis of twenty dollars a connection.[54] And Sunset Telephone required, in return for service, that the syndicate purchase $10,000 of its bonds and provide either a monthly guarantee of $150 or an initial bonus of $2,500.[55] In the end the developers accepted Southern California Edison's terms, rejected Southern California Gas's, and bought $20,000 of Sunset Telephone's securities.

Subdivision became not only increasingly competitive, but also, as Henry E. Huntington's enterprise illustrated, extremely efficient. After arriving in the city early in the 1900's, he organized the Pacific Electric Railway, Huntington Land and Improvement, and San Gabriel Valley Water companies. Pacific Electric extended its interurban tracks, throughout the county, Huntington Land purchased adjacent ranches in the San Gabriel Valley, and Valley Water developed a domestic water system. His holdings connected with transportation and provided with water, Huntington waited for an advance in the residential real estate market. Huntington Land then subdivided its acreage into suburban tracts, paid deposits to utility companies for electric, gas, and telephone service, and employed outside organizations to publicize and sell the lots.[56] Indeed, Huntington integrated his undertaking so effectively that while Pacific Electric lost millions and Valley Water thousands, Huntington Land's earnings justified the entire investment.

Subdivision, as the Los Angeles Suburban Homes Company's activities demonstrated, became more extensive too. Around 1909 this syndicate bought the southern San Fernando Valley, divided most of the 47,500 acres into small farms, and platted the rest as the towns of Van Nuys, Marion, and Owensmouth. It asked the Los Angeles Pacific to serve the territory, and, as the land contained fewer than 1,000 people and the line cost at least $200,000, it offered the corporation a $150,000 bonus. Subsequently, Los Angeles Pacific built a line to Van Nuys and Suburban Homes extended it through Marion to Owensmouth. The developers also organized subsidiary companies to tap and distribute water, hired engineering teams to subdivide the acreage, negotiated with the utility companies for connections, and employed a prominent real estate firm to market the lots. Finally, Los Angeles Suburban Homes donated lots to religious congregations, encouraged the formation of school districts, and offered discounts to builders in order, in the words of developer H. J. Whitley, to "instantaneously bring a town into existence."[57]

Subdivision, as Robert C. Gillis's improvement of Huntington Palisades indicated, also became extremely expensive after 1885. A Canadian immigrant, who, as head of the Santa Monica Land and Water Company, had successfully subdivided large sections of western Los Angeles in the early 1900's, Gillis acquired the Palisades, a 250 acre tract overlooking the Pacific Ocean, in the late 1920's. Since Huntington Palisades—part of the Westgate Addition annexed to Los Angeles in 1916—was already connected by city highways and entitled to municipal water, Gillis was spared the cost of building electric railways and developing water resources. By 1927, nonetheless, he had spent $600,000 to grade and pave the streets, construct the sidewalks, curbs, and gutters, place the utility conduits and cables, lay the water mains, sanitary sewers, and storm drains, and otherwise subdivide the property. And another $400,000 was required, it was estimated, to complete the project, making a total of $1 million— approximately $4,000 an acre or $2,000 a lot—a steep price even for one of Los Angeles' most fashionable suburbs.[58]

In these ways Los Angeles was converted into a metropolis by 1930. Municipal, county, and state highways, as well as private urban and interurban railways, extended throughout southern California. The Owens Valley Aqueduct, nearby streams, trunk mains, and local pipes provided the region with domestic water. And thousands of subdividers converted rural acreage into suburban lots from San Fernando to Long Beach, Santa Monica to Sierra Madre.[59] All in all, however, the process of transformation changed remarkably little between 1885 and 1930. True, direction of transportation shifted from private to public enterprise, from railway companies to highway departments, and control over water passed from small corporations to municipal boards and regional districts. Nonetheless, the officials labored to disperse the metropolis as well as to expedite its traffic and distribute its water, and the electorates and landholders endorsed these efforts.

14. View east on Colorado Avenue toward Pasadena, 1906

15. View east on Colorado Avenue toward Pasadena, 1928

Even more important, subdivision remained a private undertaking. Although city and county planning commissions and other regulatory bodies imposed minimal requirements, individuals and companies decided when and how to subdivide real estate. Compared with transporting commuters and supplying water, subdividing land was a rather simple matter. Also, contrasted with the municipal, county, and regional agencies the subdividers were an extremely autonomous group. Nevertheless, they, and not the authorities, evaluated the preferences of the consumers, measured the capacities of the market, and, in response to the logic of competition, completed the transformation of Los Angeles. By so influencing the pace and character of this process, the subdividers, like the immigrants whom they served, left a permanent mark on the structure of the metropolis.[60]

The most conspicuous fact about Los Angeles lies in its being a residential and not an industrial community. The half million people who reside here did not come here in any considerable numbers to engage in business; they came to reside. (H. S. McKee, 1915)

6 COMMERCIAL AND INDUSTRIAL PROGRESS

Commercial and industrial progress lagged behind population growth and urban expansion in Los Angeles at least in part because of the absence of a decent harbor nearby. Although the federal government, in response to appeals from local merchants, designated San Pedro as a port of entry in the 1850's, the roadstead was so unprotected, its channel so narrow and shallow, and its landing facilities so primitive that it accommodated only the smallest vessels. This situation so inconvenienced Los Angeles' traders that late in the 1860's Phineas T. Banning, a prominent entrepreneur who had platted the town of Wilmington near San Pedro and built a railroad connecting it with Los Angeles, asked Congress to improve the port.[1] Pressed by Senator Cornelius Cole and the California legislature, it instructed the Army Engineering Corps to investigate the petition. The corps reported that a sand bar at the entrance obstructed passage, and recommended the construction of a 6,700 foot jetty, to cost $550,000, which would generate a current capable of dredging the channel to a depth of ten feet and a width of two hundred feet.[2]

Congress adopted the corp's recommendation, allocated the necessary funds, and even before the engineers finished the jetty in 1881 the port handled the growing commerce with increasing efficiency. "Wilmington harbor, bad as its enemies may consider it," Banning boasted in 1873, "is the best in this section of the State, and must always be what it long has been, the second port in California."[3] Early in the 1880's, moreover, Congress, in response to another request by Banning, appropriated $200,000 to deepen the channel to sixteen feet by extending the old jetty and constructing a new one. Notwithstanding Banning's achievements, his claims did not pass unchallenged. Not only did San Diego promoters insist on the pre-eminence of their bay, but, in addition, Nevada Senator John P. Jones, who owned the Santa Monica Bay water front, and Oregon entrepreneur George Ainsworth, who controlled the Redondo Beach shore, championed the superiority of their own landings.[4] But though both ports gained traffic at the expense of Wilmington before 1885, the subsequent boom proved that none of them was safe or large enough to meet the requirements of trade in Los Angeles.

For commerce there—principally imported lumber and exported produce—increased considerably. Total tonnage at Wilmington, which, as Table 11 shows, registered 14,000 in 1859 and 25,000 in 1869 and advanced to 81,000 in 1879 and 285,000 in 1882, reached 466,000 in 1887 and 518,000 a year later.[5] Also, the larger ships which carried the heavier loads were unable to enter the improved channel and obliged to anchor in San Pedro Bay and transfer the cargo to small boats, known as lighters, which continued on to Wilmington. Lighterage was so expensive that many shippers wondered "whether the deep-sea freight for Los Angeles cannot be now better and more cheaply transported from the coast by way of San Diego and the new coast railroads [of the Santa Fe] than from San Pedro."[6] Several decided it could. "The apathy of the people here [in Los Angeles] in not securing a safe harbor," the British vice-consul reported, "has driven a great deal of shipping to San Diego." "If this is

TABLE 11.   Total Commerce of Port Los Angeles, 1855–1887

Year	Net tons (in thousands)	Year	Net tons (in thousands)	Year	Net tons (in thousands)
1855	6	1866	21	1877	65
1856	7	1867	23	1878	64
1857	7	1868	25	1879	81
1858	7	1869	25	1880	102
1859	14	1870	29	1881	182
1860	13	1871	55	1882	285
1861	14	1872	49	1883	206
1862	20	1873	54	1884	199
1863	17	1874	85	1885	195
1864	16	1875	95	1886	281
1865	20	1876	87	1887	466

Source: *Annual Report. Board of Harbor Commissioners of the City of Los Angeles, California* [*1924–1925*], p. 36.

to go on," the Los Angeles *Herald* warned, "then indeed we might as well not have a harbor, but become a back-country to San Diego." [7]

Local businessmen rejected this alternative, and urged Congress to provide a port capable of handling all the merchandise bound for Los Angeles and environs.[8] They also endorsed an Army Engineering Corps report which proposed not the enlargement of the inner channel, but rather the construction of an artificial harbor, to be protected by a breakwater extending 4,000 feet seaward from the northeastern corner of San Pedro Bay. The corps estimated the cost at $4 million.[9] To justify so substantial an outlay by the federal government, spokesmen for Los Angeles claimed not only that there was no safe and sufficient landing between San Francisco and San Diego, but also that only a port in the vicinity of Los Angeles could handle southern California's enormous business. Anxious to share in the trade with the Atlantic seaboard and the Orient too, Los Angeles' merchants now urged Congress to approve the corps's recommendations—unaware that in so doing they were precipitating the most bitter conflict in their city's short history.

To substantiate Los Angeles' claims, the Chamber of Commerce invited the Senate Commerce Committee to visit San Pedro Bay in 1889. Although the Senators expressed their admiration and promised their cooperation, no appropriations were forthcoming. So long as Redondo Beach and Santa Monica also requested federal aid, Congress preferred to procrastinate than to decide among them. In 1890, however, it appointed a Board of Engineers to survey the Pacific coast and determine the best location near Los Angeles for a deep-water harbor. After conducting its investigation, the board reduced the choice to San Pedro and Santa Monica and, pointing out that both were suitable, selected San Pedro. Not only was its position superior, its capacity larger, and its interior improved, the board explained, but also a breakwater there would be cheaper.[10] At the behest of Los Angeles' business leaders, California Senator Charles N. Felton then introduced into the current Rivers and Harbors Bill an appropriation implementing the board's decision. But when the Commerce Committee opened its hearings, Chairman William B. Frye abruptly announced that the Southern Pacific Railroad had recently informed him that San Pedro was unsuitable as the site for a deep-water harbor.

The Southern Pacific's intervention, while unexpected, was consistent with its determination to monopolize trade in southern California. Down through the 1880's the railroad had shipped through San Pedro. It had also eliminated all competition by acquiring the San

Pedro railway and securing the Wilmington tidelands and by purchasing the Los Angeles and Independence railway and closing its wharf at Santa Monica. Afterwards, it even extended its tracks and improved its facilities at San Pedro. At the same time, however, the Los Angeles Terminal Railway—an eastern syndicate presumably fronting for the Union Pacific (which intended to connect Los Angeles and Salt Lake City)—built a line from Los Angeles to San Pedro and bought nearby Terminal Island.[11] By 1891 it competed directly with the Southern Pacific. Huntington retaliated by beginning negotiations with Senator Jones, the owner of Santa Monica and a member of the Commerce Committee, who believed that with a breakwater his town would rival Los Angeles itself. Jones offered Huntington a right of way along the narrow shore in return for Huntington's pledge to exert his influence in order to persuade Congress to locate the harbor at Santa Monica. Jones then extended the Santa Monica branch along the beach, constructed the largest wharf in the region at its terminal, and, through Senator Frye, declared his opposition to San Pedro.[12]

16. Los Angeles, Wilmington, and Santa Monica, 1877

The committee, as a result, postponed action. To break the deadlock, Senator Felton persuaded his colleagues to instruct another board to re-examine the rival sites. The board left for southern California where it received testimony from property owners, commercial associations, governmental officials, and railroad spokesmen. Proponents of San Pedro insisted that the coastal palisades would enable the Southern Pacific to block other lines and monopolize commerce at Santa Monica. Chief Engineer William Hood, replying that ample space existed for competing railways, claimed that San Pedro's holding ground was irreparably defective. After recording these arguments, the board reviewed San Pedro's and Santa Monica's topography and hydrography and estimated their commercial and military values. It then issued a second report favoring San Pedro.[13] And Los Angeles' business leaders, who considered the contest over, confidently waited for Congress to allocate $350,000 for preliminary construction.

But Huntington informed them that the struggle was far from finished. "Well, I don't know, for sure, that I can get this money for Santa Monica," he warned. "I think I can. But I know damned well that you shall never get a cent for that other place." The magnate then circulated a petition supporting Santa Monica which was signed by so many prominent businessmen that the Chamber of Commerce had to submit the choice to its members. They voted 328 to 131 in favor of San Pedro. But the election did not faze Huntington, who, a Chamber representative from Washington warned, "will leave no effort untried to hinder and delay the construction of a harbor at any point other than Santa Monica."[14] Nor did it budge a Congress that was immobilized by its unwillingness to override either the board's recommendation for San Pedro or the Commerce Committee's preference for Santa Monica.

The deadlock persisted until late 1895 when the House Committee on Rivers and Harbors, at the request of California Representative James McLachlan, voted $390,000 to improve Wilmington's inner channel, and, on its own initiative, tied this appropriation to another for the Santa Monica breakwater. "If Los Angeles people will unite on schemes to complete inside harbor at San Pedro and to construct deep sea harbor at Santa Monica with provision to admit all railroads to Santa Monica over Southern Pacific tracks by paying pro rata costs," McLachlan wired the Chamber of Commerce "three million dollars can be procured at this session for said projects."[15] At the same time a divided Senate Commerce Committee endorsed a $3 million appropriation for Santa Monica. California Senator Stephen M.

White who voted with the minority lodged a strong protest. "This item was not placed in the bill at the suggestion of either Senator from California, nor at the instigation of the representative of the Sixth Congressional District, wherein the site is located. On the contrary both Senators and representatives objected to the construction of a breakwater at the point named in the bill and the overwhelming sentiment of the community prefers another location, namely San Pedro." [16]

If White's claim was true, the appropriation would fail; for despite the committees' actions, Congress would not force the harbor on Los Angeles. Hence it waited for a statement from the California delegation, which, in turn, awaited an expression of opinion from its constituents. They were, by and large, hostile. A few, such as former Senator Cornelius Cole, favored Santa Monica outright, and some, including the Los Angeles *Express,* feared that an adverse response would cost the city its present opportunity. But other interests, including the Los Angeles *Times* and the Chamber of Commerce, deemed the location no less important than the allocation itself and believed that by standing fast they could compel Congress to choose San Pedro. They stressed the Southern Pacific's intention to monopolize Santa Monica, and the railroad had generated so much animosity in so few years that its denials were as damaging as their allegations. "The Southern Pacific came here and had everybody for its friend," Judge Robert Widney explained, "but we have learned that when they want anything badly our interest lies the other way." [17]

The Terminal Railway and San Pedro resident John T. Gaffey were among those active in a Free Harbor League that effectively exploited this antipathy. Yet not one of them, Cornelius Cole protested, owned a vessel.[18] Neither, for that matter, did Cole, Jones, and the other Santa Monica supporters. But these people—all of whom believed that urban development set land values—did hold real estate. And they were convinced that the harbor's location would determine whether the metropolis expanded south to San Pedro or west to Santa Monica. For the protagonists the so-called "free harbor contest" was actually a struggle for speculative profits and not commercial freedom. And in the end the superior organization of the Free Harbor League and the popular suspicion of the Southern Pacific was decisive. San Pedro spokesmen persuaded the California delegates to reject the appropriation, and in May 1896, at their request, Congress committed itself to allocate funds for a site to be chosen by a final Board of Engineers. Following another extensive review, it too selected San Pedro.[19] Prodded by Senator White, Congress approved the expenditure, and, pressed by California's delegation, President William McKinley ordered the Secretary of War to let the contracts. The Engineering Corps began construction in 1899, and, when finished in 1912, the breakwater transformed San Pedro Bay into a protected and capacious harbor.

San Pedro still lacked piers, docks, wharves, and warehouses. During the 1890's, moreover, the Southern Pacific acquired additional waterfrontage, secured control over the Terminal Island corporation, and dominated the smaller landowners. The Free Harbor League notwithstanding, it now monopolized San Pedro. That corporate enterprise rather than municipal authority still shaped the harbor's development was an intolerable outcome for those who had fought so hard against the Southern Pacific.[20] They urged public ownership

17. San Pedro harbor, 1880

and operation of the port. Not only would the federal government treat a municipal undertaking more generously than a private one, they argued, but the city administration could also reduce freight rates and expand mercantile opportunities. "The time has come," Captain Amos A. Fries, one of their leaders, declared, "when Southern California must say to every son of hers, 'If you are not for a great free harbor at San Pedro, you are against us, and we will fight you no matter who you may be, what interests you represent, and what your politics are." [21]

Fries, as the Army's district engineer, objected in particular to the practice whereby the Southern Pacific blocked traffic to the independent west basin and diverted freight to its own east basin. Before the breakwater was completed, he recommended the designation of pierhead and bulkhead lines which would make access to both basins far easier and control by the railroad much harder. But the Southern Pacific, convinced that the development of the west basin would depreciate its investments in the east basin, persuaded the Army's chief of engineers to modify Fries's plans according to its own specifications. Los Angeles' commercial associations, which opposed perpetuation of the port monopoly, urged their Congressmen to press the Secretary of War to authorize the original proposals. Their intervention—which was successful—prevented deeper entrenchment by the Southern Pacific, increased the available waterfrontage at San Pedro, and justified additional improvements by the federal government.[22] But the contest consumed so much time and effort that the business leaders decided to try another approach to municipalization.

The separation of the metropolis and its harbor, they knew, was the most perplexing problem. Los Angeles commanded the wealth but not the authority to develop the port; Wilmington and San Pedro, to the contrary, possessed the right but not the resources. To resolve this dilemma, Los Angeles' leaders proposed to consolidate the city and the towns and merge the capital and the power required for a "great free" harbor. Because California law permitted the union of contiguous jurisdictions only and Los Angeles was twenty miles from San Pedro and Wilmington, the proponents of consolidation sponsored the annexation of a long narrow corridor, known as the "shoestring district," which connected the metropolis with the ports. The voters authorized it in 1906. Since the state also lacked a procedure to join freehold charter cities and sixth class towns, Los Angeles' leaders next appealed to the legislature for an appropriate enabling act. Opposed by the Southern Pacific, the bill passed two years later.[23]

LOS ANGELES HARBOR, 1932

Los Angeles then had to convince San Pedro and Wilmington of the merits of consolidation. But both towns, as a Consolidation Commission representing the city's commercial, civic, and governmental organizations learned, feared that union would shift trade from the shore to the interior and that greater Los Angeles would ignore the ports' interests. To reassure them, the Consolidation Commission promised that Los Angeles would not only spend $10 million on harbor improvements, but would also build a truck highway from the city to the waterfront, secure terminal rates for the coastal district, and allocate for public works at least as much as was collected in taxes there. The Wilmington and San Pedro spokesmen were dubious,[24] but, realizing that only the metropolis had the economic wherewithal and political influence to develop the port, they agreed to endorse consolidation. And at separate elections held in August 1909 the voters of San Pedro and Wilmington relinquished direct control over their ports and formally tied their fortunes to Los Angeles.

Yet even the consolidated city contained only about one hundred acres of waterfrontage, far too little for a regional harbor. The Southern Pacific, by contrast, owned in the Wilmington tidelands at least a thousand acres, more than enough for Los Angeles' purposes. Fortunately for the municipality, the railroad possessed an imperfect title. Hence the Los Angeles attorney, on behalf of the state, brought suit to recover the tract, and when the California Supreme Court found in his favor the Los Angeles Harbor Commission applied for the land. San Francisco's merchants, who feared that their state-operated port might lose commerce to a more aggressive municipally-owned harbor, opposed the petition. But they withdrew their opposition when a Los Angeles delegation headed by the mayor reminded them of its recent support for a bond issue to improve San Francisco Bay. Whereupon the California legislature entrusted the tidelands to Los Angeles.[25]

The United States government, Los Angeles authorities, and southern California railroads all influenced the port's subsequent progress. Early in the 1900's Congress authorized the Army Engineering Corps to deepen the entrance, widen the channel, and construct a turning basin there; the corps spent $6 million to duplicate at Los Angeles what nature created gratuitously at San Francisco. Afterwards, the enormous increase in imported lumber and exported petroleum so overwhelmed the harbor's capacity and added to the time and cost of landing that individual merchants, commercial associations, and public officials appealed for additional assistance. As a rule, the district engineer acknowledged the port's inadequacies, the corps recommended remedial improvements, and the Congress appropriated adequate funds. By 1932 the federal government had dredged the outer harbor to 35 feet, widened the main channel to 1,000 feet, enlarged the turning basin to 1,600 feet, extended the 11,000 foot breakwater another 12,500 feet, and at a cost of about $12.5 million transformed San Pedro Bay into one of the United States's principal harbors.[26]

Meanwhile, the Harbor Commission assumed responsibility to provide port facilities. Since it thought that the harbor's primary purpose was to encourage industry not produce profits, it set rates that met the expenses of operation, maintenance, depreciation, and interest, but left no surplus for improvements. And since the commission believed that the harbor raised land values and lowered commodity prices, it felt no compunction about requesting general obligation bonds for capital construction. At its prompting, the common council submitted issues in 1910, 1913, 1919, 1921, and 1923 which received the backing of the Greater Harbor Committee of Two Hundred, the endorsement of the metropolitan newspapers, and the approval of the voters. By 1932 Los Angeles had incurred a $28.9 million indebtedness to build highways, bridges, and railways, reclaim additional waterfrontage, and erect wharves, piers, and docks. It had also paid $18 million in interest, part of the price of fulfilling its obligation to Wilmington and San Pedro, the Army Engineering Corps, and Los Angeles' business community.[27]

Down into the 1920's the port lacked proper access and efficient transportation because the Southern Pacific, Santa Fe, Pacific Electric, Union Pacific, and Municipal Terminal railroads each operated independent lines on separate tracks to different wharves. To improve this situation, the Harbor Commission negotiated switching arrangements with the Pacific Electric and Union Pacific. The success of this experiment so convincingly demonstrated the desirability of complete unification of the railways that the Harbor Department and the transport companies agreed to consolidate their equipment into a single Harbor Belt Line Railroad. The city and the carriers each appointed four members to a Board of Control which directed the undertaking. The corporations divided expenses and revenues in proportion to their investments, and the Municipal Terminal received a fee for each car using its lines. By 1932 the Harbor Belt Line Railroad operated 125 miles of track which, combined with the expanding truck highways, connected the waterfront with the interior and supplied Port Los Angeles with satisfactory transportation.[28]

Port Los Angeles then consisted of an outer landing of nine hundred acres of anchorage and channels, an inner harbor of eight hundred acres with slips and turning basins, and twenty-five miles of partially developed waterfrontage which included shedded wharves for general cargo, open piers for special merchandise, and separate docks for petroleum and fishing.[29] Southern California's commerce demanded nothing less. After the boom of the 1880's collapsed, tonnage, as Table 12 shows, declined from 518,000 in 1888 to 49,000 in 1895; but, in response to the region's growth, it increased to 215,000 in 1900, and, spurred by enormous imports of lumber, advanced to 1.1 million in 1907. A decade of moderate but constant expansion followed, raising it to an all-time high of 2.4 million in 1917. Then, as a result of the region's prodigious oil strikes after the First World War, the harbor's business mounted to 10.3 million tons in 1922, climbed to 27.2 million a year later, and fluctuated from 20 million to 30 million thereafter. Between 1925 and 1931 Port Los Angeles handled almost as much freight as all the other Pacific coast ports combined by weight and slightly less than San Francisco though far more than Seattle and Portland by value.[30]

TABLE 12.   Total Commerce of Port Los Angeles, 1888–1932

Year	Net tons (in thousands)	Year	Net tons (in thousands)	Year	Net tons (in thousands)
1888	518	1903	644	1918	2,091
1889	196	1904	710	1919	3,152
1890	186	1905	916	1920	4,340
1891	250	1906	853	1921	5,253
1892	304	1907	1,084	1922	10,286
1893	280	1908	984	1923	27,155
1894	239	1909	1,268	1924	22,214
1895	49	1910	1,713	1925	20,311
1896	134	1911	1,769	1926	24,080
1897	188	1912	1,867	1927	26,231
1898	187	1913	1,728	1928	25,696
1899	200	1914	1,835	1929	29,106
1900	215	1915	2,091	1930	28,213
1901	407	1916	1,921	1931	23,098
1902	498	1917	2,409	1932	20,098

Source: Board of Economic Survey, *Economic Survey of the Port of Los Angeles, July 15, 1933,* table 54.

119

In their efforts to expand the city's range of trade, the commercial associations did not devote their attention exclusively to the creation of Port Los Angeles. They also encouraged the extension of rail and motor transportation, the removal of rate differentials that discriminated against Los Angeles, and the establishment of trade connections with other regions. Commerce, as a result, increased with the Orient directly, the eastern United States and Latin America via the Panama Canal, and the southwestern states and northern California by railroads and highways. These activities also lowered prices in Los Angeles. Between 1925 and 1932 its importers saved an estimated $1.1 million on automobiles and parts, $1.6 million on machinery, $15.4 million on iron and steel products, and $61 million on lumber—in all, well over $100 million.[31] Hence Los Angeles' emergence as jobbing center for the Southwest was not only a source of commercial profits, but also, and even more important, an impetus to industrial development.

Local business leaders had long considered industrialization essential. "It is now universally conceded," the *Times* wrote in 1882, "that the permanent growth and prosperity of any community, however favorably located geographically and otherwise it may be, depends mainly on the extent and prosperity of its manufacturing interests." [32] They also thought the region capable of sustained economic advance, and, attributing backwardness to discrimination by the railroads and extravagance of residents, urged one and all "to purchase and consume all articles produced or manufactured at home, in preference to those imported from abroad." "Let us make our own brooms," the *Herald* advised readers in 1878, "manufacture our own soap, brew our own beer from our own grain, grind our own corn into meal, manufacture our own oil, make our own shoes, manufacture our own buggies and wagons." [33] In spite of the efforts of the Home Industry Protection League in the 1870's and the Society for the Promotion of Manufactures in the 1880's, however, Los Angeles' industry lagged far behind its people's aspirations.

For, hitherto, economic conditions in Los Angeles were not conducive to extensive manufacturing. The sparse population supplied industrialists with little incentive to exploit local demand, and the region's isolation discouraged them from competing in distant markets. The shortage of labor and the paucity of capital further restricted manufacturers to modest undertakings in building trades and food processing. Even when the transcontinental railroads relieved its isolation in the 1870's and the real estate boom enlarged its population in the 1880's, moreover, Los Angeles developed little manufacturing. Property, not factories, intrigued the newcomers, the California labor commissioner explained in 1886. "There are more real estate agents to the square yard [in Los Angeles] than can be found, I believe, in any city of the world," he wrote. "The growth and development of Los Angeles has been so recent and rapid that the citizens of Los Angeles have had their hands full in attending to the business and other wants of the thousands from the East who flocked to their favored land." [34]

In 1890, therefore, Los Angeles' 50,000 people (and 750 firms) manufactured only $9.9 million in goods. This was not only less than larger western cities such as San Francisco and Denver and comparable eastern ones such as Dayton, Ohio, and Hartford, Connecticut—which was to be expected—but, as Table 13 indicates, even less than smaller western cities such as Portland and Seattle. Moreover, contrasted with San Francisco's mammoth sugar refineries, Los Angeles' principal industries—its flour mills, carpentry shops, and slaughterhouses—were small in scale, geared to the home market, and confined to consumer goods. Finally, measured against its own rapid influx of immigrants, expansion of agriculture, proliferation of services, increase in commerce, and appreciation of realty, manufacturing in Los Angeles, as Table 13 reveals, was progressing very slowly.[35] Despite the lamentations of the city's businessmen, however, the predominance of people over production, local over national undertakings, and professions over factories accurately reflected the course of Los Angeles' population growth and urban expansion.

Los Angeles still lacked capital and labor for industrialization two decades later, even though its market was enlarged by a quarter of a million newcomers and its transportation improved by a deep-water harbor. Its businessmen were simply not attracted to manufacturing. Henry E. Huntington included only one industrial enterprise among his multimillion dollar electric railway, public utility, and real estate interests. Arthur D. Letts, owner of the Broadway Department Store, channeled his fortune into merchandising and property rather than manufacturing. And H. J. Whitley, who subdivided the southern San Fernando Valley, used his profits to speculate in central California farmland and not to diversify southern California industry.[36] Nor were the newcomers drawn to work in manufacturing. The white majority, which sought a less arduous life and possessed funds and skills, preferred trade and the professions. The colored minorities,

TABLE 13. Manufacturing and Occupational Distribution in Selected Cities, 1890

| City | Population (in thousands) | Number of mfg. establishments | Value of mfg. products (in millions) | Total working force (in thousands) | Per cent in selected occupational categories | | |
					Manufacturing and mechanical industries	Trade and transportation	Professional service
San Francisco	299	4,059	$135.6	147	33.2	28.2	5.7
Denver	107	762	29.2	53	33.7	29.0	6.3
Trenton	57	885	25.6	23	55.4	20.2	3.6
Portland	46	569	25.4	n.a.	n.a.	n.a.	n.a.
Dayton	61	937	22.4	25	46.3	22.1	4.6
Hartford	53	513	17.2	24	39.6	27.5	5.2
Evansville	51	482	12.8	22	37.3	23.7	5.8
St. Joseph	52	276	11.9	22	32.1	36.2	5.0
Seattle	43	331	10.2	n.a.	n.a.	n.a.	n.a.
Los Angeles	50	750	9.9	21	25.0	31.2	10.1

Source: U.S. Census Office, *Report on Manufacturing Industries in the United States at the Eleventh Census: 1890. Part II* (Washington, 1895), pp. 166–169, 214–217, 302–305, 430–433, 462–465, 530–533, 558–561, 594–597, 634–637; U.S. Census Office, *Report on the Population of the United States at the Eleventh Census: 1890. Part II* (Washington, 1897), pp. 628–629.

n.a. denotes not available.

which lacked capital and education, suffered from racial discrimination, and would have gratefully accepted factory work, found jobs principally as common laborers and domestic servants.

Notwithstanding these obstacles, Los Angeles' tremendous population and urban growth generated a marked industrial expansion in the 1890's and early 1900's. With 1,325 establishments producing $68 million in goods in 1909, it surpassed Seattle, Portland, and Denver and, as Table 14 reveals, followed only San Francisco among far western manufacturing centers. Yet compared with such eastern and midwestern cities as Minneapolis, Kansas City (Kansas), Indianapolis, and Rochester—all of which numbered fewer people and produced more goods—Los Angeles still lagged in its industrialization. Also, by contrast with Akron's immense rubber factories, none of Los Angeles' principal industries—neither its foundries, its slaughterhouses, nor its lumber mills—was among the nation's large-scale manufacturers of capital goods. Furthermore, measured against the working force of other American cities, that of Los Angeles, as Table 14 indicates, was distributed heavily in trade and the professions and lightly in manufacturing and mechanical activities.[37]

For these reasons, a local banker wrote in 1915, "The most conspicuous fact about Los Angeles lies in its being a residential and not an industrial community . . ." Not that there is no business in Los Angeles, he explained—far from it. "Its business is well known to be so large as to require no comment, but there are two kinds of business: First, the purely local kind, which consists in mutual services performed for one another by the people of any city . . . These activities employ most of the working population. We have this in highly developed form in Los Angeles, but so have other cities." "But separate and distinct from this," he added, "is a second, and perhaps more important kind of business, which consists in carrying on, in any particular place, some large industry characteristic of that place . . . which produces a product far beyond local needs for sale and export to other localities, and which brings, in return, to that locality, a large gross income, employs and pays an industrial army and yields a net income to the proprietor." "What is meant, therefore, in saying that Los Angeles is not an industrial city," he concluded, "is that [by and large] it has not this latter form of export business."[38]

Many well-informed persons expressed reservations about the prospect of industrialization too. "I can't see any indication of it at the present time," Southern California Edison's general agent remarked. "I think Southern California will remain largely an agricultural coun-

TABLE 14. Manufacturing and Occupational Distribution in Selected Cities, 1909

City	Population (in thousands)	Number of mfg. establishments	Value of mfg. products (in millions)	Total working force (in thousands)	Per cent in selected occupational categories		
					Manufacturing and mechanical industries	Trade and transportation	Professional service
Minneapolis	301	1,102	$165.4	143	37.1	17.6	6.0
Kansas City (Kansas)	82	165	164.1	35	44.9	14.0	4.5
San Francisco	417	1,796	133.0	234	31.8	17.2	6.2
Indianapolis	234	855	126.5	108	43.7	16.0	5.7
Rochester	218	1,203	112.7	103	51.8	13.2	5.4
Akron	69	246	73.2	33	61.6	10.3	4.1
Los Angeles	319	1,325	68.6	147	31.0	20.9	8.7
Denver	213	766	51.5	97	31.5	19.2	8.5
Seattle	237	751	50.6	122	32.4	16.6	7.2
Portland	207	649	46.9	111	36.4	18.0	6.7

Source: U.S. Bureau of the Census, *Thirteenth Census of the United States. Volume IX. Manufactures 1909* (Washington, 1912), pp. 104–105, 106–107, 126–127, 332–333, 388–389, 612–613, 890–891, 990–991, 1,036–1,037, 1,306–1,307; U.S. Bureau of the Census, *Thirteenth Census of the United States. 1910. Volume IV. Population. Occupation Statistics* (Washington, 1914), pp. 152–243.

try. We can't expect any extraordinary development in manufacturing, except such manufacturing as may be for home use—for local consumption." [39] But others, who insisted that the regions prosperity ultimately depended upon industrialization, watched with increasing concern as immigrants arrived in greater numbers, realtors completed larger transactions, and contractors erected more houses, all without commensurate investments in manufacturing. "Los Angeles has carried her structure as high as it is safe to build on the present foundation," they warned. "The question that confronts us, then, is this: Shall we broaden and reinforce the foundation and push the structure upward, or shall we settle down in fatuous contentment with what has been achieved and delude ourselves with the notion that we are creating and assembling wealth by swapping jack-knives back and forth among ourselves." [40]

Los Angeles' businessmen endorsed the obvious alternative. "If we are to have an uninterrupted balanced growth," an active entrepreneur and influential publisher wrote, "there must be new industries enough constantly coming into existence to sustain our population." [41] They then inaugurated a campaign for "Balanced Prosperity." "It is our opinion," a Chamber of Commerce president remarked, "that only by LAYING A HIGH INDUSTRIAL FOUNDATION to our rapid growth can we hope to bring about a STABILIZED PROSPERITY here." [42] This appeal was novel in Los Angeles. For unlike the call for "Home Industry," which considered manufacturing an effective stimulus of progress, the demand for balanced prosperity envisioned it as an essential accompaniment of expansion. The backers of balanced prosperity were confident but not complacent. "We must not overlook the fact that other Pacific Coast cities are spending great sums of money to attract industries to their locality, and we must not assume that because of certain natural conditions which attracted population to us that these same conditions will attract industry." [43]

The Chamber of Commerce, heeding this warning, formed a Committee on Manufactures to inform businessmen of the opportunities available in Los Angeles and an Industrial Bureau to promote the industrial interests of southern California. But contrary to the Chamber's expectation, two welcome windfalls, motion pictures and oil wells, contributed far more than its promotional efforts to the economic progress of the metropolis after 1915. The movie producers, who originally settled in the region as much by coincidence as design, found its clear weather, varied topography, and abundant land particularly suited to their enterprise. Nor did the industry suffer much from

125

We Must Have a Firm Foundation!

18. Los Angeles *Times* cartoon on "Balanced Prosperity"

Los Angeles' geographic isolation; its personnel was easily assembled there, and its films were inexpensively shipped throughout the United States. The metropolis thus emerged as the nation's motion picture center, and by 1930 its fifty-two studios employed 15,000 persons, paid $72.1 million in salaries and wages, created $129.3 million of movies, and stimulated additional investment in related undertakings such as photographic equipment.[44]

Petroleum, which had long been known in southern California, was not extensively exploited there until the great expansion of the oil market early in the twentieth century. Local firms then shipped about one thousand barrels a day through Port Los Angeles. But in anticipation of even larger sources, international oil companies moved their equipment from the San Joaquin and Santa Maria fields to the Los Angeles Basin. And after World War One they made such prodigious strikes at Huntington Beach, Montebello, Seal Beach, Santa Fe Springs, and Long Beach that for a while these wells yielded almost a million barrels daily and supplied 9 per cent of the nation's and 5 per cent of the world's petroleum. These discoveries enriched a few corporations and employed many immigrants. Yet, as an even more valuable contribution to the economy of Los Angeles in 1930, they spurred the erection of thirty-two refineries which created five thousand jobs, disbursed $11 million in wages and salaries, processed $327.4 million in oil products, and, as the region's greatest industry, generated considerable activity in related enterprises such as the petro-chemicals.[45]

These windfalls notwithstanding, regional patterns of enterprise and national trends in manufacturing inhibited further industrialization in Los Angeles. Investors there still favored property development and consumer services, and companies elsewhere now dominated most major industries. Even if local entrepreneurs were convinced that rubber could be profitably produced in Los Angeles, they lacked the resources and skills to compete with the Akron oligopoly. Realizing that corporate directors rather than individual businessmen decided whether or not to establish factories in the metropolis, the Chamber of Commerce applied its promotional skills after 1915 to persuade "the man *back East* who has manufacturing abilities in these lines, who has plants now *in the East,* that he can come here and ... make good."[46] The leaders of the Chamber wooed industrialists with as much fervor as they had once coaxed immigrants. They described expanding markets, available resources, and cheaper transportation with as much enthusiasm as they had once depicted an easier life, softer climate, and more picturesque landscape.

19. Venice oil fields, ca. 1930

But national corporations established branch factories, one executive explained, only if they offered substantial advantages for manufacturing and for distribution.[47] As few sites met this criterion before 1910, most companies served the Far West from their eastern headquarters. After World War One, however, rapid population growth greatly enlarged demand on the Pacific coast, and rising transport charges markedly increased the cost of cross-country rail shipments.[48] Hence many firms decentralized production. To cite only one example, the Ford Motor Company calculated that decentralization would reduce expenses by decreasing the over-all weight of its shipments and improve service by increasing the accessibility of its distributing facilities. For these reasons Ford built regional assembly plants in Los Angeles, among other metropolises, while it maintained its central manufacturing complex at Dearborn, Michigan.[49]

Few industries other than the automotive could divide the productive process, and, compelled to concentrate their western facilities,

20. Ford Motor Company plant, 1930

most originally selected San Francisco. After the First World War, however, many national corporations favored Los Angeles. They were particularly impressed, according to a survey taken in the 1930's, by its vast and growing population, its proximity to raw materials, and its connections with other markets. When the rubber companies, for instance, decided to decentralize just before 1920, each ordered thorough studies of the respective advantages of the Pacific coast cities. These revealed that though San Francisco and Portland were more centrally situated Los Angeles afforded better access to the Far Eastern rubber plantations, the Imperial Valley cotton fields, and, even more important, the southern California tire market. Hence Goodyear, Goodrich, and Firestone all chose Los Angeles.[50] This widespread confidence in the region's future, two economists noted in 1941, made "the fundamental pattern of manufacturing expansion in Los Angeles County one of branch plant establishment."[51]

Local business leaders erroneously attributed Los Angeles' industrial progress to organized labor's impotence. Testifying before the United States Commission on Industrial Relations in 1914, F. J. Zeehandelaar, secretary of the Merchants and Manufacturers Associ-

21. Goodyear Tire and Rubber Company plant, 1925

ation, stated that the open shop was Los Angeles' most valuable asset.[52] Addressing the annual meeting of the Chamber of Commerce in 1926, President R. W. Pridham described Los Angeles as "The Citadel of the Open Shop" and claimed that its manufacturing progress was due to industrial freedom.[53] To substantiate these assertions, they pointed out that Los Angeles' previous stagnation had coincided with bitter labor conflict and that its present expansion was accompanied by duly harmonious relations. As conclusive evidence, they contrasted San Francisco, where trade unions were well established and material progress was proceeding slowly, with Los Angeles, where, in the words of organized labor's implacable foe, Harrison Gray Otis, industrial freedom reigned supreme and industrial progress advanced unobstructed.

This comparison was not wholly inaccurate. San Francisco's economy and society did facilitate active trade unionism without arousing impassioned employer opposition. Its businesses relied heavily on skilled workers with a viable tradition of organization in the United States, and its labor force included many class-conscious native Europeans favorably inclined toward cooperative action. Also, the union leaders were, with very few exceptions, honest and capable administrators who maintained a high degree of organizational coherence and even gained grudging public respect. Lastly, the employers were as confident and sophisticated as businessmen anywhere in the United States; and, though they held no deep affection for trade unions, they disapproved of unsettling and expensive antilabor crusades. For these reasons organized labor exercised as much political and economic influence in San Francisco as in any American metropolis down through the 1920's.[54]

Trade unions fared less well in Los Angeles, and even those that made modest gains in the late 1890's and early 1900's found their position precarious a decade later. They not only suffered from the influx of rural Americans who created a surplus of skilled labor and in many cases considered organized labor subversive. They also faced the determined opposition of the metropolis' manufacturers and the outright hostility of its aggressive and influential realtors and merchants. In their view rapid industrialization was Los Angeles' highest priority, and organized labor was its principal obstruction. Prodded by the Los Angeles *Times* and supported by the Chamber of Commerce, they united in the Merchants and Manufacturers Association. This association exploited the suspicions of the newcomers and the rhetoric of industrial freedom to emasculate Los Angeles' trade unions after 1915. And henceforth organized labor played so marginal a role in Los Angeles that the metropolis well deserved its reputation as the nation's open shop.[55]

The reasoning of Zeehandelaar, Pridham, and Otis was entirely wrong, however. The weakness of organized labor, according to a survey of firms operating branch facilities in Los Angeles, offered them little or no incentive to move there.[56] Their interest in workers extended only to their availability. Unlike the *Times,* they needed not skilled artisans affiliated with craft unions, but unskilled laborers unorganized everywhere in the United States. The Mexicans, Negroes, and Europeans who sought superior opportunities in southern California met this requirement after 1915. Moreover, Los Angeles and other municipalities, along with utility and petroleum companies, provided abundant and inexpensive water, gas, electricity, and oil. And local landowners offered extensive tracts connected with transcontinental railroads, truck highways, and Port Los Angeles.[57] Hence no shortage of either labor, water, power, or land prevented the scores of nation-wide corporations that were established in Los Angeles from exploiting southern California's growing markets.

In 1929, therefore, its 4,900 concerns, which employed 145,000 persons and paid $286 million in wages and salaries, manufactured $1.3 billion in goods. Despite this tremendous advance since 1909, however, Los Angeles, as Table 15 reveals, had not fully overcome the traditional disparity between population growth and industrial development. With far fewer inhabitants, such midwestern centers as St. Louis and Cleveland still produced much more than Los Angeles.[58] Nor had it greatly enlarged the scale of its industrial enterprise. With far fewer firms, such eastern cities as Detroit and Philadelphia still manufactured much more than Los Angeles. Also, measured against the labor force of other American metropolises, that of Los Angeles, as Table 15 indicates, was in 1930, as in 1890 and 1909, distributed lightly in manufacturing and mechanical industries and heavily in trade and professional service.[59]

On its own terms, though, Los Angeles had made impressive industrial progress by 1930. Its manufacturing output ranked first among the Pacific coast industrial areas, exceeding San Francisco's by $153.7 million, Seattle's by $929.6 million, Portland's by $1.1 billion, and Denver's by $1.2 billion. Los Angeles had also widely diversified its industry. Mammoth oil refineries and motion picture studios, branch automobile and rubber plants, and local furniture and clothing factories supplemented older though still valuable machine shops, slaughterhouses, publishing firms, and lumber mills. Los Angeles had even markedly enlarged its capital goods sector. Although iron and steel production lagged,[60] the electronics, chemical, and aviation industries all found conditions favorable for development.[61] Industrialization—which, though it developed principally as a result of population growth and urban expansion, provided employment and sustained prosperity in the metropolis during the 1920's—was thus a concluding but nonetheless essential element in the urbanization of Los Angeles.

In sum, despite predictions that the lack of a deep-water harbor and mineral resources would inhibit its commercial and industrial progress, Los Angeles developed a port which served as the Southwest's principal emporium and attracted the factories which formed a national manufacturing complex. Yet its achievement confounded visitors as late as the 1930's. A British visitor, who, in response to his questions about the basic sources of Los Angeles' wealth, was told by the Chamber of Commerce about "the concentration of fruit, the shipping, the Western

TABLE 15. Manufacturing and Occupational Distribution in Selected Metropolitan Areas, 1929

City	Population (in thousands)[a]	Number of mfg. establishments[b]	Value of mfg. products (in millions)[b]	Total working force (in thousands)[c]	Per cent in selected occupational categories		
					Manufacturing and mechanical industries[c]	Trade and transportation[c]	Professional service[c]
Detroit	2,100	2,806	$2,844.6	689	48.5	13.9	6.2
Pittsburgh	2,023	2,587	2,015.4	279	34.4	16.9	7.7
St. Louis	1,335	3,287	1,542.0	386	36.9	16.8	6.3
Cleveland	1,311	2,912	1,505.5	395	44.3	13.8	6.4
Los Angeles	2,208	4,908	1,319.4	581	26.2	21.8	12.2
Milwaukee	879	2,218	1,166.5	254	46.3	14.8	6.7
San Francisco-Oakland	1,307	3,903	1,165.7	334	27.1	18.5	8.3
Seattle-Tacoma	627	1,757	389.8	176	29.5	19.7	9.2
Multnomah County (Portland)	338	1,087	196.7	145	30.0	19.7	9.4
Denver County (Denver)	288	781	144.2	130	25.7	20.3	10.1

Source: U.S. Bureau of the Census, Fifteenth Census of the United States. Manufactures: 1929. Volume III (Washington, 1933), pp. 61, 69, 72, 82, 87, 250, 258, 286, 294, 402, 407, 434, 441, 454, 539, 546, 561, 568; U.S. Bureau of the Census, Fifteenth Census of the United States: 1930. Population. Volume IV (Washington, 1933), pp. 22–23.
[a] For metropolitan districts.
[b] For industrial districts.
[c] For city proper.

branch factories put up by concerns in the East," wrote that "none of these things seemed the cause of a city. They seemed rather the effect, rising from an inexplicable accumulation of people. It struck me as an odd thing that here, alone of all the cities in America, there was no plausible answer to the question, 'Why did a town spring up here and why has it grown so big?' " [62]

There was an answer, albeit an implausible one. Its components were the immigration of the midwesterners, the conversion of the coutryside, and the industrialization of the economy. Each, of course, stimulated the other, but, by and large, the newcomers antedated the subdivisions and both preceded the factories. Separately and together, they transformed greater Los Angeles into a populous, improved, and productive metropolis. Moreover, where Los Angeles corresponded with other cities in its growth, there it resembled them in its structure and its character. But where its populace and, less so, its expansion and its economy differed, there its landscape, transportation, community, politics, and planning diverged. And the essence of Los Angeles was revealed more clearly in its deviations from than in its similarities to the great American metropolis of the late nineteenth and early twentieth centuries.

PART TWO
THE FRAGMENTED METROPOLIS

This great metropolitan district [of Los Angeles] . . . shall be, not one great whole, but a co-ordination of many units, within each of which there shall be the most ideal living conditions, the most ideal conditions for business or industry, and yet with all of the individuality, with all of the characteristics and all of the ambitions that, after all, are the things that constitute real community spirit, real community pride, those things which can only be found, we discover, in the small unit that a person can intelligently comprehend. That, to me, seems the great ideal American city or community of the future; the recognition of the small unit and its perpetuation. (G. Gordon Whitnall, 1923)

In order to accommodate a great population such cities [as Los Angeles] will naturally spread over a vast area—the vaster the better. They should spread until they meet the country, and until beautiful forms of urban life blend almost imperceptibly into beautiful forms of rural life. (William B. Smythe, 1910)

7   THE URBAN LANDSCAPE

Urbanization had an overwhelming impact on the landscape of greater Los Angeles. Before 1885 the region was predominantly rural. Flocks of sheep foraged on the Santa Ana plain, and thousands of acres went uncultivated in western Los Angeles. Immense wheat fields covered the San Fernando Valley ranches, and corn stalks grew tall on the El Monte farms. Vineyards were planted symmetrically in eastern Los Angeles, and orchards were tended in clusters in the San Gabriel Valley.[1] These flourishing valleys and the nearby mountains overwhelmed small settlements such as Anaheim and Pasadena. Even in Los Angeles, then the section's first and the state's third city, more than 90 per cent of its thirty-six square miles were rustic.[2] Everywhere bountiful gardens relieved the severe earth, fragrant fruits diluted the pungent mesquite, and agriculture imposed its quiet on the region. Nowhere did the population, facilities, and businesses of the region's urban centers intrude much upon the sights, smells, and sounds of the agrarian environment.

Immigration and enterprise, of course, created a market for residential and commercial property after 1850; but the transformation of rural land into urban property was the responsibility of private enterprise not municipal authority. Corporate utilities provided service only when convinced that anticipated revenues justified initial expenditures; they made commitments cautiously even under favorable circumstances. Individual developers undertook improvements only when confident that current demand exceeded existing supply; thus their activities were limited to the minor booms of the early 1870's and 1880's.[3] For these reasons the transformed portion of Los Angeles did not extend more than two miles from the town's center before 1885.[4] And since many landholders found agriculture sufficiently

22. Rural Los Angeles, 1889 (View from San Gabriel Road, looking southwest toward Los Angeles)

profitable and conversion prohibitively expensive, subdivision proceeded sporadically and erratically even in central Los Angeles.

The separation of homes from stores and shops accompanied the expansion of Los Angeles. Unsuccessful Americans, unassimilated Chinese, and unadjusted Mexicans still rented rooms in dilapidated and overcrowded adobes and shacks amid rundown hotels, gambling dens, and houses of prostitution near the old plaza. But prosperous and respectable native Americans and European immigrants who refused to live there purchased lots and erected houses on outlying tracts in the southern and western flats and the northern and eastern hills.[5] At the same time many businessmen moved from central to southern Los Angeles. While retailers followed the residential subdivisions, wholesalers pressed towards the railroad station; while professionals concentrated in the Temple Street vicinity, craftsmen spread all over the south-central section. These enterprises extended over only a few blocks, but, dominating the town's economy, they formed its principal commercial center in 1885.[6]

Incipient industrialists who considered this district too congested and costly sought larger and cheaper parcels elsewhere. Some attempted to exploit local water power and obviate high-priced coal by constructing plants close to the Los Angeles River. Others followed their lead when the Southern Pacific routed its main line alongside the river. By 1885 a small but active manufacturing complex—made up of a gas plant, flour mills, rail yards, and slaughterhouses—had emerged there.[7] Land-use segregation did not encompass the agricultural (and thus the largest) portion of Los Angeles, however. Nor was it complete, extensive, and irreversible elsewhere. The poor and the minorities still lived in the old business center, the residential, commercial, and manufacturing areas were not yet far apart, and the inclinations of the town's entrepreneurs alone sanctioned this arrangement. From the perspective of the people of Los Angeles, however, land-use segregation was desirable and deserved encouragement.

The developers shaped the town's layout as well as its land-use. They favored the traditional American gridiron—an arrangement of perpendicularly intersecting streets—which simplified subdivision and, they believed, reduced expenses and facilitated marketing. "I have planned for straight lines and not for curved ones in the street alignments," a civil engineer reported to a San Gabriel Valley subdivider. "The advantages gained are economy of survey and platting and probably better sale for the property than if it were cut up on curves." [8] The developers divided the rest of the land into suburban lots, from 5,000 to 7,000 square feet in size and twice as deep as wide, which fronted on narrow thoroughfares and supplied space for modest houses surrounded by front lawns, small gardens, and rear yards. The developers covered the tracts with streets and lots, reserving little or no property for community purposes, and disposed of their holdings as rapidly as possible, permanently relinquishing responsibility for the subdivision's future.

The purchasers or contractors who designed the buildings faithfully reproduced the picturesque patterns then prevailing in the United States. Distinguished by wide verandas, wooden shingles, bay windows, and mansard roofs, their Victorian homes looked like country cottages fashionable in both the Pacific Northwest and northern California. Replete with Corinthian columns, iron façades, Renaissance cornices, and ornamental towers, their business blocks closely resembled commercial edifices familiar in Seattle and Sacramento alike.[9] While southern Californians boasted of their unique climate, history, and resources, nothing in the setting, structure, and materials of their architecture evoked these features—except, ironically, the deteriorating Mexican adobes. With its rustic landscape, limited dispersal, segregated land-use, gridiron layout, and picturesque aesthetic, Los Angeles differed little in appearance from the typical town of the late nineteenth-century American West.

After 1885 Los Angeles became increasingly urban. As a result of the prodigious growth of the population, the widespread demand for

23. Herman W. Hellman residence, South Hill Street

24. A. W. Potts residence, Hill and Court Streets

25. Baker Block, Main and Acadia Streets

property, and the marked advance of industry, herds were moved out of the region, crops were harvested for the last time, and orchards were relentlessly destroyed. Henceforth the landscape of greater Los Angeles was dominated by homes, offices, stores, and factories; streets, sidewalks, and railways; and water mains, gas pipes, electric lines, and sewers. The cities covered the countryside; Anaheim spread over the southeastern plain, Pasadena extended to the Sierra Madre Mountains, and the amount of land subdivided in Los Angeles proper increased more than one hundredfold.[10] Even in the distant eastern San Gabriel and western San Fernando valleys, which were still cultivated, and the steep Hollywood and Baldwin Hills, which were yet wasteland, the services and facilities requisite for development were available by 1930.

Although Los Angeles had to expand into a vast urban center—after all, two million new inhabitants and a billion dollars of additional

26. Urban Los Angeles, 1929 (Westwood Village, south of Pico Boulevard)

business had to be provided with adequate transportation, water, utilities, property, and buildings—it did not have to emerge as the dispersed metropolis par excellence. Yet with far fewer people and much less manufacturing than metropolitan Chicago and Philadelphia, greater Los Angeles, as Table 16 reveals, encompassed many more square miles. Also, with slightly more persons and much less industry than metropolitan Detroit and Boston, it numbered far fewer residents per square mile. Moreover, whereas the population ratio of central city to outlying suburbs exceeded sixteen to one in Pittsburgh and reached twenty-three to one in St. Louis, it came to fewer than three to one in Los Angeles.[11] In 1930, therefore, the structure of greater Los Angeles differed radically from that of the typical American metropolis—a divergence not wholly attributable to the material progress of southern California.

Los Angeles' chronology contributed to this incongruity. The metropolis grew slowly in the era of the horse car, rapidly during the

142

TABLE 16. Area and Density of Selected Metropolitan Districts, 1930

Metropolitan district	Population (in thousands)	Area in sq. miles	Population per sq. mile	Population per sq. mile in central city	Population per sq. mile outside central city
New York	10,901	2,514	4,336	23,179	1,001
Chicago	4,365	1,119	3,890	16,723	1,077
Cleveland	1,195	310	3,852	12,725	1,230
Milwaukee	743	242	3,076	14,056	824
Philadelphia	2,847	994	2,865	15,242	1,035
Detroit	2,105	747	2,819	11,375	881
Boston	2,308	1,023	2,257	17,795	1,560
Minneapolis-St. Paul	832	525	1,584	8,384	231[a]
St. Louis	1,294	822	1,574	13,475	573[b]
Los Angeles	*2,319*	*1,474*	*1,572*	*2,812*	*1,045*
San Francisco-Oakland	1,290	828	1,563	15,105	509[c]
Pittsburgh	1,954	1,602	1,201	13,057	815

Source: U.S. Bureau of the Census, *Fifteenth Census of the United States: 1930. Metropolitan Districts* (Washington, 1932), pp. 35, 49, 57, 73, 115, 129, 131, 140, 159, 165, 171, 193, 203, 215.

[a] Excluding St. Paul.
[b] Excluding East St. Louis.
[c] Excluding Oakland.

period of the electric railway, and even faster in the age of the private automobile. But so did Detroit and Minneapolis which, as Table 16 indicates, were less extensively and less evenly dispersed. Los Angeles' geography also expedited dispersal. The southern and western plains extended to the ocean and the northern and eastern valleys to the mountains; so no natural barriers concentrated settlement. But, except for Lakes Michigan and Erie, respectively, greater Milwaukee and Cleveland were likewise unobstructed, and they too far exceeded Los Angeles in over-all and differential densities. Hence neither timing nor nature fully accounted for the physical uniqueness of the Los Angeles landscape.[12]

Changes in the operation, management, scope, and regulation of transportation and utilities also removed restraints on expansion in Los Angeles. The connection between electric railways and real estate subdivision and the subsequent monopolization of the street and interurban lines by Huntington and Harriman spurred the creation of an extensive radial transit network. Municipalization of the waterworks supplanted a private company, responsible to its stockholders

143

and devoted to profits, with a public department, responsive to the community and committed to expansion. The highway authorities and Metropolitan Water District supplemented the corporations and the city by providing motor thoroughfares and domestic water to places off the railroads and outside Los Angeles. And both local and state commissions compelled the gas, electric, and telephone utilities to serve customers whenever they deposited funds to construct additions to the distributing systems.[13] These improvements were permissive not compulsory, however; they encouraged but did not compel subdivision.

Differences in kind among the developers fostered dispersal in Los Angeles too. There were still operators who relied upon persuasion instead of capital, amateurs who converted property in their spare time, and promoters who marketed small and cheap subdivisions. But now there were also investors such as Henry E. Huntington who possessed funds to undertake almost any project, professionals such as H. J. Whitley who made development their life's work, and entrepreneurs such as Robert C. Gillis who transformed whole sections of Los Angeles into exclusive suburbs.[14] Wealthier, more capable, and more imaginative than their predecessors, they gave an entirely new dimension to subdivision. Nevertheless, like the companies and agencies that extended facilities under pressure from consumers and voters, the Huntingtons, Whitleys, and Gillises transformed real estate according to the preferences of their prospective purchasers.

Hence the unique dispersal of Los Angeles reflected not so much its chronology, geography, or technology as the exceptional character of its population. It was not like Chicago—a typical concentrated metropolis—inhabited largely by impoverished and insecure European immigrants, who, in their attempt to find work and fellowship, were confined to the city's teeming tenements and crowded ghettos.[15] The model of the dispersed metropolis, Los Angeles was populated principally by native Americans with adequate resources and marketable skills, who faced the problems of adjustment confidently because of a common language and similar background. Relatively affluent and secure, the native Americans had a much wider choice than the European immigrants of housing and communities—to both of which, as newcomers in quest of a well-rounded life more than a remunerative occupation, they gave an extremely high priority.

Moreover, the native Americans came to Los Angeles with a conception of the good community which was embodied in single-family houses, located on large lots, surrounded by landscaped lawns, and isolated from business activities. Not for them multi-family dwellings, confined to narrow plots, separated by cluttered streets, and interspersed with commerce and industry.[16] Their vision was epitomized by the residential suburb—spacious, affluent, clean, decent, permanent, predictable, and homogeneous—and violated by the great city—congested, impoverished, filthy, immoral, transient, uncertain, and heterogeneous. The late nineteenth- and early twentieth-century metropolis, as the newcomers in Los Angeles perceived it, was the receptacle for all European evils and the source of all American sins.[17] It contradicted their long-cherished notions about the proper environment and compelled them to retreat to outskirts uncontaminated by urban vices and conducive to rural virtues. And though native Americans everywhere shared these sentiments, they formed a larger portion of the populace in Los Angeles than in other great metropolises. Here then was the basis for the extraordinary dispersal of Los Angeles.

The developers, who were predominantly native Americans, responded sympathetically. "I can't understand why anyone should oppose the expansion of the city," one remarked. "If people did not go into the outside tracts that are being opened up they would be forced into apartments." Even more important, they knew that these preferences generated profitable opportunities in subdivision, particularly in the outlying sections where real estate was still inexpensive. For these reasons they transformed southern California's vast countryside into Los Angeles' sprawling suburbs. The purchasers subsequently constructed houses there, and by 1930 Los Angeles, as Table 17 shows, had more single-family and fewer multi-family dwellings than any comparable American metropolis—except to some extent Philadelphia.[18] Since most newcomers preferred to rent accommodations until they decided where in the metropolis to settle, however, only slightly more than one-third of them owned their homes.

The developers realized that a homogeneous population and compatible land-use were no less essential than a proper layout to the suburban vision. To this end they devised appropriate deed restrictions. These not only prohibited occupancy by Negroes and Orientals in most tracts and, in the more exclusive ones, fixed minimum costs for houses so as—in one developer's words—"to group the people of more or less like income together." They also forbade commercial and industrial activities in most subdivisions, and, again in the more fashionable ones, outlawed all but the single-family houses deemed— by most Los Angeles residents—"the foundation of this country's security." (Whereas the restrictions on use, though not on race, nor-

TABLE 17.   Families and Dwellings in Selected Cities, 1930

City	Number of families (in thousands)	Number of dwellings (in thousands)	Per cent of total dwellings		
			1-family	2-family	3-or-more-family
Los Angeles	*369*	*301*	*93.9*	*3.8*	*2.4*
Philadelphia	458	398	91.6	6.1	2.3
San Francisco	179	119	88.3	5.9	5.9
Washington	126	85	87.9	8.0	4.1
Baltimore	194	163	86.7	10.8	2.5
Detroit	370	263	79.7	15.5	4.8
Pittsburgh	155	117	77.4	18.0	4.5
Cleveland	222	146	69.2	23.2	7.6
St. Louis	215	141	64.1	29.1	6.8
New York	1,723	557	52.8	24.5	22.7
Chicago	843	403	52.0	28.9	19.1
Boston	179	89	49.5	25.5	25.0

Source: U.S. Bureau of the Census, *Fifteenth Census of the United States: 1930. Population. Volume VI. Families* (Washington, 1933), p. 72.

mally expired after one or two decades in ordinary developments, they usually extended in perpetuity in more pretentious ones.) In short, deed restrictions were employed by the subdividers to ensure that most of greater Los Angeles' suburbs would stay strictly homogeneous and purely residential.[19]

Los Angeles' extraordinary dispersal was thereafter accelerated by its populace's extreme mobility. At first most newcomers found the entire region as enchanting as one woman who confided in her diary that "[southern] California seems so pretty all over that it is hard to say which is the best part."[20] But, guided by tangible considerations such as climate, topography, accessibility, and price, they eventually selected a subdivision, purchased a lot, and built a house. They rarely remained there long, however. It was not just that the influx of Mexicans, Japanese, and Negroes and the expansion of commerce and industry threatened the homogeneity and rusticity of many subdivisions. It was also that the native Americans felt little attachment to neighborhoods which, like themselves, were so new as to be devoid of any meaningful institutional ties. Thus, so long as the real estate market remained active, these people moved time and again to more prestigious, though no less homogeneous and rustic, suburbs elsewhere in Los Angeles.[21]

The aspirations of the Mexicans, Japanese, and Negroes who initially settled in the central Los Angeles ghetto also fostered residential dispersal in outlying parts of the metropolis. Although the colored minorities there lived in houses and not tenements, they, no less than the white majority, preferred modern homes in suburban settings. But developers only subdivided tracts for them which, as a result of inferior drainage or other disadvantages, were not otherwise marketable. Hence colored people with funds and determination had no alternative save to attempt to enter the few subdivisions where deed restrictions had never been applied or had already expired. But there they often encountered the opposition of white landowners who explained that, though they had—as they put it—no objection to colored people "in their place," "they must not crowd us out and lower the value of our property." [22] Still, they sometimes secured houses outside central Los Angeles, and, as their white neighbors fled in panic, other colored people succeeded them, forming suburban enclaves and furthering residential dispersal in greater Los Angeles. [23]

Los Angeles' unmatched residential dispersal was only one manifestation of the community's antiurban ethos. Its unprecedented business decentralization was another, though it was barely evident as late as 1920. By then suburbanization had brought about a thorough, extensive, and permanent land-use segregation in the metropolis. For the thousands of Mexicans, Japanese, and Negroes who lived amidst commerce and industry in the small ghettos of central Los Angeles and San Pedro there were a million white Americans who resided in the suburbs sprawling north to Hollywood, east to Pasadena, south to Long Beach, and west to Santa Monica. Moreover, greater Los Angeles extended so far into the countryside that only electric trains and motor cars connected its homes, stores, and factories—a pattern not only preferred by the populace and imposed by the developers, but also sanctioned by city and county authorities. Land-use segregation was characteristic of other American metropolises, however, and so the uniqueness of Los Angeles' landscape had not yet extended by 1920 beyond its residential dispersal.

Here as elsewhere, the downtown district dominated the region's business. It was clearly the locus of employment; according to a traffic survey conducted in January 1924, 1.2 million persons a day, or more than the entire population of the city, traveled to and from the section bounded by Temple, Figueroa, Pico, and Los Angeles Streets. [24] It was also the center of commerce. "It is a common sight on the highways," a utility company executive observed in 1915, "to see large trucks . . . headed for some town outside Los Angeles crowded, filled to the brim, but returning empty." [25] As the focus of Los Angeles' economy, moreover, downtown expanded from a few small shops and offices covering several blocks in 1885 to many large mercantile and professional buildings spread over a square mile in 1920—the most concentrated section in southern California.[26] And though most people took more pride in the outlying residential suburbs than the central business district, they believed that it had achieved a position in Los Angeles comparable to the Loop in Chicago and Lower Manhattan in New York.

Downtown also steadily shifted south and west, and its center moved from Spring and Third in 1885 to Sixth and Hill in 1920. New buildings there gained the retail trade, a banker noted in 1909, because shoppers encountered congestion further north and east.[27] The extreme fluctuations in values that accompanied this movement sorely distressed property owners, and they called on private enterprise and public authority to anchor the central business district. The construction of financial houses on Spring, utility headquarters on Fifth, department stores on Broadway, and (incipiently) a civic center at Temple permanently fixed downtown Los Angeles' location in the 1920's.[28] In the meantime, however, its function changed. Between 1885 and 1920, as Chart 1 reveals, office buildings and department stores increased their share of downtown space at the expense of hotels and stores. These changes notwithstanding, the central business district still held more than three-quarters of Los Angeles' commercial and professional enterprise in 1920.[29]

Industry, by contrast, was not concentrated downtown. This was not because the small manufacturers who operated lofts found land there too expensive. Although some who did moved to the depressed district north of Temple Street and the rundown section south of Pico Street, over half of the city's lofts were still located in the central business district in 1920.[30] It was rather because the large industrialists, who, unlike merchants, lawyers, and small manufacturers, derived few advantages from a central location, required more space than was available downtown at any price. They preferred to locate in the vicinity of the original industrial district in southeastern Los Angeles which was served by the Southern Pacific, Santa Fe, and Pacific Electric and consisted of large undeveloped tracts. When the Goodyear Tire and Rubber Company decided to establish its Pacific coast branch facilities in Los Angeles, for example, it transformed an immense parcel south of downtown and west of the railroad tracts into a massive manufacturing center.[31]

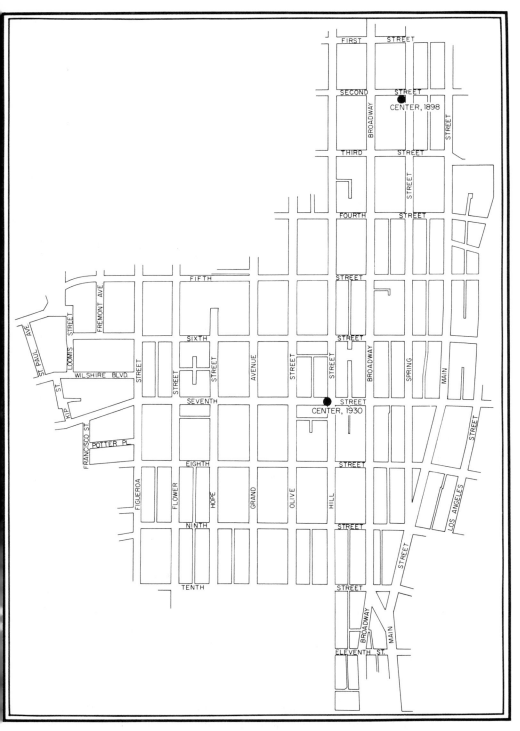

CENTRAL BUSINESS DISTRICT OF LOS ANGELES, 1898–1930

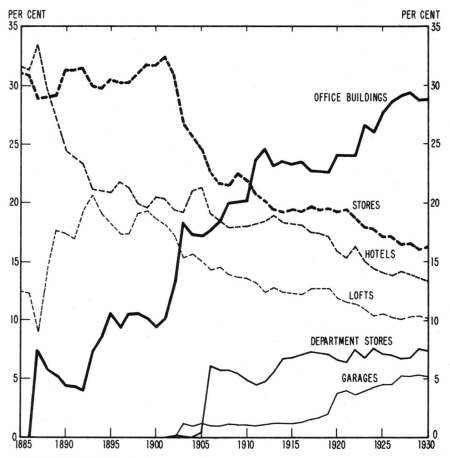

PER CENT   PER CENT

OFFICE BUILDINGS

STORES

HOTELS

LOFTS

DEPARTMENT STORES

GARAGES

CHART 1. Land-Use in Downtown Los Angeles, 1885–1930

SOURCE: Wm. H. Babcock & Sons, *Report on the Economic and Engineering Feasibility of Regrading the Bunker Hill Area* (Los Angeles, 1931), p. 21.

For other heavy industries, the waterfront district was the choice location. It had not only immediate access to the harbor and direct contact with the transcontinental lines, but also abundant water and power, adequate rail and truck connections, and inexpensive acreage, factors that strongly attracted industrialists. When the Ford Motor Company decided to abandon its downtown automobile factory, for instance, it bought property at Long Beach large enough to house its sprawling assembly plant and close enough to the water to receive parts by ship.[32] Manufacturers were able to exploit inexpensive acreage here by virtue of the existing rail transportation and public utili-

150

ties, but they were unable to build plants elsewhere in the metropolis because of the absence of these facilities. Just as commerce was concentrated in the central business district until 1920, industry, while somewhat decentralized, was confined to the downtown, southeastern, and waterfront vicinities.

Business centralization was thus far compatible with residential dispersal in Los Angeles—as in other American metropolises—because of its land-use patterns, transport facilities, and utility services. The scattered suburban population did not form a large enough market for outlying retail enterprises, and the radial electric railways, which did not supply cross-town service, provided swift and inexpensive transit in and out of downtown. Hence the metropolis' merchants felt little incentive to relocate stores and found little difficulty in attracting customers. Moreover, the transcontinental railroads (and, less important, the Pacific Electric) did not operate freight trains everywhere in Los Angeles. Nor did the private companies and public agencies distribute utilities throughout the entire metropolis. Thus, as the existing industrial districts contained enough acreage at reasonable prices, the manufacturers, like the merchants, found centralization profitable as well as obligatory.

These conditions changed soon after 1920. The retail market grew prodigiously in the suburbs, reflecting not so much the increase of immigration—which was accompanied by the expansion of territory —as the changes in the character of the populace. First, in response to the influx of single persons, entrepreneurs erected outlying apartment houses. Their proportion of new construction advanced, as Chart 2 shows, from 8 per cent in 1920 to 53 per cent in 1928.[33] An extremely small fraction of all housing in Los Angeles, apartment houses were so concentrated as to raise densities in communities such as Hollywood and on thoroughfares such as Wilshire Boulevard. Second, in response to the wealth of many residents, developers created very exclusive subdivisions such as Beverly Hills and San Marino which had enormous purchasing power.[34] Although the subdividers restricted business there, they reserved lots along major arteries for commerce. Nonetheless, these changes were essentially permissive. They generated opportunities for mercantile enterprise in the suburbs, but they did not compel established businesses to desert downtown.

The failure of the electric railways, however, did just that. The street and interurban lines were heavily congested as early as 1910: "There are times in the rush hours," the Los Angeles *Examiner* reported "when every foot of trackage in the business district is covered with trolley cars."[35] Subsequently, the electric railways had to share

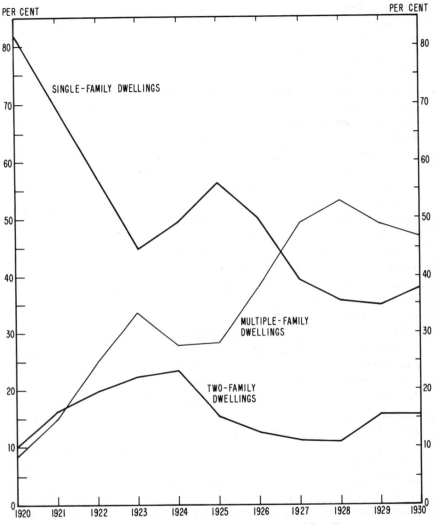

PER CENT   PER CENT

SINGLE-FAMILY DWELLINGS

MULTIPLE-FAMILY
DWELLINGS

TWO-FAMILY
DWELLINGS

1920 1921 1922 1923 1924 1925 1926 1927 1928 1929 1930

CHART 2. Annual Increase in Housing Units, by Type of Dwelling
Los Angeles, 1920–1930

SOURCE: *Annual Report. Department of City Planning. Los Angeles [1929–1930]*, p. 61.

the surface with private automobiles, the number of which in Los
Angeles County soared from under 200,000 in 1920 to over 500,000
in 1924. By then 262,000 motorcars traveled in and out of downtown
everyday and, with the trains, so tightly jammed the streets that, as
distraught witnesses complained to the California Railroad Commis-

152

sion, it was very hard to reach the central business district.[36] The municipal authorities attempted to alleviate this congestion, but to little avail. And in time the electric railways, plagued by automobile competition that increased their expenditures and reduced their revenues, so curtailed service and raised fares that the car supplanted the train as the principal means of transportation in Los Angeles.[37]

The central business district profoundly felt the repercussions. Since at least twenty autos were required to convey as many people as one train, traffic became heavier, travel took longer, and parking space became scarcer. The optimists predicted that these troubles, delays, and expenses would discourage drivers and compel them to ride the railways again. Others disagreed, arguing that the residents, faced with these alternatives, would avoid downtown before they returned to the trains.[38] The pessimists proved more perceptive. Between 1923 and 1931, while the population within ten miles of the central business district expanded 50 per cent, the number of people entering downtown Los Angeles increased only 15 per cent. "The automobile has brought a distinct change in the city building," a visitor who observed these trends predicted. "The day is not far distant when vehicular congestion will be so great down town that enterprising merchants will be establishing great department stores in outlying business centers where shoppers can be conveniently served." [39]

The triumph of motor transport facilitated the decentralization of industry too. The extensive county highway and city street systems enabled manufacturers—long dependent on the railroads—to move freight throughout the region by trucks. Widespread automobile ownership, combined with sprawling suburban subdivisions, also rendered hitherto remote and still cheap residential locations accessible to the working force.[40] The expansion of utility facilities undermined another basis for industrial concentration. The municipal authorities provided inexpensive water and power throughout the city, and regional districts and private companies supplied service at slightly higher rates elsewhere. Hence, when rapid industrial development in the 1920's made land in the still desirable downtown, southeastern, and waterfront sections extremely expensive, the industrialists had a far greater choice of sites.

The decentralization of commerce and industry followed. In response to the expansion of suburban retail markets and the inaccessibility of central Los Angeles, prominent mercantile concerns relocated old stores and opened new ones along Wilshire, Hollywood, and other fashionable boulevards.[41] Downtown, which now consisted of even fewer shops, hotels, and lofts and more office buildings, governmental structures, and garages, had only about half of the metropolis' commercial and professional enterprise and was only one, and by no means the most stylish, of its business districts. Meanwhile, in conjunction with local realtors, mammoth manufacturing firms established segregated industrial complexes throughout Los Angeles. Steelmakers constructed furnaces at Torrance, oil producers erected refineries at El Segundo, aviation companies built hangars near Santa Monica, and motion picture magnates spread studios over the San Fernando Valley.[42] Hence business decentralization, combined with residential dispersal, created an urban form in greater Los Angeles consistent with its growth and yet unique in the United States in 1930.

It was not stores, factories, or even apartment houses, however, but single-family subdivisions that characterized the Los Angeles landscape. There was, of course, considerable diversity in these developments. They were subdivided between 1900 and 1930 for, among others, retired magnates worth millions, former farmers worth thousands, and ambitious but impecunious newcomers. They were also spread over the countryside, reaching the lowlying plains and the steep hills, the cool, moist coast and warm, dry interior, and varying in accessibility to railways and highways.[43] Despite the differences in chronology, clientele, topography, climate, and location, however, the variations in subdivision design were remarkably slight in greater Los Angeles—a fact indicating that the suburban layout, like residential dispersal and business decentralization, was yet another manifestation of the community's antiurban ethos.

A description of three representative subdivisions reveals the uniformity of suburban layout in the metropolis. Oneonta Park, which was bought shortly after 1900 by the Huntington Land and Improvement Company, consisted of several small contiguous parcels situated in the western San Gabriel Valley ten miles (on the Pacific Electric) from Los Angeles. Huntington Land developed the tract for Los Angeles' middle class, platting the land with perpendicularly intersecting streets sixty to eighty feet wide and dividing the rest into one-quarter to one-half acre suburban lots. It restricted the use of the property, the cost of the buildings, and the setting of the houses. The purchaser of a one-third acre plot was forbidden to erect any but a residential dwelling worth at least $3,500, to face his home anywhere except on a specified street, to place it less than forty feet behind the front line, and to enclose the lawn with a fence or wall higher than four feet.[44]

Owensmouth, which was located in the southwestern San Fernando Valley twenty-five miles from the central business district, was acquired by the Los Angeles Suburban Homes Company around 1910. Like Huntington Land and Improvement, Los Angeles Suburban Homes subdivided its holdings according to the gridiron pattern. But as the San Fernando Valley was less accessible than the San Gabriel Valley, the company laid out lots as large as four acres that could be farmed now and divided later. Appealing to lower middle-class residents and real estate speculators, Los Angeles Suburban Homes did not rigorously restrict its property. It allowed boarding and rooming houses, apartments and hotels, and even garages, prohibited commerce and industry only until 1920, and fixed minimum costs for homes that in no case exceeded $2,000. Finally, the company stipulated that dwellings face the north-south not the east-west streets and stand no less than thirty feet from the front and ten feet from the side lines so as to conform with more exclusive suburban designs.[45]

Huntington Palisades, which was set in the Santa Monica foothills fifteen miles from downtown Los Angeles, was purchased by Robert C. Gillis in the late 1920's. Impressed by the rustic surroundings, superb views, and towering trees, he decided to transform it into a fashionable upper middle-class community. Unlike most subdividers, he adopted not the gridiron arrangement but a romantic scheme of curved streets and landscaped boulevards which followed the terrain and preserved the vegetation. Gillis also divided the property into lots from about a quarter to more than a full acre and set minimum construction costs from $5,000 for the smaller to $15,000 for the larger parcels. And he prohibited the owners from using lots for other than residential purposes, erecting dwellings of more than two stories, growing hedges to more than five feet, and placing houses without regard for setback lines. Finally, Gillis not only extended these restrictions in perpetuity, but also authorized a property-owners association to enforce them.[46]

That Oneonta Park, Owensmouth, and Huntington Palisades differed somewhat in the arrangement of streets, size of lots, value of buildings, distance of setbacks, and limitation on uses is not surprising After all, the developers, all of whom realized that the restrictions and layout tended—in their own words—"to guide and automatically regulate the class of citizens," [47] aimed at different markets. What is surprising is that, considering the varied topography, climate, and accessibility of the San Gabriel Valley, San Fernando Valley, and Santa Monica foothills, Oneonta Park, Owensmouth, and Huntington Palisades were so similar. Each was designed for single-family resi-

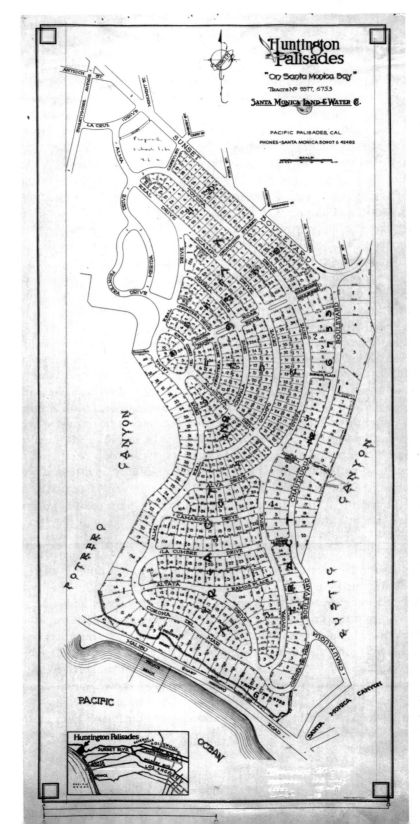

dences, set on sizable lots, fixed in two-tiered blocks, located on improved roads, and isolated from commerce and industry. None permitted any intrusions other than parks, schools, (and sometimes churches) on the domestic environment which, reflecting the suburban vision of the native Americans, everywhere dominated the layout of greater Los Angeles.

Perhaps Palos Verdes Estates, a 3,000 acre tract in the hilly southwestern corner of Los Angeles County, most clearly illustrated the pattern prevailing by the 1920's. There the developers, led by banker Frank A. Vanderlip, entrusted the subdivision to Frederick Law Olmsted, Jr., and Charles H. Cheney, two of the nation's foremost landscape architects and city planners. Olmsted and Cheney possessed an enviable opportunity—their tract was enormous, their employers wealthy, and their authority considerable—and they exploited it with professional expertise. They separated residential streets from traffic arteries, reserved eight hundred acres for parkland, designed several connecting parkways, created lots for views rather than profits, confined commerce to small centers, and prohibited industry altogether. They thus fashioned the metropolis' finest—but still only another—residential community: a "garden suburb," not, as Cheney admitted, a "garden city," [48] Palos Verdes was the quintessence of Los Angeles.

During the years that the suburban layout epitomized by Palos Verdes Estates emerged, the revival style supplanted the picturesque aesthetic in the domestic architecture of Los Angeles. There, as elsewhere in the nation around 1900, native Americans were so distressed by the discrepancies between the United States of myth and reality that they sought reassurances in the past. Northerners and southerners alike recreated colonial and plantation buildings with as much enthusiasm as they formed genealogical and historical societies. Southern Californians suffered no less from this anxiety and, even worse, had renounced the Puritans and Cavaliers, and had sunk only shallow roots in their adopted region. They tried to resolve this problem by turning to California's geography and history, and, in effect, embracing Italy and Spain. "No matter how cosmopolitan our population, our environment is definitely racial," they announced. "We are Mediterranean, in climate, in vegetation and sunlight and, deny it who will, in tradition and inheritance." [49]

They proceeded to shape Los Angeles' domestic architecture according to the Mediterranean style. This is not to deny that other fashions were popular. Most subdividers allowed their customers to choose any pattern for their homes, and many builders who found the picturesque too expensive and elaborate imitated the wooden walls,

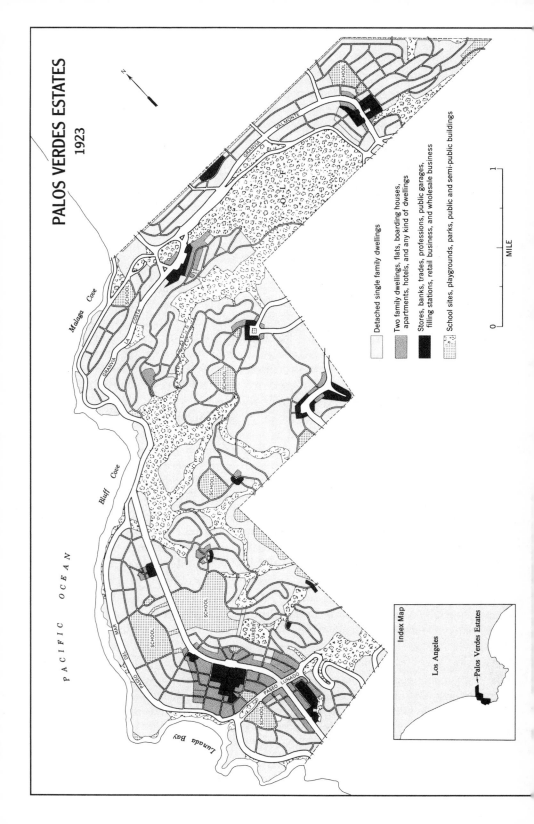

PALOS VERDES ESTATES
1923

Detached single family dwellings

Two family dwellings, flats, boarding houses, apartments, hotels, and any kind of dwellings

Stores, banks, trades, professions, public garages, filling stations, retail business, and wholesale business

School sites, playgrounds, parks, public and semi-public buildings

MILE

0   1

Index Map

Los Angeles

Palos Verdes Estates

PACIFIC OCEAN

Malaga Cove

Bluff Cove

Lunada Bay

dark colors, steep roofs, and sharp turrets of English Tudor and French Norman houses. Even the demanding Palos Verdes Art Jury, which had to approve the plans for houses built there, accepted certain northern archetypes.[50] It is rather to argue that the Mediterranean style prevailed nonetheless. Some developers discounted lots if the houses were constructed in "Moorish, Mission or Pompeian design," others simply prohibited different types, and many contractors followed plan books published by the Bungalowcraft and other companies that featured Italian and Spanish models. The Palos Verdes Art Jury clearly expressed its preference for houses of southern European inspiration too. Summing up the consequences, a highly-regarded Los Angeles architect declared: "We have arrived at a distinctive architecture which is our own, and which is a real expression of our culture and civilization."[51]

His associates defined it as "California architecture," a style which, they explained, "has been successfully developing in this state, deriving its chief inspiration directly or indirectly from Latin types which developed under similar climatic conditions along the Mediterranean." Its colors were "generally very light in tone"; its materials were "plaster, adobe or stucco" or "concrete, brick, stone or artificial stone"; its exteriors were "plaster, adobe or stucco"; and its roofs were "low-pitched [and] usually of tile laid random."[52] Following these guidelines, Los Angeles' architects replaced the verandahs, shingle sidings, protruding bays, and steep tops of the picturesque aesthetic with the patios, massive walls, arched windows, and flat roofs of California architecture. But they were not content to be mere copyists of Italy, Greece or Spain, one architect wrote in 1925. "The test of our architectural abilities is that in drawing upon the rich precedent of the Mediterranean, we should breathe into it such a spirit of originality and fitness for our own needs that we may by degrees evolve an architecture which we shall be proud to call Californian."[53]

By this criterion they failed. A few great mansions, comparable to country villas, achieved the massive simplicity and elegant ornamentation of Mediterranean architecture. But when adapted for suburban lots by uninspired builders, most houses lost all dignity and embellishment. The substitution of open lawns and auto driveways for front walls and central courtyards was particularly incongruous. A few perceived this conflict between aesthetics and culture: "Truly we are a melting pot, not of nationalities, but of architecture," one critic wrote in 1925—"an architectural anachronism, Nordic invasion of the Mediterranean, Attila again in Rome."[54] Nothing proved more

27. Hollywood Hills bungalow

28. Huntington Palisades residence

poignantly than their architecture that, however similar the climates of southern California and southern Europe, southern Californians were in heritage and character American not Mediterranean—nothing, except perhaps their indifference to such architects as Charles and Henry Greene, also midwestern immigrants, who expressed through native traditions, indigenous materials, and modern idioms the uniqueness of southern California.[55]

Meanwhile, the utilitarian replaced the picturesque in commerical architecture. In Los Angeles, as in Chicago, burgeoning business generated demand for additional space, while rising land values favored vertical not horizontal construction. Also, such technological innovations as elevators and fireproofing, iron framing and curtain walls enlarged the opportunities available to southern California (as well as midwestern) architects.[56] Following the pattern perfected by Louis Sullivan and others around the turn of the century, they designed buildings ten and twelve rather than four and six stories in the central business district. They supported them with steel skeletons instead of masonry walls, covered them with concrete and glass instead of iron façades, and capped them with flat roofs and simple cornices instead of medieval towers.[57] Although the nationwide classical reaction left a few unimpressive skyscrapers downtown and the regional Mediterranean style inspired some unattractive shops elsewhere, utilitarianism characterized commercial architecture as completely as revivalism distinguished domestic architecture in Los Angeles.

These buildings were an integral part of Los Angeles' landscape. But they were not unfamiliar elsewhere. Spanish bungalows and Italian villas covered cities in Florida and the Southwest, and modern office buildings and department stores stood in Chicago and San Francisco. Residential dispersal and business decentralization, however, were unique to Los Angeles. Nowhere else in the United States did suburbs extend so far into the countryside and downtown decline so drastically as the center of commerce and industry. This process, which reflected the newcomers' preferences, the subdividers' practices, and the businessmen's inclinations, was also self-perpetuating. Dispersal devastated the central business district, and decentralization spurred outlying subdivision. Given additional urbanization, moreover, nothing but the mountains and the sea inhibited the sprawl of the metropolis—a prospect which, whatever the attendant problems, including the failure of the electric railways, the people of Los Angeles saw as their consummate achievement.

This vision was not new in Los Angeles in 1930. Two decades before

161

29. 7th and Spring streets, c.1928

the people there decided that residential dispersal was imperative. If Los Angeles were to accommodate a large population and yet avoid undue congestion, they reasoned, the metropolis had to spread "until it meet[s] the country, and until beautiful forms of urban life blend almost imperceptibly into beautiful forms of rural life." [58] A decade later they also questioned the value of business centralization. "Is it inevitable or basically sound or desirable that larger and larger crowds be brought into the city's center," they asked; "must all large business, professional and financial operations be conducted in a restricted area[?]" [59] Most answered no. Instead, they envisioned the urban region as "Not another New York, but a new Los Angeles. Not a great homogeneous mass with a pyramiding of population and squalor in a single center, but a federation of communities co-ordinated into a metropolis of sunlight and air." [60] By 1930, however, residential dispersal and business decentralization had transformed Los Angeles into the fragmented—not the co-ordinated—metropolis.

The day is here when the smallest tradesman, builder, skilled mechanic can own an automobile ECONOMICALLY . . . And the ownership of a car, far from being an extravagance, is an actual economy. It saves time and makes money during the week. It gives happiness to the entire family on Sunday. It is a healthful, useful pleasure that discourages pleasures that are harmful. (*Los Angeles Examiner, 1914*)

8   THE FAILURE OF THE ELECTRIC RAILWAYS

The breakdown of Los Angeles' transit industry was of fundamental importance in the fragmentation of the metropolis. Yet the future of the electric railways appeared particularly promising when Huntington and Harriman consolidated the street and interurban lines in 1911. These railwaymen possessed tremendous capital resources and exceptional credit ratings, and their enterprises monopolized passenger transport in the nation's fastest growing urban area. Their companies had, of course, incurred large debts in the course of construction; the Los Angeles owed approximately $1.2 million and the Pacific Electric $3 million a year in interest alone. And as they had extended trackage even more rapidly than the region had gained population, the Los Angeles had declared few dividends before 1911 and the Pacific Electric none at all. Nevertheless, with the networks created, the competitors vanquished, and the demand established, the companies expected the returns to advance commensurate with the growth of their territories.[1]

There were still other reasons for their optimism. First, the Los Angeles and Pacific Electric supplied satisfactory service. This is not to claim that there was no room for improvement. Their lines, according to a progressive journal, were "a series of radiations from the city's center, lengthened from one real estate tract to another without the slightest consideration of the city's symmetrical and economic development."[2] Also, their trains encountered such heavy traffic in the central business district that, as the *Examiner* observed in 1911, "It [took] more time to get from the station at Sixth and Main to Aliso Street than it [did] to run the balance of the trip to Pasadena." These delays so disrupted rail operations that "there [was] no such thing as either the red or yellow cars running as per schedule." [3] Furthermore, the trains were so crowded during the morning and evening rush hours that the commuters were compelled to stand to and from work—a situation by no means unique to Los Angeles, however.

Nevertheless, the Los Angeles and Pacific Electric, which, as Huntington boasted, "extended into the open country, ahead of, and not behind, the population," had guided most subdividers and presently reached most settlements. They came to fit as they had once shaped the structure of greater Los Angeles. Their trains effectively connected the outlying residential suburbs with the central business district, running swiftly through the lightly inhabited sections and keeping time everywhere except in downtown Los Angeles. The companies, at Huntington's orders, also maintained the plants, tracks, cars, and other equipment so well that, according to an impartial expert, they were 90 per cent new. Together with the Los Angeles' traditional nickel and the Pacific Electric's equally reasonable fare, these conditions led local officials to state that "Car service has been supplied on the basis that the riding habit can be cultivated by good service and the results have justified this policy." [4]

Second, in addition to providing satisfactory service, the Los Angeles and Pacific Electric were soundly managed. Although Huntington constructed railways to develop property more than to provide transportation and Harriman regarded them as subsidiary to the Southern Pacific system, they ran transit in Los Angeles with a competence rare in the industry. In many eastern cities, where promoters built lines for speculation and bankers amalgamated them for commissions, the electric railways tended to be so excessively overcapitalized that their directors often declared dividends at the expense of proper maintenance and paid exorbitant interest charges in order to preserve credit and attract investment.[5] In Los Angeles, by contrast, the Huntington and Harriman interests retained possession of the railways and remained free from the pressures of stockholders. They were also so wealthy that they were able to conduct transit with regard for moderate rather than spectacular and long-term rather than immediate returns.

Third, the Los Angeles and Pacific Electric were to a remarkable degree independent of public authority. To be sure, many citizens protested that the railwaymen profited unconscionably from realty enterprises and that their agents used this money to wheedle special privileges out of unprincipled councilmen. These charges gained such widespread acceptance among reformers that by 1910 a southern

California banker warned his associates of "a growing tendency in every community . . . to wage war upon the public service corporations." [6] Moreover, legislative authorities responded to this discontent by expanding their regulatory functions. Los Angeles created a Board of Public Utilities in 1902, and California enlarged the jurisdiction of its Railroad Commission in 1911. These agencies had the right to fix the fares and supervise the service of the electric railways as well as to determine whether or not securities should be issued and bonds floated, grades separated and competition permitted, extensions recommended and facilities abandoned. [7]

Nevertheless, the Los Angeles and the Pacific Electric railways depended less than ever on governmental authorities for franchises. Also, the Board of Public Utilities concentrated primarily on the city's gas, electric, and telephone corporations, and the Railroad Commission directed its attention principally to the state's steam railroads. Neither was inclined to exercise its power over the electric railways. [8] Like the companies, which aspired to maintain firm credit, the agencies, which sought to prevent corporate exploitation, emphasized the promising rather than the threatening features of the metropolis' transportation business. They too believed that, as the Board of Public Utilities reported in 1914, Los Angeles' transit lines were "just emerging from the 'stage of development' onto a paying basis" and would soon "produce a *surplus* over and above the amount sufficient for interest charges and reasonable dividends." [9]

"In anticipating future development," the board added, "it is safe to conclude that earnings will increase at a remarkable rate; that the percentage of earnings required for operating expenses should gradually decrease and the ratio of investment to earnings should be reduced—thus making the burden of fixed charges relatively lighter," and the returns considerably higher. The board based these expectations upon two critical assumptions: first, that the electric railways would monopolize metropolitan transport indefinitely, and second, that transit costs would remain more or less constant in Los Angeles. Each assumption seemed incontrovertible in 1914. No railway could compete with the existing lines, only the affluent could afford private automobiles, and, according to transportation engineers, rail patronage would advance in proportion to population growth squared. [10] Also, southern California's prodigious progress notwithstanding, wages and prices there had fluctuated little in recent years.

Motor cars known as jitneys soon upset the first assumption. They initially appeared in 1914—running adjacent to the rail tracks, picking up carloads of travelers, and charging them five cents each—and by 1915 some 1,800 jitneys carried about 150,000 persons daily. Between 1914 and 1916, as a result, patronage dropped by 17.7 million and 8.6 million and operating revenue fell by $900,000 and $800,000 on the Los Angeles and Pacific Electric, respectively. Both companies warned that the jitneys could ruin but not replace the railways and demanded that the drivers, like the corporations, adhere to regular schedules, follow definite routes, and carry adequate insurance. At their behest the council passed legislation that regulated the jitneys as public utilities and thereby rendered them unprofitable. The drivers, in response, circulated a referendary petition nullifying the ordinance, but the transit companies, backed by the commercial associations, persuaded the electorate to reject it.[11] The jitneys then withdrew from the metropolis' transport industry.

America's entrance into the First World War subverted the second assumption—that transit costs would remain constant. The Los Angeles and Pacific Electric escaped little of the inflationary impact of the labor shortage and material scarcity which irreparably damaged the nation's electric railways. They too had to accept the recommendations of the National War Labor Board and purchase commodities on the spiraling market. Wages, which had ranged from twenty-five to twenty-seven cents an hour on the Los Angeles and from sixty-five to seventy-five dollars a month on the Pacific Electric between 1910 and 1916, advanced to thirty-six cents and one hundred sixteen dollars, respectively, by 1918. Prices, which had changed little in the prewar decade, also ascended according to item from 36 to 150 per cent for the Los Angeles and from 20 to 400 per cent for the Pacific Electric.[12] Without corresponding expansion of patronage, operating expenses rose $1.5 million on the local and $2.2 million on the interurban lines between 1916 and 1918.

Despite the growth of southern California, then, the companies' and authorities' anticipations were frustrated. Between 1914 and 1918, as Table 18 reveals, patronage actually fell on the Los Angeles and the Pacific Electric; operating revenue lagged, operating expenses mounted, and, after taxes, interest, and other fixed charges were deducted, net income declined sharply.[13] Furthermore, no standard indicators offered any reasons for optimism. The Los Angeles' operating ratio climbed fron 69 per cent to 83 per cent, and the Pacific Electric's rate of return dwindled from 4 per cent to 2.7 per cent.[14] Hence the Pacific Electric applied to the California Railroad Commission for permission to raise fares in May 1918, and the Los Angeles asked the

TABLE 18.   Electric Railway Operations in Los Angeles, 1913–1918

Year	Revenue passengers (in millions)	Operating revenue[a] (in millions)	Operating expenses[b] (in millions)	Total deductions[c] (in millions)	Net income (in millions)
		Los Angeles Railway			
1913	139.8	$7.0	$4.9	$1.5	$ 0.6
1914	135.0	6.8	4.7	1.6	0.5
1915	122.2	6.1	4.2	1.7	0.3
1916	117.3	5.9	4.0	1.6	0.3
1917	123.1	6.1	4.5	1.6	0.1
1918	130.4	6.6	5.5	1.5	[0.5]
		Pacific Electric Railway			
1913	68.7	$ n.a.	$ n.a.	$ n.a.	$n.a.
1914	70.3	9.0	6.6	3.5	[0.6]
1915	64.7	n.a.	n.a.	n.a.	n.a.
1916	61.2	8.3	5.9	3.8	[1.0]
1917	65.0	9.0	6.3	4.0	[0.9]
1918	67.9	10.1	8.1	4.2	[1.7]

Source: Railroad Commission of the State of California, *Case No. 4002. Report on the Local Public Transportation Requirements of Los Angeles* (Los Angeles, 1935), chart facing p. 74, p. 82; Lester S. Ready, J. O. Marsh, and Richard Sachse, *Joint Report on Street Railway Survey, City of Los Angeles* (Los Angeles, 1925), pp. 101, 171.

a Includes revenue from freight operations.
b Includes depreciation.
c Includes taxes.
[ ] denotes deficit.
n.a. denotes not available.

commission to recommend ways to alleviate its financial distress in January 1919.

The commission began gathering evidence and examining reports. Its staff corroborated the Pacific Electric's position, pointing out that were it not for the Southern Pacific's financial assistance the Pacific Electric would already have been forced into receivership. Moreover, the commission's engineers saw no alternative to a fare increase, explaining that substantial operating economies were not possible given the existing service and the current price of labor and materials. On the basis of these findings, the commission authorized the Pacific Electric's proposed charges.[15] Finding the Los Angeles' condition by no means hopeless or even serious, though, the commission rejected its projected rate increase as unnecessary and unjustifiable. It recommended instead that expenditures be reduced by more efficient operations, and that, among other changes, lines be rerouted and one-man safety cars introduced to cut material and labor costs. The commission estimated that these recommendations would save the company $1.5 million a year or enough to cover current expenses, fixed obligations, and capital improvements.[16]

The commission also urged the southern California municipalities to support the Los Angeles' and Pacific Electric's efforts to improve their earnings records. It entreated them in particular to relieve the companies of the obligation to pave the surface adjacent to their tracks. This requirement, the commission argued, was onerous and inequitable. It was onerous because it took annually at least $500,000, or more than 8 per cent of gross revenue, from the Los Angeles and over $400,000, or more than 12 per cent of net revenue, from the Pacific Electric. And it was inequitable because it assessed the railways for the benefit of the motorists and truckers who, unlike the companies, depended on and damaged the streets.[17] But this reform was outside the commission's jurisdiction and beyond the corporations' influence, and the local legislators, in response to demands from their constituents for better thoroughfares, preferred to burden the companies than to tax the landholders or deny the motorists.

The commission also asked the metropolis to simplify its franchise arrangements—which were so complex that in 1919 the Los Angeles railway operated on a score of grants that expired between 1920 and 1950—by replacing the fixed with an "indeterminate" (or "resettlement") franchise. The commission reasoned that, however unlikely that the municipality would not renew these franchises, the investors had to take that possibility into account. As a result, they rated the risks greater and set the interest higher, rendering capital more costly and refinancing less attractive. But the municipal authorities, committed to the notion that an inevitable enmity existed between business and government, were bound to a policy which obligated the antagonists to renegotiate the franchise at its expiration. Indeed, the common council, inspired by the progressive suspicion of corporate enterprise and the growing pressure for public transit, had only recently passed an ordinance that shortened the term of railway franchises in Los Angeles. Thus, despite the commission's recommendations, the metropolis refused to rationalize its franchise arrangements.[18]

The commission also proposed that outlying communities prohibit motorbus competition with the Pacific Electric. These lines were started around 1914 by local entrepreneurs tempted by the expanding transport market and by municipal authorities dissatisfied with cur-

rent rail service. Few concerns earned much of a return on their investments, even though they charged less than the interurban system and
selected only the most heavily traveled routes. According to the commission's estimates, however, the thirty-six lines which in 1920 carried
about 25,000 passengers a day deprived the Pacific Electric of nearly
$1 million in revenue a year. Like the jitneys, then, the motorbuses had
the capacity to disrupt but not supplant the railways.[19] Hence, the
commission reasoned, they should supplement and not rival the interurbans. But as most private buses were outside Los Angeles' boundaries
and the municipal ones were beyond the commission's jurisdiction,
they continued to compete directly with the Pacific Electric through
the 1920's.

The commissioners, as well as the railwaymen, realized that the
automobile, not the motorbus, was the railway's chief competitor. But
they did not consider automobile competition a permanent problem—
a conviction which reflected a crucial assumption about the nature
of metropolitan transportation. They no longer believed that the car
was exclusively for the wealthy. After all, between 1914 and 1919
registration quadrupled in the city to more than 60,000 and doubled
in the county to more than 100,000. But they were convinced that the
number of automobiles required to carry people from the outlying residential suburbs to the central business district was approaching the
"saturation point," that point at which the discomforts, delays, and
expenses of motoring would be so severe as to force drivers back to the
trains. Hence the Pacific Electric's president announced shortly after
that "the peak of the competition of the automobile, publicly or privately owned or operated, has been reached out here—and passed." [20]
For this reason the railroad commission recommended that the municipal authorities limit parking and restrict turning but not otherwise
discourage driving.

Meanwhile, the Los Angeles Railway adopted most of the commission's recommendations. Unfortunately, additional advances in the
cost of labor and power after 1919 consumed the anticipated savings,
and the company again applied to the commission for permission to
raise rates. Conceding that conditions justified the railway's request,
the commission authorized fares designed to produce a 7.4 per cent
return.[21] The Los Angeles did not raise rates, however, and retained
the same charges through the early 1920's. The Pacific Electric, in
turn, considered its recent increase insufficient, and asked the commission for another readjustment. Pasadena, Long Beach, and Santa
Monica, among other municipalities, opposed the petition on the

grounds that their branches did not lose money and urged the commission to segregate earnings by lines before allowing over-all fare hikes. But the railway objected: "I think it is possible," its attorney warned, "—if you folks want to, if you want to make a concerted action—I think it is possible for you to wreck the Pacific Electric Company." [22] And the commission, rejecting the piecemeal approach, approved another raise for the interurban system in 1922.

The electric railway's fortunes markedly improved during southern California's subsequent boom. Between 1919 and 1923, as Table 19 indicates, patronage advanced rapidly and operating revenue rose substantially on both the Los Angeles and the Pacific Electric. Even though operating expenses increased too, enough money remained to cover fixed charges and raise net income. [23] The Los Angeles by 1919 and the Pacific Electric by 1920, it appeared, had effectively reversed the downturn caused by the jitneys and the war. Moreover, the standard indicators also improved; the Los Angeles' operating ratio fell from 83 per cent to 70 per cent, and the Pacific Electric's rate of return climbed from 1.5 per cent to 6.8 per cent. [24] With the Los Angeles accumulating its largest surpluses and the Pacific Electric reporting its first profits, the prospects of the metropolis' transit industry seemed more promising in the early 1920's than at any time in the past decade.

The street railway's earnings record concealed certain unfavorable conditions, however. The Los Angeles, its enlarged patronage, revenue, and income notwithstanding, lacked the money to finance extensions; and its motorbus facilities (owned jointly with Pacific Electric) [25] provided inadequate cross-town transport. Also, the volume of riders increased less rapidly than the registration of automobiles— which now numbered over 250,000 in the city and above 400,000 in the county and aggravated the terrible congestion in the central business district. Furthermore, though the managements of the Los Angeles and the Pacific Electric maintained cordial relations, their partial overlapping produced discrimination in service and duplication in administration. [26] From the vantage of the municipality, the rider, and the commission, respectively, rail service was insufficient, slow, and inefficient; from the perspective of the companies, the returns were unsatisfactory. Thus, when the commission proposed a full-scale survey of Los Angeles' transit situation in 1923, municipal authorities and corporate directors alike offered their cooperation.

The commission investigated the Los Angeles railway, the Pacific Electric's city lines, and their motor coach subsidiary. It examined transport operations, analyzed income statements, and estimated capi-

TABLE 19. Electric Railway Operations in Los Angeles, 1919–1923

Year	Revenue passengers (in millions)	Operating revenue[a] (in millions)	Operating expenses[b] (in millions)	Total deductions[c] (in millions)	Net income (in millions)
Los Angeles Railway					
1919	145.4	$ 7.3	$ 6.1	$1.6	$[0.3]
1920	179.2	9.0	7.2	1.6	0.2
1921	200.9	10.1	8.2	1.7	0.2
1922	219.0	11.1	7.6	2.2	1.4
1923	248.6	12.6	8.8	2.2	1.5
Pacific Electric Railway					
1919	68.3	$11.3	$ 9.8	$4.4	$[2.8]
1920	84.5	15.3	12.0	4.6	[1.2]
1921	88.7	17.1	13.1	4.9	[0.8]
1922	88.1	18.3	13.8	5.1	[0.6]
1923	100.1	21.6	16.2	5.4	0.3

Source: Lester S. Ready, J. O. Marsh, and Richard Sachse, *Joint Report on Street Railway Survey, City of Los Angeles* (Los Angeles, 1925), pp. 101, 171; Railroad Commission of the State of California, *Case No. 4002. Report on the Local Public Transportation Requirements of Los Angeles* (Los Angeles, 1935), chart facing p. 74, p. 82.

a Includes revenue from freight operations.
b Includes depreciation.
c Includes taxes.
[ ] denotes deficit.

tal requirements; it measured downtown congestion, studied terminal grants, and calculated paving costs. By and large, it repeated earlier recommendations urging the Los Angeles council to regulate automobile traffic, adopt the "indeterminate" franchise, and eliminate the paving obligation.[27] In a more radical conclusion, however, it called for the unification of local transit. This, it claimed, would reduce expenses by coordinating operations and eliminating duplication, increase revenue by facilitating extensions and improving service, and revive the industry by enhancing earnings and attracting investment. The Pacific Electric could acquire the Los Angeles, the Los Angeles could purchase the Pacific Electric's branches, or a new company could consolidate all existing facilities—each alternative being preferable to the present arrangement. But even more beneficial, the commission argued, would be the municipalization of local transport.[28]

The advantages of municipalization would have been substantial.

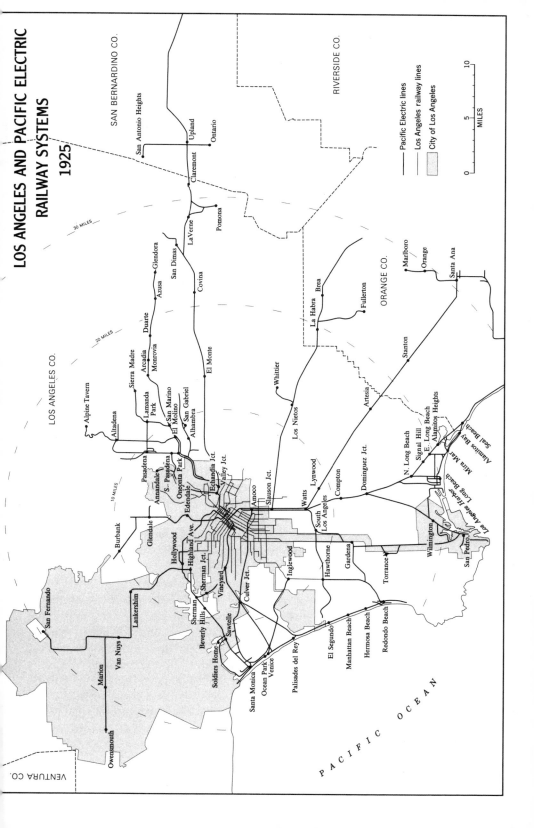

LOS ANGELES AND PACIFIC ELECTRIC RAILWAY SYSTEMS 1925

Pacific Electric lines
Los Angeles railway lines
City of Los Angeles

0   5   10
MILES

The railway would have been relieved of the state's 5¼ per cent gross revenue tax and the city's paving requirements. Together with smaller reductions in expenses due to consolidation, the savings would have totaled well over $1 million a year.[29] As a public undertaking, the railway might have received a more sympathetic hearing from the authorities, who might then have been willing to regulate the movement and storage of automobiles in order to ease traffic congestion. Also, with the city's credit, the railway could have retired the outstanding 5 per cent bonds by issuing others bearing lower rates and would thus have paid as much as 2 to 3 per cent less than it was currently paying for the use of short-term capital.[30] Here was an economically sound proposal to improve Los Angeles' street railway system—a proposal particularly appropriate in a municipality that had already assumed the ownership of its water supply, power system, and harbor.

The timing too was propitious. The city's other undertakings, whose priorities had hitherto stymied petitions for public transport, were approaching self-sufficiency. No less important, the history of rail transit in New York and San Francisco, among other metropolises, not only provided precedents for municipalization, but also demonstrated the inadequacy of private urban transportation. In 1925, therefore, prominent civic and political leaders prepared an agreement whereby the authorities would grant and the company accept a comprehensive "indeterminate" franchise. Huntington would transfer his stock to the corporation for $30 million in 4½ per cent first mortgage bonds, and the council would guarantee principal and interest and assume ownership. A commission consisting of company directors and city officials would manage the enterprise, though Huntington could terminate the agreement if earnings failed to cover obligations.[31] The arrangement was mutually beneficial; Huntington would have secured a sizable sum for a lagging investment, and Los Angeles would have gained a transportation system at a fair price. Unfortunately, the contract was not signed.

Two years later the council hired consultant Delos F. Wilcox to examine Los Angeles' transit conditions and offer recommendations for future policy. Assuming that trains were essential for urban transport, Wilcox conceived of three possibilities: the municipality could either postpone any commitment, institute the "indeterminate" franchise, or acquire the Los Angeles railway. Evaluating each alternative by the extent it enabled the community to co-ordinate operations, order extensions, and otherwise formulate policy, Wilcox decided that municipal ownership presented the best opportunity for effective rail transportation. Anticipating practical objections, he argued that the populous and prosperous metropolis had the wherewithal to finance the acquisition and that the administration of the Water and Power Department proved the responsibility of public enterprise. In closing, he recommended that as Huntington, who now devoted more attention to his library than to his railway, would be receptive to a fair offer, the authorities should act forthwith.[32] A committee headed by the mayor opened negotiations, but the magnate died soon after and his executors discontinued the discussions.[33]

None of this affected the Pacific Electric, which, in spite of its profit in 1923, was in a precarious position. Not only did patronage increases lag far behind population growth and revenue fall well below expenditures, but, despite the territorial expansion of Los Angeles, the Pacific Electric's lines extended to about the same region in 1925 as in 1915. Moreover, the company still could not attract capital, and loans from the Southern Pacific, which held its bonds as well as its stock, financed operations, but not extensions, depreciation, and improvements. Even worse, as one observer commented, service had not improved in a decade. Not only were the rides less comfortable, but, as traffic congestion intensified, the trains were interminably delayed in and around downtown Los Angeles. Lower patronage and higher expenses resulted, indicating that the Pacific Electric's crucial shortcoming, as its general superintendent acknowledged, was its inability to offer rapid transit to and from the central business district.[34]

The interurban builders had first recognized the need for rapid transit in 1906 when E. H. Harriman announced plans to construct two subways connecting the Hill Street terminal with the Hollywood and Vineyard stations. These subways would have separated the Los Angeles Pacific cars from the downtown trolley and auto traffic and reduced by half the runs of the northern lines to Hollywood and the western lines to Santa Monica. Although the municipality granted a franchise for the subways and the company earmarked $10 million of a proposed $20 million bond issue for their construction, the Los Angeles Pacific did not undertake the project.[35] Subsequently, the Pacific Electric contemplated building a subway system, but, due to its deteriorating financial condition, it completed only a one-mile tunnel from the Hill Street terminal to First Street and Glendale Boulevard. Opened in 1925, this tunnel—known as the Hollywood Subway—shortened the trips north and west by nearly a quarter of an hour; but by itself it did not provide the rapid transit required to improve appreciably the Pacific Electric's over-all service.[36]

30. Downtown traffic congestion, ca. 1920 (Hill Street north from Pacific Electric depot between Fourth and Fifth Streets)

As early as 1917, moreover, the Pacific Electric began to consider erecting elevated tracks from its Main Street terminal over the Los Angeles River to its Long Beach and Pasadena lines. But it was not until 1926 that it presented the plan, and then only as part of a Southern Pacific, Santa Fe, and Union Pacific project to eliminate grade crossings and avoid building a Union Terminal. The elevated lines, which would have removed 1,200 trains per day from the crowded downtown streets, were endorsed by the Public Utilities Board, the Chamber of Commerce, and most civic groups and metropolitan newspapers. But they were opposed by the Los Angeles *Times* and other property owners who had long contested for the construction of a Union Terminal near the plaza. They were also objected to by many residents who feared the impact of elevated railways—were they not eastern devices?—on Los Angeles' land values and landscape. Their opposition was decisive, and at a straw vote held in 1926 the electorate favored a Union Terminal at the plaza site,[37] a decision that forced the steam railroads (which were to supply the bulk of the funds) to withdraw their support and the Pacific Electric to shelve the project.

31. Outlying traffic congestion (Third and Alvarado Streets, 1932)

It was, in any case, too little and too late. For by the mid-1920's even the Pacific Electric admitted that private enterprise could not finance a rapid transit system. Hence some suggested that public authority assume the responsibility, and at their behest the common council and supervisorial board employed the engineering firm Kelker, de Leuw to prepare a comprehensive transportation plan for the metropolis. Submitted in 1925, this plan called for the creation of a unified transport network consisting of rapid transit lines, operating off-grade and supplying commuter service, interurban trains, running on the surface and connecting satellite cities, street railways, moving in congested areas and tying in with transit tracks, and motorbuses, extending into sparsely-settled sections and serving as "feeders." The Kelker, de Leuw plan also recommended that the authorities finance the system with general obligation, district assessment, and revenue bonds so that the populace, landholders, and passengers would bear the expenses together.[38] Downtown businessmen, disturbed by commercial decentralization, enthusiastically endorsed the proposal. So did disinterested citizens who, presuming that the central business

177

district was indispensable, believed that rapid transit was the only way to facilitate residential dispersal in Los Angeles.[39]

Outlying merchants and homeowners disagreed, claiming that rapid transit would benefit downtown Los Angeles and burden its suburbs. Responsible civic groups joined the opposition. "Considering the results obtained in cities like New York, Boston, and Philadelphia," the City Club wrote, "we may well ask whether Los Angeles is justified in beginning the endless chain program of expenditures in subways and elevated structures which inevitably have tended to increase the congestion in those centers of population."[40] "Is it inevitable or basically sound or desirable," a prominent resident, pursuing this theme, queried, "that larger and larger crowds be brought into the city's center; do we want to stimulate housing congestion along subway lines and develop an intensive rather than an extensive city [?]"[41] Must Los Angeles, he asked, penetrating to the core of the controversy, imitate eastern metropolises? Most residents answered no. Assuming that decentralization rendered downtown expendable and rapid transit unnecessary, the city and county governments therefore shelved the Kelker, de Leuw project.

The authorities thus refused to implement municipal ownership and rapid transit, and the incompetence of privately-operated surface railways was soon made all too obvious. Their fortunes fell sharply between 1924, a very good year, and 1926, an appallingly poor one. On both the Los Angeles and the Pacific Electric, as Table 20 shows, patronage declined, operating revenue slid, and, as operating expenses increased and fixed charges remained constant, net income dropped.[42] The standard indicators were ominous too. The Los Angeles' operating ratio climbed from 71 per cent to 85 per cent, and the Pacific Electric's rate of return dwindled from 5.5 per cent to 2.2 per cent.[43] Nevertheless, transit experts, who measured the train's safety against the automobile's flexibility and compared the inconveniences of driving with the simplicity of riding, concluded that if the costs and comforts of rail and motor transport were equal, the electric railway would attract its share of Los Angeles patronage.[44] Others, of course, disagreed.

In any case, railwaymen now understood more clearly the nature of motorcar competition. They had already realized that the auto contributed to congestion that so slowed the trains and lengthened their runs that the railways attained increasingly less mileage per kilowatt and man-hour. They had even perceived that the car offered alternative transportation, and that the companies, compelled to

TABLE 20. Electric Railway Operations in Los Angeles, 1924–1926

Year	Revenue passengers (in millions)	Operating revenue[a] (in millions)	Operating expenses[b] (in millions)	Total deductions[c] (in millions)	Net income (in millions)
			Los Angeles Railway		
1924	255.6	$13.1	$ 9.9	$2.3	$ 1.1
1925	249.1	12.9	10.5	2.3	0.2
1926	250.8	13.0	10.9	2.3	—[d]
			Pacific Electric Railway		
1924	100.9	$20.7	$15.9	$4.7	$[0.6]
1925	94.8	19.5	16.0	4.1	—[d]
1926	92.8	19.1	16.4	4.2	[1.1]

Source: Railroad Commission of the State of California, *Case No. 4002. Report on the Local Public Transportation Requirements of Los Angeles* (Los Angeles, 1935), chart facing p. 66, pp. 72, 74, 82.
  [a] Includes revenue from freight operations.
  [b] Includes depreciation.
  [c] Includes taxes.
  [d] Less than $100,000.
  [ ] denotes deficit.

share over-all patronage, suffered sharp losses in operating revenue.[45] But by the mid-1920's they also understood that the automobile competed selectively and insidiously. It diverted more travelers on the weekends than on the weekdays. Whereas the railways once carried about as many riders each day, they currently conveyed twice as many on weekdays as on Sundays. It also siphoned off more passengers in off-peak than in peak periods. The trains, as Charts 3 and 4 reveal, handled over 20 per cent of their inbound traffic in two morning hours and above 30 per cent in two afternoon hours.[46] Hence the motorcars deprived the railways of their cheap and remunerative casual business without relieving them of their expensive and unprofitable commuter service.

By now the railwaymen also doubted the validity of the "saturation theory." The automobile, as expected, stimulated residential dispersal because subdividers no longer had to locate tracts along railway tracks. And the newcomers, who relied on their autos, encountered the predicted delays, discomforts, and costs driving to downtown Los Angeles. But, instead of resorting to the electric trains, they simply avoided the central business district. Of every one hundred persons living within a ten mile radius of downtown Los Angeles, sixty-eight

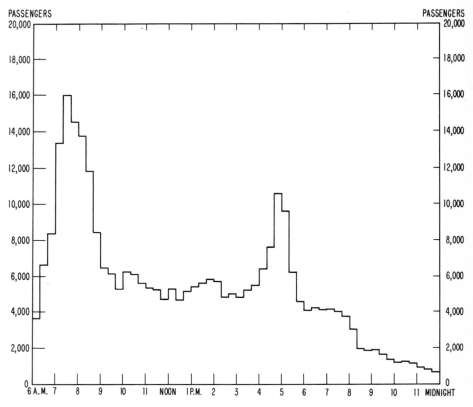

CHART 3. Peak and Off-Peak Traffic Inbound to the Central Business District on Normal Weekdays (February–May 1923) on the Los Angeles Railway

SOURCE: Joe R. Ong, "A Report on Some of the Problems of Operation of the Los Angeles Railway, July 31, 1923," chart 14.

entered it daily in 1923 and fifty-two in 1931, a decline of 24 per cent.[47] Even fewer commuted from farther away, for by the middle of the 1920's commercial and industrial decentralization enabled suburbanites to shop and work in outlying centers. And once the automobile not only competed with the railway but also established the setting for the competition, the future of urban transportation rested with the motorcar as the past had with the train.

Under such circumstances, even the Los Angeles had to request permission to raise rates from five to seven cents early in 1927. The existing fares are too low, it argued. "They do not yield over and above the amount required to pay taxes and operating charges a sum sufficient to constitute just compensation for the use of the property . . .

180

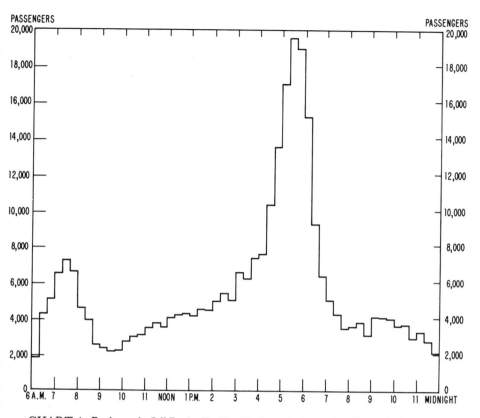

CHART 4. Peak and Off-Peak Traffic Outbound from the Central Business District on Normal Weekdays (February–May 1923) on the Los Angeles Railway

SOURCE: Joe R. Ong, "A Report on Some of the Problems of Operation of the Los Angeles Railway, July 31, 1923," chart 15.

Capacity to acquire new money for a going public utility," the company reminded the Railroad Commission, "depends upon the capacity to earn." The railway's 4.6 per cent rate of return, it added, did not attract investment.[48] The commission, calculating that the proposed increase would produce an exorbitant $15.7 million in operating revenue and an unconscionable 9.4 per cent rate of return, denied the petition. "There is no convincing evidence," it wrote, "that the present low cycle of earnings is permanent or that in the future the company will not realize as good or a better return on the average than it has during the last seven years."[49]

The Los Angeles objected to the verdict and appealed to the courts which found the denial a deprivation of property and overruled the commission's decision. The railway then instituted the revised rates, and the results initially justified its action. Although patronage declined between 1927 and 1929, operating revenue, as Table 21 reveals, advanced; and, as operating expenses and fixed charges changed little, net income increased handsomely, almost reaching its 1923 peak. Moreover, the Los Angeles' operating ratio dropped from 84 per cent to 74 per cent, and its rate of return rebounded from 4.6 per cent to 7.1 per cent.[50] In perspective, though, the railway's record was less impressive. Few improvements in service accompanied the raise in fares; the company bettered its balance at the expense of its patronage, and, despite Los Angeles' tremendous population growth and territorial expansion, the railway failed to accumulate a substantial reserve. This period of prosperity left it ill-prepared for the years of depression ahead.

The Pacific Electric also applied for permission to increase rates. Although the directors considered the application justifiable because of the company's recurrent losses, the riders deemed it indefensible because of the rush-hour congestion. If the Pacific Electric cannot operate at reasonable rates, an embittered witness testified to the Railroad Commission, "it seems to me that there is but one thing for them

TABLE 21. Electric Railway Operations in Los Angeles, 1927–1929

Year	Revenue passengers (in millions)	Operating revenue[a] (in millions)	Operating expenses[b] (in millions)	Total deductions[c] (in millions)	Net income (in millions)
		Los Angeles Railway			
1927	254.5	$13.3	$11.1	$2.3	$ 0.1
1928	248.0	13.6	11.0	2.3	0.5
1929	223.7	14.9	11.2	2.4	1.5
		Pacific Electric Railway			
1927	91.6	$19.6	$16.4	$4.1	$[0.6]
1928	93.8	18.3	15.9	4.1	[1.2]
1929	97.0	18.4	15.5	4.0	[0.7]

Source: Railroad Commission of the State of California, *Case No. 4002. Report on the Local Public Transportation Requirements of Los Angeles* (Los Angeles, 1935), chart facing p. 66, pp. 72, 74, 82.

[a] Includes revenue from freight operations.
[b] Includes depreciation.
[c] Includes taxes.
[ ] denotes deficit.

to do . . . namely, go into bankruptcy." [51] The commission, convinced that higher fares would lead to lower patronage and produce little additional revenue, persuaded the railway to reduce rates temporarily on the Burbank-Glendale line. Unfortunately, this experiment failed; the moderate increase in passengers did not compensate for the large loss in fares. Thereupon the commission authorized tariff revisions and operating efficiencies which, according to estimates, would enlarge the company's net income by more than $200,000 a year. The railway raised its rates, but, as the commission suspected, it attracted fewer passengers and received even less revenue.[52] By now the Pacific Electric's downturn was irreversible.

Its earnings record between 1927 and 1929 revealed its desperate position. Patronage, as Table 21 shows, fell short of 1923 levels, operating revenue lagged, and, even though operating expenses declined and fixed charges remained constant, net income decreased. Furthermore, the Pacific Electric's operating ratio climbed from 78 per cent to 84 per cent, and its rate of return dwindled from 2.9 per cent to 2.3 per cent.[53] This situation was so dreadful that a prominent transportation engineer who studied the interurban system a few years later concluded that "In no other line of business and on no other property in this same industry could such a history of continued and increased losses be absorbed . . . without forcing the corporation into bankruptcy." [54] Though the Southern Pacific supported the Pacific Electric through the 1930's, it was clear by now that the interurban system had failed as a transit enterprise.

For the electric railways here and elsewhere in the United States, the Great Depression was catastrophic. Between 1930 and 1933 rail patronage (see Table 22) tumbled to only a million more than in 1913 on the Los Angeles and to only a million more than in 1912 on the Pacific Electric. Operating revenue fell to less than a decade previously on the urban system and to less than two decades before on the interurban network. Though operating expenses were cut by the Los Angeles and the Pacific Electric, so little remained for fixed charges that net income dropped to historic lows on both lines.[55] Moreover, operating ratio mounted from 82 per cent to 89 per cent on the Los Angeles and from 89 per cent to 98 per cent on the Pacific Electric. Rate of return declined from 4.7 per cent to 2.1 per cent on the urban system and from 2.3 per cent to −0.2 per cent on the interurban network.[56] Although patronage, revenue, and income all advanced on the Los Angeles—though not the Pacific Electric—in 1934, the commission's expectation of a meaningful improvement in the railways'

TABLE 22. Electric Railway Operations in Los Angeles, 1930–1933

Year	Revenue passengers (in millions)	Operating revenue[a] (in millions)	Operating expenses[b] (in millions)	Total deductions[c] (in millions)	Net income (in millions)
		Los Angeles Railway			
1930	205.8	$13.7	$11.1	$2.4	$ 0.5
1931	182.5	12.2	10.7	2.2	[0.3]
1932	154.4	10.3	9.2	2.0	[0.5]
1933	140.5	9.5	8.3	1.9	[0.2]
		Pacific Electric Railway			
1930	90.5	$15.7	$14.0	$4.0	$[2.0]
1931	80.1	13.3	12.1	3.7	[2.3]
1932	67.1	10.5	10.0	3.4	[2.6]
1933	59.7	9.1	8.6	3.2	[2.6]

Source: Railroad Commission of the State of California, *Case No. 4002. Report on the Local Public Transportation Requirements of Los Angeles* (Los Angeles, 1935), chart facing p. 66, pp. 72, 74, 82.
[a] Includes revenue from freight operations.
[b] Includes depreciation.
[c] Includes taxes.
[ ] denotes deficit.

over-all position was clearly illusory. The metropolis' transit industry had exhausted all its remedies.

The abandonment of unprofitable lines was the only alternative. Heretofore the companies and the commission had withstood great pressure from outlying municipalities to consider the railways on a piecemeal basis.[57] Even now, though they conceded that those branches that operated at heavy losses jeopardized the entire industry, they were still reluctant to pursue this policy. They did not doubt that selective abandonments would save more in expenses than they lost in revenue, but they realized that service would suffer, patronage would fall, and the funded debt would not be reduced.[58] If the Los Angeles and Pacific Electric could not meet their fixed charges, how could they finance needed improvements and compete with the automobile? Abandonment was therefore a palliative not a solution; it could postpone the demise of the transit industry, but it could not restore its strength. For want of an alternative, however, the companies proposed and the commission approved the gradual abandonment and dismantling of Los Angeles' electric railways in the late 1920's and 1930's.

This futile effort to adjust transit facilities to transportation demand indicated that overbuilding was the fatal flaw in the street and interurban systems. "To a considerable extent," one expert later wrote about the Pacific Electric, its "unfavorable showing is directly attributable to the existence of too much railroad in proportion to the business available." [59] But overbuilding epitomized rail development in the metropolis. Moses Sherman, Henry Huntington, and their forgotten predecessors all considered the electric railway more a means of furthering real estate ventures than meeting transportation requirements. They constructed many lines that benefited their subdivisions but burdened their railroads. Had the transit industry not lost its monopoly after 1910, it would doubtless have overcome this handicap. The First World War would have been difficult not disastrous, and the Great Depression would have been critical not catastrophic. With the competition of the motor car, however, the electric railways in Los Angeles, thus flawed, were doomed to failure.

For this the municipal authorities were at least partly responsible. Their unwillingness to acquire the Los Angeles street system and to implement the Kelker, de Leuw rapid transit plan removed what little hope remained for the electric railways. In their defense, official inaction, however misguided, corresponded with popular opinion. The Board of Public Utilities even doubted that the voters would have endorsed bond issues to purchase old or build new mass transit facilities. [60] As residents of a dispersed and decentralized metropolis, they believed that motor cars provided better service at lower cost than electric railways. And as people of exceptional mobility and acquisitiveness, they formed intangible but by no means unimportant attachments to the private auto. From their perspective, the railway was expendable, and, with few exceptions, they wholeheartedly accepted dependence on the motor car without fully comprehending the implications of this commitment. Like suburban residences and outlying businesses, private automobiles and public highways emerged by 1930 as integral parts of the fragmented metropolis.

9 THE QUEST FOR COMMUNITY

The evolution of a fragmented community also accompanied the growth of Los Angeles. Up to 1885, Jackson A. Graves, an early settler and prominent banker, recalled, strong friendship and shared experiences tied the townspeople together. "Somehow or other, we lived nearer each other [in 1875] than we do today," he wrote in 1930. "We were more intimate, more sympathetic, there were fewer of us, and we knew each other better than we know those surrounding us at this time. It also seems that we had more leisure on our hands, time to rejoice with the fortunate, to mourn with those in affliction, to sympathize with those in distress."[1] Although Graves, a conservative appalled by the complexity of modern America, was nostalgic for the simplicity of the nineteenth century, his reminiscences accurately described the attachments of his early life and the integration of his adopted settlement. They revealed that thousands of immigrants of diverse origins, occupations, and positions were successfully assimilated into Los Angeles between 1850 and 1885.

Their assimilation was facilitated by the size, location, composition, and character of the population. After all, Los Angeles had no more than 20,000 people before the boom of the late 1880's, few of whom resided more than one mile from the town's center. Most of them—natives of the New England, Middle Atlantic, and eastern Great Lakes states and immigrants from England, Ireland, and Germany—fully adopted American aspirations and attitudes before coming to Los Angeles. Once there they engaged in commerce, crafts, industry, and the professions and attained satisfactory livelihoods. After a while they settled in desirable residential neighborhoods and adhered to prevailing mores. They were also united, as a European traveler observed in the 1870's, by "a mutual interest in the city's advancement,"[2] for they knew that their personal success depended ultimately on the town's progress. All in all, a midwestern visitor concluded in the 1870's, "The white people here are much like they are in any new and thriving town or city at the east." [3]

But this uniformity was not immediately apparent. From the perspective of the immigrant, everything and everyone seemed different; the town was strange, and the townspeople were strangers. The problems of adjustment appeared formidable. Knowing few, if any, of Los Angeles' inhabitants, how could he meet members of the community? Feeling little or no attachment to the region, how could he gain a position of respect in the town? Subjecting his fortune to precarious urban enterprises, how would he secure protection against the fluctuations of the market? And powerless among so many individuals and interests, how could he impress his designs on the fabric of life in Los Angeles?[4] Notwithstanding the newcomer's best intentions, direct entrance into the community was difficult. Fortunately, the small, compact, homogeneous, and like-minded populace facilitated the formation of voluntary associations that tied him to his fellow citizens and helped him cope with his problems.

The town's groups were legion. They included Masonic and Odd Fellow lodges, French and Italian societies, Baptist and Methodist congregations, drama and literary clubs, fire companies and military brigades, Democratic and Republican parties, Boards of Trade and Chambers of Commerce.[5] Exclusive without being invidious, they served as guideposts for the bewildered immigrant. They identified other residents with like traits and similar interests and encouraged contact on shared grounds and participation in common activities. Membership in these organizations defined the newcomer's place in Los Angeles. Furthermore, fraternal and benevolent societies alleviated his insecurity by providing funds, assistance, and insurance in case of depression, illness, and death. Political and commercial bodies promoted his aspirations in matters involving municipal authorities, transcontinental railroads, and even the federal government. Hence in Los Angeles, as elsewhere in the nation, the voluntary associations first introduced the immigrant to the community and afterwards linked him with it.

Not everyone shared in the town's community life, however. Maladjusted Mexicans, uprooted Chinese, and transient Americans all remained separate from the larger society. Few in number, these people were conspicuous by their differences. They lacked entrepreneurial and professional skills, placed a low priority on material achievement, and held modest expectations of future accomplishments. Considering Los Angeles an ancestral pueblo or a temporary settlement and not their chosen and permanent home, they felt little inclination to improve the town economically or socially. No less important, they were deemed undesirable by the Americans. To one intolerant but not untypical midwesterner, these people made up "a dirty, vile, degraded, unredeemable humanity that sits idly in the shade and suffers the rich gifts of climate and soil to go to waste unused and not even appreciated." [6] From such persons, they could expect little indeed.

Hence they earned poor livings. Most worked as laborers and domestics, some managed as gamblers and thieves, and others survived with no visible means of support whatever. They also lived in dreadful accommodations. They had no money to erect houses in fashionable neighborhoods, and in any case would not have been welcome there. They congregated in the vicinity of the old business district, where they rented crowded quarters in dilapidated dwellings. They took little interest in politics, regarding authority as a threat and avoiding it as a precaution, and politicians showed little concern for them. They did not join fraternal societies or worship in Protestant churches; nor did they cooperate with civic committees or contribute to commercial organizations. [7] Instead, the Mexicans retained and the Chinese created their own institutions, though the transient Americans relied on less formal arrangements and in particular on their wits. Unassimilated, unwelcome, and unprotected, these people were so thoroughly isolated that the American majority was able to maintain its untainted vision of an integrated community.

After 1885 the growth of Los Angeles overwhelmed the original townspeople and their descendants. Not only did the population multiply more than fifty times, and the territory expand more than a hundredfold, in the next forty-five years, but, in addition, the newcomers were far less homogeneous, and their aspirations much less unanimous, than the pioneers. The early settlers now found themselves very few among very many and watched their neighborhoods disrupted by changes in land-use. They were dismayed by the diversity of the recent immigrants and confused by the complexity of public issues. Their response to these changes was ambivalent. They admired the vast metropolis, but defended the "vanished village." "While Los Angeles was small and relatively poor in 1875," a resident wrote a half century later, "do not imagine that we did not enjoy life and have good times." [9] They approved of its material advances, but wondered, as a woman put it in 1931, "how soon the wheels of progress are going to stop rattling long enough for us to hear ourselves think, catch our breath and develop some sort of cohesive social organism." [10]

Incapable of imposing the town's coherence on the metropolis, the older residents tried instead to distinguish themselves from the newcomers. They organized pioneer and historical societies that excluded all but the earliest settlers and their families. They also resided in fashionable neighborhoods that restricted all but the acceptable and the wealthy. Yet these measures failed to set them apart and thereby tie them together. The genealogical gatherings were incidental to their members' lives, and the local subdividers were unmindful of the differences between those truly select and those merely rich. In a related attempt to perpetuate their pre-eminence by honoring the past, these people also simplified the metropolis' problems and celebrated the region's traditions. [11] But though the natives impressed their rhetoric and festivals on the newcomers, they did not control the administration of Los Angeles or the conduct of its residents.

The problems of the pioneers reflected the predominance of the newcomers. They were—admitting their numbers but excepting the Mexicans, Japanese, and Negroes—a remarkably homogeneous group. This is not to deny that they included persons as varied as prosperous farmers and hopeful actors from regions as distinct as New England and the Southwest who left for reasons as diverse as retirement and opportunity in periods as far apart as the mid-1880's and the late 1920's. It is rather to argue that most fit well within the broad range of the middle class, had rural midwestern, or at least native American backgrounds, sought a less arduous and more rewarding life, and migrated between the booms of 1904–1906 and 1920–1925. These similarities deeply impressed visitors to Los Angeles: "There is no other place in America," one wrote in 1927, "where the social stratification is so little marked, where all classes do so nearly the same thing at the same time." [12] Furthermore, these newcomers derived from their past experiences two critical, albeit contradictory, commitments which shaped their aspirations for their community.

First, having repudiated certain traditional values in choosing southern California, they felt a compulsion to justify their decision that could be relieved only by steadfast dedication to Los Angeles. They became unparalleled boosters. "Never anywhere have I seen such continual, consistent and enthusiastic 'boosting,'" an admiring Montana realtor remarked. [13] "You stop a policeman to ask a question and he answers you and then tells you what a wonderful city Los Angeles is," a Utah visitor commented in 1914. "You wait for your change in a store and the salesgirl tells you Los Angeles is a marvelous city. You get your shoes shined and the boy will state that Los Angeles' climate cannot be beaten." After that, he added, "The business man will tell you that all Los Angeles has done isn't a circumstance to what will be done." [14] Far from denying these descriptions, the promoters exulted in them. "If you do not 'come through' and tell us what a beautiful city we have, what a fine country and charming climate," the Los Angeles *Times* advised tourists in 1909, "we shall set you down as lacking in taste, intelligence and eloquence. We shall proceed to tell you, and that will be the worse for you." [15]

Boosterism inhibited dissent in Los Angeles. "There is no room for knockers here," a promoter exclaimed in 1908. "We are too busy going ahead to listen to the man with a tale of woe. The fault-finders are not going to help matters by telling us things are going from bad to worse." [16] Ironically, boosterism reflected the insecurity of the residents. Arthur Letts, a Canadian immigrant who founded the Broadway Department Store, dramatically, though unwittingly, revealed this anxiety in a sign that hung on his downtown building. "DON'T WORRY. WATCH US GROW," it read.[17] The people of Los Angeles did worry, concerned, as they were, not only about the future growth of the metropolis, but also about the inescapable evidence of modernity there. For, though as boosters they endorsed progress, as Americans they feared its consequences. They perceived in urbanization a direct conflict with their second commitment, a devotion, engendered in the country, confirmed in the city, and buttressed by tradition, to a bygone rural community.

Perhaps nothing better illustrated this attitude than their replies to an article, "Los Angeles—The Chemically Pure," published in a sophisticated eastern magazine in 1913. Its author, Willard Huntington Wright, described Los Angeles as a puritanical and ill-governed city destitute of the delights of urbanity. "The spirit of genuine gaiety is lacking," he wrote. "Enjoyment is considered the first step to perdition. Noise is the rumbling of the gates of hell. Music is a sign of immorality, and dancing is indecent." For this attitude he blamed the militant moralists from the Midwest. "These good people brought with them a complete stock of rural beliefs, pieties, superstitions and habits," he explained. "Having, by virtue of numbers, a large voice in municipal affairs, they govern Los Angeles as they would a village." Applying Sunday school precepts to their political decisions, they have transformed a once fascinating and sensible place into a "city of little sociability or hospitality, a city devoid of lenience and cosmopolitanism." [18]

The article outraged the residents of Los Angeles, but, far from denying the author's allegations, they defended the community as he described it. "Los Angeles believes in the home," a southern California spokesman answered. "She believes in the moralities; she believes in the decencies of life; she believes that children born within its precincts should be, as far as possible, freed from that familiarity with vice that renders it difficult properly to bring up children in some American cities . . . She deliberately chooses to be dubbed 'Puritan,' 'Middle-West Farmer,' 'Provincial,' etc., and glories in the fact that she has been able to sweep away many flaunting indecencies that still disgrace older and more vice-complacent communities." [19] "If anything," another Los Angeles citizen wrote, catching the quintessence of this morality, "it is our departure from these 'village ideals,' the simple, comely life of our fathers, that has nurtured the blight of demoralizing metropolitanism, a curse alike to old and young and that embodies in its spirit all those indulgences and immoralities which Mr. Wright seems to think constitute a higher phase of existence than any possible extract of a village." [20]

Thus the people of Los Angeles desired the size but not the character of a modern metropolis. They feared that as the price of progress their adopted community would lose its sense of fellow feeling and lower its standards of personal morality. As the region's population and heterogeneity increased and as its territory and industry expanded —as, in sum, Los Angeles emerged as one of the largest agglomerations in the United States—they therefore strove to recreate the cohesive communal life of their former farms and towns. They longed to perpetuate familiar rural relationships within a strange urban society, to reconcile their material ambitions with their psychic imperatives, to combine the spirit of the good community with the substance of the great metropolis.

This aspiration was faithfully reflected in the thought of the Reverend Dana W. Bartlett. Bartlett, a minister born in Maine, reared in Iowa, and then serving as clergyman, author, and social worker in Los Angeles,[21] had the utmost confidence in his adopted community. A committed environmentalist, he attributed communal deterioration elsewhere to ethnic ghettos and physical congestion; an avowed optimist, he considered Los Angeles capable of avoiding these objectionable excrescences. He appealed to his fellow citizens to design their future accordingly. Let us assimilate the immigrants, he proposed;

Americanize the Europeans, and unite the populace. "Let us have a city without tenements, a city without slums," he urged. "Ruralize the city; urbanize the country." [22] The native white majority shared Bartlett's commitments to homogeneity and rusticity. They agreed that the harmony of society depended on the uniformity of its members, and that the integrity of the community required the dispersal of its people. They believed that likeminded persons, joined in voluntary associations and settled in residential suburbs, could prevent "the blight of demoralizing metropolitanism" from spreading over Los Angeles.

From the perspective of the native white Americans, this aspiration seemed eminently practicable. After all, they came from about the same rural, middle-class, native-American backgrounds as their predecessors. They felt no less keen on joining the community and even more committed to their adopted settlement. Moreover, Los Angeles' voluntary associations actively sought their membership. Fraternal orders invited them as brothers; religious congregations welcomed them as worshippers; political clubs appealed to them as voters; commercial organizations solicited their support as businessmen; and civic groups called for their cooperation as citizens.[23] Clearly, no institutional barriers prevented the newcomers from assimilating into the communal life of Los Angeles.

Nor did any insuperable barriers prevent them from settling in the residential suburbs of the metropolis. With few exceptions, they had the necessary wherewithal. Some had enough in savings to live comfortably without working, while others had the skills, capital, and education to gain well-paying jobs, engage in business, serve in professions, and otherwise exploit the opportunities available in an expanding economy.[24] They also allocated a large share of their income to housing. Not only did a suburban home epitomize their vision of the good community, but, in choosing from the many subdivisions in Los Angeles, they encountered no obstacles other than financial in reaching a decision.[25] Sought by subdividers and welcomed by neighbors, the newcomers bought lots and built homes on suburban tracts everywhere in greater Los Angeles. Despite the homogeneity of their voluntary associations, and the rusticity of their residential retreats, however, they failed to recreate the cohesive community so crucial to their personal aspirations.

Voluntary associations integrated the community less effectively in 1930 than in 1885 because they were less relevant to the newcomers.

32. The suburban vision

33. A suburban retreat

Italian, French, and other ethnic organizations became extraneous as the United States rather than western Europe generated the vast numbers of immigrants. Benevolent societies became superfluous as economic progress, welfare legislation, and insurance companies protected residents against unemployment, accident, and death. Music, literary, and drama clubs became moribund when faced with the relentless competition of the radio, popular magazines, and movies. Commercial associations became specialized and impersonal, as they shifted their attention to the region's industrialization. And civic groups became professional and parochial when they confronted complicated policy questions and profound social conflicts.[26] Homogeneity under modern conditions was thus incompatible with traditional institutions.

The churches too fared poorly. Although most newcomers considered religion beneficial, only one in five was affiliated with a congregation in 1927.[27] "I don't know why, but l have no desire to go to church here in the city," a Protestant woman admitted. "Perhaps it is because it is so hard to get acquainted. Then, too, I thought that all people in church were friendly," she added, "but I found that they do not even bother to say 'Good Morning' to a stranger. That was a shock to me and I just didn't want to go back any more."[28] "When I first came to Los Angeles, I was delighted at the number of new members I was receiving into the church," a Protestant minister acknowledged. "I thought the church was growing very rapidly under my leadership. But when I began to check up, I discovered that the church was constantly losing so many members, that I was doing well if I kept the membership stationary."[29] To overcome the sense of anonymity and the secularization of leisure, most churches stressed social at the expense of spiritual affairs; but, except for a few revivalist cults, the congregations were incapable of binding their communicants.

Residential suburbs did not integrate the metropolis either because they discouraged contact among people. Subdivisions provided little or no acreage for common facilities such as parks and plazas. Deed restrictions prohibited the establishment of nearby commercial enterprises that served as centers of social intercourse in other American cities. Even the layouts separated inhabitants from one another, adults from churches and children from schools. Moreover, the interminable lines of streets and the monotonous rows of houses blurred boundaries between sections of the region, and the widespread use of private automobiles inhibited casual contacts that formerly stimulated personal relationships in Los Angeles. The rustic environment so conducive to community life in the tiny, compact, and well-defined town inhibited social interaction in the immense, dispersed, and sprawling metropolis.

Los Angeles' newcomers did join together on a neighborhood basis. As a means of enhancing the value of their real estate, property holders organized to demand railway connections and street improvements.[30] But these business ties rarely led to social relationships. Also, as a means of maintaining the character and structure of their blocks in the face of an alleged "invasion" of Negroes or Orientals or a projected change in the prevailing land-use, homeowners banded together to enforce deed restrictions, pressure municipal legislators, and harass prospective buyers, sellers, and builders.[31] But these outfits mobilized only in response to an immediate challenge. All in all, these associations were so motivated by a sense of exclusivity and limited to a few parts of the metropolis that they provided a poor foundation for more commendable and broader community involvement.

Residential mobility further disrupted voluntary associations and neighborhood ties in Los Angeles. As older houses deteriorated, commercial facilities expanded, and ethnic ghettos spread, homeowners in the central district, who gained from rising property values and felt little attachment to any particular tract, moved—often more than once—to outlying subdivisions. There they erected newer and more comfortable homes. For most persons in Los Angeles, the permanent thus became the utopian. Neighbors scattered all over the city, a woman lamented, and newcomers arrived only to leave, joined groups only to quit, and made friends only to part.[32] Neither extreme residential mobility, ineffective voluntary organizations, nor outlying residential subdivisions was unique to Los Angeles. But nowhere else in the United States did people change address so frequently, associations face so perplexing a task, and suburbs so completely dominate a region.

For these reasons most residents felt extremely isolated after 1900. "Why, I don't even know the name of my next door neighbor," one woman admitted. "I hear the water running in their bath tub as well as or better than I hear it in my own tub. I know what they say and can tell what they are doing, but I don't know what their name is and I have never cared to find out." [33] As a result, loneliness became endemic to Los Angeles. "It is strange not to have any home faces round," a young bride confided in her diary. "I felt so odd among so many and so many miles between me and my home folks." [34] "None of the people round here call on each other and not a single neighbor has invited us in," a middle-aged woman remarked not long after. "We don't know anybody and we don't see much sign of neighboring." Isolation and loneliness also engendered suspicion. "I don't know whether I would like to know my neighbors here," the same woman confessed. "I don't like the way some of them act." "Sometimes I think it's an advantage not to know them too well," her daughter interjected. "But we'd like to know a few real well," her mother replied. "It's lonesome when you don't." [35]

To overcome isolation and relieve loneliness, the people of Los Angeles formed other groups. Here they followed the practices of the European immigrants; but, as they were largely native Americans, membership was based on the state and not the country of birth, and as they sought companionship rather than protection, social intercourse was stressed instead of economic assistance. Pennsylvanians founded the first state society in the 1880's, Iowans organized the largest one in the early 1900's, and nearly all the native Americans established their own by the 1920's. Charles H. Parsons, who federated the state societies of Los Angeles described their appeal as follows: "There are many who come here alone, they have no relatives, possibly no immediate friends; homesickness and lonesomeness naturally follow; possibly one may be almost ready to return to the old home and former friends. Then the opportunity comes to attend one of the famous state picnics or evening social reunions." [36] For the newcomer, Parsons noted, this is the turning point.

"Often one will meet those he knew in the long ago," he explained. "He may only meet those who knew his family and friends, but it is some one from home. Immediately all the outlook changes; homesickness is forgotten, lonesomeness thrown aside. He finds he is not alone out here after all. He went to school with Billy Jones back in Warren county, Ohio. Bill is here. The world grows bright at once. Sure, he will like California and instead of buying a return ticket he buys a home, settles down and becomes a booster for Sunny Southern California." [37] Parsons' enthusiasm aside, the state societies formed only tenuous bonds. Large annual picnics in the city's parks and small monthly meetings in the downtown cafeterias did not compensate for the absence of more frequent contact and more meaningful relationships. Also, the newcomers' children, who knew no state other than California and no life other than the present, found the societies loyalties incomprehensible and its rustic gatherings dull. In time, therefore, the state societies lost their vigor and deteriorated into sanctuaries for a few elderly and uprooted persons. [38]

Hence many newcomers felt frustrated in Los Angeles. "All their lives," novelist Nathaniel West wrote (with some exaggeration), "they had slaved at some kind of labor, behind desks and counters, in the fields and at tedious machines of all sorts, saving their pennies and dreaming of the leisure that would be theirs when they had enough. Finally that day came." They left for southern California, "the land of sunshine and oranges. Once there, they discover that sunshine isn't enough, however. They get tired of oranges, even of avocado pears and passion fruit. Nothing happens. They don't know what to do with their time. They haven't the mental equipment for leisure, the money nor the physical equipment for pleasure." They become painfully disenchanted with Los Angeles. "Did they slave so long just to go to an occasional Iowa picnic? What else is there? They watch the waves come in at Venice. There wasn't an ocean where most of them came from, but after you've seen one wave, you've seen them all. The same is true of airplanes at Glendale." If only a plane would crash once in a while, West suggested, perhaps their boredom would be relieved. "But the planes never crash." [39]

West expected ennui to incite riot and violence in Los Angeles, but here he misinterpreted the character of its population. It is true that these conditions encouraged eccentric thought and erratic action, an inclination to tinker with ideas and to tamper with institutions, among those native Americans who, as one political leader observed, were "peculiarly susceptible to sentimental appeal . . . goodly people ready to accept any guaranteed panacea for peace on earth and good will to men; rather a shallow thinking lot who take their politics, as they do their religion, largely on faith." [40] These persons—among whom, some were attached to "mind cure" (or "New Thought") before coming to Los Angeles, and others were part of the metropolis' unduly large female, elderly, and otherwise uprooted populace—were particularly responsive to a host of individual cranks and organized cults. They made up the vast audiences that listened to Aimee Semple McPherson, the small congregations that chanted along with revivalist preachers, and the lonely supporters of the "Mankind United," "Mighty I Am," and other mystical movements that flourished more in Los Angeles than any other metropolis. [41]

But it is also true that these people were the exceptions. The others who failed to establish meaningful relationships through voluntary groups and suburban neighborhoods—who, as a British couple observed, "seemed to be almost as destitute of permanent friends as they were of personal furniture"—attempted to resolve the disparities between their expectations and experiences in a less aggressive fashion. They sought companionship in their immediate families and divorced their economic and civic interests from their social lives. They also derived their identities less from organizational affiliations than from material acquisitions; "the wireless, the car, the daily newspaper, or the *Saturday Evening Post,* work, cooking, 'studying how to keep thin,'" the British visitors noted, "seemed to fill their lives to the full." [42] Finally, these people intensified, rather than renounced, their commitment to homogeneity and rusticity; and instead of turning toward an activism that encouraged radical alternatives, they drifted toward a personalism that discouraged involvement per se.

The commitment of the native white majority to homogeneity undermined the position of the foreign and colored minorities in Los Angeles between 1885 and 1930. Southeastern Europeans, Mexicans, Japanese, and Negroes, not, as before, northwestern Europeans and Chinese, they numbered around 200,000 or 15 per cent of the city's population in 1930.[43] Attracted by southern California's extravagant publicity, they came not only from abroad but also from the California and Texas countrysides and from southern farms and northern ghettos. Unlike the midwesterners, they moved for traditional economic (and less political) reasons, for opportunity and a decent job rather than for comfort and a well-rounded life. Nonetheless, except for those Mexicans who intended to return home once they accumulated enough money, these people hoped to find a meaningful place in the Los Angeles community. Unfortunately, the white majority so subordinated and segregated the colored minorities—though, admittedly, not each group in the same way or to the same degree—that they were completely frustrated in this modest aspiration.

Their frustration followed in part from economic subordination. These immigrants were not the least capable of their countrymen. Among them were many Mexican mestizos from active towns, semi-skilled Russian Jews and northern Italians, ambitious American Negroes from northern metropolises, and young Japanese educated in their island's modern cities. But even they suffered severe handicaps in Los Angeles. Whatever their nationality or race, most had been common laborers or agricultural workers in their native lands; many arrived in the United States with less than forty dollars, and few came to Southern California with appreciably more. Hence they lacked the skills and capital requisite for advancement in an urban economy. "When one is blind in the house of a money-changer," one Mexican asked, commenting on his dependency, "who does the counting?"

"Aie!" his friend replied, "this is like being in the house of the soap-maker. He who does not fall, slips." [44]

A few overcame these disadvantages by grasping the opportunities generated by their own groups or, exploiting their differences, by opening ethnic restaurants and curio shops. But most had no alternative other than to compete in a labor market where, as Table 23 reveals, they qualified for only the least responsible and rewarding positions. They laid tracks, repaired pavements, slaughtered animals, hauled lumber, labored in factories, fisheries, and canneries, and served as domestics, waiters, janitors, and elevator operators.[45] Those who in time acquired the necessary skills encountered the racial prejudice of employers who claimed that white personnel would not work alongside colored persons. Thus the most capable of these immigrants entered private business when they accumulated a little capital or

TABLE 23. Nonwhite Males as a Percentage of the Male Working Force in Selected Occupational Divisions and Occupations, Los Angeles, 1930

Occupations	Negro		Other[a]	
All occupations	3.1%		9.5%	
Manufacturing and mechanical industries:	2.1		10.7	
Laborers and helpers in construction		8.2		38.0
Managers and officials		0.1		0.6
Transportation and communication:	5.6		13.0	
Chauffeurs and drivers		8.3		6.8
Owners and managers		4.3		2.5
Trade:	1.0		5.5	
Laborers, porters, and helpers in stores		18.3		25.2
Real estate agents and officials		0.8		0.7
Public service:	5.5		2.5	
Laborers		27.1		10.1
Firemen		2.0		0.6
Professional service:	1.6		2.9	
Lawyers, judges, and justices		0.5		0.8
Physicians and surgeons		1.7		2.1
Domestic and personal service:	13.8		19.1	
Janitors and sextons		31.1		14.6
Porters (not in stores)		72.7		10.3
Servants		8.0		32.0

Source: U.S. Bureau of the Census, *Fifteenth Census of the United States: 1930. Population. Volume IV* (Washington, 1933), pp. 199–202.

[a] Principally Mexicans and Japanese.

government service where official policy precluded blatant discrimination. Still, so long as they were restricted, as one Oriental complained, to those jobs unwanted by the Americans, they had to accept less challenging and remunerative employment than their abilities warranted.[46]

Their frustration resulted in part from residential segregation too. Many single men who planned to save their earnings and then return home were not inclined to spend much money on housing. Many families that did intend to settle in Los Angeles lacked the confidence to move away from their group and the wherewithal to purchase a house. Hence the Mexicans, American Negroes, Japanese, and, less so, the southeastern Europeans rented quarters in the deteriorating downtown district and outlying industrial sections. There, like immigrants in other Amercan cities, they congregated in ethnic ghettos.[47] "When I first came here," a young Japanese woman remarked about the small fishing colony off the Bay of San Pedro in which she lived, "I never thought that I was in America. Everything was the same as in my small home in Japan. All our neighbors were Japanese. We [all] knew each other."[48]

A few secure and successful Mexicans, Negroes, and Japanese, who shared with the native Americans the rustic ideal, attempted to acquire private homes in residential suburbs after the First World War. But, as the prevailing concept of the good community excluded races other than white and classes other than middle, they found themselves barred from subdivisions in greater Los Angeles by restrictive covenants. "I realize now," one Oriental lamented after a fruitless hunt for a single-family house, "that the Americans do not want to live close to us even though they want us to become Americans."[49] Even where racial covenants had never been imposed or had already expired, nonwhites often encountered the resistance of nearby property holders. "Negroes," a Santa Monica newspaper informed of a proposed development for colored people warned, "We don't want you here; now and forever, this is to be a white man's town."[50] The ethnic minorities were thus confined to undesirable districts, such as Watts, subdivided exclusively for them and to deteriorating neighborhoods, such as West Adams, where the white majority was unwilling to remain. There they formed the colored ghettos of suburban Los Angeles.[51]

The minorities also shared little in the community life of Los Angeles. This is not to deny that public discrimination decreased between 1885 and 1930. The Board of Education ceased separating schoolchildren by race; the Civil Service Commission discontinued drawing lists for nonwhites; and the Playground Board stopped closing its facilities to Negroes. But it is to say that assorted and more subtle kinds of prejudice persisted. *De facto* if not *de jure* segregation pervaded the school system; white persons secured the top positions in the local government; and a court order was required to compel the Playground Commissioners to integrate their swimming pools.[52] Even more upsetting to the Mexicans, Negroes, and Japanese, they were often refused food in restaurants, rooms in hotels, tickets at theaters, rides in jitneys, and other services in public accommodations. They were also denied communion by religious congregations, brotherhood by fraternal orders, affiliations by commercial organizations, and membership in the metropolis' other voluntary associations.[53]

The ethnic groups participated little in politics too. Transient, uninterested, and ill-informed, the Mexicans felt more concern about government in Mexico City than in Los Angeles. They do not vote or otherwise participate in politics, a prominent progressive noted; "the politicians do not base their strength upon them." [54] Deprived by Congress of the privileges of American citizenship, the Japanese refused to accept the corresponding responsibilities. As alien nationals, they sought redress for grievances through the Japanese consulate rather than the municipal legislature. Only the Negroes, who had no other outlet and no other recourse, paid much attention to public affairs in the metropolis.[55] But they had little influence in a city where the electorate was overwhelmingly white and the government was not organized by wards. The weakness of the minorities perpetuated their subordination; and from the viewpoint of the white majority, their inadequacies justified their segregation. Exploited economically, separated residentially, isolated socially, and ignored politically, these people remained entirely outside the Los Angeles community between 1885 and 1930.

Each ethnic group reacted to the situation in its own way. The southeastern Europeans, who diverged least from the native Americans, slowly but steadily assimilated into the majority. The Mexicans, who held the deepest hope and best chance to return home, retained a strong sense of nationality; so long as they could cross and recross the border, they did not feel obliged to recreate Mexico in Los Angeles. The Japanese, to the contrary, fully appreciated the distance to Japan and the irreversibility of their migration; while adhering to the materialistic ethos of their adopted nation, they tried to preserve the traditional rituals of the Orient. And the Negroes, who had no nation other than America, appealed to the native whites to acknowledge and implement their democratic heritage in Los Angeles.[56] Notwithstanding these differences, however, the minorities were all forced to mobilize their own resources and form their own communities.

Like the native Americans, the colored people sought companionship, security, protection, and unity in voluntary associations. The Mexicans established benevolent societies and attended Catholic churches; the Japanese founded nationality groups and built Buddhist shrines; and the Negroes organized state societies and formed colored congregations. These minorities also sponsored commercial organizations and supported ethnic newspapers which, in addition to binding their members socially, served as intermediaries between them and the white community. Created in response to tangible and pressing personal problems, these voluntary associations often showed exceptional vigor. Asked why the Japanese organizations were so strong, one of their leaders replied in terms almost, but not quite, as appropriate for the Mexicans and the Negroes: "If such disadvantages for them did not occur because of the fact that they are Japanese, perhaps the Japanese association would not have so firm a hold." [57]

Conditions in the metropolis were not conducive to the stability of these organizations, however. Many Mexicans left Los Angeles for their homeland, some Japanese quit their jobs to become truck farmers, and a few Negroes sought more promising opportunities in the countryside. Among those who stayed in the metropolis, the more successful moved from crowded commercial sections to outlying suburban ghettos, depriving the voluntary groups of their leaders. Even if the membership and the leadership had remained constant, moreover, these organizations would still have lacked the economic and political resources to realize their aspirations.[58] While these associations fared better than their white counterparts, then, they did not fully compensate the Mexicans, Japanese, or Negroes for the disabilities they labored under in Los Angeles.

To compound these difficulties, the voluntary associations, like the state societies, had little appeal for the second generation. Educated in the public schools and exhilarated by American freedom, the youngsters felt encumbered by the affiliations of their ancestors. The parents, as aware of the frustrations of American life as the children were of its promises, warned against this powerful attraction. But they paid them no heed. "They saw so many changes that they didn't know where to stop," one troubled woman remarked. "They didn't interfere with our plans then as they do now; they didn't talk back to us; they were obedient, but they seemed so excited. They learned English rapidly. Of course, we were glad of it, but we were also sorry. That made them too smart. But we couldn't get along without the language. Besides when they learned English they started to talk English among themselves, and we were at once divided: the 'old Russians' and the 'young Americans.' Oh they were faithful and devoted to us, but we just seemed to lose them right along. And the longer we stay here, the greater the difference between the old and young." [59]

Without the active participation of the second generation, the benevolent societies, religious congregations, and even commercial associations were less able to assimilate the newcomers, tie them together, protect their interests, and promote their goals. Without the firm support of the community organizations, the cohesive southeastern European, Mexican, Japanese (and the less stable Negro) families were gradually fragmented; their traditions were disrupted, their values undermined, and their cultures weakened.[60] In time, moreover, the children discovered that the old could not be thoroughly discarded nor the new entirely assimilated, and that they belonged to the minority they denied even more than to the majority they emulated. "Daily new philosophies are poured into my ear, and new ideas collect around me," a young woman of a separatist Russian sect remarked, "But the voices of those ancient monks rise up within me [and] compel me to admit . . . that I am a random dissatisfied soul." [61]

In response to the disintegration of their communities and cultures, the ethnic minorities also adopted the racism, nativism, and conservatism of the white majority that so effectively excluded them. The Mexicans attempted to dissociate themselves from *los tintos;* the Negroes insisted that the Japanese be treated as foreigners; and the Japanese contrasted their enterprise with the Mexicans' backwardness.[62] They exploited these ideologies as a means of elevating themselves at the expense of others, a practice that was outrageous on the part of the white Americans and pathetic on the part of their colored countrymen. Like the majority, the minorities also attempted to secure personal satisfaction by limiting their horizons to the individual and the family, the job and the home. But they were discriminated against as individuals, frustrated as spouses and parents, offered only the most menial employment, and confined to the least desirable neighborhoods. In a metropolis that promised a fuller life and opportunity to all, their subordination and segregation was particularly appalling.

Throughout these years, as an eminent sociologist wrote, Los Angeles' minority groups existed "in intimate economic dependence, but in more or less complete cultural independence of the world about them." [63] This situation was not, of course, unique here; indeed, nowhere in the United States did minorities enjoy complete equality and integration. But in Los Angeles, where they were distinguished by race rather than nationality, the majority subjugated and excluded them even more rigorously. Their plight reflected the anxieties of the native whites, and yet even they failed to recreate a coherent community. The interpersonal and institutional life of Los Angeles in the early 1930's was thus summarized, according to one scholar, in one word: disintegration.[64] Hence the fragmented society of the white majority complemented the isolated communities of the ethnic minorities and, along with the dispersal and decentralization of the metropolis, emerged as integral features of twentieth-century Los Angeles.[65]

[The progressives] came to the conclusion that the great vice in municipal politics was the mixing of national party politics with city affairs, and they concluded that what Los Angeles needed was non-partisanship in its municipal government, and decided that they would undertake to organize to that end. (Meyer Lissner, 1909)

10 THE POLITICS OF PROGRESSIVISM

Politics and government underwent profound changes in Los Angeles as the town expanded into a metropolis. Between 1850 and 1865 power was so extraneous to the interests of the townspeople that politics attracted little attention. Candidates occasionally contested for office, but citizens seldom voted in elections, and legislators rarely met to conduct public affairs.[1] After the Civil War, however, population and territorial growth compelled the authorities to assume a more active involvement in municipal affairs. They had to decide whether and on what terms to permit public utilities to operate, and whether and where to allow railway lines to run. They also had to determine whether to undertake improvements by contracting with local businessmen or by creating public departments, and how rigorously to enforce ordinances regulating and prohibiting vice. Once the actions of the mayor and common council so affected the fortunes of their constituents, political participation became as intense in Los Angeles as in other small American cities.

Government policies, to begin with, influenced the expenditures, revenues, and future prospects of the Los Angeles Water Company. By the 1868 contract, the municipal authorities reserved the right to oversee service, set rates, enfranchise competitors, revoke privileges, and extend the lease or repossess the works.[2] Los Angeles Water thus felt obliged to hold enough political power to assure favorable treatment by the town's officials. The municipality not only exercised similar authority over the charges, service, and competitive positions of the gas and electric companies, but also purchased a large block of energy for street lighting. If the common council ordered lower prices or higher quality, it would sharply reduce corporate profits; if it shifted from gas to electricity or vice-versa, it would promote the fortunes of one group of entrepreneurs at the expense of another.[3] These utilities, as a result, took a keen interest in local government; but, split between as well as within the gas and electric industries, they exerted less pressure on municipal affairs than Los Angeles Water.

Municipal action shaped the course of the street railways too. Although the council had to adhere to state specifications regarding fares, service, schedules, and routes, it retained the right to fix the tenure of the grant, choose the time for bidding, and accept or reject the offers. Its discretion not only tempted the railwaymen to compete for privileges, but also compelled the winners to remain politically active in order to protect their investments.[4] The steam railroads, which requested franchises less often, also found it advantageous to keep in contact with local legislators. Like the public utilities and street railways, they desired some check over the assessor and other officials whose decisions affected the distribution of their earnings. Even more important, the steam railroads wanted the cooperation of southern California's representatives in Sacramento and Washington.[5] Between 1865 and 1900, then, the water, gas, and electric companies, the street railway lines, and the Southern Pacific Railroad were the most influential participants in Los Angeles politics.

Municipal responsibility to improve roads, clean streets, collect garbage, preserve order, and fight fires created still other contacts between public authority and private enterprise. Although the council had to advertise for bids and accept the lowest one, the legislators set the specifications for the contracts and evaluated the responsibility of the bidders. Since the streets could be surfaced with gravel or concrete, among other coverings, the selection made bidding a formality so long as separate concerns specialized in different materials. Since the garbage collectors included special concessions in their propositions, competition in that business, one critic complained, offered "a continual temptation to use money and personal and political influence to secure contracts."[6] And since the police and fire commissioners and chiefs received appointment by reason of their political affiliations, the merchants who supplied the departments and the persons who worked for them were obliged to assist in municipal campaigns.[7]

Finally, the authorities forced a host of unsavory characters to enter politics by prohibiting gambling, restricting prostitution, and regulating saloons. While gamblers who considered protection as legitimate an expense as equipment bribed underpaid patrolmen, businessmen who rented rooms as gambling dens persuaded the police commission to tolerate lax law enforcement.[8] Though even clergymen conceded the inevitability of prostitution, the alternative policy of segregation presented opportunities galore for remunerative arrangements between pimps, policemen, landlords, and officials.[9] When the common council responded to temperance sentiment by limiting the number of saloons and granting licenses only to reputable citizens, wealthy brewers—who acquired the licenses and owned the saloons—organized to oppose prohibitionist proposals that would have depreciated their investments.[10] All these groups attempted to protect their livelihoods by devising a political accommodation between the morality and the appetites of the townspeople.

In time—in Los Angeles as in most American cities—private enterprises affected by public authority found it advantageous to form a political machine to promote their economic interests. The machine's essential task was to pick candidates and elect them to local office; its success assured regional support for the Southern Pacific, sympathetic consideration for the business concerns, and extended tenure for the officeholders.* To this end, the transcontinental railroad provided leadership, the corporate utilities, public works contractors, and liquor dealers, among many others, supplied funds, and the municipal employees donated labor.[11] Between 1865 and 1900 the machine remained in power because it managed not only to satisfy Los Angeles' major business interests (which were also its principal political forces), but also to adapt its own operations to the city's chief governmental constraints—its party system and its political localism.

The Los Angeles electorate was divided between Democrats and Republicans, even though the popular commitment to party rule was extremely pragmatic. Before the 1880's, the Democratic majority praised partisan loyalty, while the Republican minority damned it. "This is a Democratic city," the Los Angeles *Daily News* declared in 1869, "and fidelity to party organization demands that we nominate and elect a Democratic ticket entire." "If the people of this city feel that they can afford to let the control over their local government go into the hands of political parties," a Republican newspaper insisted to the contrary in 1876, "they should be prepared to see some Boss fasten himself permanently upon our public affairs and become the Dictator of our little commonwealth." [12] But afterwards, when the

---

*The machine also offered social outlets and welfare benefits, but so long as Los Angeles was small and prosperous, these functions were less important there than in larger cities inhabited by impoverished European immigrants.

influx of midwesterners increased the Republican ranks and they won complete control of the municipal government, the Democrats urged the electorate to measure the man rather than the label while the Republicans appealed for strict organizational discipline.[13]

Fortunately for the bosses, who would otherwise have been hard pressed to maintain control, ideological differences between Democrats and Republicans did not extend to municipal affairs. In basic agreement on matters of principle, the parties regularly prepared similar platforms. Each called for honest and efficient administration, reduction of taxes, and maintenance of services; each endorsed a nonpartisan school system, the development of water resources, and later municipalization of the domestic waterworks. Each also expressed concern for the workingman, urged prosecution of criminals, and promised to prevent corporate exploitation.[14] With like understanding of political realities, the parties pursued the same aims as well. Each sought to conceal the discrepancies between the exigencies of electoral financing and the rhetoric of campaign oratory; each tried to preserve the precarious balance between the pressures of the corporations and the expectations of the populace. Each, in essence, strove to meet the demands of the interests without arousing the opposition of the voters.

Still, political power in Los Angeles resided ultimately not in the parties but in the wards. For though municipal authority was vested in a mayor and common council which were in theory an independent and balanced executive and legislature, the council was in fact dominant. It enjoyed the right to appoint many of the mayor's subordinates, to order public improvements without his consent, and to override his veto of any ordinance.[15] Only occasionally, as when the mayor blocked action by the council in the controversy over the sale of the waterworks in 1868, did the executive intrude on the legislature's efforts to shape governmental policy. "While it is very necessary that first-class men should fill the charter [city-wide] offices," one citizen pointed out in 1869, "the people will not forget that the real power to do good or injury to the city reposes in the council." [16] This situation remained essentially unchanged during the next three decades.

For this reason—and also because the wards were easier to manage than the city and councilmen easier to elect than mayors—the machine operated most actively on the local level.[17] Before every municipal election, its leaders met with the party faithful of each district to select candidates for the council and representatives to the conventions that chose contenders for the city-wide offices. More often than not, the machine's nominees were endorsed. During the campaign the bosses lent them—Democrats and Republicans alike—financial and other assistance, for they cared little which party won so long as the winners acknowledged their dependence on the machine. Once in power these officials were usually receptive to its appeals. They could not always favor its requests in the face of a hostile public; nor could the machine always resolve disagreements among its constituents. But popular opinion seldom expressed itself clearly enough to preclude discretion, and internal conflict rarely exceeded the organization's capacity for compromise. By dint of hard work and shrewd strategy, the machine controlled the majority party, dominated the common council, and effectively ruled Los Angeles.

Machine rule did not pass without protest, however. "As soon as there is a chance for a change in the City Council, or any of the city officers," one resident wrote in the 1870's, "this fact is considered sufficient grounds by some for an attack on the Council, and a stranger would think, after reading our city papers and listening to our street croakers, that our Municipal Government had always been in the hands of thieves and robbers . . . [Yet] at each election," he noted, "the best talent and most honorable men are selected by the people and urged into the field and chase, by large majorities, to take care of the city interests." [18] This paradox reflected the confusion of many citizens who believed frugal administration compatible with liberal improvements and found taxes outrageously high and services incredibly inadequate. They attributed this situation to a corrupt political ring, consisting of businessmen and officials, which exploited the townspeople in order to gain profits and win elections.[19] Admittedly a simplification, this analysis reflected growing dissatisfaction with the accommodation between private enterprise and public authority in Los Angeles.

These critics attempted to reform municipal government after the boom of the 1880's by forming a Board of Freeholders and drafting a new charter which would have effectively subverted the position of the machine in Los Angeles. The board proposed to constrict the parties by placing official departments under nonpartisan commissions, to weaken the council by enlarging the mayor's powers of appointment and removal, and to eliminate the wards by reducing the number of legislators and electing them at large. Defenders of the existing governmental structure, including the bosses and the councilmen, vigorously protested these innovations, warning that a stronger executive and a smaller legislature might create an omnipotent machine. The voters, far less dissatisfied with local politics than the reformers, rejected the document. A new and more conservative Board of Freeholders then prepared another charter which stressed efficiency, avoided nonpartisanship, endorsed the common council, retained the ward system, and otherwise so respected present realities that it secured electoral approval in 1888.[20]

The dissenters renewed their efforts in the 1890's. Under the auspices of the Municipal Reform Association and the League for Better City Government, they designated reform candidates whose campaigns, though consistently unavailing, had profound implications for politics in Los Angeles. For unlike earlier reform flurries, which were primarily attempts by the minority party to divide and defeat the majority, this nonpartisan rebellion was essentially a protest by Republicans no less opposed to their own organization than to the Democrats.[21] The League for Better City Government also attempted to revise the 1889 charter. It drafted a document which would have inhibited the parties, strengthened the mayor, eliminated the wards, and applied civil service rules to subordinate officials. Although it failed of passage in 1896, it did receive substantial support. "I have the consolation," a citizen active in framing the charter wrote, "that the old political leaders declared that a document containing so many radical reforms all at once could not possibly be rammed down the throats of these people and that they are all astonished that we marshaled so many thousand votes for it." [22]

The machine remained in power in 1900, but the reformers refused to return to their party. "Locally the Republican majority is narrow," one wrote, explaining his position, "and it has a very corrupt element —an insidious kind of corruption not that of out and out rascals such as we have who give themselves completely away every time, but smooth lawyers, church-tending merchants and all that." [23] Those who agreed with him believed that these persons debased politics and demoralized society. "The best men could not be induced to enter . . . packed caucuses, primaries and conventions," one recalled, "and the men who wanted office badly enough to do so, and who had to sell their souls to a political boss to secure nominations, were usually no better than the people who tolerated such conditions deserved." [24] Concluding that politics had passed beyond popular control, the reformers decided to challenge the machine once again, hoping that it was, as one observer wrote, so "loaded down with gas meters, asphalt, saloon licenses and trolley cars," as to be vulnerable to a widespread and intensive political offensive.

This challenge marked the introduction into Los Angeles of political progressivism, an integral component of the reform movement that swept the United States after 1900. What made progressivism so vigorous there was that Los Angeles was inhabited for the most part not, as other metropolises, by European immigrants dependent on and bound to the machine,[25] but by native Americans who shared the reformers' sentiments. Like the reformers, these newcomers were revolted by the debasement and irresponsibility of local government in the United States and appalled by the prospect that the sordid political practices of corrupt eastern cities might prevail in Los Angeles. For these reasons the reformers and the newcomers—led by native Americans often prominent in business and the professions—joined forces as progressives to destroy the machine. They knew that if they were to succeed their organization had to be as efficient as the machine and their leadership as dedicated as the bosses and that lofty designs to reorganize governmental structure had to be complemented by practical schemes to gain political power.[26] At stake in this struggle, they believed, was the future of Los Angeles.

The progressives subscribed to a coherent diagnosis of politics and government in Los Angeles. They assumed that a lack not an excess of democracy and the imperfections not the inadequacies of representation rendered city government unresponsive. They also thought that the problems of urbanization required an enlargement of municipal authority which, so long as conscientious officials exercised it, would be compatible with the general welfare. Along with Theodore Roosevelt, they attributed the success of the machine to the party loyalty of the voters and considered a thorough separation of local politics from state and national affairs imperative.[27] They also postulated, without defining, so fundamental an agreement about the goals of the metropolis that the functions of city government became administrative instead of legislative, a matter of executing rather than of determining policy. For them Los Angeles was "simply a huge [business] corporation . . . [whose] citizens are the stockholders, and [whose] purpose is not to produce dividends but to promote the well-being of the community and to conserve the interests of the people as a whole."[28]

To implement these theories the progressives formed a host of reform groups, some of which attempted to revitalize democracy in Los Angeles by revising the governmental structure. Among these was the Direct Legislation League founded by Dr. John R. Haynes. The league was so confident in the electorate—it referred to it as "the honest majority"—and so suspicious of its representatives that it proposed to entrust the citizenry with the power to initiate legislation, veto laws, and remove officials—the initiative, referendum, and recall.[29] Direct legislation, Haynes and his followers insisted, was consistent with the country's political traditions: "It is simply the principle of the American town meeting applied to the conditions of city life," they explained. On these grounds the league, along with other progressive associations, persuaded a Board of Freeholders to draft a charter amendment providing for the initiative, referendum, and recall. The electorate was so impressed by direct legislation's capacity to restrain as well as to remedy governmental malfeasance that it overwhelmingly endorsed the proposition in 1900.

Other groups tried to remove the conditions that originally spawned the machine. To sever the connection between private enterprise and governmental authority—and so reduce the organization's principal source of funds—they persistently promoted municipal ownership of public utilities. They aided in municipalizing Los Angeles' water, harbor, and electric power after 1900, and planned the municipalization of its gas, telephone, and street railways in the near future.[30] To liberate city employees from political bosses—and thus curtail the organization's primary supply of labor—they successfully sponsored the establishment of nonpartisan administrative boards. At the same time they demanded the application of a civil service system so that most appointive officials would be selected by competitive examination and removed only for incompetence. In 1902, in yet another triumph, they persuaded the electorate to approve a charter amendment that created the Los Angeles Board of Civil Service Commissioners.[31]

Still other groups endeavored to reform politics by electing progressives to office. Among them was a Good Government Organization which formed a Non-Partisan City Central Committee to wrest power from the machine. The committee was, of necessity, led by Republicans. Otherwise, as Meyer Lissner, a successful attorney, explained, "the cry would at once have gone up that [the revolt] was for the purpose of boosting democrats into office in a republican municipality and it would have been doomed to failure."[32] The committee nominated a ticket led by Lee Gates that was, it promised, "unhampered by pledges, unfettered by obligations, and uncontrolled by a political master" and presented it to the Republican convention in 1906. The party regulars rudely rejected it and selected instead a ticket headed by Walter Lindley. But the progressives, who entered as independents, attracted so much support from the Republican majority that the machine jettisoned Lindley in favor of Democrat Arthur Harper. Although Harper won the mayoralty and the Republicans retained control of the council, Gates ran ahead of Lindley, and the reformers gained a few seats in the legislature[33]—an achievement of no little significance.

This victory aroused the reformers, and a group representing the city's progressive organizations and commercial associations drafted a revised charter in 1908. The machine still controlled a majority of the council, however, and the legislature refused to call a special election to choose a Board of Freeholders. The Good Government League, stymied by the council's opposition, then incorporated the cardinal provisions of this document into charter amendments and circulated an initiative proposition forcing the legislators to hold an election early in 1909. The amendments, which provided for direct primaries and nonpartisan elections as well as for a council selected at large, were as essential to the progressives' aspirations as they were subversive of the machine's operations. Both passed by handsome margins, eliminating the partisanship and localism that had characterized Los Angeles politics for a generation and strengthening the progressives in subsequent efforts to take over municipal government.[34]

A short time before this election was held, moreover, a prosecuting attorney accused the mayor of conspiring with the police chief and a notorious gangster to monopolize the city's prostitution trade. When Harper replied to this charge by appointing the police chief to the Board of Public Works—which was responsible for construction of the $23 million Owens Valley aqueduct—the progressives decided to remove him. They not only gathered enough signatures for a recall election, but, led by Edwin T. Earl, a millionaire reformer and newspaper publisher, also uncovered evidence that forced Harper to retire from politics. The bosses were completely discredited, wrote Charles D. Willard, editor of the progressive *Pacific Outlook:* "We have raided their meetings, captured their people, pulled down their leaders, taken away their newspapers, riddled them, wrecked them, as I never saw it done in any campaign." [35] The reformers, drawing support from Los Angeles' rapidly growing native-American middle class, roundly routed the machine in the election, and a progressive administration headed by Mayor George Alexander gained control of the municipal government in 1909.

The reformers had succeeded well beyond their expectations, and according to progressive social theory—which held that harmony was natural and conflict aberrant—Los Angeles should have been free of political controversy henceforth. To the dismay of the reformers, however, the metropolis was soon after sundered by even more bitter battles. The progressive victory in 1909 overshadowed but did not diminish the impressive performance of the socialists, who, appealing to municipal ownership advocates, trade union members, and Socialist party sympathizers, received far more votes than the machine and almost as many as the Good Government Organization. The Alexander administration soon after cemented the radical alliance by implementing municipalization at a pace too slow for its proponents and by passing an antipicketing ordinance which turned organized labor from economic to political action.[36] In 1911, therefore, the Socialist party and the Union Labor Political Club chose attorney Job Harriman as their mayoralty candidate, while the Republicans selected former auditor W. C. Mushet and the reformers renominated Mayor Alexander. Harriman conducted a vigorous primary campaign in which he denounced progressive management of the aqueduct and the harbor and promised more efficient and equitable administration of local government. He also stressed the Socialist commitment to municipal ownership of monopolies, not public control over production, and its dedication to improved conditions for the laboring class, not eventual expropriation of the propertied groups.

To the astonishment of the progressives, Harriman's ticket won a large plurality. "Superficially," Charles D. Willard observed, "the Socialists all but captured the city government and they may do it when the election takes place in December."[37] Although the reformers, with the Republicans, held a majority of the votes, they were exceedingly anxious about the runoff between Harriman and Alexander. For this reason the Los Angeles *Examiner,* a Hearst paper, which like almost all the metropolitan dailies opposed the Socialists, urged the formation of a nonpartisan group to help re-elect the mayor. Several reformers and regulars, in response, established a Citizens Committee of One Hundred and joined forces with the Good Government Organization. They denied that the administration had mismanaged the aqueduct and the harbor and claimed that it had approved the antipicketing law to prevent union domination. They argued that Harriman's plans for public ownership would bankrupt Los Angeles and urged the voters to overcome their differences in order, as Alexander put it, "to save the city."[38]

The city's press and commercial associations also sounded the alert, while the Socialist party and trade unions canvassed for Harriman. Then, during a campaign already complicated by the recent enfranchisement of women, the conservative Los Angeles *Times* building was dynamited. When two labor organizers confessed to the crime,

Harriman, who had made little headway among Mushet's supporters, lost any chance of victory. Alexander and the Good Government Organization won by a majority of not quite two to one.[39] Unfortunately for progressivism in Los Angeles, however, its leaders remained largely oblivious to the irreparable damage done their movement. Not only had they accepted regular assistance to re-elect reform candidates, but also, by adopting the position that Los Angeles could not survive a socialist administration, they had stressed the metropolis' conservatism at the expense of its progressivism. From this perspective, the election of 1911 was a referendum between the Republicans and the Socialists, from which the progressives, who acceded to this dichotomy, emerged as the losers.

A few reformers acknowledged this. "It seems to me," John J. Hamilton wrote, "that one more local alliance between the progressives and standpatters of Los Angeles such as that of the last municipal campaign will result in thoroughly discrediting and probably wrecking the progressive movement."[40] But not even they knew how to perpetuate their power. Clearly, the reformers could not imitate the machine. Committed to municipal ownership, they could not solicit funds from public utilities, and bound to civil service, they could not impress government employees during local elections. Nor could they count much on organizational discipline or loyalty. The leaders, for whom politics was not a livelihood, were often unwilling to compromise differences, and their followers, for whom party regularity was anathema, were—in Willard's words—always "ready to flare up at the slightest dictation." Finally, the progressives could not expect to escape future challenges. Despite their expectations, Los Angeles was still embroiled in political controversy, and despite their reforms, municipal government was still subject to political pressures.[41]

The reformers had nonetheless made considerable progress in less than a decade. They instituted direct legislation, expanded municipal ownership, established civil service, and gained control of the mayor and common council. They also inaugurated primary elections, removed party designations, increased the executive's power, and eliminated the councilmanic wards. But they now feared that the antiquated charter of 1889 jeopardized their accomplishments.[42] They believed that it obscured official responsibility, contributed to governmental complexity, and so prevented the voters from overseeing their representatives. They attributed these conditions to the separation of powers among the mayor, council, and department chiefs—a principle they considered inappropriate because it held municipal government to be a political rather than an administrative function and encouraged conflict instead of harmony in its operation.[43] They therefore called for a charter that would strengthen progressivism in Los Angeles by emphasizing agreement not contention, efficiency not compromise, and expertise not representation.

The commission form of government, which concentrated power and divided responsibility among a group of elected officials, well filled this prescription. In 1912, accordingly, the progressive council appointed a committee, dominated by Lissner and Haynes, to draft a new charter along this basis. The committee promised to clarify the fundamental principles of city government and grant Los Angeles the widest possible range of powers. It then consolidated recent reforms such as direct legislation, municipal ownership, civil service, and nonpartisanship. Even more important, it created a commission of seven members. Each member was placed in charge of a single department, and all were made responsible for public policy. The committee, Lissner announced, has devised "a businesslike system of government having a small, thoroughly responsible governing body of well paid officials who are required to give all of their time to the business of the city." [44] "It is doubtful," the other members boasted, "whether any charter ever submitted to any American city so thoroughly embodies the views of the leading authorities on municipal government as does the Los Angeles plan now proposed." [45]

The document encountered vigorous opposition from regular Republicans and Democrats who contended that it was an infamous compromise between Lissner's centralism and Haynes's socialism and warned that the progressive commission would undertake extravagant municipal enterprises. No less important, the charter suffered severe criticism from Los Angeles reformers. Some claimed that small cities alone were suited to commission government and that the metropolis' immense populace needed direct representation, while others argued that the abolition of nonpartisan boards and their replacement by individual commissioners would undermine the reformed bureaucracy. The Freeholders forcefully denied these allegations. But they could not convince the electorate that the document was not a radical departure from tradition, and to their dismay the voters decisively disapproved of their handiwork.[46]

The 1912 defeat, followed by Alexander's retirement in 1913, left the progressives poorly prepared for the forthcoming election. Lissner, who had alienated Haynes by weakening the municipal ownership provision in the abortive charter, therefore called a Municipal Conference of conservative reformers and regular Republicans. Like its predecessor, the Citizens Committee of 1911, it selected a ticket (headed by John W. Shenk), pledged to support the campaign, and planned to disband afterwards. Earl, who was not consulted by Lissner, then organized the radical reformers into a People's Campaign Committee which endorsed Shenk but chose an otherwise separate slate. The socialists renominated Job Harriman, while the regulars settled on Harry Rose. In the primary, Shenk received a plurality and Rose, who ran as an independent, secured the second spot. But in the runoff Rose, who attacked Lissner and Earl and smeared Shenk as their stooge, carried enough of Harriman's backers to triumph in a startling upset by a five to four majority. Of the councilmen-elect, five were affiliated with the Municipal Conference, four with the People's Committee, one was a socialist, and another an independent.[47] Thus the reformers lost control about as abruptly as they had won it.

The reform movement never regained its momentum. This was due in part to the passing of progressive leadership and the redirection of progressive aspirations. Willard died in 1914, and the *California Outlook,* for want of subscribers, folded four years later. Earl died in 1918, the *Tribune* ceased publication, and the *Express* turned conservative. Lissner devoted his energies to state-wide affairs, and Haynes concentrated on municipal ownership of electricity. Among the others, a few suffered misgivings about the movement, and even more believed that it had achieved its goals. After all, the reformers had destroyed the machine, defeated the parties, and, through charter amendments, increased administrative responsibility. Finally, those who felt that Los Angeles was still tainted by politics and that its government was still in need of modernization channeled the progressive impulse from a concern for democracy to a quest for efficiency, demanding not substantive reforms but procedural innovations such as an executive budget, centralized purchasing, and standardized salaries.[48]

The reform movement also failed to regain its momentum because private enterprise changed its political attitudes and techniques. By contrast with their predecessors, one councilman explained, businesses affected by municipal authority no longer "expect to 'own' or 'control' public officials exclusively." "All that [the] big interests hope for is to get a fair proportion of courtesies and favors." As important parts of the metropolitan economy, they believe that they are "entitled to [a] fair degree of consideration from public servants." Hence they contribute small sums to the favorites in the primaries and larger amounts to the winners. "A man who gets into the finals [is] not supposed to fig up for himself. But no one corporation [is] supposed to carry the burden for any candidate. Since, when he gets into office, the affairs of all the big interests will come up before him again and again, it is up to them to take out a sort of indemnity insurance." [49] This sophisticated approach, which only the most ardent progressives found objectionable, precluded implacable confrontations between business pressures and reform impulses.

The demise of reform notwithstanding, progressivism profoundly affected Los Angeles politics. True, it did not eradicate politics. Direct legislation became a political technique, municipal ownership a source of conflict, and civil servants a political force. But it did shift the locus of power in Los Angeles. The strong mayor, a large council, and appointive administrators all derived their authority from city-wide rather than ward constituencies. Reform destroyed the traditional devices for organizing politics too. With the parties defunct and the machine dismantled, the bosses had no way to reach the voters and no means to influence the government. Progressivism also compelled the candidates to appeal to the entire electorate, placing priority on publicity rather than familiarity and on finances instead of favors. Hence it weakened the position of local groups such as neighborhood associations, ethnic minorities, and radical activists and increased the importance of metropolitan institutions such as daily newspapers, civic clubs, business interests, and commercial organizations. Although other American cities were heading in this political direction, Los Angeles, with its overwhelming native-American majority, arrived there first.

These changes, which were not incompatible with reform aspirations, produced extraordinarily uneventful and unenlightened politics after 1913. The candidates were without exception men of little distinction. Their campaigns avoided such critical issues as the relationship between business and government and the incongruities of representative democracy and focused on law enforcement, personal morality, and other noncontroversial matters. Their elections, moreover, received little attention; one nonentity succeeded another as mayor nearly every other year, and, symbolically, Meredith P. Snyder, mayor during the 1890's, was again chief executive at the decade's end. Yet so long as the bureaucracy functioned smoothly, the thousands of newcomers—who, as one observer wrote later, "care little who heads the city government so long as the Southern California sun continues to shine and their real estate investments prove profitable"—were content.[50] In perspective, this equilibrium was less a

34. George E. Cryer, mayor of Los
Angeles, 1921–1929

vestige of the past than a portent of the future, revealing, in an incipient form, a consensus in Los Angeles politics.

A bitter battle over municipal electricity upset the equilibrium and obscured the consensus in the early 1920's, however. Nothing seemed less likely in 1921 when George E. Cryer replaced Snyder as mayor. A former deputy city attorney, Cryer was pressed to enter the mayoralty contest by Harry Chandler, publisher of the Los Angeles *Times,* who was a prominent businessman and leading conservative. Cryer agreed, and, guided by his mentor and manager, attorney Kent Parrott, conducted a skillful campaign which avoided divisive issues and aroused little animosity. Cryer also exploited his personal assets; simple and unassuming, even a trifle bashful, handsome, vigorous, and devout, he epitomized the midwesterner in southern California. He suited Los Angeles as well as Jimmy Walker did New York, and, after finishing second in the primary, won election in the runoff.[51]

Controversy followed Cryer into office. In order to secure an additional source of hydroelectric power, the Board of Public Service Commissioners urged Congress to build a high dam near Boulder Canyon. The Southern California Edison Company, which had filings along the Colorado River and sold its excess energy to the city, opposed this project. Cryer, under pressure from both sides, backed the

219

board, thereby infuriating Chandler. A friend of government enterprise when it advanced his interests and a foe when it did not, Chandler now objected to public power as strongly as he once favored municipal water. (For Boulder Dam detracted from the desirability of his Mexican acreage almost as much as the Owens Valley aqueduct had enhanced the value of his San Fernando Valley holdings.) He joined forces with two prominent conservative citizens' committees in opposition to Cryer; but, as they lacked the time to launch an effective challenge, the mayor was overwhelmingly re-elected in the 1923 primary.[52] By 1925, however, the conservative alliance was ready, and it selected Judge Benjamin D. Bledsoe to run against Cryer for what, by virtue of the recently-adopted charter, was a four-year term.

The mayor, advised by Parrott, supported by Haynes, and endorsed by the *Examiner,* campaigned on the issue of municipal electricity. The contest involves "public ownership for the service at cost vs. private ownership for profit at all the traffic will bear," his followers claimed. "The former means Cryer for Mayor; the latter means Bledsoe." If Bledsoe is elected, they warned, Chandler will appoint Water and Power Board members who will disrupt and discredit the department.[53] Bledsoe, seconded by the *Times,* denied that this was the issue. Summarily backing Boulder Dam, he attacked the administration—but not Cryer personally—for lax law enforcement and corrupt administrative practices. Unfortunately for the conservatives, Bledsoe could not reassure the supporters of the Los Angeles Bureau of Power and Light. Nor could he convince the voters that the mayor countenanced immorality or dishonesty in his administration. Hence Cryer gained a substantial majority in the primary, and, along with Parrott and Haynes, retained power through the decade.[54]

This conflict clarified the consensus that emerged in Los Angeles politics. The conservatives had to respect direct legislation, municipal ownership, civil service, and nonpartisanship or risk arousing the reformers. The progressives had to accept the commitment to orthodox urban development as defined in the 1911 referendum or chance antagonizing the voters. The politicians had to refrain from unduly interfering with the administrative bureaucracy which, in turn, had to resolve urban problems that would otherwise have seriously inconvenienced the residents. Finally, the officeholders had to undertake improvements for the developers and contractors without increasing the taxes of the small landowners and enforce the law in a manner which satisfied community morality without impinging too much on the underworld elements. Hence Los Angeles politics in 1930 reflected fairly well the will of the metropolis' native-American, middle-class majority even though it diverged sharply from the progressives' aspirations of 1900.

Consensus shaped the structure of municipal authority too. Following the resounding rejection of the 1912 charter, the reformers were too disorganized to attempt any comprehensive governmental revision.[55] In 1914, however, the common council ordered the newly-formed Bureau of Efficiency to recommend measures to expedite official business. Notwithstanding its instruction, the bureau prepared a host of radical amendments which included, among other innovations, a city manager and proportional representation. Whereupon the legislators refused to submit the proposals to the voters and instead authorized a Board of Freeholders to draft another charter. The board, selected in June 1915, was dominated by moderate progressives who assumed from the start that "what the citizens of Los Angeles most particularly desire in a new charter is increased business efficiency."[56] Conceding that politics was the one thing the Freeholders could not have agreed upon, it accepted the existing governmental reforms, but dismissed the radical city manager and commission plans. Then to the question, "Can the city be administered as an efficient business corporation?" the board offered the charter of 1915 as an affirmative answer.

The charter retained the mayor and council, but extended their terms to four years. It divided the rest of the government into twelve departments, keeping unsalaried, rotating, and amateur commissioners on humanitarian ones and replacing them with paid, permanent, and professional administrators on business ones. To enhance the prospects of passage, the board included alternatives for the more controversial provisions such as two-year terms, councilmanic districts, proportional representation, and departmental managers.[57] Although the Freeholders urged the voters to consider the result as an administrative not a political document, it was criticized on both grounds. Some objected to the substitution of managers for commissioners, while others claimed that the changes would encourage bureaucratic extravagance. The opposition, organized in an Anti-Charter League and supported by the Los Angeles *Times*, prevailed by a narrow margin. Though the alternative propositions were therefore voided, the electorate rejected departmental managers and proportional representation and approved a four-year term for the mayor and district organization for the council.[58]

The defeat of the 1912 and 1915 charters, along with the success of the earlier amendments, revealed a basic agreement about the appropriate government for Los Angeles. The citizens favored preserving the progressive heritage, but opposed eliminating the mayor and common council or altering the structure of the administrative bureaucracy. To these ends, they subsequently extended the application of civil service, opposed the establishment of municipal boroughs, and endorsed the reorganization of the Harbor Commission.[59] By 1923 many believed that it was time to incorporate this consensus into a more efficient charter. Hence the Chamber of Commerce organized a charter study group whose membership ranged over the political spectrum—from the Merchants and Manufacturers Association to the Central Labor Council and from the League for Better Public Service to the City Club. Their representatives later campaigned for election to a Board of Freeholders. Though the Municipal League deemed some reactionaries and the Better America Federation called others radicals, both associations supported most of the candidates, who, almost without exception, won positions on the board.[60]

These Freeholders not only represented diverse viewpoints; they were also far less visionary than their predecessors. They found the charter, as amended, reasonably satisfactory, doubted that the citizenry desired any fundamental changes,[61] and ignored administrative innovations adopted elsewhere. They retained the progressive reforms and mayor and council arrangement, merely extending the executive's term to four years and offering the voters a choice between at large and district representation. They also entrusted municipal administration to professional managers under the supervision of citizen commissioners, denying that involvement had to be sacrificed for expertise.[62] The Freeholders concluded by expressing the hope that the voters would regard the revision as an improvement over the present charter, a wish which was clearly gratuitous. For by adhering so closely to the consensus, the document provoked almost no dissent, and, supported by the metropolitan press, it gained overwhelming approval in May 1924.

By a smaller but still substantial majority, the electorate adopted councilmanic districts.[63] This protest against the incongruity of at large representation and decentralized development reflected a widespread reversion to localism in the politics and government of Los Angeles. It also coincided with the reversal of the reform aspiration to unify the city and county so that a greater Los Angeles would emerge administratively as well as economically—a goal towards which much progress had been made heretofore. The enthusiasm for governmental consolidation first appeared in the 1890's among citizens who proposed to obviate tax increases by eliminating duplication of local offices. It then spread in the early 1900's among promoters who envisioned a greater Los Angeles of seven hundred square miles united by the aqueduct and the harbor. And it received support in the 1910's from progressives who were committed to the concept of a community of interests in metropolitan Los Angeles.[64]

Despite this backing, consolidation advanced little before 1913. The city and the county remained distinct units, though both the common council and the supervisorial board favored state legislation permitting the merger of their assessors' offices. Long Beach, Pasadena, and other incorporated communities objected so strenuously to relinquishing their autonomy that comprehensive consolidation was impossible. There was, nonetheless, one encouraging trend. In a series of annexations—prompted by court decisions depriving outlying communities of their water supply—and consolidations—facilitated by economic inducements offered to Wilmington and San Pedro—Los Angeles, as shown in Table 24, expanded from 29 to 108 square miles.[65] Hence the advocates of unification now trusted their hopes to the piecemeal expansion of the metropolis, confident that this pragmatic approach would lead in time to *de facto* consolidation.

Their optimism was heightened in 1913 when the Municipal Annexation Commission advised that annexation or consolidation be prerequisite to supplying water and power to outlying communities. Subsequently, the municipality adopted not only this recommendation, but also another requiring these districts to assume a proportionate share of Los Angeles' water, power, and harbor bonds. Notwithstanding this condition, unincorporated territories short of water, such as the San Fernando Valley and the Westgate section, were anxious to tap the Owens Valley aqueduct. Led by large-scale developers (among them the Los Angeles Suburban Homes Company and the Santa Monica Land and Water Company) these areas joined the metropolis. Thus between 1915, and 1925, by virtue of nearly three score annexations and consolidations, Los Angeles, as Table 24 shows, increased its territory from 108 to 415 square miles—far more than any other American city.[66] The metropolis, it now seemed, would soon implement the reformers' aspiration for greater Los Angeles.

Shortly after Los Angeles voted to return to the ward system, however, the trend towards consolidation by annexation was sharply reversed. This occurred in part because the Department of Water and

MAP SHOWING

TERRITORY ANNEXED

TO THE

CITY OF LOS ANGELES
CALIFORNIA

J. J. JESSUP   CITY ENGINEER

SCALE 0 ½ 1 2 3 MILES

224

TERRITORIAL EXPANSION OF LOS ANGELES, 1850–1930

TABLE 24. Territorial Expansion of Los Angeles, 1850–1930

Number	Date	Name	Sq. miles[a]	Total sq. miles[a]
1	1781	Los Angeles (before expansion)	28	28
2	1859	Southern Extension	1	29
3	1895	Highland Park	1	31
4	1896	Southern & Western	10	41
5	1899	Garvanza	1	41
6	1899	University	2	43
7	1906	Shoestring	19	62
8	1909	Wilmington[b]	10	72
9	1909	San Pedro[b]	5	76
10	1909	Colegrove	9	85
11	1910	Hollywood[b]	4	90
12	1910	East Hollywood	11	101
13	1912	Arroyo Seco	7	108
14	1915	Palms	7	115
15	1915	San Fernando	170	285
16	1915	Bairdstown	3	288
17	1916	Westgate	49	337
18	1916	Occidental	1	338
19	1917	Owensmouth	1	339
20	1917	West Coast	12	351
21	1918	West Adams	1	352
22	1918	Griffith Ranch	*	352
23	1918	Hansen Heights	8	360
24	1918	Ostend	*	360
25	1918	Orange Grove	*	360
26	1919	West Lankershim	1	362
27	1919	Dodson	1	363
28	1919	Fort McArthur	1	363
29	1919	Peck	*	364
30	1919	Harbor View	*	364
31	1920	St. Francis	*	364
32	1920	Hill	*	364
33	1920	Chatsworth	*	364
34	1922	La Brea	2	366
35	1922	Manchester	*	366
36	1922	Melrose	1	367
37	1922	Sawtelle[b]	2	369
38	1922	Angeles Mesa	1	370
39	1922	Angeles Mesa No. 2	*	370
40	1922	Rimpau	*	370
41	1923	Hancock	*	370
42	1923	Evans	*	371

TABLE 24. Territorial Expansion of Los Angeles, 1850–1930 (*cont.*)

Number	Date	Name	Sq. miles[a]	Total sq. miles[a]
43	1923	Ambassador	3	373
44	1923	Laurel Canyon	14	387
45	1923	Hyde Park[b]	1	388
46	1923	Eagle Rock[b]	3	391
47	1923	Vermont	*	391
48	1923	Laguna	*	391
49	1923	Carthay	*	392
50	1923	Rosewood	1	392
51	1923	Agoure	*	392
52	1923	Lankershim	8	400
53	1924	Providencia	5	405
54	1924	Cienega	1	406
55	1924	Annandale	1	406
56	1924	Clinton	*	406
57	1924	Wagner	1	407
58	1924	Fairfax	2	409
59	1925	Holabird	*	409
60	1925	Danziger	*	409
61	1925	Hamilton	*	410
62	1925	Martel	*	410
63	1925	Santa Monica Canyon	*	410
64	1925	Beverly Glen	1	410
65	1925	Venice[b]	4	415
66	1926	Green Meadows	4	419
67	1926	Buckler	*	419
68	1926	Watts[b]	2	420
69	1926	Sunland	6	427
70	1926	Tuna Canyon	8	434
71	1927	Mar Vista	5	439
72	1927	Barnes City[b]	2	441
73	1927	Brayton	*	441
74	1928	Wiseburn	*	441
75	1928	White Point		441
76	1930	Classification Yard	*	442
77	1930	View Park	*	442
78	1930	Sentney	*	442
79	1930	Tobias	*	442

Source: J. J. Jessup, City Engineer, "Map showing Territory Annexed to the City of Los Angeles California."

[a] To the nearest square mile.

[b] Indicates acquisition by consolidation, all others by annexation.

* Less than one square mile.

Power doubted its capacity to serve newly-annexed territory, and the incorporated cities surrounding the metropolis objected as vigorously as ever to consolidation. Yet even more important were changes in the unincorporated areas which had contributed so much to the expansion of Los Angeles. Not only were the services for which they formerly joined the metropolis now provided by the county and special assessment districts, but, in addition, the decentralization of business brought merchants and manufacturers who opposed unification as insistently as realtors favored it to positions of leadership. To add to this, the residents of these communities extended their antipathy to the metropolis in general to Los Angeles in particular. As a result, the metropolis annexed so few parcels and gained so little territory during the next five years that all hope of further consolidation through annexation was frustrated.[67]

Accordingly, the number of governmental jurisdictions—which, including the county, the metropolis, other cities, and special districts, was in the hundreds—increased in greater Los Angeles. Not only were their functions distinct and their activities fragmented, but often their leaders were more remote and their constituents less well informed than their progressive counterparts. For though the reformers were disconcertingly naïve, postulating a simplicity and harmony which had never existed in any American metropolis, at least they acted as if the urban region were an integral unit and not merely a collection of contiguous jurisdictions. Whereas their successors, who were perhaps more sophisticated, preferred to avoid than to confront metropolitan Los Angeles and confined their political involvement, like their social relationships, to their suburban retreats. By doing so—by, in effect, denying the metropolis they had created—these people circumscribed their civic consciousness in a way that emphasized the progressive's commitment.

11   THE MUNICIPAL OWNERSHIP MOVEMENT

No issue revealed more about the nature of politics in Los Angeles than the struggle over municipal ownership of public utilities, a controversy which divided the progressive metropolis from the early 1900's through the mid-1930's. When municipal ownership emerged as a major issue at the turn of the century, private enterprise provided all the public utilities in Los Angeles. Los Angeles Water, Los Angeles Lighting, Los Angeles Electric, and Sunset Telephone and Telegraph controlled the water, gas, electricity, and communication businesses, respectively. The Los Angeles, Pacific Electric, and Los Angeles Pacific railways dominated urban transit, and the Southern Pacific and Los Angeles and Salt Lake railroads owned most of the San Pedro waterfrontage.[1] Amid the confusion that followed the expiration of Los Angeles Water's franchise, however, there was mounting pressure for the local authorities to provide these facilities.

It came less from the Populist, Socialist, Nationalist, and other fringe parties that favored municipal ownership as an alternative to corporate concentration than from thousands of ordinary citizens uncommitted to radicalism of any sort but dissatisfied with private service.[2] They protested against the irregular distribution of water and the periodic shortages of gas, complained about the excessive costs of electricity and the absence of a telephone interchange, and criticized the street railways as uncomfortable and the port tariffs as exorbitant. They urged the government to alleviate these conditions by municipalizing these facilities. From its inception, therefore, the municipal ownership movement had a pragmatic cast. Its rationale was economic rather than political—better service at lower charges, not public supervision of urban development. "The thing we want to consider is, in each case, is the proposition a good one, and, if run on business principles, can it be run successfully?" the mayor of Los Angeles stated in 1899. "If it can, then it is a proper measure for the municipality." [3]

Prospects for municipal water were particularly promising. Inasmuch as the plant had only been leased, the authorities had merely to repurchase it; and since other American cities operated waterworks, Los Angeles found many precedents for municipalization. Hence the city bought back the property, and the subsequent success of the enterprise—in terms of service, rates, integrity, and foresight—not only convinced many sceptics that public administration was as efficient as private direction, but also reinforced practicality as the cardinal measure of municipal ownership. The assumption of other utilities, which involved a departure from the traditional relationship between government and business, faced far greater obstacles, however. For these undertakings required the diversion of funds needed for other purposes, and the corporations possessed enough power to block adverse action by the council. Also, municipal ownership was still "commonly set down as expensive and unsatisfactory," one resident recalled. "The superiority of private initiative and management over public was generally accepted." [4]

An abortive attempt to municipalize electricity at the turn of the century illustrated these difficulties. Early in the 1880's the common council, disregarding the objections of the Los Angeles Gas Company, decided to light the streets with electricity and signed a contract with the Los Angeles Electric Company. Although the streets were well lit thereafter, many citizens considered the charge excessive. When the company, in defiance of public sentiment, refused to reduce the rate in the 1890's, a few councilmen proposed that Los Angeles erect its own lines and lamps and solicit bids for current from competing concerns. Some critics insisted that this proposal was too limited, asking why, if municipal water was advantageous, public power would be any less so. "Anyone who has the slightest knowledge of these matters," a conservative councilman answered, "is aware that, other things being equal, municipal ownership does not compare with private ownership from the standpoint of economy." [5] It was for political not economic reasons, however, that the legislature shelved this modest proposal in 1899 when Los Angeles Electric, responding to an offer by a newly-formed firm to erect a lighting system and supply cheap electricity, revised its charges.

A more ambitious effort to municipalize gas failed no less completely shortly after. Under pressure from residents who had long suffered poor service and high prices, the mayor urged the council to buy or build a municipal gas works. He declared that the enterprise would not unduly tax Los Angeles' resources, and could be as efficiently and honestly administered as the Water Department. The legislators rejected his plea, passing instead an ordinance fixing minimal requirements for heat content and candle power. The mayor denounced the law, arguing that its standards were too low, but the council overrode his veto. A reform representative then proposed that the legislature authorize a $2.5 million bond issue for the construction of a public gas plant. He claimed that the undertaking would remedy the present situation without exceeding the city's legal debt limit, and urged his colleagues to refer the motion to the Municipal Ownership Committee. By a six to three margin, however, they sent it to the hostile Finance Committee.[6]

The committee, dominated by machine candidates, reported adversely. Conceding that the consumers' complaints were well founded, it insisted that the council had an obligation to protect the Gas Company's investment and that the recent regulatory legislature would assure satisfactory service. Admitting that the city could increase its debt by $2.5 million, it contended that the future requirements of the waterworks precluded the municipality from assuming another obligation when less expensive alternatives were available. The Finance Committee then endorsed the principle of municipal ownership, but concluded that the circumstances were not propitious for the erection of a public gas works.[7] The council agreed, and in 1905, despite the protests of the progressives and the *Examiner*, filed the motion—a decision that indicated the influence of corporate utilities in a period of machine rule.

Two years later, in the course of an exceptionally cold winter, the Gas Company unexpectedly suspended service. The mayor promptly ordered an investigation to determine liability for the shutdown and to estimate the company's ability to serve the city. The council's Gas and Light Committee hired two San Francisco engineers who reported that though the corporation had been negligent it still had adequate generating and distributing capacity.[8] To meet future demand, they recommended that the legislature prescribe minimal pressures for gas pipes, impose penalties for lapses in service, and appoint inspectors to enforce these regulations. The Municipal Gas League denounced these suggestions: "Permanent relief from the miserable situation now being endured by the people of the city," it argued, "will never come until Los Angeles owns her own gas plant."[9] But the Gas and Light

Committee adopted the suggestions, and the council, ignoring the league's petition for municipalization, incorporated the engineers' recommendations into yet another ordinance.

Meanwhile, several Los Angeles businessmen lost patience with such private incompetence and public procrastination. Led by John R. Haynes, the wealthy reformer, and James F. Sartori, a prominent banker, they organized the City Gas Company. They intended to establish a competing gas works and later sell it to Los Angeles at cost plus 10 per cent. "There is no use of having any new companies at all," Haynes pointed out in 1907, "unless the city will eventually own its municipal gas plant." Despite City Gas's intentions, the Municipal Gas League opposed its application for a franchise on the grounds that the award would impede municipalization. But the council made the grant anyway, and the league's prediction proved accurate. After spending more than $1 million, the promoters lost interest, and, approached by the new Domestic Gas Company, disposed of their franchise and equipment. Subsequently, Southern California Gas took control of Domestic Gas and gained second place, behind Los Angeles Gas and Electric, in the metropolis' gas industry.[10]

Few reformers trusted the legislature to regulate these companies. They believed that most councilmen were bound to the corporations and that the others lacked the staff and expertise to oversee them. Once in power the progressives therefore drafted an initiative petition proposing the formation of a Board of Public Utilities. Passed by the electorate in 1909, the ordinance created a three-man commission, appointed by the mayor, to regulate the utility companies. It was empowered to examine earnings and propose rates, check complaints and suggest remedies, and make recommendations on all applications for franchises. The board labored under severe disadvantages, however. Its personnel was insufficient, and its authority merely investigatory and advisory; it could be pressured by the companies, and overruled by the council.[11] Contrary to progressive expectations, the creation of the Public Utilities Board simply forced the utility corporations to engage more actively in Los Angeles politics.

The reformers therefore became disenchanted with regulation. "The great interests which the private companies have at stake compel them to use all sorts of means to protect these interests," one commented. "Their efforts to control men in office who have charge of the regulation of their affairs is demoralizing the whole scheme of government." As appointive officials submitted to the pressures of private utilities, he added, "Public regulation [came to be] regarded by many as a futile compromise, and municipal ownership advocated as the only means whereby the cause of corruption and demoralization could be removed." [12] Municipalization was consistent with the progressive notion that the utilities were cardinal components of the machine, and suited to the reform strategy to dam the flow of funds from the corporations to the parties. Asked if the departments and chiefs would be the basis for new machines and bosses, proponents of municipalization replied no—so long as nonpartisanship was applied to managers, civil service to employees, and direct legislation to officials. [13] Municipal ownership thus emerged as an integral part of progressivism.

Although the reformers adopted the movement, municipal ownership retained its pragmatic base—its piecemeal approach and profit and loss calculus. To the question "Do you believe in municipal ownership?" even the progressive Municipal League observed that "owners of public utility securities may answer 'no' unequivocally" and "Socialists can answer 'Yes' readily enough. [But] for the average, sane, disinterested business-like citizen, the proper answer . . . would seem to be: 'Yes, at some times, in some places, of some things' . . . Municipal ownership is fundamentally a local issue," the league insisted. "Each city has its peculiar needs and problems to meet, and these vary from year to year. It is quite conceivable that a city should need to take over the electric business for a time and dispose of it again later, and both operations might be wise and not operate as an argument for or against municipal ownership of other things." [14] Pragmatism and progressivism thus formed the foundation for the monuments to municipal ownership.

The projected Owens Valley aqueduct, whose waters would fall several thousand feet and generate at least a million kilowatts, presented the next opportunity to extend municipal ownership in Los Angeles. While the aqueduct was under construction, the council hired a team of consulting engineers to evaluate the prospects of a public power project. It reported that the venture "should prove a safe and remunerative undertaking [and provide], at reasonable rates, large supplies of electrical energy." [15] Hence the legislature drafted a charter amendment in 1909 which entrusted responsibility for the enterprise to the Bureau of Aqueduct Power of the Board of Public Works. The electorate endorsed it, and the board asked the council to authorize a $3.5 million bond issue for the construction of generating plants along the aqueduct route. The legislature submitted the proposition to the voters, indicating the progressive administration's willingness to challenge the local power companies. These included Los

Angeles Gas and Electric, the successor to Los Angeles Lighting and Los Angeles Electric, Pacific Light and Power, organized by Henry E. Huntington to supply energy for his railway networks, and Southern California Edison, the result of a score of consolidations guided by John B. Miller and backed by Chicago financiers.[16]

The companies vigorously opposed the proposition. But they offered no constructive alternatives, and in a region that lacked other sources of energy the aqueduct power was deemed too valuable to be wasted. Thus the electorate endorsed the bond issue by a majority of more than seven to one in 1910.[17] In conjunction with the Board of Public Service—created in 1911 to operate municipal water and electricity—the Board of Public Works then built the power plants. Meanwhile, in an effort to limit municipalization, the corporations offered to purchase and market the city's power. This arrangement, they claimed, would assure Los Angeles a handsome income without compelling it to construct an expensive distributing system. By a majority of almost nine to one, however, the voters rejected their proposal in 1911. The companies also proposed to buy 35,000 horsepower from the municipality for $1 million per annum. But the Public Service Board, on the advice of its chief electrical engineer, Ezra F. Scattergood, declined this offer.[18]

The board then advised the council to authorize a $6.5 million bond issue to acquire or erect distributing facilities. Whereupon Los Angeles Gas and Electric and the other companies sought another way to maintain their control over the metropolis' power business. They realized that outright competition would be disastrous against an opponent that generated current less expensively, attracted capital at lower interest, and paid no taxes. And they perceived that they could not convince a populace proud of the achievements of its waterworks and harbor that private management was inherently superior to public administration. Yet they also knew that the investors would accept only general obligation, as opposed to revenue, bonds from the Public Service Department until it increased its earnings and improved its credit. Since these securities required electoral approval, the corporations reasoned, they could obstruct municipal ownership most effectively by opposing the department's bond issues and depriving it of funds for expansion.

The progressives, their fortunes still high, had different plans. At the meetings of the 1912 Board of Freeholders, Haynes and his colleagues drafted a declaration that would have committed Los Angeles to municipal ownership of all public utilities. The commercial associations protested, criticizing the Freeholders for discouraging the investment of private capital and calling for an enumeration of powers in place of a statement of intent. "What our policy should be in carrying these powers into effect should be left for the citizens to determine from time to time," they argued. "The city policy, with reference to one utility, would not be its policy towards some other utility. Its policy should be subject to change, and its determination left to the people as occasion arises." [19] Decrying this pragmatic approach, Haynes defended the progressive petition on the grounds that the declaration of intent would commit the legislators to municipalization and undermine the opposition of the corporations.[20] But the board, anxious that the business leaders might refuse to endorse the charter, substituted a less binding provision.

Business pressure also forced the board to weaken progressive proposals that would have facilitated municipalization. The reformers urged that the city be authorized to exempt general obligation bonds for self-supporting undertakings from the debt limit. But the commercial associations, which claimed that Los Angeles' credit would be ruined, persuaded the Freeholders to retain this restriction on these securities. The progressives demanded that the municipality be empowered to assess real estate for the acquisition and extension of utility facilities. But the business groups, which argued that the taxpayers would be unduly burdened, forced the board to grant the landholders a veto. The reformers insisted that a city amortization fund be created and later transferred to the Los Angeles railway as payment for its plant. But the commercial organizations, which feared that improvements would be inhibited, prevailed on the Freeholders to delete this provision too.[21] Although the electorate rejected the 1912 charter, these proceedings presaged the crucial part that the Chamber of Commerce and the other commercial and civic associations would play in the municipal ownership movement.

They also indicated that municipalization would have to be implemented piecemeal, and the progressives, overcoming their disappointment, formed a Power Bond Campaign Committee in 1913 to promote the $6.5 million bond issue for the distributing network. The electric companies, through a Voters Educational Association, led the opposition. They not only entered the contest better prepared than in 1911, but also presented reasonable alternatives. They offered to purchase the aqueduct electricity, distribute it for the city, lease the board their own equipment, or join in partnership with Los Angeles. They contended that these proposals would provide income for the city without wasting its resources and reduce rates for the consumers without raising their taxes. Disenchanted with the reform administration and confronted by other issues totaling $11 million, the citizens refused to vote the power bonds the necessary two-thirds majority.[22] The companies' strategy had achieved a resounding success.

The progressives promptly reminded the electorate of its $3.5 million investment in generating facilities. "The city must, as a simple business move, finish its power plant and get it producing," they said. "Not to do this would be utter folly."[23] The Public Service Commissioners then persuaded the council to resubmit the issue in 1914. To generate popular support in a municipality without political parties and ward clubs, they appealed to the voluntary associations and metropolitan newspapers. In response, the Chamber of Commerce, Municipal League, and Central Labor Council (though not the Realty Board and Merchants and Manufacturers Association) formed a People's Power Bond Campaign Committee. The committee promoted the issue on the grounds that "No one of the plans presented by the Companies would yield as great a net profit to the city as would be received from the sale ... of its electricity through its own distributing system."[24] The *Examiner* and *Tribune* agreed, but the corporations and the *Times*—a journal as reactionary in its philosophy as it was regular in its politics—urged the voters to reject the bonds.

The proposition carried by a two-thirds majority, providing the Public Service Board with enough capital to construct a distributing system and compete with the electric companies. Los Angeles Gas and Electric, Pacific Light and Power, and Southern California Edison therefore proposed the gradual transfer of their lines to the city. The commissioners rejected their offer, insisting on an immediate sale, but, in deference to the Chamber of Commerce, which vigorously objected to the duplication of existing facilities, agreed to open negotiations. A Committee of Five met with the corporate representatives, and, though Los Angeles Gas and Electric withdrew, it reached an accord with the others in 1916. The municipality would buy their equipment at a price set by the California Railroad Commission, and the companies would distribute the aqueduct electricity until the authorities made payment.[25] A long step toward public power in Los Angeles, the contract was subsequently ratified by the corporations, the commissioners, the Chamber of Commerce, and the council.

At about the same time, a committee of the Los Angeles City Club undertook a survey of municipal ownership. It reported that American cities lagged behind European ones in public enterprise—which, it believed, reduced rates, improved service, and liberated government and the press from corporate influence. It also measured the progress made thus far in Los Angeles—which, in fact, was considerable in the waterworks and harbor, modest in electricity, and negligible in gas, telephone, and transportation. The committee recommended that the municipality acquire all self-sustaining utilities immediately, assume the developing ones thereafter, and in time even operate terminals, markets, and slaughterhouses.[26] The City Club committee's report, which did little to implement municipalization in Los Angeles, revealed that, the recent progress of public power excepted, the municipal ownership movement had not extended far from its traditional strongholds—the waterworks and the harbor.

An unsuccessful attempt to municipalize the telephone business—then dominated by Home Telephone and Pacific Telephone—revealed some of the reasons why. Home Telephone had been organized by local businessmen in 1902 to compete with Sunset Telephone (the successor to Los Angeles Telephone) and to introduce the dial system into Los Angeles. Pacific Telephone, the west coast affiliate of the Bell network, had purchased the franchises and properties of Sunset Telephone four years later.[27] As competitors, the corporations did not interchange calls; and as the telephone became a necessity, subscribers had to keep two instruments. Thus, when Sunset Telephone's franchise expired in 1916 and Pacific Telephone applied for renewal, the council insisted that the companies meet with the Public Utilities Board to devise a remedy for this inconvenience. The legislators also drafted a proposition that withheld a franchise from any telephone company unwilling to interchange its service, and the electorate endorsed it by a four to one majority.[28]

Meanwhile, several improvement associations petitioned the authorities to purchase the Pacific and the Home systems, arguing that the investment would be profitable for the city. The council, repeating its preference for municipal enterprise, rejected their requests. It contended that the voters would not support the venture until the water, power, and harbor projects were self-sufficient and that an effectively regulated merger would eliminate the dual phone service more rapidly than municipalization.[29] Nonetheless, the People's Telephone Committee exerted so much pressure that the legislators agreed to pose the following questions to the Public Utilities Board. Could Pacific Telephone be the basis for a municipal system? Would $8 million adequately compensate the company? Could a public plant be connected with Home Telephone? and Would the result improve service and reduce rates? The board replied yes to each,[30] proving the feasibility of municipal ownership, but the council nonetheless filed the report and dismissed the subject.

The People's Telephone Committee, in response, prepared an initiative petition calling for a municipal telephone network and an $8 million bond issue and secured enough signatures to place it on the ballot. Conservative interests opposed the proposition, taking the position that public regulation would assure an interchange arrangement and public operation would perpetuate separate service. They also stressed that taxes were already excessive, and that, if an additional indebtedness were to be incurred, Los Angeles should improve its sewers before municipalizing its telephone.[31] The People's Telephone Committee challenged these assertions, contending that public ownership would guarantee a unified telephone system and that the enterprise would be a "PAYING INVESTMENT FROM THE START." "No more effective opportunity has ever been offered citizens for transferring big corporation profits to their own pockets," the committee declared, "than the present opening for the substitution of a city phone system for a corporation-owned one."[32]

The committee could not persuade the commercial and civic associations to support the proposition, and, against an extensive campaign waged by the telephone companies, it failed to win even a simple majority. Hence Pacific Telephone and Home Telephone proceeded with plans to consolidate and reorganize as Southern California Telephone. The California Railroad Commission approved the merger, contingent on the assignment of the Home franchise to Southern California Telephone, and the council referred the application to the Board of Public Utilities. The board favored the petition, provided the company agreed to connect all phones in the city, relinquish any other grants, use the most modern equipment, and extend service throughout Los Angeles.[33] The Council adopted this advice, the corporation accepted these conditions, and, once the consolidation was consummated and the franchise transferred, Southern California Telephone, not the city of Los Angeles, dominated the metropolis' communications industry.

Meanwhile, Pacific Light and Power and Southern California Edison merged in 1916 to form a new Southern California Edison that combined Pacific's hydroelectric capacity with Edison's expanding market.[34] The California Railroad Commission then valued the merged company's distributing facilities at around $11 million, and the council, after canceling one bond issue in 1917, authorized another for $13.5 million in 1919.[35] The Public Service Board, supported by the voluntary associations and the *Examiner,* promoted the proposition, while Los Angeles Gas and Electric, backed by a Municipal Taxpayers League and the *Times,* opposed it. The campaign also attracted nationwide attention—which intensified the conflict—because Los Angeles operated the largest municipal power plant in the United States.[36]

Nonetheless, the protagonists refused to debate the merits of private and public enterprise. Los Angeles Gas and Electric charged that the Public Service Department had promised to finance its expansion out of earnings, and that the issue would raise the already exorbitant tax rate. The Public Service Board insisted that municipal distribution would improve service and reduce costs, and that revenue from operations would cover debt charges and obviate higher taxes.[37] More important than these claims was the fact that the timing of the election coincided with the industrial promotion of Los Angeles. Many businessmen, who would otherwise have sympathized with the companies, supported the board because they attributed the lag in manufacturing to the high price of power. Without committing themselves to any theories for or against municipal ownership, their spokesmen explained, they favored a public distributing system in order to reduce the cost of electricity.[38]

The Chamber of Commerce supported the bonds, and the electorate endorsed the issue. The municipality then brought a friendly suit to validate the bonds, but, before a decision was reached, Los Angeles Gas and Electric challenged their validity. Although the court confirmed the issue, the delay prevented the authorities from making payment to Southern California Edison by the deadline. Thus the parties extended the temporary operating agreement until March 1921. The board then sold the offering to a local syndicate, paid the Edison Company, and acquired a distributing system.[39] A major advance toward public power, this achievement proved that, given the leadership of the reformers, the cooperation of the Chamber of Commerce, and the endorsement of the *Examiner,* effective coalitions could be created out of the political disorganization that followed the progressive reformation.

The struggle was far from over in 1921, however. Both the Public Service Board and Southern California Edison, as the Chamber of Commerce reported in 1920, had fully exploited the available supplies of hydroelectric power.[40] Neither the corporation, which had filings along the Colorado, nor the department, which had no additional sources, believed that it could meet future demand. Fortunately for Los

Angeles the federal government then decided to finance the construction of Boulder Dam by wholesaling electricity to southern
California.[41] To demonstrate its interest and competence, the Public
Service Board persuaded the council to authorize a $35 million in-
debtedness, $25 million of which was earmarked for hydroelectric
development in conjunction with Boulder Canyon. The utility companies, the *Times,* and the reactionary Committee of Ten Thousand
denounced the proposition, and the commercial associations, which
deemed the issue premature and excessive, refused to campaign for
passage. Hence the bonds failed by a substantial margin.[42]

Encouraged by this election, the power corporations launched for
the first time an offensive against the principle of municipal ownership.
Private enterprise differs from public operation in the character, policy, and purpose of its management, their spokesmen contended. "One
is responsible and can be held to the performance of duty; the other
cannot. One must keep its engagements, fulfill its promises, or lose
money, while the other has no money to lose, no investment to safe-
guard, and can, therefore, promise anything under the dome of
heaven, trusting that the people may forget, and if they don't, that
they will have to pay anyhow."[43] "Out of all the experiments from
Pharaoh to Pinchot, there is not a single known instance where government ownership, national, state, municipal or otherwise, has been
beneficial," Southern California Edison's president claimed. "It is
known that the system cannot continue in a democracy. Either the
democracy or the system must go."[44] This propaganda, which ignored the municipality's commitment to efficiency, its responsibility
to the consumer, and its dependence on the electorate, impressed
many citizens during the 1920's.

Instead of answering these charges, the Public Service Board,
against the advice of the Chamber of Commerce, asked in 1924 for the
largest issue yet—$25 million to build a Boulder Canyon transmission
line, $6 million to erect a standby steam plant, and $24 million to
acquire Los Angeles Gas and Electric's system and extend its own
distributing facilities. But the council authorized only $21 million in
bonds for improvements, though it also submitted two referenda as
to whether Los Angeles should contract for Boulder Canyon power
and whether it should purchase Los Angeles Gas and Electric. The
voters affirmed the questions but rejected the proposition. Discouraged
by two successive defeats, the board reconsidered its position. It could
offer the plant for sale, and, with the consent of two-thirds of the electorate, dispose of it to the highest bidder, thereby abandoning munic-

ipal ownership. It could also refuse new business or raise its rates in order to finance expansion out of earnings, thereby inconveniencing prospective customers or inhibiting industrial progress.[45] Since neither alternative was acceptable, the board decided to appeal to the citizens again.

Aware that failure might be fatal, it proceeded with extreme caution. On its instructions, Scattergood estimated that $24 million would be required just to extend and improve the power system in the immediate future. Los Angeles Gas and Electric and Southern California Edison challenged his figures and denied that the department needed more than $8 million.[46] The board therefore requested prior endorsement from the Chamber of Commerce, which asked if, in return, it would abide by the Railroad Commission's recommendations. Trusting Scattergood's estimate and the commission's impartiality, the board accepted this arrangement. The commission confirmed Scattergood's figures, but, anticipating $8 million in earnings over the next four years, it recommended a $16 million instead of a $24 million indebtedness. The council then submitted the issue to the electorate in 1924.

The Chamber of Commerce honored its pledge and endorsed the bonds. Pressed by the business community, Southern California Edison agreed to remain neutral.[47] Assured that the issue would not be used to acquire its lines, Los Angeles Gas and Electric withdrew its opposition too. Promoters of the proposition claimed that the municipality alone could supply cheap power for industrial expansion and that it would suffer severe losses if forced to sell the plant to the companies. This pragmatic appeal was effective. Conservative businessmen, who at heart believed that private enterprise was more efficient and economical than public operation, conceded that the Public Service Department was an exception.[48] With even the *Times* grudgingly concurring, the bonds received an eight to one majority. When the voters authorized another $11 million for further extentions and improvements two years later, the municipal utility fully overcame the gravest threat thus far to its existence.

The entire community, and especially its businessmen, longed for a respite from this struggle and urged the electric companies and the power bureau to settle their differences. It was convinced that private and public agencies would have to combine resources to meet future demands, and impressed with such advantages of cooperation as an interconnected network available in emergencies.[49] Unfortunately, the situation precluded a mutually satisfactory resolution. Los Angeles

Gas and Electric, which served 30 per cent of the city, still competed with the Bureau of Power and Light, and Southern California Edison, which supplied the suburbs, still hoped to acquire the municipal plant at a deflated price. The Water and Power Department, in turn, planned to extend its distributing facilities into Los Angeles Gas and Electric's territory and to enlarge its generating capacity until it no longer had to purchase current from Southern California Edison. Thus the contest continued.

But its character changed. Having failed to defeat the Bureau of Power and Light's bond issues, the corporations now attempted to take over the Board of Water and Power. Since the commissioners were appointed by the mayor with the consent of the council, Haynes and his associates had held a veto over the selection through the 1920's. Had either Bert Farmer or Benjamin Bledsoe defeated George Cryer, Chandler and his conservative allies would doubtless have reconstituted the board.[50] Now, after three terms in office, Cryer retired from politics. Among those who sought to succeed him in 1929, John C. Porter, a former grand jury chairman, and William G. Bonelli, a college professor now council president, emerged as the strongest candidates. Both promised to support public power, and in a close contest the citizens elected Porter.[51] Whereupon the new mayor precipitated Los Angeles into a political crisis comparable in intensity to the conflict between the progressives and the socialists two decades ago.

Porter's first two appointments pleased the Water and Power Department, and the board remained unanimous in its commitment to public power. But subsequently the mayor accepted resignations from two commissioners, forced a third to retire, dismissed a fourth outright, and reluctantly reappointed a fifth.[52] With only one exception, Porter's replacements were indifferent to municipal ownership and antipathetic to the electrical division. A majority, they not only subordinated the Power Bureau to the water division, but also continued to rely on Southern California Edison for current and refused to compete with Los Angeles Gas and Electric for customers.[53] In protest, several dedicated progressives and pragmatic businessmen formed a Municipal Light and Power Defense League and entered the 1931 municipal election. They called on the citizens to return those representatives who opposed the mayor and to renounce those who supported him. Denounced by the companies and the *Times,* the league and the department—by now an effective political organization— nonetheless persuaded the voters to choose a legislature committed to reversing the Porter administration's policy.

35. Harry Chandler, publisher of the Los Angeles *Times*

36. John R. Haynes, reformer and supporter of municipal ownership

The council promptly demanded the removal of the majority commissioners. When the mayor refused, it undertook an investigation of the Water and Power Board and found it was being operated for the benefit of the companies not the city. An independent study by the Lawyers Club of Los Angeles substantiated this conclusion.[54] Under mounting pressure one commissioner resigned, and at the same time another's term expired. Porter's first nomination displeased defenders of the electrical division, and the council compelled him to propose a more agreeable appointee. With the board evenly divided on the issue of public power, the mayor submitted another candidate antagonistic to the Haynes faction. The legislators refused to confirm him too, and, when Porter defiantly presented another unsatisfactory nominee, municipal government reached an impasse. Finally, amid hostilities which culminated in an unsuccessful mayoralty recall, Porter appointed a commissioner acceptable to the council. And Haynes and his associates, again in full control of the situation, restored the power division to its rightful position in the department.[55]

Next the commission implemented its designs for an entirely independent generating system. By now the federal government had resolved the conflicts over Boulder Dam; and with the earlier endorsement of the electorate, the board contracted for its allotment of electricity. As the contract obligated it to erect a transmission line from the dam to the city, the board applied to the Reconstruction Finance Corporation for a $22.8 million loan in 1932. Porter objected, but when he attempted to remove the commissioners, the council upheld them. The R.F.C. approved the petition in 1933, the department began work soon after, and two years later, in accord with a recent charter amendment, the voters authorized $23 million in *revenue bonds* to repay the corporation.[56] When the federal government finished its dam in 1936, the department transmitted the energy of the Colorado River to Los Angeles and achieved independence of Southern California Edison.

The board also implemented its plans to acquire Los Angeles Gas and Electric's distributing facilities. It had already offered to buy the company's power system and challenged the validity of its gas franchise—but to no avail. However, prospects were measurably improved when Frank Shaw, who succeeded John Porter in 1933, officially endorsed the course of the commissioners. The board then prepared a charter amendment enabling it to issue revenue bonds to purchase Los Angeles Gas and Electric's power facilities. The corporation, in turn, drafted a proposition authorizing the council to grant it another franchise for its gas business. The electorate approved the board's petition, but rejected the company's. After spending more than $200,000 to destroy the power bureau, Los Angeles Gas and Electric had no alternative other than to open negotiations.[57] The competitors reached agreement in 1936. The city secured the right to acquire the company's electric plant for $46 million; if it failed to exercise this option, the council had to award the corporation a new franchise to market light and power in Los Angeles for thirty-five years.[58]

As part of the compromise, the authorities offered Los Angeles Gas and Electric and Southern California Gas long-term grants to distribute gas. They wrote these provisions, including the $46 million revenue bonds, into a charter amendment that was submitted to the electorate in 1936. They thereby sacrificed whatever chance remained for a municipal gas works to enhance the prospects of the public power project—a strategy that forced even Chandler's Los Angeles *Times* to withdraw its opposition. The Water and Power Department, seeking the broadest possible backing, then justified the acquisition as a sound business practice. "The proposal to acquire the electric system," it assured the citizenry, "does not involve the question of public versus private power." [59] The department's statement revealed that municipal ownership had lost its momentum and changed from an expansive to a defensive movement. In any event, the voters approved the amendment and completed the municipalization of electricity in Los Angeles.

From a progressive perspective, the long struggle was paradoxical. After all, regulars as well as reformers had exploited direct legislation, civil servants had campaigned in councilmanic elections, and non-partisanship had rendered it difficult to generate popular support. Municipalization also contradicted progressivism's fundamental assumptions. It had provoked rather than eliminated conflict, intensified instead of depressed political activity, and even brought out divergent interpretations of the general welfare. Nevertheless, this bitter contest was consistent with the character of politics in Los Angeles. Municipal ownership was a clear issue; its protagonists were easily identifiable, their positions were well articulated, the decisions were electoral, and the constituency was city-wide. Yet public power succeeded only because its pragmatic approach was in accord with the aspirations of the commercial and civic associations and the majority of the leading newspapers, the cardinal forces in the reformed metropolis.

Measured against the ambitions of the progressive freeholders in 1912 or the City Club in 1917, the accomplishments of the municipal ownership movement in Los Angeles were at most moderately impressive. The city took possession of the waterworks, the harbor, and the power plant (which alone encountered serious opposition), and the corporations retained control over gas, telephone, and the electric railways. That the municipality failed to assume direction of the gas and telephone business was not crucial. Although municipalization would probably have reduced rates, Southern California Gas and Southern California Telephone, regulated by the Public Utilities Board and the Railroad Commission, supplied satisfactory service. But that the municipality failed to assume responsibility for the electric railways was disastrous. For not only did commercial associations tender the railways little of the support they lavished on the harbor and individual residents presume that automobiles alone could meet the transportation demands of the metropolis, but, in addition, transit, unlike gas and telephone, was unprofitable.

Hence public ownership of the electric railways was not merely desirable; it was indispensable. It required scant intelligence to claim, as the *Examiner* did, that since a "privately owned public utility of necessity stands on its own feet, a publicly owned utility must do as well or better." [60] But it demanded exceptional perception to comprehend that municipal ownership justified itself best when undertaking a task that exceeded the resources of private enterprise. Neither the pragmatic base nor the progressive buttress of municipal ownership could support this idea. Thus the metropolis, adhering instead to a concept of municipal ownership that precluded unprofitable ventures, did little to prevent the deterioration of the electric railways.[61] The achievements of Los Angeles' power plant notwithstanding, the predicament of its electric railways revealed the limitation of a movement whose criterion was self-sustenance. The history of municipal ownership underscored the desirability of a program for civic reform that depended less on a profit and loss calculus than on the community's determination to shape its destiny.

*Right from the start, we must understand that we are not the conserv-
ative branch of the City Government . . . We are the ones who should
'Dream dreams and see Visions'—visions of the better City to be. (Los
Angeles City Planning Commission, 1920)*

12   CITY AND REGIONAL PLANNING

City and regional planning, like municipal ownership, emerged as an
integral part of progressivism in Los Angeles after 1900. Hitherto, not
only did private enterprise shape Los Angeles' landscape, but the
inhabitants took deep pride in its residential dispersal, segregated
land-use, and single-family houses. They insisted on the priority of improvements, admitted the risks of development, and, so long as expansion remained the desideratum, equated criticism with ingratitude.
By 1900, however, many progressives realized that Los Angeles was
already a metropolis, that the returns from subdivision were commensurate with the investments, and that their environment was deficient
more in quality than in size. Hence they felt free—even obliged—to
express their doubts that private enterprise, alone and unrestrained,
could transform Los Angeles into an economically, communally, and
aesthetically satisfying metropolis.

The progressives claimed that under the prevailing arrangements
the subdividers gained the profits and left the community the losses.
For proof they pointed to irregular thoroughfares and premature subdivisions and estimated the expenses in terms of traffic congestion and
extra services.[1] They also feared that as a consequence of uncontrolled
development, commerce and industry would encroach on their suburban retreats. To them it seemed that private enterprise could now
ruin residential neighborhoods as easily as it had once created them.[2]
They complained about the absence of spacious parks, handsome
boulevards, and majestic monuments in Los Angeles too. For this they
blamed private enterprise's single-minded devotion to profits and
public authority's exclusive dedication to material progress.[3] By 1910
the progressives were so emboldened by their recent political achievements that they forthrightly challenged the tradition of unregulated

development. They demanded a more efficient, orderly, and attractive metropolis—one designed as a prominent city planner urged "Not to be simply big; but to be beautiful as well." [4]

The progressives were aware that both private enterprise and municipal authority already regulated urban development. In order to preserve the rusticity and homogeneity of their suburban tracts, subdividers applied deed restrictions that forbade buyers to improve lots for other than residential purposes and to erect on them other than single-family homes.[5] This device was quite effective when the developers extended the prohibitions in perpetuity and organized homeowners associations to enforce them. But the subdividers usually set expiration dates, and, in a region where the inhabitants moved so often, the neighbors rarely attained the unanimity required to renew them. Even when they did, they frequently lacked the money and knowhow to bring suit against violators. Hence private regulation was not altogether adequate; it tended to be most effective where it was least necessary—in sections where the terrain or the location precluded business undertakings and multi-family dwellings.

Likewise, the common council excluded saloons and slaughter-houses from residential neighborhoods, established building codes and fire districts, and improved streets, acquired parks, and erected official buildings. In spite of all this, however, it did not alter the prevailing patterns of urban development. Because it had to justify prohibitions by the common law, its jurisdiction covered only those activities recognized as nuisances.[6] Because it based regulations on a narrow interpretation of the police power, its authority extended only to ordering adherence to minimal specifications. And because it undertook public works piecemeal, its projects did not conform to any over-all design for Los Angeles. Thus those reformers anxious about the future cast of the metropolis concluded that public officials could shape the landscape of Los Angeles only by assuming additional responsibility to oversee and supplement private enterprise. Here was the foundation for city and regional planning in the metropolis.

To build on it, the progressives formed a City Planning Association in 1915. The association, which was voluntary in organization, advisory in capacity, and influential only through its personnel, promoted planning until 1920 when the council established a City Planning Commission. The commission was, if nothing else, ambitious. "Right from the start, we must understand that we are not the conservative branch of City Government," its president announced. "We are the ones who should 'Dream dreams and see Visions'—visions of the better City to be." [7] The commission was initially hampered by too many members, too little money, and limited powers. But in the charter of 1925 it was changed into a small board, provided with adequate funds, and given far greater authority. Like Los Angeles' other administrative agencies, the City Planning Department consisted of a paid, permanent professional staff under the supervision of an unsalaried, rotating citizens commission. It was designed, according to director G. Gordon Whitnall, "as a coordinating medium thru which all agencies . . . which contribute to the physical development of the community shall be focused in a single attack upon the task of building the city of tomorrow." [8]

Other municipalities, some of which bordered on Los Angeles, followed suit. After all, their residents relied on the same railways and highways, and their governments faced similar exigencies of urbanization. Moreover, their planners agreed with Whitnall that these communities faced common problems which could only be resolved through cooperative efforts.[9] Hence, in the early 1920's Whitnall and his colleagues asked the Los Angeles Board of Supervisors to invite representatives from the county's municipalities to a convention to discuss planning. There the members formed a Regional Planning Conference, a voluntary association composed of civic and governmental groups that set an important precedent even though it lacked any real authority. It was supplanted in 1923 by the Los Angeles County Regional Planning Commission, an official agency empowered by the supervisors to advise local governments on matters affecting the county as a whole.[10] The formation of the Regional Planning Department indicated the widespread acceptance of planning in greater Los Angeles.

A reform aspiration, city planning was not a radical venture. Its sponsors reflected the conservative inclinations of progressivism: "City planning," one spokesman remarked in 1914, "is but one phase of this larger movement for efficiency." Its defenders denied charges that planning was visionary: "City planning is not a fad," the Municipal League insisted, "but a sound self-sustaining business proposition whenever seriously undertaken." Its practitioners conceived of its implementation circumspectly: "A city plan should be prepared from the economic standpoint first, the social or human standpoint second, and the aesthetic standpoint last," a professional planner explained, "not in the reverse order." And its overseers defined its criterion conservatively: "The benefits to be gained from an improvement must equal or exceed the cost," the Los Angeles City Planning Commission declared, "or the work should not be done." All in all, the rationale for planning was in full accord with progressivism in Los Angeles: "The 'city practical' no less than the 'city beautiful,'" the Municipal League pointed out in 1914, "has become the slogan of this work." [11]

Utilitarian in its profession, city planning was environmental in its approach. It accepted as its fundamental axiom the idea that appropriate physical surroundings would assure personal morality and communal coherence. From their conception of congested eastern and midwestern metropolises, the planners assumed that the great city was no longer the most pleasant place for living or the most efficient location for working. They proposed as an alternative residential dispersal and business decentralization—carefully supervised so as to foster self-sufficient satellite cities instead of sprawling suburban subdivisions. They committed themselves, in Whitnall's phrase, to "the recognition of the small unit and its perpetuation," [12] and they confidently expected each community to complement not compete with Los Angeles. In all essentials the planners shared the populace's suburban ideals, and the populace agreed with the planners' metropolitan aspirations—a congruity that reflected their common native-American middle-class backgrounds.

The planners realized that dispersal and decentralization depended on an efficient transit system. Yet they also knew that traffic congestion was so acute that, as the City Planning Commission reported in 1923, transportation in Los Angeles was more difficult than ever.[13] The increasing number of motor cars and electric trains made travel to and from downtown and in and around the region slower, costlier, and more dangerous every year. The indiscriminate mix of autos, buses, trucks, and trains, business and pleasure vehicles, and through and local traffic greatly aggravated the situation. For a while the planners envisioned the improvement of the urban and interurban lines as the solution. But the Los Angeles and the Pacific Electric could not raise capital; and the Public Utilities Board and the Railroad Commission could not compel extensions. Nor could the city and the county assume responsibility. Hence the planners, hoping that dispersal and decentralization would obviate rapid transit, concentrated thereafter on facilitating the flow of private automobiles.[14]

The authorities tried to ease congestion by a variety of technical devices and police measures. They assumed that traffic moved more rapidly at a moderate but constant than at a fast but irregular pace, that the tighter the regulation the swifter the progress, that delays occurred at intersections and when motorists turned against oncoming cars, and that streets served to expedite movement not to store vehicles. They concluded that traffic would be eased if drivers were forced to heed speed limits and signal lights, grade crossings were eliminated wherever possible, left-hand turns were prohibited on crowded thoroughfares, and parking was restricted during rush hours.[15] The council passed the necessary ordinances, but the results were disappointing. Maximum speeds and traffic signals made passage more orderly but little faster; separate grades and fewer turns promoted safer but not quicker travel; and parking regulations did not measurably accelerate movement. By the mid-1920's, as more and more motor cars jammed downtown streets and tied up outlying arteries, the City Planning Commission decided that nothing less than enlarged surface capacity would afford permanent relief.

The commission, backed by an unofficial traffic association, persuaded the council to employ three well-known planners to study Los Angeles' traffic problem. Postulating that auto travel would increase so long as rapid growth continued, they recommended that old streets be widened and new ones opened and that main and supplementary, through and local, and business and pleasure roads be differentiated.[16] The electorate subsequently approved a bond issue to implement their Major Traffic Street Plan. Soon after, the Board of Supervisors, which was responsible for transportation elsewhere in the county, instructed the Regional Planning Commission to design a highway system to connect the smaller municipalities and circumvent the crowded metropolis. The commission prepared several plans which called for major highways (one hundred feet wide) along section lines, secondary highways (eighty feet wide) along half-section lines, and intermediary bypasses (sixty feet wide).[17] Toward the end of the decade, the commission located the routes and the supervisors authorized the projects.

The city and county arterial networks encouraged dispersal and decentralization, but, as the increase of automobiles kept pace with the expansion of highways, they did not ease congestion. Some planners acknowledged the contradiction inherent in this approach to urban transportation. "If, then, no matter what we do about increasing street capacity, we must approach the same degree of almost but not quite intolerable congestion," they asked, "why not be fatalistic and do nothing?" They replied that a modern roadway system which utilized all its components to the utmost allowed for greater over-all movement.[18] Yet justifying their expenditures on this basis, the planners ignored another paradox. For, as one perceptive observer pointed

251

out, "Building a new highway 'farther out' to relieve localized congestion on an established thoroughfare does not solve the problem. By the time the situation has forced action, expanded development has usually created the necessity for a new highway, not as a substitute, but as an additional artery." "But," he asked, penetrating to the crux of the matter, "what will happen when the gaps are closed?" [19]

If few planners had an answer to that question, most realized that the subdivision was no less important than the highway in shaping the metropolis. "A subdivision is not merely a means for marketing land," they claimed; "it is far more, a process in community building." "The fleeting economic effect of the act of selling," they explained, "soon gives way to the permanent, inexorable economic and social effect of the layout as a part of the form and life of the community." [20] The planners argued that most developers ignored this responsibility, and regarded subdivision solely as "speculation in pyramiding prices of home property—a vicious thing." They reasoned that if the region's tracts were effectively regulated prior to development each new parcel would contribute to a more efficient metropolis, coherent community, and attractive landscape. In these aspirations the planners received the unqualified endorsement of the City and the Regional Planning Commissions.

The planners, whose regulatory authority here came from local and state legislation, designated the city's major traffic and the county's regional highway schemes as the bases for subdivision in Los Angeles. They required that through most tracts the developers reserve rights of way of one hundred feet for major highways and eighty feet for secondary arteries. They also demanded that within other tracts the developers plat streets at least sixty feet wide and align them with adjacent thoroughfares. Moreover, the planners discouraged dead-end roads, limited the grade to 6 per cent on through streets and to 15 per cent on local ones, and called for curbs with a minimal radius of from ten to twenty feet. At the rear of property fronting on highways eighty feet or more in width, they insisted on alleys twenty feet wide in order to expedite deliveries and reduce the number of driveways.[21] Indeed, in one regulation after another the planners revealed an overriding concern for automobile transport.

They also required that all streets intersect at ninety degree angles wherever practicable and that no blocks extend for more than six hundred feet in length or more than two tiers in width. Although these restrictions did not preclude layouts other than the gridiron, they did encourage subdividers to repeat traditional patterns rather than devise more imaginative arrangements. As the minimum size for lots, the Regional Planning Commission fixed 5,000 (50 by 100) square feet, and the City Planning Commission set 6,750 (50 by 135) square feet for residences and 4,800 (40 by 120) square feet for businesses.[22] Although a few smaller plots would doubtless have been platted if not for these requirements, the intense competition in the 1920's would have deterred developers from marketing many such parcels. The planners also urged the subdividers to dedicate parts of their tracts for such public purposes as parks. But so long as the subdivisions satisfied the requirements concerning streets and lots, neither the City nor the Regional Planning Commission had the authority to disapprove them.

All in all, the results of subdivision regulation were unimpressive. The planners seldom exploited the opportunity to promote suburban settings comparable to, say, Palos Verdes Estates, and the commissions, by basing their restrictions on prevailing practices, merely reinforced existing patterns with governmental sanctions. The planners also failed to control excess subdivision.[23] Although they accurately estimated the burdens it placed on the community, they remained quiet before claims that any enterprise that fostered dispersal and decentralization, no matter how premature, should be free from public interference. In sum, the planners imposed minimal standards for tolerable conformity. Hoping to facilitate motor transportation and prevent egregious abuses, they settled for a mediocrity and congruity far from the innovation and excellence achieved at the better subdivisions in Los Angeles. That the council or the courts might have opposed a more aggressive policy was no reason for the planners, as professionals called to "Dream dreams and see Visions," to have demanded so little of the developers.

If private enterprise retained full control over the lots afterwards, public supervision of urban expansion would have been severely limited. For the planners it followed that municipal authority also had to regulate land-use if Los Angeles were to become more efficient, orderly, and attractive. The common council had already divided the metropolis proper into one large residential and several small industrial districts.[24] And although the boundaries were fixed to fit rather than alter the city's structure, this legislation had profound implications for planning in Los Angeles. It discarded the traditional concept of nuisance in favor of the radical notion that businesses per se were detrimental to residences.[25] As the original categories were crude and the administrative machinery cumbersome, the planners now appealed for more sophisticated classifications and more flexible procedures—for, in effect, zoning. That zoning was called for (and adopted) so early in Los Angeles was because no other American metropolis—not even New York—experienced more rapid population growth, more serious social disorientation, and more violent fluctuations of property values.

As the planners conceived it, zoning's purpose was twofold: to promote the widest possible segregation of land-use and to foster the most rational utilization of real estate. From the assumption that all cities tend to zone themselves, they reasoned that zoning's task was to encourage this tendency in accord with the expansion of the metropolis. Yet in their endeavor to establish the validity of zoning—which was, at least in theory, a great innovation—they felt obliged to exercise caution in implementing it. As pioneers with few precedents to guide them, the planners only gradually enlarged the scope of zoning; not until 1925 did they draft a comprehensive ordinance. Every advance was challenged, but the California Supreme Court ruled that zoning, even for single-family dwellings, was a reasonable exercise of the police power. Zoning's rationale must be the welfare not merely the appearance of the community, the court declared, and its application must be neither retroactive nor discriminatory.[26]

In an effort to buttress zoning—which was, again in theory, a major reform—the planners considered it essential to secure the support of the developers. A former president of the Los Angeles Realty Board carefully enumerated the terms that would have to be met before the realtor would endorse zoning. "First, he expects that those persons dealing with zoning shall be practical and sane in their thought and that they shall be willing to give and take . . . Second, the realtor fears the theorist—fears the man who has some theoretical plan whereby the ills of society may be rectified . . . Third, the zoning power should be able to demonstrate that in addition to having relation to good morals, health, protection, and general welfare of the community, zoning has some relation to the general prosperity and to the general land values of the community as well." [27] The planners accepted these conditions, but, stressing zoning's capacity to stabilize realty values, they limited its efficacy to supervise urban expansion.

Lastly, in an attempt to overcome the objections to zoning—which did, after all, modify property rights—the planners allowed the landholder to appeal their classifications. He could challenge the staff's preliminary findings at an open hearing, and if not satisfied he could request an *exception* for his plot. He could carry his case to the commission and then to the council, and if both upheld the planners he could ask them for a *variance*. The burden of proof rested with the petitioner who had to demonstrate not only that his parcel was subject to exceptional circumstances, but also that a variance was essential for its utilization and neither injurious to the adjacent realty nor detrimental to the general welfare.[28] The legislators, however, were so receptive to pleas for zone changes that by 1925 the Municipal League observed a "marked tendency on the part of the City Council to set at naught the well-considered plans and work of our City Planning Commission . . . A continuance of this practice," it warned, "may mean the complete breakdown of zoning legislation." [29]

None of these matters prevented zoning from promoting the widest possible land-use segregation. First in the city and later in the county, the planners devised classifications ranging from single-family to residential income, commercial, limited industrial, and unlimited industrial.[30] They believed that individual homes, as somehow morally superior, should be carefully protected, and that apartment houses should serve as buffers between them and businesses. Accordingly, the planners restricted commerce to the downtown district and the major thoroughfares and confined manufacturing to the industrial sections near the river and the water front. They set aside the surrounding property for residential income property and reserved the remaining land—which was the least accessible in the metropolis—for one- and two-family houses.[31] In sum, zoning reinforced land-use segregation in Los Angeles by investing the patterns imposed by private enterprise with governmental sanctions.

But these changes did preclude zoning from fostering the most rational utilization of real estate. As a result of their caution, the planners started to zone Los Angeles when southern California was in the midst of the most prodigious boom in its history. The growth of population and industry generated extraordinary demands for urban property that presented unparalleled chances for speculative profits.[32] The developers, who had endorsed zoning as a way to stabilize values, now feared that its implementation might act as a brake on the appreciation of realty. They strenuously objected to any official action designed to fix the character of their property and prevent its exploitation for heavier uses. Most residents also preferred the opportunity that came with higher classifications to the security that was assured by appropriate zoning. And they were willing to exert political pressure in order to secure whichever ratings enhanced the speculative possibilities of their holdings. Hence the same people who supported zoning in principle challenged it, if it ran counter to their interests, in practice.

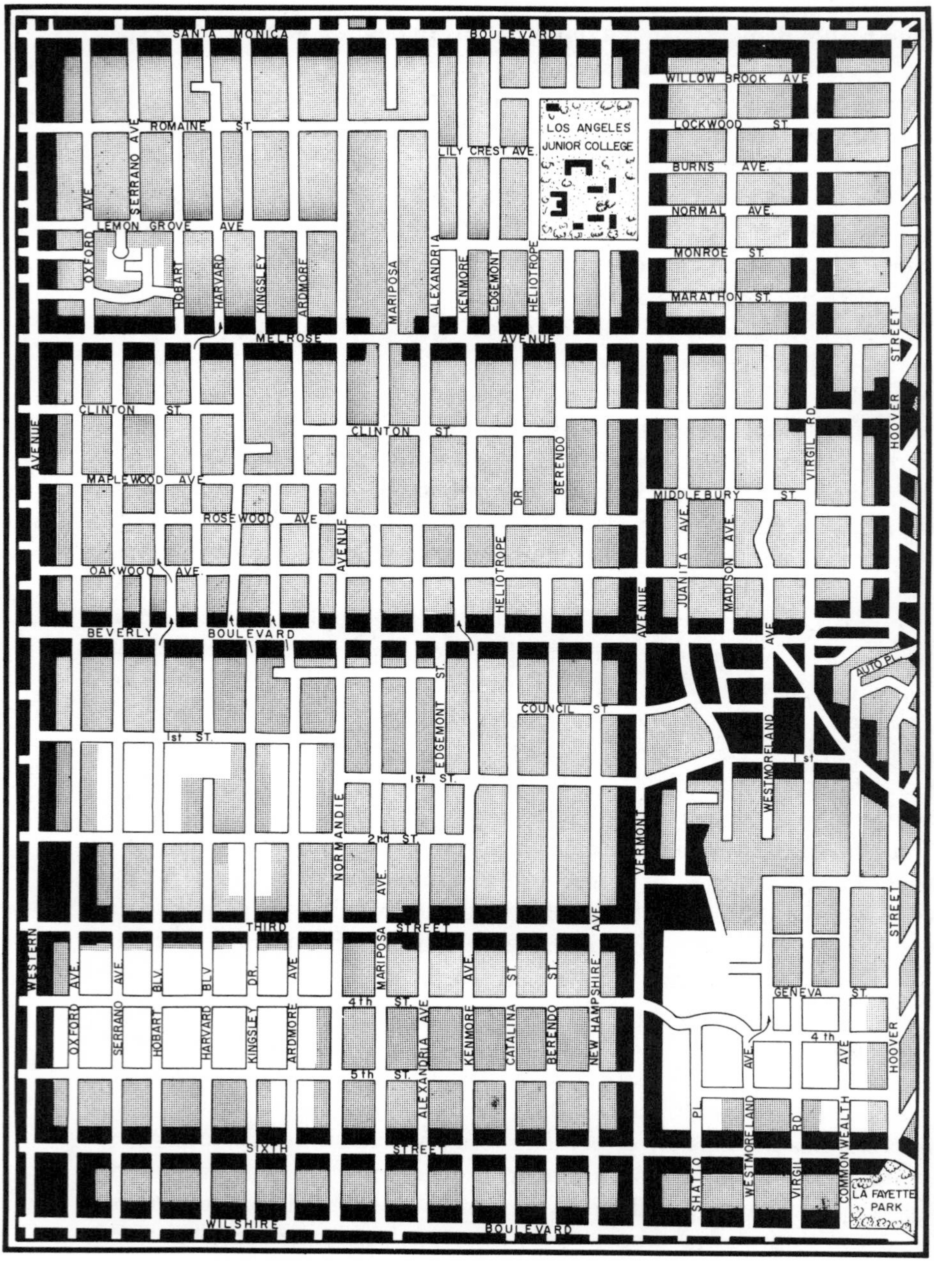

SANTA MONICA BOULEVARD
WILLOW BROOK AVE
LOCKWOOD ST
BURNS AVE
NORMAL AVE
MONROE ST
MARATHON ST
ROMAINE ST
SERRANO AVE
LOS ANGELES JUNIOR COLLEGE
LILY CREST AVE
OXFORD AVE
LEMON GROVE AVE
HOBART
HARVARD
KINGSLEY
ARDMORE
MARIPOSA
ALEXANDRIA
KENMORE
EDGEMONT
HELIOTROPE
MELROSE AVENUE
CLINTON ST
CLINTON ST
MAPLEWOOD AVE
ROSEWOOD AVE
OAKWOOD AVE
AVENUE
BERENDO
DR
MIDDLEBURY ST
VIRGIL RD
HOOVER STREET
JUANITA AVE
MADISON AVE
AVENUE
HELIOTROPE
BEVERLY BOULEVARD
AUTO PL
COUNCIL ST
EDGEMONT ST
1st ST
1st ST
WESTMORELAND AVE
1st
NORMANDIE AVE
2nd ST
VERMONT AVENUE
THIRD STREET
WESTERN AVENUE
OXFORD AVE
SERRANO AVE
HOBART BLV
HARVARD BLV
KINGSLEY DR
ARDMORE AVE
MARIPOSA
KENMORE AVE
CATALINA ST
BERENDO ST
NEW HAMPSHIRE AVE
4th ST
ALEXANDRIA AVE
GENEVA ST
4th
AVE
AVE
HOOVER STREET
5th ST
SHATTO PL
WESTMORELAND
VIRGIL RD
COMMONWEALTH
SIXTH STREET
LA FAYETTE PARK
WILSHIRE BOULEVARD

"A" ZONE – SINGLE FAMILY DWELLINGS "B" ZONE – RESIDENTIAL INCOME USES "C" ZONE – COMMERCIAL-BUSINESS USES

Zoning, after a short struggle, succumbed to this onslaught. By virtue of concessions by planners, exceptions by commissioners, and variances by councilmen, Los Angeles was egregiously overzoned for residential-income, commercial, and industrial purposes. Of the lots improved in 1926, for example, 69 per cent were used for private homes, 16 per cent for multi-family dwellings, 7 per cent for stores and offices, and 8 per cent for shops and factories. But of the parcels zoned in that year 10 per cent were classified for single-family residences, 59 per cent for residential-income purposes, 13 per cent for commerce, and 18 per cent for industry.[33] As the land reserved for private homes consisted mainly of hillsides unsuited for any other purpose, nearly every neighborhood unprotected by deed restrictions was open to the encroachment of apartment houses. And as the commercial frontage stretched along the highways in an uneconomical, disorderly, and unattractive fashion, the planners were already urging that these business "shoestrings" be replaced by shopping "centers."[34]

Between 1910 and 1930, then, zoning in Los Angeles was fully adopted but extensively modified. Originally conceived as a means of sound and strong land-use regulation, it was compromised in its formulation and emasculated in its implementation. Initially considered as an instrument of planning subject to administrative control, it was changed into a method of promoting property interests through political influence.[35] The zoners also failed to recognize the dynamic character of urban development. In their commitment to the idea that different uses were inherently incompatible, they ignored the more profound problem of how they were related to one another. In their insistence on complete segregation of residential and commercial property, they neglected to examine how these uses might be better integrated.[36] In its short history, zoning, far from guiding the expansion of the metropolis, merely sanctioned the preferences of private enterprise; and as the excessive number of business lots indicated, few realtors found zoning an insuperable obstacle to their exploitation of Los Angeles.

The planners were dismayed by the extent to which zoning dominated their activity. The City Planning Department, Whitnall lamented in 1925, "is almost exclusively occupied with work incident to zoning."[37] They believed that land-use regulation was only one of their responsibilities and that among the others was the preservation and beautification of open spaces. They agreed with the donor of Griffith Park that "fresh air, communion with nature and amusements other than those afforded by the cheap theater, moving picture show

257

or saloon are requisite to public health." [38] They also realized that as the size of a community increases, the ability of its residents to provide their own recreation decreases. [39] And they feared, with Frederick Law Olmsted, Jr., lest Los Angeles become "a place to be escaped from whenever wealth permits, as a thousand times a thousand makes a million in the addition of urban subdivision lots cheek by jowl without interruption or relief." [40] For these reasons the planners took the initiative to expand and improve the metropolis' park system.

That Los Angeles was not destitute of open spaces was in part because the council, as successor to the ayuntamiento, had inherited several thousand acres of pueblo land. Although it later offered the legacy for sale, the bidders considered some of the tracts valueless. The authorities subsequently allocated public funds or accepted private contributions to convert these parcels into Elysian, Westlake, and other handsome parks. Even more important, a few wealthy residents had granted park land to the city. Although most of these benefactors gave less than one hundred acres, Griffith J. Griffith donated to Los Angeles three thousand acres for the largest municipal park in the nation. [41] By the turn of the century, however, the pueblo land was distributed, and civic generosity waned because of the improved opportunities for profitable subdivision. Also, the migration to Los Angeles and the expansion of the metropolis so accelerated afterwards that by the 1920's even the Chamber of Commerce conceded that Los Angeles desperately needed more parks and playgrounds. [42]

This deficiency was more easily diagnosed than remedied. To acquire additional open space for the city, the planners realized, other sources of land and funds would have to be tapped. If civic devotion could no longer be counted on, they reasoned, perhaps enlightened self-interest could be exploited instead. Thus they endeavored to persuade the large-scale developers that the dedication of a few parcels for a park would enhance the value of the adjacent lots. Occasionally, as when the Janss Investment Corporation reserved part of a tract in Westwood for Holmby Park, the subdividers heeded their pleas. [43] But few developers were so cooperative, and, as the planners lacked the authority to order donations, the appeal gained Los Angeles few new parks. (Ironically, when the real estate market lagged in the late 1920's and subdividers offered more property for park purposes, the authorities were so concerned about the dwindling tax rolls that they were reluctant to accept these gifts.)

The planners also urged the municipal authorities to appropriate funds for the acquisition of park sites. But time after time the legisla-

37. Central Park (now Pershing Square), 1887

38. Westlake Park, 1929

tors replied that Los Angeles simply could not spare the money. Population growth, they explained, generated a need for other public improvements with higher priorities. They therefore refused to raise taxes and risk arousing the voters for any but indispensable facilities. True, the planners occasionally convinced the legislators to authorize bond issues for the purchase of park properties, and, with the cooperation of the voluntary associations, persuaded the electorate to approve propositions.[44] But all too often the authorities were so anxious about physical improvements, the organizations so worried about the municipality's credit, and the voters so concerned about increased realty taxes that they were unreceptive to the planners' appeals. To overcome these obstacles required a combination of foresight, determination, and sacrifice that was exhibited no more frequently in Los Angeles than in most other American metropolises in the early twentieth century.

From time to time the planners also called on the residents to form assessment districts and issue improvement bonds for local parks. Unfortunately, property-holders associations which objected to higher taxes vigorously opposed these proposals on the grounds that the existing parks were adequate, that the projected ones were poorly located, or that the current levies were already burdensome. In one neighborhood after another they persuaded at least one-third of the voters that the parks were either unnecessary, improperly placed, or unreasonably priced.[45] As a result of the indifference of the home owners, the municipal authorities, and the private developers, Los Angeles lost one opportunity after another to preserve its open spaces. In 1930, it possessed about 5,300 acres of parks (of which more than 3,000 had been donated by Griffith J. Griffith), a total which compared favorably with that of other metropolises but fell far short of the planners' aspirations for Los Angeles.[46]

The planners hoped to link the parks together by a network of parkways (or boulevards) which, unlike ordinary highways, were envisioned as recreational facilities and not traffic arteries. As designed elsewhere in the United States, a parkway was isolated from heavy traffic; its route was laid out indirectly, and its access was limited to pleasure vehicles.[47] Although several landscape architects, including some of national renown, submitted parkway plans to the council after 1900, the legislature refused to implement them. (It is true that many ambitious real estate developers appropriated the terms "parkway" and "boulevard" when naming roadways, but these were highways in structure as well as function.[48]) So notwithstanding the planners' visions, Los Angeles was almost as destitute of parkways in 1930 as in 1910.

Nothing illustrated their difficulties as well as the abortive attempt to transform Wilshire Boulevard—which ran from Los Angeles to Santa Monica—into a parkway connecting the downtown district with the Pacific Ocean. The common council and the Board of Supervisors first proposed to develop Wilshire Boulevard as a parkway early in the twentieth century. But the project remained in abeyance until the City Planning Commission zoned its frontage for residential income (or "B") usage in the early 1920's. By then Wilshire was a main traffic artery, and property owners there, protesting that it was far too valuable for any but business purposes, requested a commercial (or "C") classification. The commission urged the council to reject the petition, insisting that the landholders knew of the restrictions when they purchased their realty and that nearby residents counted on zoning when they bought their lots. It also contended that downtown Los Angeles deserved protection, that the metropolis had excessive business frontage, and that reclassification, by generating additional traffic along the boulevard, would disrupt plans for the parkway.[49] Nevertheless, the council bowed before the pressure of the property owners and, overruling the commission, rezoned Wilshire Boulevard from Westlake to Western Avenues for commercial use.

This decision distressed the planners not only because it jeopardized the prospects for the parkway, but also because it undermined the position of the commission. Backed by downtown realty and commercial interests, which feared competition from outlying businesses, they therefore decided to challenge the legislature. They circulated a referendary petition nullifying its action and authorizing the electorate to choose between "B" and "C" zoning for eastern Wilshire Boulevard. The Wilshire Boulevard Association, representing the landholders, responded by denouncing the planners for their interference. Claiming that its members acquired their real estate anticipating a zone change, it warned that they would oppose further widening of Wilshire if the rezoning were disallowed, and promised that they would spend millions to improve the boulevard if the reclassification were approved. This approach was effective in a community so concerned about traffic congestion and land values, and, to the dismay of the planners, the voters endorsed commercial use for eastern Wilshire Boulevard by a three to two majority.[50]

Western Wilshire property owners then demanded that their holdings be rezoned too, and when the commission refused their request they appealed to the council. The Municipal League condemned their action, arguing that the eastern section had ample commercial frontage and that the western portion could be used for apartment houses. It insisted that additional business on Wilshire would preclude the creation of a parkway and that another reversal of the commission's recommendations would subvert zoning. When the legislature ordered the change any way, the league prepared a second referendum. The West Wilshire Development Association replied that the frontage was unsuitable for residences because of the continuous flow of traffic outside. It added that Wilshire landholders unanimously favored reclassification, and urged each voter to place himself in their position. "Suppose you yourself purchased a lot tomorrow in a district zoned for business," it wrote and "then suppose by means of a referendum such as this, your zoning was changed overnight." [51] Curiously, the electorate rejected this reasoning and, overruling the council, classified western Wilshire Boulevard for "B" use.

But ultimate authority rested with the legislators and not their constituents; for while the voters could zone the entire frontage, the councilmen could reclassify any particular parcel. After the election west Wilshire property owners petitioned for variances, demanding the same opportunities as east Wilshire realty holders and exerting intense political pressure on the elected officials. In one instance after another the legislature granted their requests. Every favorable decision was then cited to justify every subsequent appeal, and the remaining frontage was rezoned piecemeal for commercial use.[52] The emergence of Wilshire Boulevard as a business stretch second to none in the metropolis revealed the process whereby the authorities—acknowledging that as the automobile converted wide thoroughfares into traffic arteries it rendered them less desirable for residences and more valuable for businesses—allowed the landowners to exploit their frontage so that the few roads in Los Angeles planned as rustic parkways emerged as commercial highways.[53]

The planners included a civic center in their vision of a more efficient, orderly, and attractive metropolis. They felt that grouping Los Angeles' administrative and cultural facilities together at a central location would facilitate public affairs, stabilize downtown values, and form a regional monument. Yet they knew that without a comprehensive plan the city and the county office buildings, libraries, and museums would be scattered all over the urban area.[54] Hence, at the insistence of the City Planning Association, Mayor Frederick T. Woodman appointed a special committee in 1918 to investigate possible

39. Wilshire Boulevard, 1930

sites for an administrative and cultural center. Interested property owners suggested, among other places, the southern periphery of the business district, the Pershing Square and Normal Hill area, and the northern section of downtown Los Angeles. The committee, after evaluating each for accessibility, availability, and cost, recommended that an administrative complex be erected at the northernmost site and a cultural center created at the central one. [55]

The council referred the committee's report to the Planning Commission for further consideration. The commission accepted the division of the administrative and cultural facilities and, confining its attention to the former, examined the prospective locations not only according to the committee's criteria but also for visibility, surroundings, and capacity for expansion. It too selected a northern site—bounded by Hill, First, and Los Angeles Streets and Sunset Boulevard—and in 1922 the council authorized the citizens to choose between this and a more southerly location and to vote on a $7.5 million bond issue for a city hall. The Planning Commission vigorously campaigned for its site. "Shall Los Angeles continue its haphazard growth with its public buildings scattered to the four winds," it asked the voters, "—or—Shall Los Angeles demand the economy, efficiency, and sightliness in its public buildings that can be secured only by intelligent grouping in an Administrative Center built to a definite plan?" [56] The electorate, endorsing the commission's decision, placed the civic center north of First Street and authorized the construction of the city hall there.

Soon after, on the instructions of the city and county authorities, Cook and Hall, Landscape Architects and City Planners, submitted preliminary drawings. The firm based its design on a north-south axis formed by Broadway, Spring, and Main Streets, each widened to one hundred feet with Spring depressed for a short distance. These thoroughfares, which connected with First Street and Sunset Boulevard, provided both sites for the government buildings and surface for the automobile traffic. Cook and Hall completed its modest scheme with a decorative circle at the intersection of Spring and Sunset and a small park to the west of Broadway. [57] The city and county officials solicited other plans too, and among them, the one prepared by Allied Architects Association of Los Angeles was by far the most impressive. It covered nearly a square mile, preserving the Mexican plaza to the east as a historic landmark and developing Bunker Hill to the west as a landscaped park. It fixed an east-west axis, placed the lots along First, Temple, and Sunset, and separated the buildings from the cars by depressing the north-south arteries. [58] The association's design integrated the structures and spaces as imaginatively as it tied the administrative complex to the cultural facilities.

A bitter controversy ensued. Cook and Hall claimed that the Allied Architects plan required too much land and provided too few lots, that the east-west axis deprived the civic center of the mountain vistas to the north, that the underground thoroughfares were extravagant, and that the total costs were prohibitive. Allied Architects replied that the scope of its scheme matched the size of Los Angeles, that the east-west axis capitalized on Bunker Hill as a backdrop, that the depressed streets expedited and isolated traffic, and that the project could be undertaken in sections as funds permitted. It also charged that the Cook and Hall civic center was uninspired in conception, that the north-south axis inhibited a distinctive architectural composition, that the surface arteries did not separate buildings and automobiles, and that the over-all design created little open space. [59] The Southern California Chapter of the American Institute of Architects agreed with Allied Architects, and the Board of Supervisors adopted its plan. But the city council deemed the proposal too expensive and ordered construction of the city hall according to the Cook and Hall drawings.

The resulting deadlock continued until the board and the council, at the insistence of the commercial and civic associations, instructed the City and the Regional Planning Commissions to arrange a mutually satisfactory compromise.[60] Their staffs hoped to combine the best features of both designs, but bound by traffic requirements and property costs, they prepared a plan that in every way compared poorly with its predecessors. It encompassed only the territory bordered by Hill, Main, First, and Ord Streets, neglected the plaza as a landmark and Bunker Hill as a park, and widened and extended all the streets through the administrative center.[61] It thereby dissected the project into assorted building lots separated from one another by a continuous flow of automobiles and detached from the historical, recreational, and cultural institutions of the metropolis. Opposed by the regional branch of the American Institute of Architects but supported by the Chamber of Commerce and other business organizations, the plan was accepted by the city and county authorities—revealing the aesthetic shortcomings of an urban policy based on the primacy of transportation and the parsimony of government.

Over-all, city planning in Los Angeles was not so simply evaluated. From the perspective of Charles Mulford Robinson, the well-known planner who, on his visit there in 1909, objected to the sprawling residences and crowded businesses and envisioned a metropolis not only large but distinguished, full of parks, parkways, and imposing monuments, the accomplishments of planning were undeniable.[62] During the next two decades the City and the Regional Planning Commissions remedied some of these deficiencies and implemented some of these aspirations. Highway planning, subdivision regulation, and land-use restriction rationalized suburban expansion and alleviated downtown congestion while the newly acquired parks and the civic center scheme fashioned an environment at once more rustic and more urbane. To the extent that efficiency, order, and quality could be attained through dispersal, decentralization, and congruity, to that extent city planning in Los Angeles achieved its aims by 1930.

Nevertheless, these achievements indicated merely that city planning was in some ways consonant with the ambitions and attitudes of the developers and residents. Efforts to regulate transportation, subdivision, and land-use were effective only when they corresponded to the preferences of the subdividers. They sanctioned the patterns al-

265

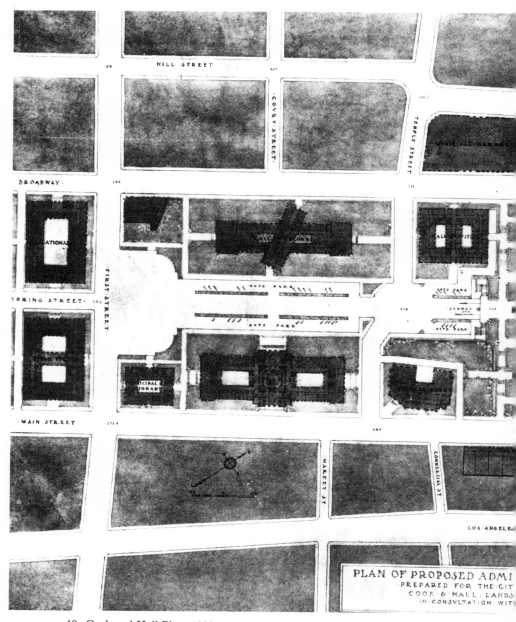

40. Cook and Hall Plan, 1923

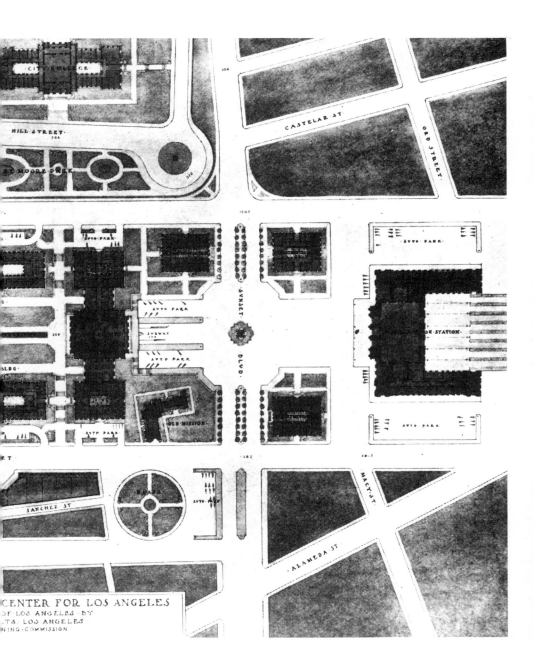

CIVIC BLDG·

HILL STREET·

MOORE PARK·

CASTELAR ST·

ORD STREET·

AUTO PARK·

AUTO PARK·

SUBWAY·

AUTO PARK·

OLD MISSION·

AUTO PARK·

AUTO PARK·

STATION·

AUTO PARK·

BLDG·

PLAZA·

SANCHEZ ST·

AUTO PARK·

MACY ST·

ALAMEDA ST·

CENTER FOR LOS ANGELES
OF LOS ANGELES · BY
TS· LOS ANGELES
NING · COMMISSION

41. Allied Architect's Plan, 1924

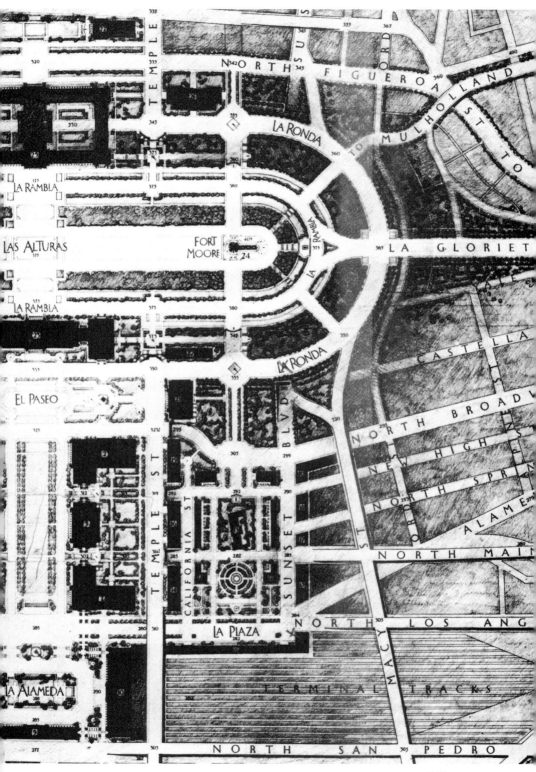

ADMINISTRATIVE CENTER
FEDERAL · STATE · COUNTY · CITY & OTHER PUBLIC BUILDINGS
LOS ANGELES ~ CALIFORNIA

1 COUNTY COURTS
2 STATE BUILDING
3 CITY HALL (built up)

4 TRAFFIC SAFETY
5 HALL of JUSTICE (built)
6 FEDERAL BUILDING

7 ENGINEERING BLDG
8 CONSULAR OFFICES
9 PLAZA CHURCH (built 1861)

10 HEALTH · EDUCATION
11 LATIN-AMERICAN HALL
12 FOREIGN TRADE BLDG

WEBBER · SPAULDING · LANDSCAPE ARCHITECT

42. Official Civic Center Plan, 1927

43. Los Angeles Civic Center, early 1930's

ready imposed by private enterprise far more often than they shaped the cast of future development. Attempts to provide parks, parkways, and a civic center succeeded only where they were adjusted to the priorities of physical improvements, low taxes, and automobile traffic. More often than not, they failed to overcome these obstacles and to supplement the activities of the developers. Planning also transferred certain decisions from the marketplace to the political arena. But this shift just created another setting for the conflict of property interests; it wrought a change of tactics rather than tacticians. In sum, nothing in Los Angeles demonstrated the tenacity of private development as convincingly as the course of public planning.

From the vantage of the metropolitan region, moreover, planning was severely undermined. The planners hoped that their labors would foster a sense of cooperation rather than competition among the communities of Los Angeles County. But, to their despair, the outlying municipalities exploited the techniques of planning to avoid its principles. True, they delegated authority over public facilities to organiza-

271

tions such as the Metropolitan Water District of Southern California which respected the region's environmental unity. But they refused to relinquish their control over land-use regulation and implemented zoning with a parochialism that subverted over-all planning. The prosperity of the 1920's effectively concealed the consequences, but the depression that followed rendered them all too evident. Only then did the people of Los Angeles realize that a unique opportunity to shape their physical environment was lost forever.

Once a rustic, always a rustic—the simple life for me—but living the simple life in these days is a very complicated proposition. It isn't any easy process this getting away from the stream of civilization to live in a sphere of beauty and contentment as one's imagination attempts to picture it. (Ernest C. Steele, 1928)

Conclusion: "THE SIMPLE LIFE"

The Great Depression had a profound impact on Los Angeles. After nearly half a century of persistent and prodigious growth, immigration halted, subdivision subsided, and industry contracted.[1] The depression did not diminish Los Angeles' prior material progress; in terms of population, territory, and productivity, it still stood well in the forefront of American metropolises in 1930. Nor did the depression obscure Los Angeles' unique character. With regard to landscape, community, and government, it realized the aspirations of the native-American middle class more fully than any other urban center. The Great Depression did, however, bring the respite from change which provided the perspective necessary to determine how effectively the people of Los Angeles had reconciled their ambitions for a great metropolis with their visions of the good community.[2]

The immigrants who transformed Los Angeles derived from their antipathy to the late nineteenth-century metropolis a common attitude toward the urban landscape. They thought that the small suburb was more conducive to the maintenance of family life and community ties than the great city and that commercial and industrial decentralization was as necessary for the preservation of a rustic environment as residential dispersal. In the proliferation of business complexes surrounded by single-family subdivisions, they envisioned an alternative to the congested metropolis more consistent with the American past. Unfortunately, though Los Angeles was shaped accordingly, the suburbs intensified the sense of personal isolation, and the houses, highways, and factories overran rural southern California. The depression aggravated these problems. Dissatisfied persons could not flee their neighborhoods for outlying districts, and governmental agencies could not afford to acquire additional open space. The people of Los An-

273

geles reached their suburban retreats, but they did not find in them the bases for a coherent and rustic metropolis.

Dispersal and decentralization, the residents of Los Angeles realized, depended first and foremost on effective transportation. Most expected that the motor car, whose flexibility so well suited the sprawling metropolis, would attract an increasingly large share of over-all patronage. But few expected the electric railways to curtail service, and not even they doubted that the automobile and the highway alone could integrate Los Angeles. After the depression struck, however, the trains deteriorated so seriously that automobiles accounted for about 80 per cent of all passenger miles in the 1930's.[3] Yet even the Automobile Club of Southern California admitted that, extensive highway construction notwithstanding, traffic was highly congested and delays very common. Each year motorists caused 18,000 accidents that injured or killed 34,000 persons and damaged millions of dollars of property in Los Angeles County. And those who arrived safely and on time faced a parking shortage that, as the Automobile Club reported, extended to every commercial section of the metropolis.[4] For better or worse, however, greater Los Angeles was too firmly committed to the automobile by now to essay any alternatives.

Bound by both their faith in equality and their quest for homogeneity, the people of Los Angeles were divided in their attitudes toward ethnic minorities. They believed that racial minorities should assimilate into American society, but felt that their own residential suburbs should remain exclusively white. They urged that all citizens be judged on their character and ability alone, but regarded as inviolable the individual's freedom of association and the employer's choice of personnel. Although some perceived ethnic cultures as a means of enriching American civilization, most considered alien habits peripheral and possibly detrimental to American life. The white majority thus resolved its dilemma by segregating and subordinating the Mexicans, Japanese, and Negroes with a thoroughness that belied America's pluralistic culture and democratic legacy. This was tragic not only for the colored peoples, the chief victims, but also for the white residents, who, as one perceptive observer wrote, neglected "the wealth of cultural heritage waiting to be appropriated by and incorporated into our American culture."[5]

Although they often disagreed on particular issues and personalities, the citizens of Los Angeles were fundamentally progressive in political outlook. They attributed municipal corruption and irresponsibility to machines that retained power through undemocratic procedures, corporate influence, official patronage, and partisan loyalty. They also postulated such an integral agreement about the aims of local government that its essence became business not politics, its function administration not legislation, and its leaders bureaucrats not representatives. Yet though many progressive proposals were adopted, few progressive aspirations were achieved. Direct legislation was exploited by the irresponsible as well as the responsible; municipal ownership exacerbated rather than alleviated political conflict; civil service merely entrenched the administrative bureaucracy; and nonpartisanship forced public servants onto a course of continual campaigning.[6] Charter revisions not only failed to transform Los Angeles into a business corporation, but, by making appointive officials independent of elective officials, also inhibited popular involvement. The rules were changed, but the game was much the same.

Although the people of Los Angeles were impressed with plans for a more efficient, orderly, and attractive metropolis, they were too devoted to development to accept stringent restrictions on private enterprise. They were confident that the subdividers would realize that in the long run proper planning would enhance not jeopardize their interests. They were certain that Los Angeles' environment was so sound that it required oversight rather than overhauling, improvement instead of alteration. The legislators therefore refused to entrust far-reaching powers to the planners, a decision which undermined their position vis-à-vis the subdividers. Also, the differences between private and public welfare became evident as those who supported planning in principle often opposed it in practice. Finally, the fundamental satisfaction with the physical surroundings compelled the planners to circumscribe the range of their regulatory authority. For these reasons the planners succeeded only where their goals corresponded with those of the developers, and planning, instead of guiding private development, merely sanctioned it.

These disparities between conception and realization reflected in part the rapid pace of immigration, subdivision, and industrialization in Los Angeles. Indeed, the inhabitants had only limited control over the way whereby the newcomers as well as technological and economic changes affected the metropolis. Nevertheless, their aspirations were often inconsistent. If residential dispersal were encouraged in order to depress population density, how were the electric railways to avoid ruin and the motor cars to escape congestion? If the ethnic minorities were segregated and subordinated, how were they to assimilate into American society and enter the middle class? If independent satellite

275

cities spread all over greater Los Angeles, how was the region, unified economically, to be cemented politically? And if the party organizations were destroyed and the administrative bureaucracy reinforced, how were the citizens to impress their will on the municipal government? The people of Los Angeles were by no means free of responsibility as these questions became more difficult to answer and these inconsistencies more difficult to deny.

Nor were they without liability for certain misconceptions about urbanization that shaped the structure, character, and culture of Los Angeles. In their reaction against congestion, they failed to realize that concentration in the city permitted spaciousness in the country and unlimited dispersal facilitated limitless sprawl. In their rejection of rapid transit, they ignored the efficacy with which railways moved millions of passengers and the inefficiencies that resulted from total reliance on automobiles. In their revulsion against ethnic minorities, they disregarded the contributions these groups made to community life and the potentialities they offered to metropolitan civilization. In their antagonism to machine rule, they ignored the fact that though a disinterested electorate is an ideal, an interested electorate is more desirable than an uninterested one. And in their objection to rigorous planning, they refused to recognize how staunchly conservative were the professional planners, how deeply entrenched the private developers, and how politically sensitive the planning commissioners.

There was, however, a more profound reason why the people of Los Angeles were unable to reconcile their ambitions for a great metropolis with their visions of the good community. They were severely handicapped by a chronic nostalgia for a bygone world. "Once a rustic, always a rustic—the simple life for me," one resident confided in his diary, "—but living the simple life in these days is a very complicated proposition." "It isn't," he complained, "any easy process this getting away from the stream of civilization to live in a sphere of beauty and contentment as one's imagination attempts to picture it." [7] How presumptuous to think it should be easy! And how misguided those who, on finding it otherwise, retreated to suburbs where they revised their visions and reduced their expectations, turned towards themselves and away from society, abdicated responsibility and accepted fragmentation. The history of Los Angeles revealed above all that this was not the way to resolve satisfactorily the problems of the late nineteenth- and early twentieth-century American metropolis.

BIBLIOGRAPHY   NOTES   INDEX

BIBLIOGRAPHY

I. MANUSCRIPT COLLECTIONS

Ackerman, Fremont. Papers. Special Collections Division, University of California Library, Los Angeles.

Cole, Cornelius. Papers. Special Collections Division, University of California Library, Los Angeles.

Couts, Cave J. Papers. Henry E. Huntington Library, San Marino, California.

Crank, J. F. Papers. Henry E. Huntington Library, San Marino, California.

Dalton, Henry. Papers. Henry E. Huntington Library, San Marino, California.

Dickson, Edward A. Papers. Special Collections Division, University of California Library, Los Angeles.

Elliott, Thomas B. Papers. Henry E. Huntington Library, San Marino, California.

Emery, Mrs. Ernest T. Diary. Special Collections Division, University of California Library, Los Angeles.

Ford Motor Company Archives, Dearborn, Michigan.

Freeman, Daniel. Papers. Special Collections Division, University of California Library, Los Angeles.

Gaffey, John T. Papers. Henry E. Huntington Library, San Marino, California.

Gillis, Robert C. Papers. Mr. Arthur L. Loomis, Pacific Palisades, California.

Graves, Jackson A. Papers. Henry E. Huntington Library, San Marino, California.

Greater Harbor Committee of Two Hundred Records, Los Angeles Chamber of Commerce.

Haynes, John R. Papers. Government and Public Affairs Reading Room, University of California Library, Los Angeles.

Huntington, Henry E. Ledgers and Journals. Huntington Land Companies, San Marino, California.

Huntington Land and Improvement Company Ledgers, Journals, and Records. Huntington Land Companies, San Marino, California.

Huntington-Hopkins Correspondence, Stanford University Library, Stanford, California.

Jones, John P. Papers. Henry E. Huntington Library, San Marino, California.

——— Papers. Special Collections Division, University of California Library, Los Angeles.

Kimball, Frank A. Papers. Public Library, National City, California.

Lesperance, Leo B. Papers. Special Collections Division, University of California Library, Los Angeles.

Lissner, Meyer. Papers. Stanford University Library, Stanford, California.

Lord, Isaac W. Papers. Special Collections Division, University of California Library, Los Angeles.

Los Angeles Board of Harbor Commissioners Files, City Hall, Los Angeles.

Los Angeles Chamber of Commerce Files, Los Angeles Chamber of Commerce.

Los Angeles Chamber of Commerce Minutes, 1889–1930, Los Angeles Chamber of Commerce.

Los Angeles City Planning Department Files, City Hall, Los Angeles.

Los Angeles Common Council Files, City Hall, Los Angeles.

Los Angeles County Law Library Files, County Law Library, Los Angeles.

Los Angeles County Records, Henry E. Huntington Library, San Marino, California.

Los Angeles County Regional Planning Department Files, County Office Building, Los Angeles.

Los Angeles Department of Public Utilities and Transportation Files, City Hall, Los Angeles.

Los Angeles Department of Sewage Design Files, City Hall, Los Angeles.

Maclay, Charles. Papers. Henry E. Huntington Library, San Marino, California.

Miscellaneous Manuscripts, Special Collections Division, University of California Library, Los Angeles.

Morse, Ephraim W. Papers. Junipero Serra Museum, San Diego, California.

Palos Verdes Estates Art Jury Minutes, 1922–1930, City Hall, Palos Verdes Estates, California.

Porphyry Paving Company Records, Special Collections Division, University of California Library, Los Angeles.

Rosecrans, William S. Papers. Special Collections Division, University of California Library, Los Angeles.

San Diego and Gila Southern Pacific and Atlantic Railroad Company Minutes, 1854–1878, Junipero Serra Museum, San Diego, California.

Santa Monica Land and Water Company Ledgers, Journals and Records, Santa Monica Land and Water Company, Pacific Palisades, California.

Sherman, Moses H. Papers. Mr. Arnold Haskell, Los Angeles.

Shorb, J. de Barth. Papers. Henry E. Huntington Library, San Marino, California.

Southern California Edison Company Files, Southern California Edison Company, Los Angeles.

Stearns, Abel. Papers. Henry E. Huntington Library, San Marino, California.

Steele, Ernest C. Diary. Henry E. Huntington Library, San Marino, California.

Stimson, Marshall. Papers. Henry E. Huntington Library, San Marino, California.

Title Insurance and Trust Company Files, Title Insurance and Trust Company, Los Angeles.

White, Stephan M. Papers. Borel Collection, Stanford University Library, Stanford, California.

Whitley, H. J. Papers. Special Collections Division, University of California Library, Los Angeles.

Willard, Charles D. Papers. Henry E. Huntington Library, San Marino, California.

Wilson, Benjamin D. Papers. Henry E. Huntington Library, San Marino, California.

Woods, Reverend James L. Diary. Henry E. Huntington Library, San Marino, California.

II. UNITED STATES GOVERNMENT DOCUMENTS

United States Bureau of Immigration. *Annual Reports of the Commissioner-General of Immigration to the Secretary of Labor*, 1900–1930.

United States Census Office. *The Seventh Census of the United States: 1850*. Washington, 1853.

———— *Population of the United States in 1860 . . . the Eighth Census*. Washington, 1864.

———— *Agriculture of the United States in 1860 . . . the Eighth Census*. Washington, 1864.

———— *Census Reports: Statistics of the Population of the United States . . . the Ninth Census (June 1, 1870)*. Washington, 1872.

——— *Census Reports: Statistics of the Population of the United States at the Tenth Census (June 1, 1880).* Washington, 1883.

——— *Census Reports: Report on the Statistics of the Production of Agriculture at the Tenth Census (June 1, 1880).* Washington, 1883.

——— *Report on the Population of the United States at the Eleventh Census: 1890. Parts I, II.* Washington, 1895–1897.

——— *Report on Manufacturing Industries in the United States at the Eleventh Census: 1890. Part II.* Washington, 1895.

——— *Census Reports. Volume I. Twelfth Census of the United States. 1900. Part I.* Washington, 1901.

United States Bureau of the Census. *Thirteenth Census of the United States. Volumes I, IV. Population. 1910.* Washington, 1913–1914.

——— *Thirteenth Census of the United States . . . Volume IX. Manufactures 1909.* Washington, 1912.

——— *Fourteenth Census of the United States. 1920. Volume II. Population.* Washington, 1922.

——— *Fifteenth Census of the United States: 1930. Population. Volumes I, II, III, IV, VI.* Washington, 1931–1933.

——— *Fifteenth Census of the United States 1930. Metropolitan Districts Population and Area.* Washington, 1932.

——— *Fifteenth Census of the United States. Manufactures: 1929. Volume III.* Washington, 1933.

United States Congress: House Committee on Immigration and Naturalization. Hearings. *Japanese Immigration.* Washington, 1921.

——— *House Executive Documents,* 31st Congress, 1st Session, Number 17, "General Rules and Regulations for the Colonization of Territories of the Republic Mexico, November 21, 1828."

——— *House Executive Documents,* 50th Congress, 1st Session, Number 191, "Survey of San Pedro Bay, California."

——— *House Executive Documents,* 52d Congress, 2d Session, Number 17, H. W. Halleck, "Report on the Laws and Regulations Relative to Grants or Sales of Public Lands in California."

——— *House Executive Documents,* 56th Congress, 2d Session, Number 2, *Report of the Chief of Engineers,* Part 6, Captain James J. Meyler, "Preliminary Examination of Inner Harbor at San Pedro, 1899."

——— *House Executive Documents,* 60th Congress, 2d Session, Number 1,114, Captain Amos A. Fries, "Survey of Wilmington Harbor, California, 1907."

——— *House Executive Documents,* 61st Congress, 2d Session, Number 896, Lieutenant-Colonel C. H. McKinstry, "Preliminary Examination of Los Angeles and Long Beach Harbors, California, 1913."

——— *House Executive Documents,* 62d Congress, 3d Session, Number 1,013, Major Frederick B. Downing, "Preliminary Examination of Los Angeles and Long Beach Harbors, California, 1919."

——— *House Executive Documents,* 68th Congress, 1st Session, Number 349, Colonel Herbert Deakyne, "Preliminary Examination of Los Angeles and Long Beach Harbors, California, 1923."

——— *House Miscellaneous Documents,* 43d Congress, 2d Session, Number 6, "Memorial of the Texas Pacific Railroad Company and the Atlantic and Pacific Railroad Company."

——— *House Miscellaneous Documents,* 43d Congress, 2d Session, Number 36, "Argument of the Texas Pacific Railroad Before the House Committee of the Pacific Railroads, January 18, 1875."

——— *Senate Documents,* 61st Congress, 2d Session, Number 663, "Reports of the Immigration Commission."

———— *Senate Documents,* 64th Congress, 1st Session, Number 415, Commission on Industrial Relations, "Open and Closed Shop Controversy in Los Angeles."

———— *Senate Documents,* 70th Congress, 1st Session, Number 92, Federal Trade Commission, "Hearing on Public Utility Corporations."

———— *Senate Executive Documents,* 50th Congress, 1st Session, Number 51, "Hearings of the United States Pacific Railway Commission."

———— *Senate Executive Documents,* 52d Congress, 1st Session, Number 39, "Report of Board of Engineers on Deep Harbor on Pacific Coast between Points Dume and Capistrano, California."

———— *Senate Executive Documents,* 55th Congress, 1st Session, Number 18, "Report of Board for Locating a Deep-Water Harbor in Southern California."

———— *Senate Miscellaneous Documents,* 41st Congress, 2d Session, Number 121, "Southern Transcontinental Railway Company."

United States Department of the Interior. *The Hoover Dam. Power and Water Contracts and Related Data.* Washington, 1933.

United States District Court, Southern District of California. *Transcript of the Record from the Board of Land Commissioners.* Henry E. Huntington Library, San Marino, California.

III. STATE OF CALIFORNIA DOCUMENTS

California State Legislature. *The Statutes of California,* 1850–1930.

Commission of Immigration and Housing of California. *A Survey Made in Los Angeles City.* San Francisco, 1910.

Constitution of the State of California Adopted . . . 1879. Edward F. Treadwell, ed. San Francisco, 1923.

Railroad Commission of the State of California. *Application 21656. Report on Engineering Survey of Pacific Electric Railway Company.* Los Angeles, 1938, California Public Utilities Commission Files, Sacramento, California.

———— *Archives:* Application 894. "In the Matter of the Application of the Los Angeles Railway Corporation, and the City Railway Company of Los Angeles, for Authority to Transfer Property and Issue Stocks and Bonds," Public Utilities Commission Files.

———— *Archives:* Application 1424. "In the Matter of the Application of the City of Los Angeles and the Board of Public Service Commissioners of the City of Los Angeles to Have the Railroad Commission Fix and Determine the Compensation to be Paid the Southern California Edison Company for Its Electric Distributing System," Public Utilities Commission Files.

———— *Archives:* Application 3791. "In the Matter of the Application of the Pacific Electric Railway Company for an Order Granting Permission to Increase Rates for the Transportation of Passengers between Points on the Pacific Electric Railway in the State," Public Utilities Commission Files.

———— *Archives:* Application 4238. "In the Matter of the Application of the Los Angeles Railway Corporation for an Order Authorizing It to so Operate Its System and Change Its Rates that the Income Will be Sufficient to Pay the Cost of the Service," Public Utilities Commission Files.

———— *Archives:* Application 5806. "In the Matter of the Application of Pacific Electric Railway Company, a Corporation, for an Order Granting Permission to Increase Rates and to Establish Just and Reasonable Rates for the Transportation of Persons and Property between Points in the State of California," Public Utilities Commission Files.

———— *Archives:* Case 1602. "In the Matter of the Commission's Investigation into the Electric Railway Service of the Pacific Electric Company and the Los Angeles

Railway Corporation in the Hollywood District of the City of Los Angeles," Public Utilities Commission Files.

—— *Archives:* Application 13323. "In the Matter of the Application of Los Angeles Railway Corporation for an Order Readjusting Rates and Establishing Just and Reasonable Rates for the Transportation of Persons on the Company's Lines in the State of California," Public Utilities Commission Files.

—— *Archives:* Application 13460. "In the Matter of the Application of the Pacific Electric Railway Company, a Corporation, for an Order Granting Permission to Increase Rates and Fares between Points in the State of California," Public Utilities Commission Files.

—— *Decisions, 1911–1935.*

—— *Report on Financial, Operating and Service Conditions of the Pacific Electric Railway,* Los Angeles, 1928, Mr. Lawrence Veysey, Cambridge, Massachusetts.

—— *Report on the Local Public Transportation Requirements of Los Angeles.* Los Angeles, 1935, Los Angeles Department of Public Utilities and Transportation Files, City Hall, Los Angeles.

Railroad Commission of the State of California Engineering Department. *Application 4238. Report on Service, Operating and Financial Conditions of the Los Angeles Railway Corporation,* Los Angeles, 1919, Department of Public Utilities Files.

—— *Application 5806. Report on Financial, Operating and Service Conditions of Pacific Electric Railway Company.* San Francisco, 1921, Department of Public Utilities Files.

Ready, Lester S., J. O. Marsh, and Richard Sachse, *Joint Report on Street Railway Survey, City of Los Angeles to Railroad Commission of the State of California.* Los Angeles, 1925, Department of Public Utilities Files.

IV. CITY AND COUNTY OF LOS ANGELES DOCUMENTS

Los Angeles (City). Board of City Planning Commissioners, *Annual Reports,* 1929–30—1933–34.

—— Board of City Planning Commissioners Minutes, 1920–1930, Department of City Planning, City Hall, Los Angeles.

—— Board of Harbor Commissioners, *Annual Reports,* 1914–15—1932–33.

—— Board of Harbor Commissioners Minutes, 1914–1930, Harbor Department, City Hall, Los Angeles.

—— Board of Los Angeles Aqueduct Power, *First Annual Report,* 1909–1910.

—— Board of Playground and Recreation Commissioners Minutes, 1920–1930, Department of Parks, City Hall, Los Angeles.

—— Board of Public Service Commissioners, *Annual Reports,* 1911–1925.

—— Board of Public Service Commissioners Minutes, 1911–1925, Department of Water and Power, Los Angeles.

—— Board of Public Utilities and Transportation Commissioners, *Fiftieth Annual Report,* 1958–1959.

—— Board of Public Utilities Commissioners, *Annual Reports,* 1909–10—1929–30.

—— Board of Public Utilities Commissioners Minutes, 1909–1930, Department of Public Utilities and Transportation, City Hall, Los Angeles.

—— Board of Water and Power Commissioners, *Annual Reports,* 1926–1935.

—— Board of Water and Power Commissioners Minutes, 1926–1935, Department of Water and Power, Los Angeles.

—— Board of Water Commissioners, *Annual Reports,* 1902–1910.

—— Board of Water Commissioners Minutes, 1902–1910, Department of Water and Power, Los Angeles.

—— *Charter and Revised Ordinances of the City of Los Angeles.* Compiled by William McPherson. Los Angeles, 1873.

———— *Charter and Compiled Ordinances and Resolutions of the City of Los Angeles.* Compiled by Freeman G. Teed. Los Angeles, 1889.

———— *Charter of the City of Los Angeles as Adopted January, 1889 . . . and Amended January, 1917.* Los Angeles, ca. 1917.

———— *Charter of the City of Los Angeles Annotated. As Adopted January 22, 1925 [and] Amended May 15, 1933.* Compiled by Ray Chesebro et al. Los Angeles, 1933.

———— Chief Engineer of the Los Angeles Aqueduct, *First Annual Report,* 1907.

———— City Engineer, *Annual Reports,* 1921–22—1922–23.

———— Common Council, *Archives: Records: Petitions,* 1850–1930, Office of the City Clerk, City Hall, Los Angeles.

———— *Compiled Ordinances and Resolutions of the City of Los Angeles.* Compiled by W. W. Robinson. Los Angeles, 1884.

———— *Compiled Ordinances and Resolutions of the City of Los Angeles.* Compiled by Freeman G. Teed, Los Angeles, 1887.

———— Department of Parks, *Annual Report,* 1925–1926.

———— Department of Playground and Recreation, *Annual Report,* 1929–1930.

———— Housing Commission, *Annual Reports,* 1909–10—1913–14.

———— *Municipal Reports,* 1879–1886, Public Library, Los Angeles.

———— *Ordinances and By-Laws of the City of Los Angeles, Los Angeles Star,* June 3, 1860.

———— *Revised Charter and Compiled Ordinances of the City of Los Angeles.* Compiled by William M. Caswell. Los Angeles, 1878.

Los Angeles (County). Office of the County Surveyor. *The Official Subdividers Guide.* Los Angeles, ca. 1927.

———— Regional Planning Commission. *A Comprehensive Report on the Regional Plan of Highways. Section 2-E San Gabriel Valley.* Los Angeles, 1929.

———— ———— *A Comprehensive Report on the Regional Plan of Highways. Section 4 Long Beach-Redondo Area.* Los Angeles, 1931.

———— ———— *First Annual Report,* 1924 (Hugh Pomeroy, "Regional Planning in Practice").

———— ———— *Report of a Highway Traffic Survey in the County of Los Angeles.* Los Angeles, 1934.

———— Regional Planning Commission Minutes, 1927–1930, County Office Building, Los Angeles.

V. NEWSPAPERS AND PERIODICALS

Allied Architects Association of Los Angeles, *Bulletin,* 1924–1926.

California Eagle (Los Angeles), 1910–1930.

California Outlook, 1911–1918.

California Southland, 1918–1929.

Department of Research and Service, *Industrial Surveys of Los Angeles,* Los Angeles, 1923–1928.

Eberle Economic Service, 1924–1935.

Electric Railway Journal, 1909–1930.

The Golden West. A Magazine of Progress, 1919–1925.

El Heraldo de Mexico (Los Angeles), 1920.

Historical Society of Southern California, *Annual Publications,* 1884–1934.

Historical Society of Southern California, *Quarterly Publications,* 1935–1963.

Los Angeles Chamber of Commerce, *Members Annuals,* 1900–1930.

Los Angeles City Club, *Bulletin,* 1920–1930.

Los Angeles *Daily News,* 1868–1873.

Los Angeles *Evening Express,* 1873–1880, 1883–1885, 1891–1902.

Los Angeles *Examiner,* 1903–1930.

Los Angeles *Herald,* 1874–1891.
Los Angeles *Morning Journal,* 1879–1885.
Los Angeles Realtor, 1921–1930.
Los Angeles *Semi-Weekly News,* 1862–1863.
Los Angeles *Socialist,* 1902–1909.
Los Angeles *Star,* 1852–1855, 1859–1863, 1868–1879.
Los Angeles *Times,* 1883–1930.
Los Angeles *Tri-Weekly News,* 1863–1868.
Municipal League of Los Angeles, *Municipal Affairs,* 1905–1909.
Municipal League of Los Angeles, *Bulletin,* 1913–1923.
Municipal League of Los Angeles, *Bulletin. Light on Your City's Affairs,* 1924–1931.
National City *Record,* 1880–1886.
La Opinion (Los Angeles), 1927.
Pacific Municipalities, 1899–1930.
Pacific Outlook, 1895–1911.
Palos Verdes Estates Homes Association, *Bulletin,* 1924–1930.
San Diego *Herald,* 1851–1860.
San Diego *Union,* 1868–1885.
Southern California Business, 1922–1930.
Traffic Commission of the City and County of Los Angeles, *Annual Reports,* 1925–1930.

VI. CONTEMPORARY ACCOUNTS

Adamic, Louis. *Laughing in the Jungle: The Autobiography of an Immigrant in America.* New York and London, 1932.
———— *The Truth about Los Angeles.* Girard, Kansas, 1927.
Adams, Emma H. *To and Fro in Southern California.* Cincinnati, 1887.
Agriculture Department of Los Angeles Chamber of Commerce. *What the Newcomer should know about the Small Farm in Los Angeles County.* 1927.
Alderman, N. *General Industrial Report of Burbank.* Burbank, 1924.
Allen, Hugh. "California, VII," in Goodyear Tire and Rubber Company, *The Wing-foot Clan,* no. 9, p. 80.
Annual Report of the Los Angeles County Pioneers of Southern California for the Year 1909–1910.
Automobile Club of Southern California, *A Report on Los Angeles Traffic Problems with Recommendations for Relief.* Los Angeles, 1922.
Ayers, James J. *Gold and Sunshine: Reminiscences of Early California.* Boston, 1922.
Babcock, Wm. H. & Sons. *Report on the Economic and Engineering Feasibility of Regrading the Bunker Hill Area.* Los Angeles, 1931.
Baker, Donald, M. *A Rapid Transit System for Los Angeles California: A Report to Central Business District Association.* Los Angeles, 1933.
Bartlett, Dana W. *The Better City: A Sociological Study of a Modern American City.* Los Angeles, 1907.
Bass, Charlotta. *Forty Years: Memoirs from the Pages of a Newspaper.* Los Angeles, 1960.
Bell, Horace. *Reminiscences of a Ranger or Early Times in Southern California.* Santa Barbara, California, 1927.
Bliven, Bruce. "Los Angeles: The City That Is Bacchanalian—In a Nice Way," *The New Republic,* 2: 197–200 (July 13, 1927).
Board of Economic Survey. *Economic Survey of the Port of Los Angeles, July 15, 1933.* Los Angeles Chamber of Commerce Files.
Bond, J. Max. "The Negro in Los Angeles," University of Southern California Doctoral Dissertation, 1936.
Brace, Charles Loring. *The New West: or California in 1867–1868.* New York, 1869.
Brewer, William. *Up and Down in California in 1860–1864.* Francis P. Farquhar, ed. Berkeley and Los Angeles, 1949.

Brook, Harry Ellington. *The Land of Sunshine: Southern California.* Los Angeles, 1893.

Bryant, Edwin. *What I Saw in California: Being the Journal of a Tour . . . in the Years 1846, 1847.* Santa Ana, California, 1936.

Bryce, James. *The American Commonwealth.* 3d ed. New York, 1895.

Carr, Harry. *Los Angeles City of Dreams.* New York, 1935.

Caughey, John Walton, ed. *The Indians of Southern California in 1852: The B. D. Wilson report and a selection of contemporary comment.* San Marino, California, 1952.

Cheney, Charles H. "Zoning in Practice." *Proceedings of the Eleventh National Conference on City Planning. Niagara Falls and Buffalo, May 26-28, 1919.* Boston, 1920, pp. 162–185.

Citizens Transportation Survey Commission. *Report on Traffic and Transportation Survey.* Berkeley, 1940.

Committee on Municipal Ownership, City Club of Los Angeles. *Report on Government Ownership of Public Utility Service Undertakings.* Los Angeles, 1917.

Cook and Hall to the City Council of Los Angeles, January 28, 1925, Municipal Reference Library, City Hall, Los Angeles.

Damon, George A. "Inter and intra Urban Transit and Traffic as a Regional Planning Problem." *Proceedings of the Fifteenth National Conference on City Planning, Baltimore, Md., April 30—May 1-2, 1923.* Baltimore, 1923, pp. 45-54.

———— "Relation of the Motor Bus to Other Methods of Transportation." *Proceedings of the Sixteenth National Conference on City Planning. Los Angeles, California, April 7-10, 1924.* Baltimore, 1924, pp. 79–90.

Dana, Richard Henry, Jr. *Two Years before the Mast and Twenty-four Years After.* New York, 1909.

Day, George M. "Races and Cultural Oases," *Sociology and Social Research*, 18: 326–339 (March-April 1934).

Dillon, Richard H., ed. *California Trail Herd: The 1850 Missouri to California Diary of Cyrus C. Loveland.* Los Gatos, California, 1961.

Douglas, H. Paul. *The Church in the Changing City.* New York, 1927.

Douglas, J. R. "Report on Conditions Affecting the Real Estate Business in Los Angeles." 1923. Security-First National Bank Research Department, Los Angeles.

Dresser, Horatio W. *Human Efficiency: A Psychological Study of Modern Problems.* New York and London, 1912.

Duflot de Mofras, Eugene. *Travels on the Pacific Coast.* Marguerite Eyer Wilbur, ed. and tr. 2 vols. Santa Ana, California, 1937.

Dykstra, Clarence A. "Los Angeles Returns to the Ward System," *National Municipal Review*, 14: 210–214 (May 1925).

———— "The Pending Los Angeles Charter," *National Municipal Review*, 13: 148–151 (March 1924).

Edgell, G. H. *The American Architecture of To-day.* New York, 1928.

Egleston, Nathaniel H. *The Home and Its Surroundings or Villages and Village Life.* New York, 1884.

Engineering Department Automobile Club of Southern California. *Traffic Survey, Los Angeles Metropolitan Area Nineteen Hundred Thirty-Seven.* Los Angeles, ca. 1937.

Ervin, J. McFarline. "The Participation of the Negro in the Community Life of Los Angeles," University of Southern California Masters Thesis, 1927.

Finck, Henry T. *The Pacific Coast Scenic Tour.* London, 1891.

Forbes, Alexander. *California: A History of Upper and Lower California.* Reprinted from the 1839 edition. San Francisco, 1937.

Frank, Herman. *Scrapbook of a Western Pioneer.* Los Angeles, 1934.

Fukuoha, Fumiko. "Mutual Life and Aid Among the Japanese in Southern California with Special Reference to Los Angeles," University of Southern California Masters Thesis, 1937.

Gamio, Manuel, comp. *The Mexican Immigrant. His Life Story. Autobiographical Documents.* Chicago, 1921.

Garland, Hamlin. *A Son of the Middle Border.* New York, 1924.

Gordon, Jan, and Cora Gordon. *Star-Dust in Hollywood.* London, 1931.

Graves, Jackson A. *California Memories 1857–1927.* 2d ed. Los Angeles, 1930.

—— *My Seventy Years in California 1857–1927.* Los Angeles, 1927.

Great Britain Foreign Office. *Accounts and Papers.* 1884 (Volume XXXV), 1886 (Volume XXIX), 1888 (Volume XXXIX), 1889 (Volume XXXV), 1890 (Volume XXXVII).

Gregg, Gardner W. "Los Angeles' Bold Plan for a Civic Center," *National Municipal Review,* 14: 406–409 (July 1925).

Griffith, Griffith J. *Parks, Boulevards and Playgrounds.* Los Angeles, 1910.

Hall, Bolton. *Thrift.* New York, 1916.

Hill, Joseph A. "Interstate Migration." United States Bureau of the Census. *Special Reports. Supplementary Analysis and Derivative Tables. Twelfth Census of the United States: 1900.* Washington, 1906.

Historical Society of Southern California, Los Angeles, 1887. San Francisco, 1888.

Howe, E. W. *The Story of a Country Town.* New York, 1926.

Hutton, William Rich. *Glances at California 1847–1853. Diaries and Letters.* San Marino, California, 1942.

"Interlocking Specifications for the Regional Plan of Los Angeles County." City Planning Department, Los Angeles.

Irvine, Alexander. *Revolution in Los Angeles,* 1911.

James, George Wharton. *Out West,* 5: 208–209 (March 4, 1913).

Jenkins, Arthur C. "Preliminary Report on Engineering and Economic Analysis of Operations, Facilities and Financial Status of Pacific Electric Railway Company, Los Angeles, California." (July 15, 1948). California Public Utilities Commission.

Jessup, Walter A., and Albert Shiels. *Report of the Advisory Committee to the Board of Education of the City of Los Angeles . . .* Los Angeles, 1916.

Johnson, Arthur T. *California: An Englishman's Impression of the Golden State.* New York, ca. 1910.

Kawasaki, Kanichi. "The Japanese Community of East San Pedro, Terminal Island, California," University of Southern California Masters Thesis, 1931.

Kelker, de Leuw & Company. *Report and Recommendations on a Comprehensive Rapid Transit Plan for the City and County of Los Angeles.* Chicago, 1925.

Kenderdine, T. S. *California Revisited, 1857–1897.* Newton, Pennsylvania, 1898.

—— *A California Tramp . . . Life on the Plains and in the Golden State Thirty Years Ago.* Newton, Pennsylvania, 1888.

Kip, William Ingraham. *The Early Days of My Episcopate.* New York, 1894.

Kirkham, Stanton Davis. *Resources: An Interpretation of the Well-Rounded Life.* New York and London, 1910.

Lewis, Edwin L. "Street Railway Development in Los Angeles and Environs." 2 vols. Possession of Mr. John Curtis, Los Angeles Metropolitan Transit Authority, Los Angeles.

Linklater, Eric. *Juan in America.* New York, 1931.

Los Angeles Board of City Planning Commissioners. *Conference on the Rapid Transit Question.* (January 21, 1930). Public Library, Los Angeles.

—— *Second Conference on Mass Transportation.* (May 16, 1930). Public Library, Los Angeles.

Los Angeles Board of Public Service Commissioners. *Complete Report on Construction of the Los Angeles Aqueduct.* Los Angeles, 1916.

Los Angeles Board of Trade. *Annual Report for 1887–1888.*

Los Angeles Chamber of Commerce Industrial Department. *General Industrial Report of Los Angeles County.* Los Angeles, 1929.
—————— *General Industrial Report of Los Angeles County.* Los Angeles, 1930.
Louis, Kit King. "Study of American-Born and American-Reared Chinese in Los Angeles," University of Southern California Masters Thesis, 1931.
Low, George P. "The Generating, Transmission and Distribution Systems of the Edison Electric Company of Los Angeles, Cal.," *Journal of Electricity, Power and Gas,* 12: 9–46 (January 1903).
Luther, Mark Lee. *The Boosters.* Indianapolis, 1923.
McClintock, Miller. *A Proposed Traffic Ordinance for the City of Los Angeles, with Annotations and Recommendations for the Remedy of Street Traffic Conditions.* Los Angeles, 1924.
Markey, Morris. *This Country of Yours.* Boston, 1932.
Metropolitan Water District of Southern California. *History and First Annual Report [1938].* Los Angeles, 1939.
Mohler, Charles K. "Public Utility Regulation by Los Angeles," *The Annals of the American Academy of Political and Social Sciences,* 53:108–118 (May 1914).
Morgan, John T. "Our American Mayors: VIII. Mayor George E. Cryer of Los Angeles," *National Municipal Review,* 17: 27–32 (January 1928).
Morris, Howard L., and Thomas Wright. *Los Angeles City Directory for 1879-1880.* Los Angeles, 1879.
Municipal League of Los Angeles. *Statement of the Facts Pertaining to the Present Election . . . November 18th, 1911.* 1911.
Newmark, Harris. *Sixty Years in Southern California 1853-1913.* Maurice H. and Marco R. Newmark, eds. 2d ed. New York, 1926.
Newmark, Maurice H., and Marco R., eds. *Census of the City and County of Los Angeles for the Year 1850.* Los Angeles, 1929.
Nordhoff, Charles. *California for Health, Pleasure, and Residence: A Book for Travellers and Settlers.* New York, 1874.
Norton, R. H. *Reminiscences of an Agitator.* Los Angeles, 1912.
Office of the Chief Engineer, Pacific Electric Railway Company. "Corporate History of the Pacific Electric as of June 30, 1914." Mr. James Gibson, California Public Utilities Commission, San Francisco.
Ogden, Adele, ed. "Business Letters of Alfred Robinson," *California Historical Society Quarterly,* 23: 301–344 (December 1944).
Olin, Blaine. "Municipal Buses: Santa Monica Solves Its Transportation Problem," *Public Ownership of Public Utilities,* 17: 3–4 (January 1935).
Olmsted, Frederick Law. "Palos Verdes Estates," *Landscape Architecture,* 17: 255–290 (July 1927).
Olmsted, Frederick Law, Harland Bartholemew, and Charles Henry Cheney. *A Major Traffic Street Plan for Los Angeles.* Los Angeles, 1924.
Olmsted Brothers, and Bartholemew and Associates. *Report to the Citizens Commission on Parks, Playgrounds and Beaches Los Angeles Region.* Los Angeles, 1931.
Ong, Joe R. "A Report on Some of the Problems of Operation of the Los Angeles Railway, July 31, 1923." Mr. John Curtis, Los Angeles Metropolitan Transit Authority.
Park, Robert Ezra. "Education and the Cultural Crisis," *American Journal of Sociology,* 48: 728–736 (May 1943). Reprinted in Robert Ezra Park. *Race and Culture.* Glencoe, Illinois, 1950.
Pierce, Buford E. *Illustrated Annual: Federation of State Societies of Southern California 1914.* Los Angeles, 1914.
Pomeroy, Hugh. "Los Angeles Civic Center Street Plan," *Community Builder,* 1: 18–25.
"Report of the Allied Architects Association of Los Angeles on an Administrative Center for the County of Los Angeles and the City of Los Angeles, December 31, 1924."

"Report of Aqueduct Investigation Board." Public Library, Los Angeles.

"Report of the City Planning Association on our New City Hall and Administration Center." (1922). Municipal Reference Library, City Hall, Los Angeles.

Revere, Joseph Warren. *A Tour of Duty in California* . . . . New York, 1849.

Richards, Eugene S. "The Effects of the Negro's Migration to Southern California upon His Socio-Cultural Patterns," University of Southern California Doctoral Dissertation, 1941.

Robinson, Alfred. *Life in California before the Conquest.* Reprinted from the 1847 edition. San Francisco, 1925.

Robinson, Charles Mulford, "The City Beautiful." Los Angeles Municipal Art Commission. *Report . . . to the Mayor, the City Council and Board of Public Works.* Los Angeles, 1909.

Salvator, Ludwig Louis. *Los Angeles in the Sunny Seventies: A Flower from the Golden Land.* Marguerite Eyer Wilbur, tr. Los Angeles, 1929.

Search, P. W., Superintendent of Schools. *Los Angeles City Schools. Report of Conditions with Recommendations.* Los Angeles, 1895.

Security Trust and Savings Bank. *Industrial Survey of Los Angeles.* 1923–1928.

Simpson, George. *An Overland Journey Round the World during the Years 1841 and 1842.* Philadelphia, 1847.

Sinclair, Upton. *Autobiography.* New York, 1962.

Skinner, Emory Fiske. *Reminiscences.* Chicago, 1908.

Smith, Clara G. "The Development of the Mexican People in the Community of Watts," University of Southern California Masters Thesis, 1933.

Smith, Sarah Bixby. *Adobe Days: A Book of California Memories.* Los Angeles, 1931.

Smutz, Huber Earl. "City Planning Impressions." Nos. 1–3.

——"Zoning Facts." Nos. 1–6.

Smythe, William E. "Significance of Southern California," *Out West,* 32: 287ff (April 1910).

Southern California Bureau of Information. *Southern California: An Authentic Description for the Homeseeker, Tourist, and Invalid.* Los Angeles, 1892.

"Southwestern Economic Conference Transcript, June 15–17, 1925." Bancroft Library, University of California, Berkeley.

Spalding, William Andrew. *Los Angeles Newspaperman: An Autobiographic Account.* Robert V. Hine, ed. San Marino, California, 1964.

Sparks, Frank H. "The Location of Industry: An Analysis of Some of the Factors which have Affected the Location of Industry in the Ten Southern Counties of California," University of Southern California Doctoral Dissertation, 1941.

Thomas, Don. "In Competition for American Tourists and Capital," *California Journal of Development,* 20: 11–12 (April 1930).

Thompson and West. *History of Los Angeles County California, 1880.* Reprinted from the 1880 edition. Berkeley, 1959.

Trine, Ralph Waldo. *The Land of Living Men.* New York, 1910.

Truman, Ben C. *Homes and Happiness in the Golden State of California.* San Francisco, 1885.

—— *Semi-Tropical California.* San Francisco, 1874.

Uono, Kiyoshi, "The Factors Affecting the Geographical Aggregation and Dispersion of the Japanese Residences in the City of Los Angeles," University of Southern California Masters Thesis, 1927.

Van Dyke, T. S. *Millionaires of a Day: An Inside History of the Great Southern California "Boom."* New York, 1890.

Warner, Charles D. *Our Italy.* New York, 1891.

Wells, Carl Douglas. "A Changing Social Institution in an Urban Environment: A Study of the Changing Behavior Patterns of the Disciples of Christ in Los Angeles," University of Southern California Doctoral Dissertation, 1931.

West, Nathaniel. *The Day of the Locust.* New York, 1939.

Wheat, Carl I., et al. *Public Utility Regulation by the California Railroad Commission.* San Francisco, 1927.

Whitnall, G. Gordon. "The Experience in the Los Angeles Region." *Planning Problems of Town, City, and Region. Papers and Discussions at the Nineteenth National Conference on City Planning, Washington, D.C., May 9–11, 1927.* Philadelphia, 1927, pp. 126–130.

Whitworth, L. *Los Angeles City and County Directory for 1881–1882.* Los Angeles, 1882.

Wilcox, Delos F. *Analysis of the Electric Railway Problem. Report to the Federal Electric Railways Commission with Summary and Recommendations.* New York, 1921.

——— *Preliminary Report on Local Transportation Policy Submitted to the City Council of the City of Los Angeles* (April 28, 1927).

Willard, Charles D. *The Free Harbor Contest at Los Angeles.* Los Angeles, 1899.

Woods, S. D. *Light and Shadows of Life on the Pacific Coast.* New York, 1910.

Wright, Willard Huntington. "Los Angeles—The Chemically Pure," *The Smart Set* (March 1913). *The Smart Set Anthology.* Burton Rascoe and Graff Conklin, eds. New York, 1934, pp. 90–102.

Zoning in the United States. The Annals of the American Academy of Political and Social Sciences. No. 155, pt. II (March 1931).

VII. GRAPHIC MATERIALS

Atchison and Eshelman. *Los Angeles Then and Now.* Los Angeles, 1897.

Baist, George William. *Baist's Real Estate Atlas of Surveys of Los Angeles.* Philadelphia, 1889.

——— *Real Estate Atlas of Surveys of Los Angeles.* Philadelphia, 1921.

The Bungalowcraft Company. *Homes of the Moment.* 3d ed. Los Angeles, 1931.

The Bungalowcraft Company. *New Spanish Bungalows.* 6th ed. Los Angeles, 1930.

Ferrell, W. R. "The Merchants' Map of the Los Angeles Market" (1930). Chamber of Commerce, Los Angeles.

Los Angeles Department of Water and Power. "City of Los Angeles and Vicinity Showing the Percentage of the Area Occupied by the Different Classes of Improvements as of January 1925." Department of Water and Power, Los Angeles.

——— "City of Los Angeles and Vicinity Showing the Percentage of the Area Occupied by the Different Classes of Improvements as of January 1934." Department of Water and Power, Los Angeles.

"Los Angeles Metropolitan and ABC City Market by Family Expenditures" (ca. 1935). Chamber of Commerce, Los Angeles.

The Los Angeles Zoning Atlas. Los Angeles, 1930.

"Map of the City of Los Angeles California by H. J. Stevenson, U.S. Dept. Surveyor, 1884." Department of Water and Power, Los Angeles.

"Map of the City of Los Angeles California by H. J. Stevenson, U.S. Dept. Surveyor, 1876." Department of Water and Power, Los Angeles.

Metropolitan Surveys. *"Industrial Guide" and Street Index of Los Angeles and Its Environs.* Los Angeles, ca. 1935. Chamber of Commerce, Los Angeles.

Morehouse, A. G., and C. E. Elstner, *Pen Sketches of Los Angeles.* Los Angeles, 1896.

"The Old Spanish and Mexican Ranchos of Los Angeles County." Title Insurance and Trust Company, Los Angeles.

Security-First National Bank Photograph Collections, Security-First National Bank, Los Angeles.

Title Insurance and Trust Company Photograph Collection, Title Insurance and Trust Company, Los Angeles.

Weston, Rex D. *Weston's Double Bungalows.* Los Angeles, 1924.

VIII. SECONDARY SOURCES

Atherton, Lewis. *Main Street on the Middle Border.* Bloomington, Indiana, 1954.

Bancroft, Hubert H. *California Pastoral, 1769-1848.* San Francisco, 1881.

Barsness, Richard W. "Railroads and Los Angeles: The Quest for a Deep-Water Port," *Southern California Quarterly,* 47: 379–391 (December 1965).

Baur, John E. *The Health Seekers of Southern California, 1870-1900.* San Marino, California, 1959.

Bean, Walton. *Boss Ruef's San Francisco.* Berkeley and Los Angeles, 1952.

Bemis, George W., and Nancy Basche. *Los Angeles County as an Agency of Municipal Government.* Los Angeles, 1946.

Bernstein, Irving. *The Lean Years: A History of the American Worker 1920-1933.* Boston, 1960.

Blackmar, Frank W. "Spanish Colonization in the Southwest," *Johns Hopkins University Studies in Historical and Political Science,* VIII (1890).

———— "Spanish Institutions of the Southwest," *Johns Hopkins University Studies in Historical and Social Sciences,* Extra Volume 10 (1891).

Blegen, Theodore C. "The Competition of the Northwestern States for Immigrants," *Wisconsin Magazine of History,* 3: 3–29 (September 1919).

Blow, Ben. *California Highways.* San Francisco, 1920.

Bogardus, Emory F. *The Mexicans in the United States.* Los Angeles, 1934.

Bolton, Herbert E. "The Mission as a Frontier Institution in the Spanish-American Colonies," *American Historical Review,* 23: 42–61 (October 1917).

Braden, Charles S. *Spirits in Rebellion: The Rise and Development of New Thought.* Dallas, 1963.

Bradley, Glenn D. *The Story of the Santa Fe.* Boston, 1920.

Brown, Arthur J. "The Promotion of Emigration to Washington," *Pacific Northwest Quarterly,* 36: 3–18 (January 1945).

Bystrom, Shirley C. "Los Angeles, 1846–1860," University of California at Berkeley Masters Thesis, 1951.

Caughey, John Walton. *California.* New York, 1940.

———— *Gold is the Cornerstone.* Berkeley, 1948.

Cleland, Robert Glass. *The Cattle on a Thousand Hills: Southern California, 1850-1880.* San Marino, California, 1941.

———— *From Wilderness to Empire: A History of California, 1542-1900.* New York, 1944.

———— *The Irvine Ranch of Southern California 1810-1950.* San Marino, California, 1952.

Clodius, Albert Howard. "The Quest for Good Government in Los Angeles 1890–1910," Claremont Graduate School Doctoral Dissertation, 1953.

Condit, Carl. *The Rise of the Skyscraper.* Chicago, 1962.

Cook, S. F. "The Conflict between the California Indian and White Civilization: I. The Indian versus the Spanish Mission," *Ibero-Americana,* 21 (1943).

———— "The Conflict between the California Indian and White Civilization: III. The American Invasion," *Ibero-Americana,* 23 (1943).

———— "Population Trends among the California Mission Indians," *Ibero-Americana,* 17: 5–9 (1940).

Coons, Arthur G., and Arjay R. Miller. *An Economic and Industrial Survey of the Los Angeles and San Diego Areas.* Sacramento, 1941.

Cross, Ira B. *A History of the Labor Movement in California.* Berkeley, 1935.

Crouch, Winston W., and Beatrice Dinerman. *Southern California Metropolis: A Study in Development of Government for a Metropolitan Area.* Berkeley and Los Angeles, 1964.

Crump, Spencer. *Ride the Big Red Cars: How Trolleys Helped Build Southern California.* Los Angeles, 1962.

Daggett, Stuart. *Chapters on the History of the Southern Pacific.* New York, 1922.

Dakin, Susanna Bryant. *A Scotch Paisano: Hugo Reid's Life in California, 1832-1852.* Berkeley, 1939.

De Graaf, Lawrence Brooks. "Negro Migration to Los Angeles, 1930–1950," University of California at Los Angeles Doctoral Dissertation, 1962.

Delafons, John. *Land-Use Controls in the United States.* Joint Center for Urban Studies of the Massachusetts Institute of Technology and Harvard University, 1962.

Dick, Everett. *The Sod-house Frontier 1854–1890.* New York, 1938.

Dohrman, H. T. *California Cult: The Story of "Mankind United."* Boston, 1958.

Dumke, Glenn S. *The Boom of the Eighties in Southern California.* San Marino, California, 1944.

Engelhardt, Fr. Zephyrin. *The Missions and Missionaries of California.* 4 vols. San Francisco, 1908–1915.

Ferrier, William W. *Ninety Years of Education in California 1846–1936.* Berkeley, 1937.

Findley, James Clifford. "The Economic Boom of the 'Twenties in Los Angeles," Claremont Graduate School Doctoral Dissertation, 1958.

Forbes, B. C. *Men Who Are Making the West.* New York, 1923.

Fowler, Frederick Hall. *Hydroelectric Power Systems of California and Their Extensions into Oregon and Nevada.* Washington, 1923.

Francis, Jessie D. "An Economic and Social History of Mexican California (1822–1846)," University of California at Berkeley Doctoral Dissertation, 1936.

Gates, Paul. "Adjudication of Spanish-Mexican Land Claims in California," *Huntington Library Quarterly,* 21: 213–236 (May 1958).

———— *The Illinois Central Railroad and Its Colonization Work.* Cambridge, Mass., 1934.

Grodinsky, Julius. *Transcontinental Railway Strategy, 1869–1893: A Study of Businessmen.* Philadelphia, 1962.

Guinn, J. M. *A History of California and an Extended History of Los Angeles and Environs.* 3 vols. Los Angeles, 1915.

Hancock, Ralph. *Fabulous Boulevard.* New York, 1909.

Handlin, Oscar. "The Social System," *Daedelus* (Winter 1961), pp. 11–30.

———— *The Uprooted.* Boston, 1951.

Hansen, Marcus Lee. "Official Encouragement of Immigration to Iowa," *Iowa Journal of History and Politics,* 19: 159–195 (April 1921).

Hedges, James B. *Building the Canadian West: The Land and Colonization Policies of the Canadian Pacific Railway.* New York, 1939.

———— "Promotion of Immigration to the Pacific Northwest by the Railroads," *Mississippi Valley Historical Review,* 15: 180–203 (September 1928).

Hilton, George W., and John F. Due. *The Electric Interurban Railways in America.* Stanford, California, 1960.

Hittell, Theodore H. *History of California.* 4 vols. San Francisco, 1885.

Hoyt, Franklin. "The Los Angeles and San Gabriel Valley Railroad," *Pacific Historical Review,* 20: 227–240 (August 1951).

———— "Railroad Development in Southern California, 1868–1900," University of Southern California Doctoral Dissertation, 1951.

Hoyt, Homer. *One Hundred Years of Land Values in Chicago.* Chicago, 1933.

Ichihashi, Yamato. *Japanese in the United States.* Stanford, California, 1932.

Ingersoll, Luther. *Ingersoll's Century History: Santa Monica Bay Cities.* Los Angeles, 1908.

Jermain, Nina Lauretta. "The History of the Los Angeles Civic Center," University of Southern California Masters Thesis, 1934.

Journal of Electricity, Power and Gas, 13: 10ff (January 1903).

Kidston, William. "The Oil Fields of Southern California. A History of the Los Angeles Oil Basin." 1936. 2 vols. Special Collections Divisions, University of California Library, Los Angeles.

Kilner, William H. B. *Arthur Letts 1862–1923.* Los Angeles, 1927.

Kirker, Harold. *California's Architectural Frontier: Style and Tradition in the Nineteenth Century.* San Marino, California, 1960.

Kleinsorge, Paul L. *The Boulder Canyon Project: Historical and Economic Aspects.* Stanford, California, 1941.

Knight, Robert E. L. *Industrial Relations in the San Francisco Bay Area, 1900-1918.* Berkeley and Los Angeles, 1960.

Krythe, Mamie. *Port Admiral: Phineas Banning.* San Francisco, 1957.

Kuznets, Simon, and Dorothy Swaine Thomas. *Population Redistribution and Economic Growth. United States, 1870-1950.* Philadelphia, 1957.

Layton, Edward. "The Better America Federation: A Case Study of Superpatriotism," *Pacific Historical Review*, 30: 137-147 (May 1961).

Lesley, Lewis Burt. "San Diego and the Struggle for a Southern Transcontinental Railroad Terminus." *Greater American Essays in Honor of Herbert Eugene Bolton.* Berkeley and Los Angeles, 1945, pp. 499-518.

———— "The Struggle of San Diego for a Southern Transcontinental Railroad Connection, 1854-1891," University of California at Berkeley Doctoral Dissertation, 1934.

McClenahan, Bessie Arverne. "The Changing Nature of an Urban Residential Area," University of Southern California Doctoral Dissertation, 1928.

———— *The Changing Urban Neighborhood: From Neighbor to Nigh-Dweller.* Los Angeles, 1929.

McCoy, Esther. *Five California Architects.* New York, 1960.

McGroarty, John S. *Los Angeles from the Mountains to the Sea.* 3 vols. Chicago and New York, 1921.

McWilliams, Carey. *Prejudice. Japanese Americans: Symbol of Racial Intolerance.* Boston, 1944.

———— *Southern California Country: An Island on the Land.* New York, 1946.

Mason, Edward S. *The Street Railway Industry in Massachusetts: The Rise and Decline of an Industry.* Cambridge, Mass., 1932.

Matson, Clarence S. *Building a World Gateway: The Story of Los Angeles Harbor.* Los Angeles, 1945.

Mavitz, Nancy. *Sister Aimee.* Garden City, New York, 1931.

Mayo, Morrow. *Los Angeles.* New York, 1933.

Meyer, Donald. *The Positive Thinkers.* New York, 1965.

Mittelbach, Frank G. "Dynamic Land Use Patterns in Los Angeles. The Period 1924-1954." Possession of the author, Real Estate Research Institute, University of California at Los Angeles.

Moe, Edward O., and Carl C. Taylor. *Culture of a Contemporary Rural Community: Irwin, Iowa.* Washington, 1942.

Mowry, George. *The California Progressives.* Berkeley and Los Angeles, 1951.

Nadeau, Remi A. *City-Makers: The men who transformed Los Angeles from village to metropolis during the first great boom, 1868-1876.* Garden City, New York, 1948.

———— *Los Angeles: From Mission to Modern City.* New York, 1960.

———— *The Water Seekers.* Garden City, New York, 1950.

Nettels, Curtis. *The Emergence of a National Economy 1785-1815.* New York, 1962.

Nevins, Allan. *Ford: The Times, the Man, the Company . . . 1863-1915.* New York, 1954.

Ogden, Adele. "Alfred Robinson, New England Merchant in Mexican California," *California Historical Society Quarterly*, 23: 193-218 (September 1944).

Ostrander, Gilman M. *The Prohibition Movement in California, 1848-1933.* Berkeley and Los Angeles, 1957.

Ostrom, Vincent. *Water and Politics: A Study of Water Policies and Administration in the Development of Los Angeles.* Los Angeles, 1953.

Overton, Richard C. *Burlington West: A Colonization History of the Burlington Railroad.* Cambridge, Mass., 1941.

Parker, Edna Monch. "The Southern Pacific Railroad and Settlement in Southern California," *Pacific Historical Review*, 6: 103-120 (June 1937).

293

Paul, Rodman. *California Gold.* Cambridge, Mass., 1947.

Perry, Louis B., and Richard S. *A History of the Los Angeles Labor Movement, 1911–1941.* Berkeley, 1963.

Peterson, Harold F. "Early Minnesota Railroads and the Quest for Settlers," *Minnesota History,* 13: 25–44 (March 1932).

———— "Some Colonization Projects of the Northern Pacific Railroad," *Minnesota History,* 10: 127–144 (June 1929).

Pierce, Bessie L. *A History of Chicago.* Volume III. New York, 1957.

Pomeroy, Earl. *In Search of the Golden West: The Tourist in Western America.* New York, 1957.

Priestly, Herbert Ingram. "Spanish Colonial Municipalities," *California Law Review,* VII (1918–19), pp. 397–416.

Robinson, W. W. *Land in California.* Berkeley and Los Angeles, 1948.

———— *Ranchos Become Cities.* Pasadena, California, 1939.

Rolle, Andrew F. *An American in California: The Biography of William Heath Davis, 1822–1909.* San Marino, California, 1956.

Rose, L. J., Jr. *L. J. Rose of Sunny Slope 1827–1899, California Pioneer, Fruit Grower, Wine Maker, Horse Breeder.* San Marino, California, 1959.

Sanchez, Nellie Van de Grift. *Spanish Arcadia.* Los Angeles, 1929.

Schlesinger, Arthur M. *The Rise of the City 1878–1898.* New York, 1933.

Scruggs, Barton S. *A Man in Our Community: The Biography of L. G. Robinson of Los Angeles.* Gardena, California, 1937.

Scully, Vincent J., Jr. "Romantic Rationalism and the Expression of Structure in Wood: Downing, Wheeler, Gardner, and the 'Stick Style,' " *Art Bulletin,* 35: 121–142 (1953).

Shannon, Fred A. *Farmers' Last Frontier: Agriculture, 1860–1897.* New York, 1951.

Smith, Clifford M. "The History of the San Fernando Valley with Special Emphasis on the City of San Fernando," University of Southern California Masters Thesis, 1930.

Smith, Luke Mader. "Relations between the Territorial Structuring and the Local Government of a Metropolitan Suburb: The Sunland-Tujunga Valley, Los Angeles," Harvard University Doctoral Dissertation, 1948.

Smutz, Huber Earl. "The Department of City Planning of the City of Los Angeles." (September 1935). Possession of the author, City Planning Department, Los Angeles.

Smythe, William E. *History of San Diego 1542–1907.* San Diego, 1907.

Spalding, William A. *History and Reminiscences, Los Angeles City and County, California.* 3 vols. Los Angeles, 1931.

Stilwell, Louis D. *Migration from Vermont.* Montpelier, Vermont, 1948.

Stimson, Grace Heilman. *Rise of the Labor Movement in Los Angeles.* Berkeley and Los Angeles, 1955.

Swett, Ira, ed. "Los Angeles and Redondo," *Interurbans,* special no. 20 (1957).

————, ed. Los Angeles Railway History," *Interurbans,* special no. 11 (1951).

Tuck, Ruth D. *Not with the Fist: Mexican-Americans in a Southwest City.* New York, 1946.

Van Valen, Nelson S. "Power Politics: The Struggle for Municipal Ownership of Electric Utilities in Los Angeles, 1905–1937," Claremont Graduate School Doctoral Dissertation, 1964.

Walker, Franklin A. *A Literary History of Southern California.* Berkeley and Los Angeles, 1950.

Weiss, Richard. "The American Myth of Success, 1865 to the Present: A Study in Popular Thought," Columbia University Doctoral Dissertation, 1966.

Willard, Charles D. *History of Los Angeles.* Los Angeles, 1901.

———— *History of the Los Angeles Chamber of Commerce.* Los Angeles, 1899.

Wilson, Carol Green. *California Yankee: William R. Staats—Business Pioneer.* Claremont, California, 1946.

Winther, Oscar Osburn. "The Use of Climate as a Means of Promoting Migration to Southern California," *Mississippi Valley Historical Review,* 33: 411–424 (December 1946).

Woodward, C. Vann. *Reunion and Reaction: The Compromise of 1877 and the End of Reconstruction.* Rev. ed. Garden City, New York, 1956.

Young, Pauline V. *The Pilgrims of Russian-Town.* Chicago, 1934.

IX. WORKS ON THE HISTORY OF LOS ANGELES
PUBLISHED AFTER 1966

Banham, Reyner. *Los Angeles: The Architecture of the Four Ecologies.* Harmondsworth, 1971.

Bottles, Scott L. *Los Angeles and the Automobile: The Making of the Modern City.* Berkeley and Los Angeles, 1987.

Brodsly, David. *L.A. Freeway: An Appreciative Essay.* Berkeley and Los Angeles, 1983.

Bunch, Lonnie G. *Black Angelenos: The Afro-American in Los Angeles, 1850–1950* Los Angeles, 1988.

Cohen, Jerry, and William S. Murphy. *Burn, Baby, Burn! The Los Angeles Race Riot, August, 1965.* London, 1966.

Davis, Mike. *City of Quartz: Excavating the Future in Los Angeles.* London 1990.

Engh, Michael E., S. J. *Frontier Faiths: Church, Temple, and Synagogue in Los Angeles, 1846–1888.* Albuquerque, 1992.

Fishman, Robert. *Bourgeois Utopias: The Rise and Fall of Suburbia.* New York, 1987.

Fogelson, Robert M. *Violence as Protest: A Study of Riots and Ghettos.* Garden City, New York, 1971.

Foster, Mark S. "The Decentralization of Los Angeles during the 1920s." University of Southern California Doctoral Dissertation, 1971.

Griswold del Castillo, Richard. *The Los Angeles Barrio, 1850–1890: A Social History.* Berkeley and Los Angeles, 1980.

Jaher, Frederic Cople. *The Urban Establishment: Upper Strata in Boston, New York, Charleston, Chicago, and Los Angeles.* Urbana, 1982.

Kaplan, Sam Hall. *L.A. Follies: A Critical Look at Growth, Politics, and Architecture.* Santa Monica, 1989.

Klein, Norman M., and Martin J. Schiesl, eds. *20th-Century Los Angeles: Power, Promotion, and Social Conflict.* Claremont, 1990.

Light, Ivan, and Edna Bonacich. *Immigrant Entrepreneurs: Koreans in Los Angeles, 1965–1982.* Berkeley and Los Angeles, 1988.

Lo, Clarence. *Small Property versus Big Government: Social Origins of the Property Tax Revolt.* Berkeley and Los Angeles, 1990.

Modell, John. *The Economics and Politics of Racial Accommodations: The Japanese of Los Angeles, 1900–1942.* Urbana, 1977.

Mullins, William H. *The Depression and the Urban West Coast, 1929–1933: Los Angeles, San Francisco, Seattle, and Portland.* Bloomington, Indiana, 1991.

Raftery, Judith Rosenberg. *Land of Fair Promise: Politics and Reform in Los Angeles Schools, 1855–1941.* Stanford, California 1992.

Rieff, David. *Los Angeles: Capital of the Third World* New York, 1991.

Rios-Bustamente, Antonio, and Pedro Castillo. *An Illustrated History of Mexican Los Angeles, 1781–1985.* Los Angeles, 1986.

Romo, Ricardo. *East Los Angeles: History of a Barrio.* Austin, 1983.

Singleton, Gregory H. *Religion in the City of Angels: American Protestant Culture and Urbanization, Los Angeles, 1850–1930.* Ann Arbor, Michigan, 1979.

Weiss, Marc A. *The Rise of the Community Builders: The American Real Estate Industry and Urban Land Planning*. New York, 1987.

Woods, Gerald. *The Police In Los Angeles: Reform and Professionalization*. New York, 1992.

Yu, Eui-Young, et al, eds. *Koreans in Los Angeles: Prospects and Promises*. Los Angeles, 1982.

NOTES

CHAPTER 1: FROM PUEBLO TO TOWN

1. Frank W. Blackmar, "Spanish Institutions of the Southwest," *Johns Hopkins University Studies in Historical and Political Science,* extra vol. 10: 85–87, 94–101, 112–115 (1891); Hubert Howe Bancroft, *California Pastoral, 1769–1848* (San Francisco, 1888), chap. vii; Theodore H. Hittell, *History of California* (San Francisco, 1885), II, chap. viii; Herbert E. Bolton, "The Mission as a Frontier Institution in the Spanish-American Colonies," *American Historical Review,* 23: 42–61 (October 1917).

2. S. F. Cook, "Population Trends among the California Mission Indians," *Ibero-Americana,* 17: 48 (1940); S. F. Cook, "The Conflict between the California Indian and White Civilization: I. The Indian Versus the Spanish Mission," *Ibero-Americana,* 21: 5–11 (1943); Carey McWilliams, *Southern California Country: An Island on the Land* (New York, 1946), pp. 21–37. For a dissenting opinion, see Eugene Duflot de Mofras, *Travels on the Pacific Coast,* ed. and trans. Marguerite Eyer Wilbur (Santa Ana, Calif., 1937), I, 183.

3. Blackmar, "Spanish Institutions of the Southwest," chap. vii; for the most extensive survey of the California missions, see Fr. Zephyrin Engelhardt, *The Missions and Missionaries of California,* 4 vols. (San Francisco, 1908–1915).

4. Felipe de Neve, "Regulations and Instructions for the Garrisons of the Peninsulas of California . . . June 1, 1779," trans. Charles F. Lummis, *Annual Publications of the Historical Society of Southern California,* XV (1931), Part II: Documents Pertaining to the Founding of Los Angeles, pp. 180–185. See also, Blackmar, "Spanish Institutions of the Southwest," pp. 163–164, 192–193.

5. See de Neve, "Regulations and Instructions," pp. 180–185; Blackmar, "Spanish Institutions of the Southwest," pp. 164–165.

6. "Translation of Portion of Order of Governor Felipe de Neve for Founding of Los Angeles," *Annual Publications of the Historical Society of Southern California,* XV (1931), Part II: Documents Pertaining to the Founding of Los Angeles, pp. 154–155; Blackmar, "Spanish Institutions of the Southwest," pp. 181–183. A vara is a Spanish and Portuguese measure of length, varying in different localities from about 32 inches to about 43 inches.

7. For the standard surveys of early Los Angeles history, see J. M. Guinn, *A History of California and an Extended History of Los Angeles and Environs* (Los Angeles, 1915), I, chap. xxxix; John S. McGroarty, *Los Angeles from the Mountains to the Sea* (Chicago and New York, 1921), I, chaps. ii, iii; Morrow Mayo, *Los Angeles* (New York, 1933), pp. 3–15; Remi A. Nadeau, *Los Angeles: From Mission to Modern City* (New York, 1960), chap. i.

8. H. W. Halleck, "Report on the Laws and Regulations Relative to Grants or Sales of Public Lands in California," United States Congress, *House Executive Documents,* 31 Congress, 1 Session, Number 17, Appendix 13, pp. 148–149. See also, Robert Glass Cleland, *The Cattle on a Thousand Hills: Southern California, 1850–1880* (San Marino, Calif., 1941), pp. 27–29.

9. Halleck, "Report," Appendix 5, pp. 141–142; "Marginal Decrees of Jose Figueroa, Superior Chief of the Territory, November 26, 1833," *Quarterly Publications of the Historical Society of Southern California,* 19: 135 (September-December 1937); Cleland, *Cattle on a Thousand Hills,* pp. 5, 26.

10. W. W. Robinson, *Land in California* (Berkeley and Los Angeles, 1948), chap. vi; Cleland, *Cattle on a Thousand Hills,* p. 46; "The Old Spanish and Mexican Ranchos of Los Angeles County," a map prepared by the Title Insurance and Trust Company, Los Angeles.

11. George Simpson, *An Overland Journey Round the World during the Years 1841 and 1842* (Philadelphia, 1847), pp. 166–167; Alexander Forbes, *California: A History of Upper and Lower California* (San Francisco, 1937), p. 155. See also, David W. Cheesman, "By Ox Team From Salt Lake City to Los Angeles, 1850. A Memoir," ed. Mary E. Foy, *Annual Publications of the Historical Society of Southern California,* 14: 271–337 (1930); Hittell, *History,* II, 471, 497.

12. Don Jose del Carmen Lugo, "Life of a Rancher," translated from an interview by Thomas Savage, *Quarterly Publications of the Historical Society of Southern California,* 37: 351 ff (December 1955). See also, Cleland, *Cattle on a Thousand Hills,* chap. ii; Susanna Bryant Dakin, *A Scotch Paisano: Hugo Reid's Life in California, 1832–1852* (Berkeley, 1939), pp. 71–73.

13. Henry Dalton's Diary (or "Daily Life at Azusa"), passim, Henry Dalton Papers, Henry E. Huntington Library, San Marino, Calif.; S. F. Cook, "The Conflict between the California Indian and White Civilization: III. The American Invasion," *Ibero-Americana,* 23: 52–54 (1943).

14. "Invoice of Sundries Shipped on Board the Brig 'Sun,'" Dalton Papers; Alfred Robinson, *Life in California before the Conquest* (San Francisco, 1925), chap. iii; Adele Ogden, ed. "Business Letters of Alfred Robinson," *California Historical Society Quarterly,* 23: 301–344 (December 1944); Richard Henry Dana, Jr., *Two Years before the Mast and Twenty-four Years After* (New York, 1909), p. 81.

15. Nellie Van de Grift Sanchez, *Spanish Arcadia* (Los Angeles, 1929), pp 195–196; see also, Ethel Shorb, "The Home and Home Life of an Early Spaniard in California," J. de Barth Shorb Papers, Henry E. Huntington Library, San Marino, Calif.

16. Maurice H. and Marco R. Newmark, eds., *Census of the City and County of Los Angeles for the Year 1850* (Los Angeles, 1929), passim; United States Census Office, *The Seventh Census of the United States: 1850* (Washington, 1853), pp. 970–972. See also, Edwin Bryant, *What I Saw in California: Being the Journal of a Tour . . . in the Years 1846, 1847* (Santa Ana, Calif., 1936), pp. 405–406; Robinson, *Life in California,* 55–56; Duflot de Mofras, *Travels on the Pacific Coast,* pp. 1, 184.

17. Lugo, "Life of a Rancher," p. 236. A few wealthy rancheros such as Abel Stearns resided in the pueblo and employed overseers to manage their estates.

18. Dana, Jr., *Two Years before the Mast,* chaps. xiii, xiv; Robinson, *Life in California,* pp. 67, 72, 88; Adele Ogden, "Alfred Robinson, New England Merchant in Mexican California," *California Historical Society Quarterly,* 23: 193–218 (September 1944).

19. Robert Glass Cleland, *From Wilderness to Empire: A History of California, 1542–1900* (New York, 1944), chaps. v–vii; John Walton Caughey, *California* (New York, 1940), chaps. viii–xi.

20. Joseph Warren Revere, *A Tour of Duty in California . . .* (New York, 1849), p. 25; see also, S. W. Kearney, "Proclamation to the People of California" (March 1, 1847), United States Congress, *House Executive Documents,* 31 Congress, 1 Session, Number 17, pp. 288–289; Hittell, *History of California,* II, 70–71.

21. R. B. Mason, "Proclamation to the People of California" (August 7, 1848), United States Congress, *House Executive Documents,* 31 Congress, 1 Session, Number 17, pp. 650–651.

22. Jessie D. Francis, "An Economic and Social History of Mexican California

(1822–1846)" (University of California at Berkeley Doctoral Dissertation, 1936), pp. 33–34; Hittell, *History,* II, 58.

23. "Annual Message of the Governor of California, 1856," quoted in Cleland, *Cattle on a Thousand Hills,* p. 165.

24. Los Angeles *Star,* September 16, 1851; see also, Antonio Pico et al., "A Petition to the Honorable Senate and House of Representatives of the United States of America, February 21, 1849," Abel Stearns Papers, Henry E. Huntington Library, San Marino, Calif. This document is also printed in Cleland, *Cattle on a Thousand Hills,* Appendix II. pp. 238–243, and is hereafter referred to as Petition of the California Landowners.

25. Juan Bandini to the *Southern Californian,* April 11, 1855, quoted in Cleland, *Cattle on a Thousand Hills,* pp. 59–60; see also, the testimony of Jose Antonio Yorba et al., November 19, 1847, in *Los Angeles County Records,* p. 418, in translation and on microfilm, Henry E. Huntington Library, San Marino, Calif.

26. United States District Court, Southern District of California, *Transcript of the Record from the Board of Land Commissioners,* Henry E. Huntington Library, San Marino, Calif. For the traditional view of the Land Commission, see Robinson, *Land in California,* chap. viii. For a recent revision, see Paul Gates, "Adjudication of Spanish-Mexican Land Claims in California," *Huntington Library Quarterly,* 21: 213–236 (May 1958). By placing the commission in historical perspective, Gates provides a more accurate appraisal; but he underestimates the burdens attendant upon litigation. See, for example, S. S. Robinson to Henry Dalton, August 31, 1866, November 10, December 12, 1866, March 8, 1867, Dalton Papers.

27. Abel Stearns to John B. Weller, ca. 1855, Stearns Papers; see also, "Petition of the California Landowners," Stearns Papers.

28. Cook, "California Indian and White Civilization: I. The Indian versus the Spanish Mission," p. 4.

29. John Walton Caughey, ed., *The Indians of Southern California in 1852: The B. D. Wilson report and a selection of contemporary comment* (San Marino, California, 1852), pp. 25–26, et passim.

30. On the gold rush, see John Walton Caughey, *Gold is the Cornerstone* (Berkeley, 1948), passim; Rodman Paul, *California Gold* (Cambridge, Mass., 1947), passim.

31. Cave J. Couts to Abel Stearns, February 14, February 19, April 14, 1852; Abel Stearns to L. Belcher, April 28, 1852, Stearns Papers; Cleland, *Cattle on a Thousand Hills,* pp. 137–143.

32. Horace Bell, *Reminiscences of a Ranger or Early Times in Southern California* (Santa Barbara, Calif., 1927), p. 10.

33. Charles Nordhoff, *California for Health, Pleasure, and Residence: A Book for Travellers and Settlers* (New York, 1874), p. 244.

34. Los Angeles *Star,* August 10, 1854; Richard H. Dillon, ed., *California Trail Herd: The 1850 Missouri to California Journal of Cyrus C. Loveland* (Los Gatos, Calif., 1961), passim; Gilbert Cureton, "The Cattle Trail to California, 1840–1860," *Quarterly Publications of the Historical Society of Southern California,* 35: 99–109 (June 1953).

35. For price lists in the mid-1850's, see Los Angeles *Star,* August 31, 1854, April 21, 1855.

36. Los Angeles *Star,* March 1, 1856; see also, Cleland, *Cattle on a Thousand Hills,* pp. 144–147.

37. Southern Californian, April 11, 1855, quoted in Cleland, *Cattle on a Thousand Hills,* p. 59; see also, Los Angeles *Star,* January 19, 1856.

38. William P. Reynolds to Edward J. Reynolds, June 28, 1859, Stearns Papers; see also, San Francisco *Bulletin,* March 31, 1860, quoted in Los Angeles *Star,* April 7, 1860; United States Census Office, *Agriculture of the United States in 1860 . . . the Eighth Census* (Washington, 1864), CIXXI.

39. F. D. Atherton to Abel Sterns, August 16, 1861, and Robert Burnett to Abel Stearns, September 7, 1861, Stearns Papers; Abel Stearns to Cave J. Couts, February 16, 1863, Cave J. Couts Papers, Henry E. Huntington Library, San Marino, Calif.; Los Angeles *Star,* December 25, 1860, July 21, 1861.

40. "Petition of the California Landowners," Stearns Papers; see also, Harris Newmark, *Sixty Years in Southern California 1853–1913,* ed. Maurice H. and Marco R. Newmark, 2d ed. (New York, 1926), pp. 130–131.

41. See, for example, the activities of Henry Dalton (Dalton Papers) and Abel Stearns (Cleland, *Cattle on a Thousand Hills,* chap. x).

42. Los Angeles *Star,* January 11, 1862; William Brewer, *Up and Down in California in 1860–1864,* ed. Francis P. Farquhar (Berkeley and Los Angeles, 1949), p. 25.

43. Charles S. Johnson to Abel Stearns, February 6, 1863, March 14, 1863, Stearns Papers; see also, Cleland, *Cattle on a Thousand Hills,* pp. 173–175.

44. Los Angeles *Star,* January 23, 1864; see also, Los Angeles *Tri-Weekly News,* January 22, 1864.

45. *Southern News,* April 6, 1864, quoted in Cleland, *Cattle on a Thousand Hills,* p. 179; see also, Los Angeles *Star,* November 26, 1864.

46. Guinn, *Los Angeles,* I. chap. xlii; Cleland, *Cattle on a Thousand Hills,* chap. vii; W. W. Robinson, *Ranchos Become Cities* (Pasadena, Calif., 1939), passim.

47. Luther Ingersoll, *Ingersoll's Century History: Santa Monica Bay Cities* (Los Angeles, 1908), pp. 128–131.

48. Robert Glass Cleland, *The Irvine Ranch of Southern California 1810–1950* (San Marino, Calif., 1952), pp. 75–80.

49. Robinson, *Ranchos Become Cities,* pp. 88–89; Clifford M. Smith, "The History of the San Fernando Valley . . ." (University of Southern California Masters Thesis, 1930).

50. See the letters of Evan J. Coleman to J. de Barth Shorb, 1880–1885, Shorb Papers.

51. W. A. Dalton to Henry Dalton, December 21, 1873, April 16, 1875, Dalton Papers; see also, E. F. Notham to Abel Sterns, May 10, 1870, Stearns Papers; Los Angeles *Star,* April 30, 1874.

52. Isaac W. Lord to Mrs. G. Sackey, February 28, 1876, and Lord to Mrs. C. S. Storm, March 17, 1786, Isaac W. Lord Letterbook, pp. 83, 128, Isaac W. Lord Papers, Special Collections Division, University of California Library, Los Angeles; Rev. William Ingraham Kip, *The Early Days of My Episcopate* (New York, 1894), p. 214.

53. Los Angeles *Star,* December 20, 1874.

54. Los Angeles *Evening Express,* January 23, 1877; see also, *ibid.,* February 17, 1875; Los Angeles *Star,* November 28, 1868; Los Angeles *Herald,* November 4, 1875; Daniel Freeman's statement about the subdivision of his ranch by the Centinela Land Company, Daniel Freeman Papers, Special Collections Division, University of California Library, Los Angeles.

55. James Clark to Mrs. James Clark, March 17, 1856, in "An Emigrant of the Fifties," ed. David Davies, *Quarterly Publications of the Historical Society of Southern California,* 19: 118–119 (September-December 1937).

56. *Seventh Census: 1850,* pp. 976–977; United States Census Office, *Census Reports: Report on the Statistics of the Production of Agriculture at the Tenth Census (June 1, 1880)* (Washington, 1883), pp. 34, 106, 180, 256–257; Guinn, *Los Angeles,* I, 252–254.

57. Sarah Bixby Smith, *Adobe Days: A Book of California Memories* (Los Angeles, 1931), chap. vii. The Dalton Papers and the Freeman Papers are also illuminating about southern California ranch life in these years.

58. Duflot de Mofras, *Travels on the Pacific Coast,* pp. 1, 163–164; *Seventh Census: 1850,* pp. 970–972; United States Census Office, *Population of the United States in 1860 . . . the Eighth Census* (Washington, 1864), pp. 29, 31; United States Census Office, *Census*

Reports: Statistics of the Population of the United States . . . the Ninth Census (June 1, 1870) (Washington, 1872), pp. 90–91. United States Census Office, *Census Reports: Statistics of the Population of the United States at the Tenth Census (June 1, 1880)* (Washington, 1883), p. 91.

59. Los Angeles *Evening Express,* April 19, 1873; Los Angeles *Herald,* February 4, 1877; Los Angeles *Star,* January 4, 1884; Howard L. Morris and Thomas Wright, *Los Angeles City Directory for 1879–1880* (Los Angeles, 1879), passim; L. Whitworth, *Los Angeles City and County Directory for 1881–1882* (Los Angeles, 1882), passim; see also, Ludwig Louis Salvator, *Los Angeles in the Sunny Seventies: A Flower from the Golden Land,* trans. Marguerite Eyer Wilbur (Los Angeles, 1929), pp. 97–108; Newmark, *Sixty Years,* chaps. vi, xxiv; Remi A. Nadeau, *Citymakers: The men who transformed Los Angeles from village to metropolis during the first great boom, 1868–1876* (New York, 1948), chaps. vii, xi.

60. Los Angeles *Star,* April 25, 1874; see also, *ibid.,* May 16, 1868.

61. Guinn, *Los Angeles,* I, 277–281.

CHAPTER 2: PRIVATE ENTERPRISE, PUBLIC AUTHORITY, AND URBAN EXPANSION

1. Blackmar, "Spanish Institutions of the Southwest," chap. viii; Frank W. Blackmar, "Spanish Colonization in the Southwest," *Johns Hopkins University Studies in Historical and Political Science,* 8: 48–67 (1890); Herbert Ingram Priestly, "Spanish Colonial Municipalities," *California Law Review,* 7: 397–416 (1918–19).

2. Newmark, *Sixty Years,* pp. 116–117; Bancroft, *California Pastoral,* pp. 355–356; Vincent Ostrom, *Water and Politics: A Study of Water Policies and Administration in the Development of Los Angeles* (Los Angeles, 1953), pp. 27–37.

3. Los Angeles *Star,* August 24, 1854.

4. Felipe de Neve, "Regulations and Instructions for the Garrisons of the Peninsula of California," p. 179.

5. Los Angeles *Star,* July 17, 1852; Los Angeles *Semi-Weekly News,* December 24, 1867.

6. Guinn, *Los Angeles,* I, 118–119; Francisco Coronel Augustin Olvera's statement, July 22, 1847, Los Angeles County Records, pp. 543–544, Henry E. Huntington Library, San Marino, Calif.; S. D. Woods, *Light and Shadows of Life on the Pacific Coast* (New York, 1910), pp. 27–29.

7. Los Angeles *Daily News,* January 8, 1869, September 1, 1871.

8. Guinn, *Los Angeles,* I, 118–119.

9. Los Angeles *Daily News,* January 21, 1871; Los Angeles *Star,* June 13, 14, 18, 1867; Newmark, *Sixty Years,* pp. 119–120. For illustrations of the new buildings, see Thompson and West, *History of Los Angeles County California, 1880* (Berkeley, 1959).

10. J. R. Stevenson to First Alcalde of the City of Los Angeles, November, 5, 1857, *Los Angeles County Records,* pp. 592–593; Stephen Foster to the Army, February 20, 1850, *ibid.,* pp. 833–834.

11. Rev. James L. Woods, Diary, November 24, 1854, Henry E. Huntington Library, San Marino, Calif.; *ibid.,* November 19, 29, December 10, 24, 1854. See also, Los Angeles *Star,* October 9, 1854; Newmark, *Sixty Years,* pp. 205–207.

12. Issac W. Lord to R. Ludlow, March 24, 1874, Lord Letterbook, p. 825, Lord Papers; John E. Baur, *The Health Seekers of Southern California, 1870–1900* (San Marino, Calif., 1959), chap. iii.

13. Newmark, *Sixty Years,* p. 118; for reports of the epidemics, see Los Angeles *Star,* November 22, 1862, February 7, March 7, 1863, May 22, July 3, 1869, February 10, 1877.

14. Los Angeles *Star,* August 16, 1856, September 25, 1869; Guinn, *Los Angeles,* I, chap. lvii.

15. Los Angeles *Star,* May 10, 1856. For the municipality's earlier involvements in education, see William W. Ferrier, *Ninety Years of Education in California 1846–1936* (Berkeley, 1937), pp. 77–78, 154–158; Guinn, *Los Angeles,* I, chap. liv.

16. "An act to provide for the Incorporation of Cities," *The Statutes of California Passed at the First Session of the Legislature (1849–1850)* (San Jose, Calif., 1850), pp. 87–91; Thomas F. Barbee *v.* Joseph Huber, Jr., cited in Los Angeles *Evening Express,* June 19, 1876; Edward F. Treadwell, ed., *The Constitution of the State of California Adopted . . . 1879* (San Francisco, 1923), Article XI, pp. 485–651.

17. Los Angeles *Daily News,* August 10, 1871, March 2, 1872; Los Angeles *Evening Express,* November 16, 1876. For an example of the practical limitations on the state's power, note the conflict provoked by the Governor's Board of Public Works (Los Angeles *Herald,* April 8, 11, June 20, 1876).

18. Los Angeles *Star,* March 9, 1861; *ibid.,* January 5, 1861. Certain annual messages of Los Angeles mayors are revealing; see *ibid.,* May 17, 1851, May 10, 1856, January 4, 1862, January 2, 1869.

19. *Ordinances and By-Laws of the City of Los Angeles,* Article V, printed in Los Angeles *Star,* June 3, 1860; William McPherson, comp., *Charter and Revised Ordinances of the City of Los Angeles* (Los Angeles, 1873), pp. 54–73.

20. *Ordinances,* article V, Los Angeles *Star,* June 3, 1860; William M. Caswell, comp., *Revised Charter and Compiled Ordinances and Resolutions of the City of Los Angeles* (Los Angeles, 1878), pp. 163–164; Freeman G. Teed, comp., *Compiled Ordinances and Resolutions of the City of Los Angeles* (Los Angeles, 1887), pp. 190–191.

21. *Ordinances,* article X, Los Angeles *Star,* June 3, 1860; McPherson, *Ordinances and Resolutions,* pp. 47–59; Caswell, *Ordinances and Resolutions,* pp. 217–220; Robinson, *Ordinances and Resolutions,* pp. 135–138, 299–309.

22. *Ordinances,* article V, Los Angeles *Star,* June 3, 1860; Caswell, *Ordinances and Resolutions,* pp. 261–262, 443–445, 489–490; Robinson, *Ordinances and Resolutions,* pp. 210–211; Teed, *Ordinances and Resolutions,* pp. 108–109, 159–160.

23. *Ordinances,* article V, Los Angeles *Star,* June 3, 1860; Caswell, *Ordinances and Resolutions,* pp. 233–238, 459–460; Teed, *Ordinances and Resolutions,* pp. 37–38, 289; Freeman G. Teed, comp., *Charter and Compiled Ordinances and Resolutions of the City of Los Angeles* (Los Angeles, 1889), pp. 192–193.

24. Los Angeles *Star,* November 22, 1862, February 7, March 7, 1863, May 22, July 3, 1869, January 12, February 10, 1877; McPherson, *Ordinances and Resolutions,* pp. 102–104; Caswell, *Ordinances and Resolutions,* pp. 231–234.

25. Los Angeles *Evening Express,* January 2, 1874, April 2, 1877, July 27, September 25, 1877; Los Angeles *Times,* October 19, 1883; "Annual Reports of the Water Overseer, 1879–1886," *Los Angeles Municipal Reports, 1879–1886,* Public Library, Los Angeles. See also, F. H. Olmsted's tracing of the original zanja system on "Map of the City of Los Angeles California by H. J. Stevenson, U.S. Dept. Surveyor, 1876," Department of Water and Power, Los Angeles.

26. "An Act to amend the Charter of the City of Los Angeles," *The Statutes of California . . . Nineteenth Session . . . 1871–72* (Sacramento, 1872), pp. 128–130; "An Act to amend the charter of the City of Los Angeles . . . ," *The Statutes of California . . . Twentieth Session . . . 1873–74* (Sacramento, 1874), pp. 633–659; "An Act to provide for work upon streets . . . and for the construction of sewers within municipalities," *Laws and Resolutions Passed by the Legislature of 1883–84 at its Extra Session* (Sacramento, 1885), pp. 147–165.

27. Los Angeles *Daily News,* January 8, 1869; Los Angeles *Evening Express,* January 20, 1874; "Annual Reports of the Street Superintendent, 1879–1886," *Los Angeles Municipal Reports, 1879–1886.*

28. Los Angeles *Daily News,* March 3, 1871; Los Angeles *Star,* March 28, April 4, 1873; Los Angeles *Evening Express,* December 27, 1872, October 1, December 27, 1875, March 15, 16, April 20, 1877; "Annual Reports of the City Engineer, 1879–1886," *Los Angeles Municipal Reports, 1879–1886;* "Report of the Sewer Committee, 1884," *ibid.;* Caswell, *Ordinances and Resolutions,* pp. 425–429; Robinson, *Ordinances and Resolutions,* pp. 95, 342–344.

29. "Report of Fred Eaton, City Surveyor, May 3, 1887," and "Report of Rudolph Herring, Consulting Engineer, September 6, 1887," Department of Sewage Design, City Hall, Los Angeles; See also, Teed, *Ordinances and Resolutions* (1889), pp. 152–159.

30. Los Angeles *Star,* May 20, 1887; Los Angeles *Herald,* June 26, 30, July 4, 1888; Teed, *Ordinances and Resolutions* (1889), pp. 196–197.

31. Los Angeles *Herald,* September 13, 16, November 14, 15, 19, December 18, 26, 31, 1888, January 1, 8, 1889.

32. *Ibid.,* January 17, April 3, 30, June 1, 4, July 13, 1889.

33. *Ibid.,* July 26, 1889; for the arguments favoring the project, see *ibid.,* August 3, 8, 11, 1889.

34. *Ibid.,* August 31, September 18, October 5, 12, 24, 26, 28, November 6, 9, 1889.

35. *Ibid.,* December 24, 1889.

36. *Ibid.,* January 14, March 14, 15, 16, 1890, September 2, 11, 19, October 15, 18, November 1, 2, 9, 10, 1891, April 18, June 7, 8, July 6, 12, August 31, 1892.

37. Los Angeles *Star,* August 7, 1852, August 7, 1855, April 28, 1860, August 8, 1868; see also, Guinn, *Los Angeles,* I, chap. liv.

38. Los Angeles *Tri-Weekly News,* June 18, 1867; Los Angeles *Star,* November 13, 1869; Los Angeles *Daily News,* September 26, 1871; Los Angeles *Evening Express,* April 6, 1874; Newmark, *Sixty Years,* p. 405; Thompson and West, *Los Angeles,* chap. xxxii.

39. Los Angeles *Star,* August 10, 31, October 5, 1854, September 9, October 4, December 27, 1870; Bell, *Reminiscences of a Ranger,* chap. vii; Thompson and West, *Los Angeles,* chap. xxxii; Newmark, *Sixty Years,* pp. 139, 207.

40. McPherson, *Ordinances and Resolutions,* pp. 96–98, Appendix Three, pp. 165–167; Teed, *Ordinances and Resolutions,* pp. 130–133.

41. "Annual Reports of the Auditor, 1879–1886," *Los Angeles Municipal Reports, 1879–1886;* McPherson, *Ordinances and Resolutions,* pp. 11–16.

42. Los Angeles *Star,* November 16, 1854, February 12, March 12, May 7, 1859, December 24, 1864, January 14, 21, 1865, April 13, 1866, May 22, September 23, 1869, December 15, 1870; Salvator, *Los Angeles in the Sunny Seventies,* p. 131; McGroarty, *Los Angeles,* I, 308.

43. Salvator, *Los Angeles in the Sunny Seventies,* pp. 131–132; Thompson and West, *Los Angeles,* chap. xxxii. For a fuller consideration of the voluntary associations, see Chap. 9, below.

44. Los Angeles *Star,* February 21, 1857; December 25, 1858, February 6, 1859, April 7, 1860, February 15, 1862; Guinn, *Los Angeles,* I, chap. lvi; Ostrom, *Water and Politics,* pp. 40–41.

45. McPherson, *Ordinances and Resolutions,* pp. 110–118; City of Los Angeles *v.* Los Angeles City Water Company, 124 Cal. 368, Transcript on Appeal 6–7, 91–94, County Law Library, Los Angeles.

46. Los Angeles *Weekly News,* January 31, 1868; see also, Los Angeles *Tri-Weekly News,* January 10, 14, 1868; Newmark, *Sixty Years,* pp. 365–366.

47. Los Angeles *Daily News,* February 7, 1868; Los Angeles City, *Archives* (the Minutes of the Common Council), vol. 6, February 4, 1868, pp. 197–198, February 10, 1868, p. 200, City Hall, Los Angeles.

48. *Ibid.,* April 23, 1868, p. 225, June 1, 1868, pp. 237–238, June 8, 1868, p. 239; Los Angeles *Weekly News,* June 5, 12, 1868; Los Angeles *Star,* June 6, 13, 1868.

49. Los Angeles *Weekly News,* June 19, 1868.

50. Los Angeles City, *Archives,* vol. 6, July 10, 1868, p. 249, July 20, 1868, pp. 251–252; Los Angeles *Star,* July 18, 25, 1868; Ostrom, *Water and Politics,* pp. 42–44.

51. Los Angeles *Star,* July 17, 1852; Los Angeles *Semi-Weekly News,* December 24, 1867; McPherson, *Ordinances and Resolutions,* Appendix One, pp. 151–154.

52. Los Angeles *Daily News,* March 3, 1869; Los Angeles *Herald,* December 28, 1873, November 6, 1874, April 15, May 30, 1875; Newmark, *Sixty Years,* p. 362; William A. Spalding, *Los Angeles Newspaperman. An Autobiographic Account,* ed. Robert V. Hine (San Marino, Calif., 1961), pp. 63, 64, 80, 96, 97, 110, 111, 136, 137.

53. Los Angeles *Evening Express,* December 10, 1877; *ibid.,* July 29, 1875; Los Angeles *Star,* November 1, 1872, February 12, 1874; Los Angeles *Herald,* December 28, 1873, November 6, 1874.

54. Newmark, *Sixty Years,* p. 81.

55. Morris and Wright, *Los Angeles Directory 1879–80,* passim; Whitworth, *Los Angeles Directory 1881–82,* passim.

56. Los Angeles *Evening Express,* July 2, 1875; see also, *ibid.,* December 5, 1873, September 8, 1874, March 21, 1875.

57. "An Act concerning street railways," *The Statutes of California . . . Eighteenth Session . . . 1869–1870* (Sacramento, 1870), pp. 481–484; Caswell, *Ordinances and Resolutions,* pp. 264–266; Robinson, *Ordinances and Resolutions,* pp. 181–183; Teed, *Ordinances and Resolutions,* pp. 255–258.

58. Haines W. Reed, "The Relation of Municipal Public Utility Corporations to the Public," *Pacific Municipalities,* 26: 647 (December 1912).

59. Los Angeles *Star,* August 8, 1868; Los Angeles *Evening Express,* October 27, 1873; McPherson, *Ordinances and Resolutions,* pp. 106–107; Newmark, *Sixty Years,* p. 349; Board of Public Utilities and Transportation, City of Los Angeles, *Fiftieth Annual Report [1958–1959],* p. 22.

60. Robinson, *Ordinances and Resolutions,* p. 297; Newmark, *Sixty Years,* p. 535; Board of Public Utilities and Transportation, City of Los Angeles, *Fiftieth Annual Report [1958–1959],* p. 59.

61. Robinson, *Ordinances and Resolutions,* pp. 159–160; Board of Public Utilities and Transportation, City of Los Angeles, *Fiftieth Annual Report [1958–1959],* p. 40.

CHAPTER 3: THE RIVALRY BETWEEN LOS ANGELES AND SAN DIEGO

1. Los Angeles *Star,* March 24, 1868, September 25, 1869, January 8, March 5, July 2, 1870; Los Angeles *Evening Express,* December 26, 1871. On urban rivalry in the American West, see James Bryce, *The American Commonwealth,* 3d ed. (New York, 1895), II, 833–834.

2. Forbes, *California,* pp. 102–103; Duflot de Mofras, *Travels on the Pacific Coast,* I, 168–172; Simpson, *Journey Round the World,* p. 219; Dana, Jr., *Two Years before the Mast,* pp. 100–102, 119; Brewer, *Up and Down in California,* pp. 8–9.

3. Los Angeles *Star,* August 14, 1869; see also, San Diego *Union,* January 13, December 29, 1870; Ephraim W. Morse to J. S. Mofford, August 6, 1870, Ephraim W. Morse Papers, Junipero Serra Museum, San Diego.

4. Dana, Jr., *Two years before the Mast,* p. 410. See also, *Seventh Census: 1850,* pp. 970–972; *Population at the Eighth Census: 1860,* p. 31.

5. William E. Smythe, *History of San Diego 1542–1907* (San Diego, 1907), p. 249; William S. Rosecrans to Mrs. William S. Rosecrans, April 11, 1866, William S. Rosecrans Papers, Special Collections Division, University of California Library, Los Angeles.

6. D. M. Berry to Helen Elliott, October 1, 1873, Thomas B. Elliott Papers, Henry E. Huntington Library, San Marino, Calif.; Andrew F. Rolle, *An American in California:*

The Biography of William Heath Davis, 1822-1909 (San Marino, Calif., 1956), chap. viii.

7. Thomas Ryland Darnell to James Darnell, October 18, 1855, in "San Diego in 1855 and 1856," *Annual Publications of the Historical Society of Southern California*, 16: 61–62 (1934); see also, Los Angeles *Star*, November 27, 1869; Smythe, *San Diego*, p. 337; Hine, *William Andrew Spalding*, pp. 10–14; Herman Frank, *Scrapbook of a Western Pioneer* (Los Angeles, 1934), pp. 51–52.

8. San Diego and Gila Southern Pacific and Atlantic Railroad Company Minutes, 1854–1878, Junipero Serra Museum, San Diego; San Diego *Herald*, May 21, 1853, October 20, November 8, December 6, 1855, August 9, 1856; Lewis Burt Lesley, "The Struggle of San Diego for a Southern Transcontinental Railroad Connection, 1854–1891" (University of California at Berkeley Doctoral Dissertation, 1934), chap. i–iv.

9. William S. Rosecrans to William J. Palmer, December 18, 1867, Ephraim W. Morse to William S. Rosecrans, January 15, 1868, William S. Rosecrans to J. Edgar Thompson, February 15, 1868, all in Rosecrans Papers; San Diego and Gila Company Minutes, March 5, 1868; Smythe, *San Diego*, pp. 336–337.

10. William J. Palmer to William S. Rosecrans, February 21, 1868, Rosecrans Papers.

11. Thomas S. Sedgwick to William S. Rosecrans, April 20, 1869, Rosecrans Papers.

12. William J. Galewood to William S. Rosecrans, August 9, 1869, Ephraim W. Morse to William S. Rosecrans, August 9, 1869, William S. Rosecrans to John C. Fremont, February 11, 1870, all in Rosecrans Papers; San Diego and Gila Company Minutes, June 27, September 23, 1869; Los Angeles *Star*, September 18, October 9, 1869; "Southern Transcontinental Railway Company," United States Congress, *Senate Miscellaneous Documents*, 41 Congress, 2 Session, Number 121, passim.

13. Ephraim W. Morse to Frank A. Kimball, May 6, 1880, Frank A. Kimball Papers, Public Library, National City, Calif. On the company's monopoly in California, see Stuart Daggett, *Chapters on the History of the Southern Pacific* (New York, 1922), chap. vii, xxiv.

14. "Hearings of the United States Pacific Railway Commission," United States Congress, *Senate Executive Documents*, 51 Congress, 1 Session, Number 51, p. 3, 614; see also, *ibid.*, pp. 2,505–2,509, 3,683, 4,035; J. B. Cox to William S. Rosecrans, November 29, 1865, Rosecrans Papers. See also, Collis P. Huntington to Mark Hopkins, April 14, 1868, to Leland Stanford, July 17, 1868, Huntington-Hopkins Correspondence, Stanford University Library, Stanford, Calif.

15. J. B. Cox to William S. Rosecrans, October 8, 1868, Rosecrans Papers; see also, Thomas S. Sedgwick to William S. Rosecrans, August 21, 1868, Rosecrans Papers.

16. William S. Rosecrans to Board of Directors of the California Southern Coast Railroad Company, January 1871, William Hale to William S. Rosecrans, March 2, 1870, L. C. Gunn to Board of Directors of the Los Angeles and San Diego Railroad Company, May 9, 1870, Martin J. O'Connor to William S. Rosecrans, April 15, 1870, William S. Rosecrans to Mrs. William S. Rosecrans, June 30, 1870, all in Roescrans Papers; San Diego *Union*, December 9, 30, 1869, March 31, 1870.

17. William S. Rosecrans to Martin J. O'Connor, April 4, 1871, Rosecrans Papers. See also, Ephraim W. Morse to Morton Hunter, November 16, 1870, to Thomas Whaley, November, 25, 1870, Morse Papers; Los Angeles *Star*, November 25, 1870.

18. William S. Rosecrans to Board of Directors of the California Southern Coast Railroad Company, January 1871, Rosecrans Papers; see also, William S. Rosecrans to Martin J. O'Connor, May 5, 1870, Morse Papers; Los Angeles *Star*, July 2, 9, 1870.

19. Ephraim W. Morse to Thomas Whaley, March 23, 1871, Morse Papers; see also, Ephraim W. Morse to Friend Sherman, January 17, 1871, to Colonel Ferrell, July 31, 1871, Morse Papers; William S. Rosecrans to Martin J. O'Connor, February 18, 1871, Rosecrans Papers; San Diego *Union*, January 26, 1871.

20. "We have rumors," Ephraim W. Morse wrote to George D. Marston, "that a consolidation is being effected between the Texas Pacific and the Southern Pacific of California by which they leave San Diego out until the whole road is built." July 23, 1871, Morse Papers. Rumors of a deal between Huntington and Scott also circulated two years later. Michael J. O'Connor to William S. Rosecrans, May 16, 1873, Rosecrans Papers. That they were not unfounded is revealed in Collis P. Huntington to Mark Hopkins, September 28, 1872, February 15, 1875, Huntington-Hopkins Correspondence.

21. Ephraim W. Morse to his father, August 21, 1872, Morse Papers; see also, Ephraim W. Morse to Thomas S. Sedgwick, May 22, 1871, to George D. Marston, July 23, 1871, Morse Papers; William S. Rosecrans to Martin J. O'Connor, April 20, 1870, Thomas S. Sedgwick to William S. Rosecrans, February 14, March 10, 1872, Rosecrans Papers; San Diego *Union*, March 13, 19, 23, 24, April 11, 18, 26, 1872.

22. Ephraim W. Morse to Thomas S. Sedgwick, September 1, 1872, Morse Papers; see also, San Diego *Union*, August 27, 28, 1872.

23. Ephraim W. Morse to Friend Howard, November 13, 1873, Morse Papers; see also, Ephraim W. Morse to Friend Terrell, October 12, 1872, to J. L. Bleeker, October 16, 1872, to Friend Chase, November 12, 1872, Morse Papers; Thomas S. Sedgwick to William S. Rosecrans, November 12, 1872, John McManus to William S. Rosecrans, March 30, 1874, Rosecrans Papers; San Diego and Gila . . . Company Minutes, December 6, 1872; San Diego *Union*, January 14, November 7, December 12, 1873. For a general survey of Scott's activities, see C. Vann Woodward, *Reunion and Reaction: The Compromise of 1877 and the End of Reconstruction* (New York, 1956), chap. iv.

24. The bonds were to be issued upon the completion of every ten miles. See "Memorial of the Texas Pacific Railroad Company and the Atlantic and Pacific Railroad Company," United States Congress, *House Miscellaneous Documents*, 43 Congress, 2 Session, Number 6; "Argument on the Texas Pacific Railroad before the House Committee on Pacific Railroads," United States Congress, *House Miscellaneous Documents*, 43 Congress, 2 Session, Number 36, Part 2; John McManus to William S. Rosecrans, March 30, 1874, Rosecrans Papers.

25. Julius Grodinsky, *Transcontinental Railway Strategy, 1869–1893: A Study of Businessmen* (Philadelphia, 1962) pp. 41–44, 49–54.

26. "Hearings of the United States Pacific Railway Commission," pp. 2,505–2,509.

27. "Argument on the Texas Pacific Railroad before the House Committee on Pacific Railroads," pp. 1–8.

28. Collis P. Huntington to Leland Stanford, September 18, 1874, Huntington-Hopkins Correspondence; see also, Collis P. Huntington to Charles Crocker, November 30, 1874, Huntington-Hopkins Correspondence.

29. Woodward, *Reunion and Reaction*, chap. iv; Grodinsky, *Transcontinental Railway Strategy*, chap. iv. Morse interpreted the situation perceptively. "You can see," he wrote to D. Felsenheld (March 3, 1876, Morse Papers), "that Stanford would prefer to *Scotch* but not kill Scott's bill, leave him to hope for success year after year so that he will not apply for private capital to build the road and in the meantime, by using the Government money in his hands & some of his enormous profits, he will push forward his road into Arizona so far that Scott never could get private capital."

30. Ephraim W. Morse to [?], March 1875, Morse Papers; see also, Ephraim W. Morse to Friend Howard, March 20, 1876, to D. Felsenheld, March 7, 1876, Morse Papers.

31. Ephraim W. Morse to Friend Pierce, July 25, 1876, Morse Papers. See also, Ephraim W. Morse to D. Felsenheld, April 1876, May 21, 1876, to Friend Pierce, July 18, 1876, Morse Papers. Morse also noted that San Francisco persistently opposed San Diego's interests. Ephraim W. Morse to Friend Whaley, September 23, 1876,

Morse Papers. Stanford spared no effort to foster this opposition. San Diego *Union*, June 6, 1875.

32. "Hearings of the United States Pacific Railway Commission," pp. 1,750, 1,794–1,795; Ephraim W. Morse to J. Chauncey, May 3, 1878, to L. B. Caswell, March 14, 1878, Morse Papers; see also Woodward, *Reunion and Reaction*, pp. 120–124; Grodinsky, *Transcontinental Railway Strategy*, pp. 64–66; Daggett, *Southern Pacific*, chap. vii; Lewis Burt Lesley, "San Diego and the Struggle for a Southern Transcontinental Railroad Terminus," *Greater American Essays in Honor of Herbert Eugene Bolton* (Berkeley and Los Angeles, 1945), pp. 499–518. It is true that the mountains due east of San Diego would have made the construction of a direct line to Fort Yuma difficult and expensive. The Central Pacific even argued that the route was not feasible, though Sedgwick and Rosecrans offered proof to the contrary. Scott also believed that the direct line was impracticable, though later Texas Pacific officials were convinced otherwise. But none of this—not even the fact that Rudolph Spreckles eventually built a San Diego-Fort Yuma railroad—is essential to the argument here. The San Gorgonio Pass was as accessible to San Diego as to Los Angeles, and Scott was firmly committed to San Diego if ultimately destined for San Francisco. In the face of political and economic realities, especially the power and wealth of the Central Pacific, this geographic handicap was irrelevant. See Ephraim W. Morse to Friend Sherman, December 12, 1870, to Mrs. M. A. Burton, January 28, 1873, Morse Papers; "Argument on the Texas Pacific Railroad Before the House Committee on Pacific Railroads"; Thomas S. Sedgwick to William S. Rosecrans, August 30, 1868, Frank S. Bond to William S. Rosecrans, September 18, 1876, Rosecrans Papers.

33. Los Angeles *Herald*, August 11, 1878; Los Angeles *Star*, May 18, 1873.

34. Los Angeles *Star*, December 23, 28, 1872; see also, *Population at the Ninth Census: 1870*, pp. 90–91.

35. Los Angeles *Star*, May 8, 16, 1872; *ibid.*, March 26, July 9, 1870; Los Angeles *Evening Express*, May 18, 1872; Los Angeles *Daily News*, May 19, 1872; John S. Griffin to Benjamin D. Wilson, February 16, 1872, Benjamin D. Wilson Papers, Henry E. Huntington Library, San Marino, Calif.

36. Los Angeles *Daily News*, July 7, 1872; Newmark, *Sixty Years*, pp. 502–503; Daggett, *Southern Pacific*, chap. vii.

37. Los Angeles *Daily News*, July 23, 1872. The Southern Pacific agreed to accept as partial payment $250,000 in Los Angeles and San Pedro Railroad bonds owned by the county and city; for an account of this enterprise, see "Report on the Present Conditions of the Los Angeles and San Pedro Railroad Company," Los Angeles *Star*, July 6, 1870, Supplement.

38. "I *feel* that by keeping perfectly cool, quiet and firm," Hyde explained to Mark Hopkins, "I am gradually getting the whip hand and will drive the entire team." William B. Hyde to Mark Hopkins, July 27, 1872, Huntington-Hopkins Correspondence.

39. Los Angeles *Daily News*, July 26, August 7, 1872; Los Angeles *Evening Express*, August 24, 1872.

40. Los Angeles *Evening Express*, July 29, 1872; Los Angeles *Daily News*, July 31, August 13, 1872; Los Angeles *Star*, October 30, 1872; Phineas Banning to Benjamin D. Wilson, December 21, 1871, Wilson Papers.

41. Los Angeles *Daily News*, August 30, 1872; Los Angeles *Star*, August 26, 1872; Los Angeles *Evening Express*, August 24, 1872.

42. Los Angeles *Daily News*; September 7, 1872. The bonds referred to in note 37 constitute the $250,000 differential.

43. Los Angeles *Star*, September 9, 1872; *ibid.*, September 7, 1872; Los Angeles *Evening Express*, September 5, 1872.

44. Los Angeles *Daily News*, September 5, 8, 13, 14, 1872.

45. William B. Hyde to Mark Hopkins, September 4, 1872, Huntington-Hopkins Correspondence.

46. Los Angeles *Daily News,* September 28, October 3, 1872; San Diego *Union,* October 5, 1872.

47. R. M. Widney, "Los Angeles County Subsidy. Which Subsidy Shall I Vote For, or Shall I vote Against Both . . . ," *Quarterly Publications of the Historical Society of Southern California,* 38: 347–362 (December 1956). For San Diego's reply, see San Diego *Union,* October 26, 1872.

48. Los Angeles *Star,* October 28, 1874; *ibid.,* September 5, 6, 1872; Los Angeles *Evening Express,* November 1, 6, 11, 1872, January 12, 18, 23, 27, February 2, 1875, September 6, 1876; Collis P. Huntington to Leland Stanford, January 18, 1875, Huntington-Hopkins Correspondence.

49. Salvator, *Los Angeles in the Sunny Seventies,* pp. 109–112; Los Angeles *Star,* January 8, 1875; Franklin Hoyt, "Railroad Development in Southern California, 1868–1900" (University of Southern California Doctoral Dissertation, 1951) passim.

50. Los Angeles *Herald,* September 23, 1877, October 14, 1877; see also, *ibid.,* September 27, 30, 1877, April 27, 1878; Los Angeles *Evening Express,* August 21, 1875.

51. Frank A. Kimball to Ephraim W. Morse, July 25, 1879, Kimball Papers; see also, Ephraim W. Morse to J. L. Pearson, July 5, 1879, to Frank A. Kimball, August 20, August 23, 1879, Morse Papers; Frank A. Kimball to Ephraim W. Morse, August 8, 1879, Kimball Papers.

52. Grodinsky, *Transcontinental Railway Strategy,* pp. 95–100; Glenn D. Bradley, *The Story of the Santa Fe* (Boston, 1920), chaps. iii, vi, vii.

53. Grodinsky, *Transcontinental Railway Strategy,* pp. 165–170; Bradley, *Santa Fe,* chap. ix.

54. Frank A. Kimball to Ephraim W. Morse, July 25, 1879, Kimball Papers.

55. Los Angeles *Herald,* January 25, 1880; Ephraim W. Morse to D. T. Phillips, November 27, 1879, Morse Papers; Frank A. Kimball to Thomas Nickerson, August 11, 1879, Kimball Papers; Smythe, *San Diego,* pp. 401–404.

56. Ephraim W. Morse to Frank A. Kimball, May 31, 1880, Morse Papers; see also, Ephraim W. Morse to George S. Foster, November 29, 1879, to D. Felsenheld, November 29, 1879, Morse Papers; Frank A. Kimball to Ephraim W. Morse, May 13, 1880, Kimball Papers.

57. On the California Southern, see Frank A. Kimball to Ephraim W. Morse, July 15, 1880, to Thomas Nickerson, August 13, 1880, to David K. Horton, April 30, 1883, Kimball Papers; Ephraim W. Morse to Thomas L. Rogers, October 3, 1881, to Dr. Allen, December 15, 1882, Morse Papers; Los Angeles *Evening Express,* April 4, 1884.

58. Ephraim W. Morse to Thomas Whaley, January 20, 1884, Morse Papers; see also, Grodinsky, *Transcontinental Railway Strategy,* pp. 168–169.

59. San Diego *Union,* December 2, 1885; Ephraim W. Morse to Thomas Whaley, January 20, 1884, Morse Papers; San Diego *Union,* November 19, 1885; National City *Record,* November 26, 1885; Smythe, *San Diego,* pp. 405–406.

60. Los Angeles *Times,* January 12, 1886; see also, Grodinsky, *Transcontinental Railway Strategy,* pp. 216–218; Bradley, *Santa Fe,* chap. x.

61. Los Angeles *Times,* November 29, 1885; see also, *Population at the Tenth Census: 1880,* pp. 108, 109.

62. Los Angeles *Herald,* March 12, 1886; Los Angeles *Times,* November 21, 1885; San Diego *Herald,* March 9, 1888; J. F. Crank to Leonard Caruen, June 26, 1884, J. F. Crank Papers, Henry E. Huntington Library, San Marino, Calif.; Franklin Hoyt, "The Los Angeles and San Gabriel Valley Railroad," *Pacific Historical Review,* 20: 227–240 (August 1951).

63. Los Angeles *Times,* August 27, 1885; see also, "Report by Vice-Consul Win-

chester on the Trade and Commerce of San Diego for the Year 1883," Reports from Her Majesty's Consuls on the Manufactures, Commerce, etc., of the Consular Districts, Great Britain Foreign Office, *Accounts and Papers,* 1884, volume XXXV, part VIII, p. 1,494.

64. Ephraim W. Morse to Friend Pierce, July 18, 1876; see also, Ephraim W. Morse to S. Felsenheld, April ?, 1876, Morse Papers.

65. Los Angeles *Times,* January 12, 1886.

CHAPTER 4: THE GREAT MIGRATION

1. Los Angeles *Star,* January 13, 1872.

2. Los Angeles *Herald,* August 22, 1879; Los Angeles *Evening Express,* September 9, 1879; Los Angeles *Herald,* January 4, 1878.

3. Los Angeles *Star,* May 2, 1878; Los Angeles *Evening Express,* September 19, 1876; Los Angeles *Morning Journal,* October 12, 1879; Ben C. Truman, *Semi-Tropical California* (San Francisco, 1874), p. 88.

4. Daniel Freeman to Park Terrell, May 6, 1895, to W. G. Pollock, February 6, 1896, both in Freeman Papers; George H. Bonebrake to J. de Barth Shorb, December 27, 1884, Fred L. Alles to J. de Barth Shorb, April 11, 1885, both in Shorb Papers; Los Angeles *Herald,* July 30, 1879; Los Angeles *Morning Journal,* August 5, 1879.

5. Salvator, *Los Angeles in the Sunny Seventies,* pp. 3, 21, 115, 235; Nordhoff, *California,* pp. 18, 19, 51, 123; Ben C. Truman, *Homes and Happiness in the Golden State of California* (San Francisco, 1885) pp. 12, 24, 34; Henry T. Finck, *The Pacific Coast Scenic Tour* (London, 1891), p. 40.

6. Fred W. Mitchell to Benjamin D. Wilson, October 17, 1872, J. W. Dallas to Benjamin D. Wilson, December 2, 1872, C. G. Blauvett to Benjamin D. Wilson, April 11, 1873, Jonathan D. Thorne to Benjamin D. Wilson, July 30, 1877, all in Wilson Papers; Fred C. Muller to J. de Barth Shorb, October 16, 1883, Shorb Papers; Los Angeles *Star,* April 16, 1870; Los Angeles *Herald,* February 9, 1876.

7. William S. Rosecrans to Mrs. William S. Rosecrans, April 11, 1866, J. M. Trowbridge to William S. Rosecrans, August 14, 1869, both in Rosecrans Papers; John G. Pearce to Charles Maclay, October 6, 1875, Charles Maclay Papers, Henry E. Huntington Library, San Marino, Calif.; Gardner C. Geer to Daniel Freeman, June 10, 1884, Freeman Papers; Emma H. Adams, *To and Fro in Southern California* (Cincinnati, 1887), pp. 73–74; Baur, *Health Seekers,* pp. 33–48.

8. H. H. Spaulding to Benjamin D. Wilson, December 23, 1876, Wilson Papers; Los Angeles *Evening Express,* March 11, 1878; Hine, *William Andrew Spalding,* pp. 12–13.

9. *Population at the Eighth Census: 1860,* pp. 29, 31; *Population at the Tenth Census: 1880,* pp. 447, 483, 492–495, 498, 649.

10. Theodore C. Blegen, "The Competition of the Northwestern States for Immigrants," *Wisconsin Magazine of History,* 3: 3–29 (September 1919); Marcus Lee Hansen, "Official Encouragement of Immigration to Iowa," *Iowa Journal of History and Politics,* 19: 159–195 (April 1921); see also, Paul Gates, *The Illinois Central Railroad and Its Colonization Work* (Cambridge, Mass., 1934), passim; Richard C. Overton, *Burlington West: A Colonization History of the Burlington Railroad* (Cambridge, Mass., 1941), passim; Harold F. Peterson, "Some Colonization Projects of the Northern Pacific Railroad," *Minnesota History,* 10: 127–144 (June 1929).

11. Simon Kuznets and Dorothy Swaine Thomas, *Population Redistribution and Economic Growth. United States, 1870–1950, I, Methodological Considerations and Reference Tables* (Philadelphia, 1957); Joseph A. Hill, "Interstate Migration," United States Bureau of the Census, *Special Reports. Supplementary Analysis and Derivative Tables. Twelfth Census of the United States: 1900* (Washington, 1906).

12. Curtis Nettels, *The Emergence of a National Economy 1775–1815* (New York, 1962), pp. 158–159.

13. Kuznets and Thomas, *Population Redistribution and Economic Growth,* passim; Hill, "Interstate Migration," passim.

14. Los Angeles *Herald,* March 18, 1881.

15. *Ibid.,* November 5, 1880.

16. Los Angeles *Star,* January 13, 1872.

17. William S. Rosecrans to Leland Stanford, March 4, 1881, Rosecrans Papers; Los Angeles *Times,* May 18, 1883; James B. Hedges, "Promotion of Immigration to the Pacific Northwest by the Railroads," *Mississippi Valley Historical Review,* 15: 180–203 (September 1928); Arthur J. Brown, "The Promotion of Emigration to Washington," *Pacific Northwest Quarterly,* 36: 3–18 (January 1945).

18. Los Angeles *Evening Express,* September 1, 1884; see also, Los Angeles *Herald,* June 17, 1887, December 10, 1889; Brewer, *Up and Down in California,* p. 48; Edna Monch Parker, "The Southern Pacific Railroad and Settlement in Southern California," *Pacific Historical Review,* 6: 103–120 (June 1937).

19. T. S. Van Dyke, *Millionaires of a Day: An Inside History of the Great Southern California "Boom"* (New York, 1890), pp. 38, 39; see also, Glenn S. Dumke, *The Boom of the Eighties in Southern California* (San Marino, Calif., 1944), chap. v.

20. Los Angeles *Herald,* February 19, 1886, January 1, December 10, 1889; Leland Stanford to William S. Rosecrans, March 1, 1881, Rosecrans Papers; Dumke, *Boom of the Eighties,* chaps. iii, iv.

21. Van Dyke, *Millionaires of a Day,* p. 45.

22. "Report of Vice-Consul Mortimer," *Diplomatic and Consular Reports on Trade and Finance. United States. Report for the Year 1887 on the Trade of the Consular Districts of San Francisco,* Great Britain Foreign Office, *Accounts and Papers,* 1888, volume XXXIX, p. 14.

23. Van Dyke, *Millionaires of a Day,* p. 208; *ibid.,* pp. 92–93, 145–153, 160–161; Dumke, *Boom of the Eighties,* chap. xviii; see also, "Report of Vice-Consul Mortimer," *Diplomatic and Consular Reports on Trade and Finance. United States. Report for the Year 1888 on the Trade of the Consular Districts of San Francisco,* Great Britain Foreign Office, *Accounts and Papers,* 1889, volume XXXV, p. 30.

24. Guinn, *Los Angeles,* I, 254–255; "Report of Vice-Consul Mortimer on the Trade and Commerce of Los Angeles and Wilmington, California, for the Year 1885," *Reports from Her Majesty's Consuls on the Manufactures, Commerce, etc., of the Consular Districts,* Great Britain Foreign Office, *Accounts and Papers,* 1886, volume XXIX, part IV, p. 610.

25. Los Angeles *Herald,* February 21, 1888. The remarks of one visitor were particularly revealing: "My [previous] impressions of the city of Los Angeles were that it was a place of some 25,000 people, mostly of the migratory, restless class, induced to emigrate to it by exaggerated stories of its healthfulness and beauty; that it was situated in a sandy, sterile region of country, with an occasional spot of rich soil requiring irrigation to produce either fruits, grain or vegetables; . . . [and] that water for irrigation could not be had . . . To my mind yours was a city in something of a desert waste and therefore would soon fall back to its original significance." Los Angeles *Herald,* June 17, 1888. Needless to say, he fully recanted.

26. Baur, *Health Seekers,* pp. 175–176.

27. Emory Fiske Skinner, *Reminiscences* (Chicago, 1908), pp. 326–327.

28. Los Angeles Board of Trade, *Annual Report for 1887–1888;* see also, Charles Dwight Willard, *History of the Los Angeles Chamber of Commerce* (Los Angeles, 1899), pp. 143–145.

29. Los Angeles *Herald,* November 15, December 8, 1888.

30. Los Angeles *Evening Express,* January 2, 1886.

31. Nathaniel H. Egleston, *The Home and Its Surroundings or Villages and Village Life* (New York, 1884), pp. 31–34.

32. Louis Adamic, *The Truth about Los Angeles* (Girard, Kan., 1927), p. 41; see also, E. W. Howe, *The Story of a Country Town* (New York, 1926), p. 150; Everett Dick, *The Sod-House Frontier 1854–1890* (New York, 1938), passim; Lewis Atherton, *Main Street on the Middle Border* (Bloomington, Ind., 1954), passim.

33. Hamlin Garland, *A Son of the Middle Border* (New York, 1924), pp. 86, 129, 365; see also, Arthur M. Schlesinger, *The Rise of the City 1878–1898* (New York, 1933), pp. 60–69.

34. Lucy Coit to Fremont Ackerman, August 3, 1890, Fremont Ackerman Papers, Special Collections Division, University of California Library, Los Angeles.

35. Louis D. Stilwell, *Migration from Vermont* (Montpelier, Vt., 1948), p. 160; Egleston, *Village and Village Life*, p. 42.

36. Los Angeles *Examiner,* September 6, 1910.

37. *Ibid.,* September 14, 1910.

38. Willard, *Chamber of Commerce,* pp. 76–77, 89–96, 147–151, 154–157, 163–165.

39. Here I am indebted to Richard Weiss who has described this change in "The American Myth of Success, 1865 to the Present: A Study in Popular Thought" (Columbia University Doctoral Dissertation, 1966).

40. Stanton Davis Kirkham, *Resources: An Interpretation of the Well-Rounded Life* (New York and London, 1910), p. 212, chaps. xiv, xv; Ralph Waldo Trine, *The Land of Living Men* (New York, 1910), chaps. vii, x; Horatio W. Dresser, *Human Efficiency: A psychological Study of Modern Problems* (New York and London, 1912), p. 365; Bolton Hall, *Thrift* (New York, 1916), chaps. i, xxiii; Charles S. Braden, *Spirits in Rebellion: The Rise and Development of New Thought* (Dallas, 1963), part I; Donald Meyer, *The Positive Thinkers* (New York, 1965), part two; Weiss, "American Myth of Success."

41. Southern California Bureau of Information, *Southern California: An Authentic Description . . . for the Homeseeker, Tourist, and Invalid* (Los Angeles, 1892), passim.

42. Los Angeles Chamber of Commerce Minutes, September 1, 1909, Chamber of Commerce Building, Los Angeles.

43. Charles Dudley Warner, *Our Italy* (New York, 1891), pp. 87–89, 146–147; Harry Ellington Brook, *The Land of Sunshine: Southern California* (Los Angeles, 1893), passim, which was originally published by the Southern California Bureau of Information and frequently reissued by the Los Angeles Chamber of Commerce between 1900 and 1920. See also Oscar Osburn Winther, "The Use of Climate as a Means of Promoting Migration to Southern California," *Mississippi Valley Historical Review*, 33: 411–424 (December 1946).

44. Fredric Keffer to Fremont Ackerman, December 14, 1931, Ackerman Papers.

45. Los Angeles *Examiner,* March 3, 1912; Arthur T. Johnson, *California: An Englishman's Impression of the Golden State* (New York, ca. 1910), pp. 17–18.

46. "Ray & I are thinking seriously of moving to your section after prosperity returns," a Nebraska man wrote to a friend in Los Angeles in 1896. "It is too hard to make a living down there now, otherwise I would be ready to leave as soon as I could dispose of my home. I am well acquainted here & can make a good living for my family as well as care for my Cal[ifornia] property. We will come anyhow when our orchard commences bearing if it produces even half of what people say it will. That ho[w]ever will be four years more. McKinley & Prosperity will reach us before that." Charles W. Helmick to Fremont Ackerman, June 27, 1896, Ackerman Papers.

47. Jackson A. Graves to I. W. Hellman, October 2, 1914, Jackson A. Graves Papers, Henry E. Huntington Library, San Marino, Calif. See also James Diller to J. de Barth Shorb, December 22, 1885, Shorb Papers; Edward O. Moe and Carl C. Taylor, *Culture of a Contemporary Rural Community: Irwin, Iowa* (Washington, 1942), pp. 9–10.

48. Harry Carr, *Los Angeles City of Dreams* (New York, 1935), pp. 126–129.

49. Mark Lee Luther, *The Boosters* (Indianapolis, 1923), pp. 161–162; see also, Los Angeles *Examiner,* August 31, 1910.

50. Louis Adamic, *Laughing in the Jungle: The Autobiography of an Immigrant in America* (New York and London, 1932), p. 218.

51. Mrs. William A. Rolfe to Fremont Ackerman, November 14, 1927, Ackerman Papers.

52. McWilliams, *Southern California Country*, p. 135.

53. Don Thomas, "In Competition for American Tourists and Capital," *California Journal of Development*, 20: 11–12 (April 1930); Earl Pomeroy, *In Search of the Golden West: The Tourist in Western America* (New York, 1957).

54. United States Census Office, *Census Reports. Volume I. Twelfth Census of the United States. 1900. Population, Part I* (Washington, 1901), p. 609.

55. United States Bureau of the Census, *Fifteenth Census of the United States: 1930. Population, Volume III, Part 1* (Washington, 1932), pp. 267–269; "Reports of the Immigration Commission. Immigrants in Industries," Part 25, Volume III, United States Congress, *Senate Documents*, 61 Congress, 2 Session, Number 663, pp. 445–461.

56. *Fifteenth Census: 1930. Population, Volume III, Part 1*, p. 266; "Reports of the Immigration Commission. Immigrants in Industries," Part 25, Volume I, pp. 5–33, 223–224; Yamato Ichihashi, *Japanese in the United States* (Stanford, California, 1932), chap. iv; Carey McWilliams, *Prejudice. Japanese Americans: Symbol of Racial Intolerance* (Boston, 1944), pp. 73–77.

57. *Fifteenth Census: 1930. Population, Volume III, Part 1*, pp. 252, 260; United States Bureau of Immigration, *Annual Reports of the Commissioner General of Immigration to the Secretary of Labor, 1900–1930;* Manuel Gamio, comp., *The Mexican Immigrant. His Life Story. Autobiographical Documents* (Chicago, 1921), passim; Emory F. Bogardus, *The Mexicans in the United States* (Los Angeles, 1934), chap. i; Ruth D. Tuck, *Not with the Fist: Mexican-Americans in a Southwest City* (New York, 1946), pp. 56–61.

58. *Fifteenth Census: 1930. Population, Volume III, Part 1*, p. 266; Lawrence Brooks de Graaf, "Negro Migration to Los Angeles, 1930–1950" (University of California at Los Angeles Doctoral Dissertation, 1962), chaps. i, ii; Eugene S. Richards, "The Effects of the Negro's Migration to Southern California upon His Socio-Cultural Patterns" (University of Southern California Doctoral Dissertation, 1941), pp. 42–49.

59. United States Bureau of the Census, *Fifteenth Census of the United States: 1930. Population, Volume I* (Washington, 1931), pp. 18–19; United States Bureau of the Census, *Fifteenth Census of the United States: 1930. Metropolitan Districts* (Washington, 1932), pp. 10–12.

60. *Fifteenth Census: 1930. Population. I*, pp. 18–21; *Fifteenth Census: 1930. Metropolitan Districts*, pp. 10–12.

61. United States Bureau of the Census, *Thirteenth Census of the United States. 1910. Volume I. Population* (Washington, 1913), pp. 207–213; United States Bureau of the Census, *Fourteenth Census of the United States. 1920. Volume III. Population.* (Washington, 1922), pp. 40–45; United States Bureau of the Census, *Fifteenth Census of the United States: 1930. Population. Volume II* (Washington, 1932), pp. 73–78.

62. United States Census Office, *Report on Population of the United States at the Eleventh Census: 1890. Part I* (Washington, 1895), pp. 580–583; *Twelfth Census. 1900. Population. Part I*, pp. 706–713; United States Bureau of the Census, *Thirteenth Census of the United States. Volume I. Population. 1910* (Washington, 1913), pp. 770–771; United States Bureau of the Census, *Fourteenth Census of the United States. 1920. Volume II. Population* (Washington, 1922), pp. 661–668; *Fifteenth Census: 1930. Population. Volume II*, pp. 204–215.

63. *Eleventh Census: 1890. Part I*, pp. 580–583; *Twelfth Census. 1900. Population. Part I*, pp. 706–709; *Thirteenth Census. Volume I. Population. 1910*, p. 770; *Fourteenth Census. 1920. Volume II. Population*, p. 666; *Fifteenth Census: 1930. Population. Volume II*, p. 212. The census figures are a bit misleading here, for they indicate only in which states the residents were born and not from which states they emigrated. A person who was born

in New York and reared in Iowa and then moved to California is considered a New Yorker not an Iowan. These figures can be refined only when the detailed household returns for the twentieth century are made available. (See Newmark and Newmark, *Census of Los Angeles 1850*, passim, for an earlier period.) They should not markedly alter the conclusions reached here—except that as internal migration proceeded mainly from east to west, the numbers from the East and east north-central states are probably exaggerated while the numbers from the West and west north-central states are probably underestimated. This problem, needless to say, is not unique to Los Angeles.

64. *Thirteenth Census. 1910. Volume I. Population*, pp. 207–213; *Fourteenth Census. 1920. Volume III. Population*, pp. 40–45; *Fifteenth Census: 1930. Population. Volume II*, pp. 73–78.

65. United States Census Office, *Report on Population of the United States at the Eleventh Census: 1890. Part II* (Washington, 1897), pp. 115–130; United States Census Office, *Census Reports. Volume II. Twelfth Census of the United States. 1900. Population. Part II* (Washington, 1902), pp. 123–145; *Thirteenth Census. Volume I. Population. 1910*, pp. 278–283, 437–462; *Fourteenth Census. 1920. Volume II. Population*, pp. 288–358; *Fifteenth Census: 1930. Population. Volume II*, pp. 115, 724–793; United States Bureau of the Census, *Fifteenth Census of the United States: 1930. Population. Volume VI* (Washington, 1933), p. 71.

CHAPTER 5: TRANSPORTATION, WATER, AND REAL ESTATE

1. Edwin L. Lewis, "Street Railway Development in Los Angeles and Environs. Volume I, 1873–1895," in the possession of Mr. John Curtis of the Los Angeles Metropolitan Transit Authority, Los Angeles. A vice-president of the Los Angeles Railway, Lewis prepared this manuscript from the corporation's records before they were destroyed. See also, Ira Swett, ed., "Los Angeles Railway History," *Interurbans*, special no. 11 (1951).

2. Los Angeles *Examiner*, December 12, 1904.

3. Edward S. Mason, *The Street Railway Industry in Massachusetts: The Rise and Decline of an Industry* (Cambridge, Mass., 1932), chap. ii.

4. Lewis, "Street Railway Development," I, 35–42, 46–49; Swett, "Los Angeles Railway," p. 9; Guinn, *Los Angeles*, I, 280–281.

5. Lewis, "Street Railway Development," I, 54–62, 105–111, 194–207; Swett, "Los Angeles Railway," pp. 12–13.

6. J. F. Crank to S. D. Hoevy, May 16, 1888, to C. B. Holmes, May 10, 1890, August 12, 1890, to Thomas Addison, October 15, 1890, to M. B. Hull, March 21, 1891, to Thomas Brown, July 21, 1891, August 6, 1891, Crank Papers.

7. Lovell White to John J. Mitchell, February 25, 1892, J. F. Crank to Louis Coburn, October 26, 1891, to John J. Mitchell, December 31, 1891, to Edwin Burritt Smith, April 7, 1892, to James J. Houghteling, June 2, 1892, to C. B. Holmes, August 1, 1892, Crank Papers.

8. Edwin L. Lewis, "Street Railway Development in Los Angeles and Environs. Volume II, 1895–1938," pp. 3–12; Swett, "Los Angeles Railway," p. 15.

9. Office of the Chief Engineer, Pacific Electric Railway Company, "Corporate History of the Pacific Electric as of June 30, 1914," pp. 72–74, 224–250, in the possession of Mr. James Gibson of the California Public Utilities Commission, San Francisco.

10. Cornelius Cole to Olive Cole, September 1, 1890, Cornelius Cole Papers, Special Collections Division, University of California Library, Los Angeles; see also, R. C. Shaw to Cornelius Cole, May 28, 1887, M. L. Wicks to Cornelius Cole, June 26, 1888, Cole Papers; Roy F. Jones to John P. Jones, January 8, 1900, John P. Jones Papers, Special Collections Division, University of California Library, Los Angeles; Chief Engineer, "Corporate History," pp. 296–297.

11. Cahuenga Valley *Sentinel,* January 27, 1900, Whitley Papers; Robert C. Gillis to Moses H. Sherman, ca. 1904, Robert C. Gillis Papers, in the possession of Mr. Arthur L. Loomis, Pacific Palisades, Calif.; Roy F. Jones to John P. Jones, October 29, 1899, Jones Papers. Perhaps the most illuminating remarks on this matter were made by Moses H. Sherman in a letter to Robert C. Gillis, November 29, 1907: "We want to buy 12,000 acres at once, and put the [rail] road right through the middle of it. Also, the property owners in that locality would subscribe enough money to build the road the whole distance so that the L[os] A[ngeles] P[acific] Co. would not have to put in a dollar. We might build five or six, or even seven miles of road, and we might build less, according to the amount of money they raise, but the understanding is that the Railway Company does not put in anything." Moses H. Sherman Papers, in the possession of Mr. Arnold Haskell, Los Angeles.

12. Huntington Land and Improvement Company Ledgers and Journals, Huntington Land Companies, San Marino, Calif.; see also, Chief Engineer, "Pacific Electric," pp. 228–243; Ira Swett, ed., "Los Angeles and Redondo," *Interurbans,* special no. 20 (1957), p. 7.

13. Los Angeles *Times,* April 3, 6, 9, May 6, 9, 1903; Los Angeles *Examiner,* December 12, 1903; Swett, "Los Angeles Railway," p. 19.

14. Moses H. Sherman to Dear Friend, November 12, 1902, enclosed in Thomas C. Bundy to Robert C. Gillis, November 12, 1902, Gillis Papers.

15. Robert C. Gillis to Moses H. Sherman, July 17, 1905, Moses H. Sherman to Robert C. Gillis, November 14, 1905, Moses H. Sherman to Robert Sherman, November 15, 1905, Robert C. Gillis to Paul Shoup, April 8, 1914, all in Gillis Papers; Robert C. Gillis to Henry E. Huntington, September 24, 1909, to C. E. Seger, February 26, 1910, both in Sherman Papers. See also, *Electric Railway Journal,* 35: 957 (May 28, 1910); P. H. Albright, "Reconstruction and Improvements of the Los Angeles Pacific Company," *ibid.,* 34: 930–936 (October 30, 1909).

16. Los Angeles *Examiner,* November 9, 19, 1910; Lewis, "Street Railway Development," II, 69–71; Chief Engineer, "Pacific Electric," pp. 329–367. See also, *Electric Railway Journal,* 34: 566–570 (October 2, 1909); 36: 1,007 (November 12, 1910); 36: 1,079 (November 26, 1910); 37: 182 (January 28, 1911).

17. Frederick Law Olmsted, Harland Bartholemew, Charles H. Cheney, *A Major Traffic Street Plan for Los Angeles* (Los Angeles, 1924), p. 17; Los Angeles *Examiner,* January 15, 1914.

18. *Ibid.,* July 6, 1924; Los Angeles Board of City Planning Commissioners Minutes, January 10, 1922, Department of City Planning, City Hall, Los Angeles.

19. *Annual Report of the City Engineer Los Angeles, California [1921-1922],* pp. 10–13, 38–40.

20. H. H. Merrick to Santa Monica Mountain Park Company, April 9, 1923; Municipal Improvement District No. 22 Memorandum; Mulholland Highway Files, Gillis Papers; *Annual Report of the City Engineer Los Angeles, California [1922-1923],* pp. 48–49.

21. Los Angeles Board of City Planning Commissioners Minutes, December 12, 1922; Municipal League of Los Angeles, *Bulletin. Light of Your City's Affairs,* vol. 5, no. 5 (December 28, 1927), vol. 5, no. 6 (January 21, 1928).

22. Ben Blow, *California Highways* (San Francisco, 1920), pp. 1–12, 162–167; *Annual Report of the Engineering Department of the City of Los Angeles [1924-1925],* p. 85.

23. Los Angeles *Herald,* February 18, 1882; Daniel Freeman to [?], September 22, 1896; City of Los Angeles *v.* Los Angeles City Water Company, Transcript on Appeal; Ostrom, *Water and Politics,* p. 44.

24. Los Angeles *Herald,* June 19, 1890; see also, *ibid.,* August 27, September 18, 1889, May 18, 24, 26, June 12, November 14, 1890; Los Angeles *Evening Express,* October 20, 1890, February 21, 1891; Ostrom, *Water and Politics,* pp. 45–46.

25. Los Angeles *Evening Express,* March 4, 1890; Los Angeles *Herald,* December 30, 1891. The courts refused to allow the forfeiture. Los Angeles *Evening Express,* January 4, 1892.

26. Los Angeles *Evening Express,* March 17, 23, August 25, 29, September 26, October 13, 24, 1892. The vote was 4,980 to 1,896. *Ibid.,* November 3, 1892.

27. *Ibid.,* June 20, August 14, October 7, 9, November 7, 14, 1893, January 6, 1894, January 19, 1895, January 13, 1896. For the best description of the domestic water system, see the city engineer's report in *ibid.,* July 26, 1897.

28. *Ibid.,* January 3, 1898.

29. City of Los Angeles *v.* Los Angeles City Water Company, 124 Cal. 368; Board of Arbitrators Minutes and Proceedings, p. 66, Department of Water and Power, Los Angeles; Los Angeles *Evening Express,* April 4, May 13, 1899.

30. *Final Report of the Compromise Committee,* July 19, 1901, Department of Water and Power Files; Los Angeles *Evening Express,* June 14, August 28, 1901; Los Angeles *Times,* July 12, 20, August 16, 20, 25, October 22, November 17, 19, 1901, February 4, 1902; Ostrom, *Water and Politics,* pp. 47–48.

31. *First Annual Report of the Board of Public Utilities of the City of Los Angeles* [*1909–1910*], p. 36; Seward Cole to Board of Public Service Commissioners of the City of Los Angeles, January, 1917, Cole Papers; Van Nuys Water Company Journals, Owensmouth Water Company Journals, Los Angeles Suburban Homes Company Minutes, March 7, 1910, February 17, 1912, all in Whitley Papers.

32. Huntington Land and Improvement Company Ledger 1, p. 264, Ledger B, pp. 279–280, Ledger C, p. 421, Ledger D, Account 251, Huntington Land Companies Files; Santa Monica Land and Water Company Ledger, p. 176; Santa Monica Land and Water Company Journal 180, Santa Monica Land and Water Company, Pacific Palisades, Calif.

33. Los Angeles City, *Archives,* vol. 585, p. 33; Los Angeles Board of Public Utilities Minutes, July 13, July 19, 1912, Department of Public Utilities, City Hall, Los Angeles; see also, Accounting Record of Acquired Water Systems, Department of Water and Power Files.

34. Los Angeles Board of Water Commissioners Minutes, September 22, 1902, March 23, 1911; *Second Annual Report of the Board of Water Commissioners of the City of Los Angeles, California* [*1903*], pp. 4–5, 9–10; Los Angeles *Times,* December 18, 21, 1901, February 6, 1902.

35. "Report on Water Supply by Wm. Mulholland Superintendent and Lippincott & Parker Consulting Engineers," *Fourth Annual Report of the Board of Water Commissioners of the City of Los Angeles, California* [*1905*], pp. 79–80.

36. *Third Annual Report of the Board of Water Commissioners of the City of Los Angeles, California* [*1904*], p. 23; *First Annual Report of the Chief Engineer of the Los Angeles Aqueduct* [*1907*], pp. 17–21; Ostrom, *Water and Politics,* pp. 11–15; Remi A. Nadeau, *The Water Seekers* (Garden City, N.Y., 1950), pp. 21–28.

37. Los Angeles *Examiner,* August 17, 25, September 3, 8, 1905; Los Angeles Chamber of Commerce Minutes, July 11, 1906; Nadeau, *Los Angeles,* pp. 161–180; Ostrom, *Water and Politics,* pp. 54–56.

38. *First Annual Report of the Chief Engineer of the Los Angeles Aqueduct* [*1907*], passim.

39. Los Angeles *Examiner,* May 24, 1907.

40. Los Angeles Board of Public Service Commissioners, *Complete Report on Construction of the Los Angeles Aqueduct* (Los Angeles, 1916), pp. 266–269, passim; Ostrom, *Water and Politics,* pp. 93–95; Nadeau, *The Water Seekers,* pp. 44–63.

41. Los Angeles Board of Water Commissioners Minutes, February 6, 1905, August, 29, 1912, December 22, 1922, June 18, 1929.

42. *Tenth Annual Report of the Board of Public Service Commissioners of the City of Los Angeles, California* [*1911*], pp. 41–59; *Eleventh Annual Report of the Board of Public Service*

Commissioners of the City of Los Angeles, California [*1912*], pp. 3–4; Los Angeles Board of Public Service Commissioners Minutes, September 25, 1912, December 26, 1913, June 27, 1916, April 11, 1919.

43. Louis C. Hill, J. B. Lippincott, A. L. Sonderegger, "Summary of Report on the Water Supply for the City of Los Angeles and the Metropoltian Area, August 14, 1924," Department of Water and Power Files; *Twenty-Third Annual Report of the Board of Public Service Commissioners of the City of Los Angeles* [*1924*], pp. 7–10.

44. *Twenty-Ninth Annual Report of the Board of Water and Power Commissioners of the City of Los Angeles* [*1930*], pp. 3, 5; Ostrom, *Water and Politics,* pp. 20–22; Nadeau, *The Water Seekers,* pp. 131–132.

45. Nadeau, *The Water Seekers,* pp. 147–171; Kleinsorge, *Boulder Canyon Project,* pp. 15–51; The Metropolitan Water District of Southern California, *History and First Annual Report* [*1938*] (Los Angeles, 1939), pp. 26–32.

46. Nadeau, *The Water Seekers,* pp. 172–191; Kleinsorge, *Boulder Canyon Project,* pp. 55–74; Metropolitan Water District, *History and Report,* pp. 32–37; United States Department of the Interior, *The Hoover Dam: Power and Water Contracts and Related Data* (Washington, 1933), pp. 1–42.

47. The corporation lobbied for a low dam which would allow it to generate electricity at other filings, whereas the board appealed for a high dam which would favor governmental enterprise. For a discussion see Los Angeles Board of Public Service Commissioners Minutes, June 12, 1923; Los Angeles Chamber of Commerce Minutes, December 9, 1924; Nadeau, *The Water Seekers,* pp. 191–217; Kleinsorge, *Boulder Canyon Project,* pp. 89–92, 113–116.

48. Ostrom, *Water and Politics,* pp. 18–19; Nadeau, *The Water Seekers,* pp. 218–244; Kleinsorge, *Boulder Canyon Project,* pp. 236–242; Metropolitan Water District, *History and Report,* pp. 57–271.

49. Huntington-Redondo Company Minute Book B, Huntington Land Companies Files; Los Angeles Suburban Homes Company Minutes, March 15, 1912, Whitley Papers; Contract between Title Insurance and Trust Company and Meyerling and Lawrence Company, December 29, 1921, Emery Park Subdivision Trust, Title Insurance and Trust Company Files.

50. Los Angeles City, *Archives,* vol. 585, p. 52.

51. *First Annual Report of the Board of Public Utilities of the City of Los Angeles* [*1909–1910*], pp. 11–12, 168, 170, 171, 189; Los Angeles Board of Public Utilities Minutes, August 15, 1913, October 2, 1919; Los Angeles City, *Archives,* vol. 585, p. 28.

52. Los Angeles Board of Public Service Commissioners Minutes, April 3, 1923; see also, Rules and Regulations, Electric Extensions, No. 20, Southern California Edison Company, Los Angeles; Contingent Refund Book, Huntington Land Companies Files; Subdivision Trust S 7663, Title Insurance and Trust Company, Los Angeles.

53. Los Angeles Suburban Homes Company Minutes, November 6, November 11, 1911, January 10, June 14, 1913, Whitley Papers.

54. *Ibid.,* February 3, February 10, 1913, Whitley Papers.

55. *Ibid.,* November 13, November 17, November 25, 1911, Whitley Papers.

56. Huntington Land and Improvement Company Ledgers and Journals, Huntington Land Companies Files.

57. Los Angeles Suburban Homes Company Minutes, Whitley Papers; Los Angeles *Times,* August 23, 1912; "Report of Aqueduct Investigation Board," pp. 89–92, Public Library, Los Angeles.

58. "Estimate to Complete Improvements—Huntington Palisades, September 30, 1927," Santa Monica Land and Water Company Files. For Gillis' earlier activities, see Santa Monica Land and Water Company Ledgers and Journals, Santa Monica Land and Water Company Files; and for his relationship with the Los Angeles Pacific

Railway, see Robert C. Gillis to Moses H. Sherman, ca. 1904, Gillis Papers, and Moses H. Sherman to Robert C. Gillis, November 29, 1907, Sherman Papers.

59. Donald M. Baker, *A Rapid Transit System for Los Angeles California. A Report to Central Business District Association* (Los Angeles, 1933), plate 2.

60. No mention has been made here of police, fire, and sanitation because provision of these services, as pointed out in Chap. 2, above, followed rather than preceded urban expansion. The history of the sewer system, which was particularly important, can be traced in the *Sewer Facilities Record,* Books 1–4, and the "Report of the Special Sewage Disposal Commission," Parts I, II (April 16, 1921), and III (August 10, 1921)—both in the Department of Sewage Design—and in the *Annual Reports of the City Engineer of Los Angeles,* passim.

CHAPTER 6: COMMERCIAL AND INDUSTRIAL EXPANSION

1. Los Angeles *Star,* October 2, 1858; Board of Economic Survey, *Economic Survey of the Port of Los Angeles, July 15, 1933,* p. 48, Los Angeles Chamber of Commerce Files; Mamie Krythe, *Port Admiral: Phineas Banning* (San Francisco, 1957), chaps. x, xi; Guinn, *Los Angeles,* I, 326–328.

2. Amos A. Fries, "Preliminary Examination of Wilmington Harbor, California, 1907," United States Congress, *House Executive Documents,* 60 Congress, 2 Session, Number 1,114, p. 3; Phineas Banning to Cornelius Cole, October 12, November 2, 1871, Cole Papers; Los Angeles *Star,* October 30, 1869, February 24, April 23, July 30, 1870; Krythe, *Phineas Banning,* pp. 171–198.

3. Los Angeles *Star,* November 14, 1873; see also, *ibid.,* May 5, 1875, February 16, November 15, 1876; Los Angeles *Evening Express,* December 23, 30, 1873; Salvator, *Los Angeles in the Sunny Seventies,* pp. 185–186.

4. Los Angeles *Herald,* February 22, March 23, 1878; Eugene Germain to Board of Directors of the Redondo Beach Company, December 10, 1887, to Charles Silent, January 11, 1888, Freeman Papers; Fries, "Examination of Wilmington Harbor, 1907," p. 3; Salvator, *Los Angeles in the Sunny Seventies,* p. 179.

5. *Annual Report. Board of Harbor Commissioners of the City of Los Angeles, California [1924–1925],* p. 36; Board of Economic Survey, *Port of Los Angeles,* Table 54.

6. Los Angeles *Herald,* January 11, 1887; "Report of a Board of Engineer Officers on Deep-Water Harbor at San Pedro or Santa Monica Bays, California," United States Congress, *House Executive Documents,* 52 Congress, 2 Session, Number 41, Appendix 1, pp. 30–31 (hereafter, "1892 Board"); "Report of Vice-Consul Allen," *Diplomatic and Consular Reports on Trade and Finance. United States. Report for the Year 1888 on the Trade of the Consular District of San Francisco,* Great Britain Foreign Office, *Accounts and Papers,* 1889, volume XXXV, p. 33; "Report of Vice-Consul Mortimer," *Diplomatic and Consular Reports on Trade and Finance. United States. Report for the Year 1889 on the Trade of the Consular District of San Francisco,* Great Britain Foreign Office, *Accounts and Papers,* 1890, volume XXXVII, p. 37.

7. Los Angeles *Herald,* October 21, November 14, December 14, 1887; "Survey of San Pedro Bay, California," United States Congress, *House Executive Documents,* 50 Congress, 1 Session, Number 191, pp. 1–7.

8. Los Angeles *Herald,* October 21, 1887; see also, Los Angeles *Evening Express,* June 30, 1884.

9. "Survey of San Pedro Bay, California," pp. 2–7; "Report of Board for Locating a Deep-Water Harbor in Southern California," United States Congress, *Senate Executive Documents,* 55 Congress, 1 Session, Number 18, Appendix F, p. 158 (hereafter, "1897 Board").

10. "Report of Engineers on Deep Harbor on Pacific Coast between Points Dume and Capistrano, California," United States Congress, *House Executive Documents,* 52

Congress, 1 Session, Number 39, pp. 1–9 (hereafter, "1891 Board"); Los Angeles *Herald,* May 15, 1890, November 7, March 21, 1890; Charles Dwight Willard, *The Free Harbor Contest at Los Angeles* (Los Angeles, 1899), chap. vi.

11. Los Angeles *Evening Express,* October 13, 23, December 20, 1887; "1892 Board," p. 68; I. A. Pritchard to John P. Jones, August 21, 1891, John P. Jones Papers, Henry E. Huntington Library, San Marino, Calif.; "1897 Board," pp. 59–60. See also, Richard W. Barsness, "Railroads and Los Angeles: The Quest for a Deep-Water Port, *Southern California Quarterly,* 47: 379–391 (December 1965).

12. John P. Jones to Georgina Jones, August 24, 1890, September 24, October 9, 18, 21, 1891, February 7, 1892, March 1892, September 7, 1895; Collis P. Huntington to John P. Jones, June 26, June 27, 1892, Jones Papers (Huntington Library); Los Angeles *Herald,* July 24, 1891.

13. "1892 Board," pp. 2–23; Los Angeles *Evening Express,* May 14, 30, September 8, 9, 1892; Willard, *Free Harbor Contest,* chaps. viii, ix.

14. Los Angeles *Evening Express,* October 4, 1894; see also, *ibid.,* March 11, 1893, March 12, April 6, 1894; Los Angeles Chamber of Commerce Minutes, March 14, 1892, April 7, 1894; Willard, *Free Harbor Contest,* p. 107 and chap. x.

15. Los Angeles *Evening Express,* April 4, 1896; John P. Jones to Georgina Jones, September 7, 1895, May 1, 1896, Jones Papers; Stephen M. White to John T. Gaffey, January 14, 1895, John T. Gaffey Papers, Henry E. Huntington Library, San Marino, Calif.

16. Los Angeles *Evening Express,* April 29, 1896; *ibid.,* April 17, 18, 19, 27, 1896.

17. A supporter of the Southern Pacific in the 1870's, Widney had written the most influential pamphlet in favor of the subsidy; for his position, see "1892 Board," p. 68. See also, Daggett, *Southern Pacific,* chap. xxiv.

18. Cornelius Cole Memorandum, Cole Papers; see also, Daniel Freeman to Park Terrell, February 6, 1896, Freeman Papers; Stephen M. White to Thomas E. Gibbon, April 7, 1896, Stephen M. White Papers, Borel Collection, Stanford University Library, Stanford, Calif.; Willard, *Free Harbor Contest,* chaps. xiii, xiv.

19. "1897 Board," pp. 3–29, 142–143, 161–167; Los Angeles *Evening Express,* May 8, 9, 13, 14, 22, 29, 1896, March 25, May 20, July 14, 31, 1897, July 1, 6, 29, 1898; Willard, *Free Harbor Contest,* chap. xviii.

20. Los Angeles *Examiner,* March 22, 1905, January 14, 1908; Los Angeles Chamber of Commerce Minutes, November 18, 1905, January 23, 1907; Fries, "Survey of Wilmington Harbor, California, 1907," p. 13.

21. Los Angeles *Examiner,* November 7, 1908; Los Angeles *Times,* April 9, 1903; Los Angeles Chamber of Commerce Minutes, February 23, 1911; Captain Amos A. Fries, "Survey of Wilmington Harbor, California, 1907," United States Congress, *House Executive Documents,* 60 Congress, 2 Session, Number 1,114, pp. 7–20.

22. Captain James J. Meyler, "Preliminary Examination of Inner Harbor at San Pedro, 1899," United States Congress, *House Executive Documents,* 56 Congress, 2 Session, Number 2, *Report of the Chief of Engineers,* Part 6, pp. 4,194–4,198; Captain Amos A. Fries, "Preliminary Examination of Wilmington Harbor, California, 1909," United States Congress, *House Executive Documents,* 61 Congress, 2 Session, Number 768, pp. 3–8; Los Angeles Board of Harbor Commissioners Minutes, March 23, August 8, 1908, Los Angeles Harbor Department, City Hall, Los Angeles; Los Angeles Chamber of Commerce Minutes, June 17, 1908; Los Angeles *Examiner,* January 14, 19, 25, February 21, March 20, May 24, 26, 27, June 19, 23, 25, July 30, 1908.

23. Los Angeles Board of Harbor Commissioners Minutes, August 23, 1909; see also, Los Angeles *Examiner,* September 17, 18, November 17, 18, December 28, 1906, January 8, 1907; Los Angeles *Times,* June 19, 21, 22, 1909.

24. John T. Gaffey's Speech, Gaffey Papers; Los Angeles Board of Harbor Commissioners Minutes, November 12, 1908, June 18, 1909; Los Angeles *Examiner,* Janu-

ary 27, 31, February 5, 17, 25, 27, March 1, 3, 5, 9, 10, 12, 1909; Los Angeles *Times,* August 5, 18, 1909; Board of Economic Survey, *Port of Los Angeles,* Exhibit 1, pp. 1–16.

25. Los Angeles Board of Harbor Commissioners Minutes, August 10, 1909; Los Angeles Chamber of Commerce Minutes, February 23, March 1, March 15, 1911; Los Angeles *Examiner,* November 10, 14, 17, 1908, February 19–25, March 21, 1911; Board of Economic Survey, *Port of Los Angeles,* p. 60.

26. Lieutenant-Colonel C. H. McKinstry, "Preliminary Examination of Los Angeles and Long Beach Harbors, California, 1913," United States Congress, *House Executive Documents,* 63 Congress, 2 Session, Number 896, pp. 11–23, 24–25; Major Frederick B. Downing, "Preliminary Examination of Los Angeles and Long Beach Harbors, California, 1919," United States Congress, *House Executive Documents,* 66 Congress, 3 Session, Number 1,013, pp. 9–20; Colonel Herbert Deakyne, "Preliminary Examination of Los Angeles and Long Beach Harbors, California, 1923," United States Congress, *House Executive Documents,* 68 Congress, 1 Session, Number 349, pp. 17–23.

27. *Annual Reports. Board of Harbor Commissioners of the City of Los Angeles, California* [*1914-1915—1929-1930*]; Los Angeles Board of Harbor Commissioners Minutes, July 28, 1914; Analysis of Bond Redemption and Interest Fund Requirements of Principal and Interest, October 5, 1949, Los Angeles Harbor Department, San Pedro; Board of Economic Survey, *Port of Los Angeles,* pp. 72–75, plate 76; Clarence S. Matson, *Building a World Gateway: The Story of the Los Angeles Harbor* (Los Angeles, 1945), passim.

28. Los Angeles Board of Harbor Commissioners Minutes, December 9, 17, 1913, January 19, December 10, 1915, June 5, 1920; J. W. Ludlow to Board of Harbor Commissioners, September 14, 1922; Joint Committee on the Los Angeles Harbor Transportation Development to Major Charles T. Leeds, March 1, 1924, Los Angeles Chamber of Commerce Files; Los Angeles Board of Harbor Commissioners, "The Facts Concerning the Unification of Railroad Facilities at Los Angeles Harbor," Los Angeles Harbor Department Files (City Hall).

29. *Annual Report. Board of Harbor Commissioners of the City of Los Angeles, California* [*1931-1932*], passim.

30. Board of Economic Survey, *Port of Los Angeles,* tables 1, 2, 54.

31. *Ibid.,* table 50; Los Angeles Board of Harbor Commissioners Minutes, December 24, 1913; "Preliminary Examination of Los Angeles and Long Beach Harbors, California, 1923," Appendix, pp. 54–56, 58; Los Angeles Chamber of Commerce Minutes, April 26, 1911, April 16, 1913, September 28, 1922; "Southwestern Economic Conference (Los Angeles, June 15–17, 1925)," Bancroft Library, University of California at Berkeley; Willard, *Chamber of Commerce,* pp. 200–202.

32. Los Angeles *Times,* March 24, 1882.

33. Los Angeles *Herald,* March 30, April 28, 1878; Los Angeles *Evening Express,* April 1, 8, 13, 25, 1878; Los Angeles *Times,* December 24, 1881, March 24, April 11, 19, May 2, 1882.

34. Los Angeles *Herald,* January 21, 1888.

35. United States Census Office, *Report on Manufacturing Industries in the United States at the Eleventh Census: 1890. Part II* (Washington, 1895), pp. 166–169, 214–217, 302–305, 430–433, 462–465, 530–533, 558–561, 594–597, 634–637; *Eleventh Census: 1890. Population. Part II,* pp. 628–629.

36. Henry E. Huntington's Ledgers, Huntington Land Companies Files; William H. B. Kilner, *Arthur Letts 1862-1923* (Los Angeles, 1927); Corporate Records, Whitley Papers.

37. United States Bureau of the Census, *Thirteenth Census of the United States. Volume IX. Manufactures 1909* (Washington, 1912), pp. 104–105, 106–107, 126–127, 322–323, 388–389, 612–613, 890–891, 990–991, 1,036–1,037, 1,306–1,307; United States Bureau of the Census, *Thirteenth Census of the United States. 1910. Volume IV. Population* (Washington, 1914), pp. 142–243.

38. H. S. McKee, "Business Conditions and the Outlook," Los Angeles, July 1915, Gillis Papers.

39. The exchange continued as follows:

"Q. Are there reasons, geographical and economic, that suggest themselves to you for that position?

"A. There are very decided reasons. In the first place, we haven't the raw materials here to develop a great manufacturing area, and even if we had the raw materials here, we would be handicapped to a large extent in manufacturing more than we need locally because of the high freight rates between here and the middle west or the east where the centers of population are the greatest."

Quoted in "In the matter of the application of the City of Los Angeles . . . that the Railroad Commission fix and determine the compensation to be paid the Southern California Edison Company . . . for its distribution system," California Railroad Commission, *Archives*, Application 1424, Reporter's Transcript, pp. 1,161–1,163, California Public Utilities Commission, Sacramento.

40. Los Angeles *Examiner*, May 12, 1907; Los Angeles Chamber of Commerce Minutes, January 21, 1914, August 9, 1916; Atchison and Eshelman, *Los Angeles Then and Now* (Los Angeles, 1897), p. 108.

41. "Harry Chandler's Statement," *Southern California Business*, 2: 13–16 (November 1923).

42. W. T. Bishop to Robert C. Gillis, August 21, 1923, Gillis Papers.

43. *Ibid.*

44. Harry D. Brown, "Why Movies Stay in Hollywood," *Southern California Business*, 4: 18ff (January 1926); McWilliams, *Southern California Country*, chap. xvi; United States Bureau of the Census, *Fifteenth Census of the United States. Manufactures: 1929. Volume III* (Washington, 1933), p. 70.

45. "Preliminary Examination of Los Angeles and Long Beach Harbors, California, 1923," Appendix, pp. 68–70; *Fifteenth Census. Manufactures: 1929. Volume III*, p. 70; William Kidston, "The Oil Fields of Southern California. A History of the Los Angeles Oil Basin," 1936, 2 vols., Special Collections Division, University of California Library, Los Angeles.

46. "Preliminary Examination of Los Angeles and Long Beach Harbors, California, 1923," Appendix, pp. 81–82 (my italics); see also, Los Angeles Chamber of Commerce Minutes, July 5, 1905, January 23, 1912, February 3, 1913, February 11, 1926; Los Angeles Chamber of Commerce, *Members Annual*, 1900–1930, Los Angeles Chamber of Commerce Files; Willard, *Chamber of Commerce*, pp. 171–178.

47. C. B. Seger to W. J. Doran, August 13, 1919, Gillis Papers.

48. Los Angeles Chamber of Commerce Industrial Department, *General Industrial Report of Los Angeles County, California* (Los Angeles, 1929). The completion of the Panama Canal placed the midwestern manufacturers at an even greater disadvantage; see Los Angeles Chamber of Commerce Industrial Department, *General Industrial Report of Los Angeles County, California* (Los Angeles, 1930).

49. "Memorandum of Interview with Wm. S. Knudson . . . by Sydney T. Miller and F. D. Jones, June 25, 1926," Ford Motor Company Archives, Dearborn, Mich.; Allan Nevins, *Ford: The Times, the Man, the Company . . . 1863-1915* (New York, 1954), pp. 500–502.

50. Hugh Allen, "California, VII," in Goodyear Tire and Rubber Company, *The Wingfoot Clan*, no. 9, p. 80; Los Angeles *Herald*, August 5, 1927 (referred to me by William D. Overman, Firestone Tire and Rubber Company); *Fifteenth Census. Manufactures. Volume III*, p. 70.

51. Arthur G. Coons and Arjay R. Miller, *An Economic and Industrial Survey of the Los Angeles and San Diego Areas* (Sacramento, 1941), p. 127.

52. Commission on Industrial Relations, "Open and Closed Shop Controversy in

Los Angeles," United States Congress, *Senate Documents,* 64 Congress, 1 Session, Number 415, pp. 5,493–5,518; Los Angeles Chamber of Commerce Minutes, July 30, 1910.

53. Los Angeles Chamber of Commerce, *Members Annual [1926]*, pp. 139–140; Commission on Industrial Relations, "Open and Closed Shop Controversy in Los Angeles," pp. 5,518–5,536; see also, McWilliams, *Southern California Country,* pp. 275–276.

54. Robert E. L. Knight, *Industrial Relations in the San Francisco Bay Area, 1900–1918* (Berkeley and Los Angeles, 1960), chap. ix; on organized labor's troubles in the 1920's, see Irving Bernstein, *The Lean Years: A History of the American Worker 1920–1933* (Boston, 1960), pp. 154–155.

55. Grace Heilman Stimson, *Rise of the Labor Movement in Los Angeles* (Berkeley and Los Angeles, 1955), passim; see also, Jackson A. Graves, *California Memories 1857–1927,* 2d ed. (Los Angeles, 1930), chap. xviii; Baur, *Health Seekers,* pp. 49–50; Ira B. Cross, *A History of the Labor Movement in California* (Berkeley, 1935), passim. For the subsequent history of Los Angeles' unions, see Louis B. and Richard S. Perry, *A History of the Los Angeles Labor Movement, 1911–1941* (Berkeley, 1963), passim.

56. Frank H. Sparks, "The Location of Industry: An Analysis of Some of the Factors which have Affected the Location of Industry in the Ten Southern Counties of California" (University of Southern California Doctoral Dissertation, 1941), passim.

57. Chamber of Commerce Industrial Department, *Industrial Reports of Los Angeles County,* passim; Department of Research and Service, Security Trust and Savings Bank, *Industrial Survey of Los Angeles* (Los Angeles, 1923–1928), passim.

58. United States Bureau of the Census, *Fifteenth Census of the United States. Manufactures: 1929. Volume III* (Washington, 1933), pp. 61, 69, 71, 82, 250, 258, 286, 294, 402, 407, 434, 439, 441, 454, 539, 546, 561, 568.

59. *Ibid;* United States Bureau of the Census, *Fifteenth Census of the United States: 1930. Population. Volume IV* (Washington, 1933), pp. 22–23.

60. Los Angeles Chamber of Commerce Industrial Department, "Report to Henry M. Robinson, April, 1930," Chamber of Commerce Files; Security Trust and Savings Bank, *Industrial Survey, 1924,* pp. 12–15. See also, miscellaneous reports on steel production, Gillis Papers; *Fifteenth Census. Manufactures: 1929. Volume III,* p. 69.

61. Arnold T. Anderson, "Commercial Aviation in Southern California," Security Trust and Savings Bank, *Industrial Survey, 1928,* pp. 28–31; Lloyd Parke Hamilton, "Coming to the Front in Furniture," *Southern California Business,* 3: 15ff (January 1925); *Fifteenth Census. Manufactures: 1929. Volume III,* pp. 69–70.

62. Morris Markey, *This Country of Yours* (Boston, 1932), pp. 226–227.

CHAPTER 7: THE URBAN LANDSCAPE

1. Issac W. Lord to Mrs. Nealy, March 17, 1876, Lord Letterbook, p. 130, Lord Papers; Los Angeles *Journal,* November 2, 1879; Brewer, *Up and Down in California,* p. 13; Smith, *Adobe Days,* chap. ix; Robinson, *Ranchos Become Cities,* pp. 86–90, 182–184.

2. "Map of the City of Los Angeles California by H. J. Stevenson, U.S. Dept. Surveyor, 1884," Department of Water and Power Files; Salvator, *Los Angeles in the Sunny Seventies,* p. 124; Thompson and West, *Los Angeles,* illustration facing p. 16.

3. Los Angeles *Herald,* December 10, 1877.

4. "Map of the City of Los Angeles California, 1884"; "Map of the City of Los Angeles California, 1876."

5. Los Angeles *Daily News,* March 8, 1869; Los Angeles *Herald,* December 28, 1873; Los Angeles *Star,* April 25, 1874; Newmark, *Sixty Years,* p. 112; Salvator, *Los Angeles in the Sunny Seventies,* p. 136; Woods, *Pacific Coast,* pp. 27–29; James J. Ayres, *Gold and Sunshine: Reminiscences of Early California* (Boston, 1922), pp. 225–226.

6. Jackson A. Graves, *My Seventy Years in Southern California 1857–1927* (Los Angeles,

1927), pp. 105–115; George William Baist, *Baist's Real Estate Atlas of Surveys of Los Angeles* (Philadelphia, 1889), pp. 4–6.

7. Los Angeles *Star*, July 16, 1870; Los Angeles *Herald*, February 4, 1877; Los Angeles *Evening Express*, July 26, 1880; Baist, *Real Estate Atlas* (1889), pp. 36–39, 51, 61, 64.

8. William Hamilton Hall to J. de Barth Shorb, January 4, 1892, Shorb Papers. For a protest against the gridiron pattern, see Los Angeles *Herald*, April 24, 1890.

9. Carr, *Los Angeles*, pp. 136–137; Lord Letterbook, pp. 49–50, Lord Papers; Thompson and West, *Los Angeles*, illustrations facing pp. 38, 44, 60, 76. See also, Harold Kirker, *California's Architectural Frontier: Style and Tradition in the Nineteenth Century* (San Marino, 1960); Vincent J. Scully, Jr., "Romantic Rationalism and the Expression of Structure in Wood: Downing, Wheeler, Gardner and the 'Stick Style,'" *Art Bulletin*, 35: 121–142 (1953).

10. Wm. H. Babcock & Sons, *Report on the Economic and Engineering Feasibility of Regrading the Bunker Hill Area* (Los Angeles, 1931), plate 2; Baker, *Rapid Transit System for Los Angeles*, plate 2; Olmsted Brothers and Bartholemew and Associates, *Report to the Citizens Committee on Parks, Playgrounds and Beaches Los Angeles Region* (Los Angeles, 1931), plate 16; Metropolitan Surveys, *"Industrial Guide" and Street Index of Los Angeles and Its Environs* (Los Angeles, ca. 1935), Los Angeles Chamber of Commerce Files; Jackson A. Graves, *California Memories 1857–1927*, 2d ed. (Los Angeles, 1930), pp. 5–6; Regional Planning Commission County of Los Angeles, *Report of a Highway Traffic Survey in the County of Los Angeles* (Los Angeles, 1934), passim.

11. *Fifteenth Census: 1930. Metropolitan Districts*, pp. 10–12, 35, 39, 73, 115, 165, 171.

12. *Ibid.*, pp. 56–57, 114–115, 128–129, 130–131, 214–215. Although these figures are somewhat misleading because the central cities vary so much in territory, the description presented here, even adjusted for Los Angeles' vast corporate expanse, requires little change.

13. Chap. 5, above. It should be stressed, if only to correct a common misconception, that residential dispersal in Los Angeles was not due to the automobile. That pattern was fixed by the radial routes of the electric railways fully ten years before the widespread ownership of the motor car. The automobile certainly contributed to urban sprawl, but largely because it fit so well the existing pattern of residential dispersal and the prevailing notion of the good community.

14. Santa Monica Land and Water Company Corporate Records, Santa Monica Land and Water Company Files; Huntington Land and Improvement Company Ledgers and Journals, Huntington Land Companies Files; Los Angeles Suburban Home Company Minutes, Whitley Papers.

15. Bessie L. Pierce, *A History of Chicago*, III (New York, 1957), passim; Homer Hoyt, *One Hundred Years of Land Values in Chicago* (Chicago, 1933), chaps. iv, v.

16. Los Angeles *Examiner*, April 11, 1924; Los Angeles *Herald*, March 21, 1891; Mrs. Ernest T. Emery Diary, passim, Special Collections Division, University of California Library, Los Angeles; *Cahuenga Suburban*, April 1895, Cole Papers; Agricultural Department of Los Angeles Chamber of Commerce, *What the Newcomer should know about the Small Farm in Los Angeles County* (1927).

17. *Report of the Housing Commission of the City of Los Angeles [1909–1910]*, p. 26; Finck, *Pacific Coast Tour*, pp. 31–33.

18. *Fifteenth Census: 1930. Population. Volume VI*, p. 72; George William Baist, *Real Estate Atlas of Surveys of Los Angeles* (Philadelphia, 1921), passim.

19. "Tract No. 6753. Restrictions for the Huntington Palisades," Santa Monica Land and Water Company Files; Huntington Land and Improvement Company Minute Book C, Huntington Land Companies Files; "Tract 6882. Protective Restrictions Palos Verdes Estates, Los Angeles California," City Hall, Palos Verdes Estates; Los Angeles Suburban Homes Company Minutes, February 8, 1912, Whitley Papers.

See also, Siegfried Goetze, "Towards Better Housing in Los Angeles," Lissner Papers; Charles H. Cheney to Edgar F. Conant, October 8, 1928, Palos Verdes Homes Associations Files.

20. October 22, 1905, September 24, 1906, Mrs. Ernest T. Emery's Diary.

21. J. R. Douglas, "Report on Conditions Affecting the Real Estate Business in Los Angeles" (1923), Security-First National Bank Research Department, Los Angeles; Bessie Averne McClenahan, *The Changing Urban Neighborhood: From Neighbor to Nigh-Dweller* (Los Angeles, 1929), pp. 35, 47, 84.

22. Bessie Averne McClenahan, "The Changing Nature of an Urban Residential Area" (University of Southern California Doctoral Dissertation, 1928), p. 218.

23. Kiyoshi Uono, "The Factors Affecting the Geographical Aggregation and Dispersion of the Japanese Residences in the City of Los Angeles" (University of Southern California Masters Thesis, 1927), pp. 124ff; J. Max Bond, "The Negro in Los Angeles" (University of Southern California Doctoral Dissertation, 1936), pp. 68ff.

24. Kelker, de Leuw & Company, *Report and Recommendations on a Comprehensive Rapid Transit Plan for the City and County of Los Angeles* (Chicago, 1925), p. 37, plate 17.

25. California Railroad Commission, *Archives,* Application 1,424, Reporter's Transcript, pp. 1,163–1,165.

26. Babcock & Sons, *Regrading the Bunker Hill Area,* plate 29; on the expectations for the central business district, see Chap. 8, below.

27. Jackson A. Graves to I. W. Hellman, November 15, 1909, Graves Papers; see also, Los Angeles *Times,* July 25, 1909; Los Angeles *Examiner,* November 17, 1911.

28. Harrison Lewis to F. E. Lee, February 6, 1919; John P. Kennedy to Robert C. Gillis, March 19, 1926, Gillis Papers; Los Angeles *Examiner,* May 1, 1914, May 14, 1915.

29. Babcock & Sons, *Regrading the Bunker Hill Area,* plates 4, 6; Baist, *Real Estate Atlas* (1921), pp. 2, 3.

30. Babcock & Sons, *Regrading the Bunker Hill Area,* plates 4, 9; Los Angeles Department of Water and Power, "City of Los Angeles and Vicinity Showing the Percentages of the Areas Occupied by the Different Classes of Improvements as of Jan. 1925," Department of Water and Power Files; Baist, *Real Estate Atlas* (1921), pp. 2, 3.

31. Hugh Allen, "California," p. 80; Frank G. Mittelbach, "Dynamic Land Use Patterns in Los Angeles. The Period 1924–1954," in possession of the author, Real Estate Research Institute, University of California, Los Angeles.

32. "The Reminiscences of Mr. M. L. Wiesinger," p 51, Ford Motor Company Archives, Oral History Section, Dearborn, Mich. See also, Kelker, de Leuw & Co., *Rapid Transit Plan for Los Angeles,* plate 9; Department of Water and Power, "City of Los Angeles . . . Jan. 1925."

33. *Annual Report. Department of City Planning. Los Angeles [1923–1930],* p. 61. Los Angeles Department of Water and Power, "City of Los Angeles and Vicinity Showing the Percentages of the Area Occupied by the Different Classes of Improvements as of January 1934," Department of Water and Power Files.

34. W. R. Ferrell, "The Merchants' Map of the Los Angeles Market" (1930); Division of Business and Market Research of the Los Angeles *Examiner,* "Los Angeles Metropolitan and ABC City Market by Family Expenditures" (ca. 1935), Los Angeles Chamber of Commerce Files.

35. Los Angeles *Examiner,* November 17, 1911; see also, Los Angeles *Times,* July 25, 1909; Automobile Club of Southern California, *A Report on Los Angeles Traffic Problems with Recommendations for Relief* (Los Angeles, 1922), passim.

36. "In the Matter of . . . Railway Service in the Hollywood District of the City of Los Angeles," California Railroad Commission, *Archives,* Case 1602, Reporter's Transcript, pp. 128ff; Kelker, de Leuw & Co., *Rapid Transit Plan for Los Angeles,* p. 36; Baker, *Rapid Transit System for Los Angeles,* plate 9.

37. *Annual Reports of the Traffic Commission of the City and County of Los Angeles* [*1925–1930*]; Olmsted, Bartholomew and Cheney, *Major Traffic Street Plan,* pp. 11–16.

38. Hale H. Huggins, "Decentralization of Shopping," *Los Angeles Realtor,* 3: 4 (January 1924); "In the Matter of the Application of Los Angeles Railway Corporation, for an Order Readjusting Rates . . .," California Railroad Commission, *Archives,* Application 13, 323, Reporter's Transcript, pp. 594–596.

39. Stanley McMichael, "Los Angeles as it Appears to an Eastern Realtor," *Los Angeles Realtor,* 2: 21 (January 1923).

40. "The Industrial Land Situation in Los Angeles," *Eberle & Riggleman Economic Service,* III, 7 (February 15, 1926), Part II, pp. 29–32.

41. Department of Water and Power, "City of Los Angeles . . . 1934"; California Railroad Commission, *Archives,* Case 1602, Reporter's Transcript, passim; Babcock & Sons, *Regrading the Bunker Hill Area,* plate 6.

42. Department of Water and Power, "City of Los Angeles . . . 1934"; Los Angeles Chamber of Commerce Minutes, January 10, 1924; N. Alderman, *General Industrial Report of Burbank* (Burbank, 1924), passim; "Industrial Land Situation in Los Angeles," Part II, p. 30.

43. Kelker, de Leuw & Company, *Rapid Transit Plan for Los Angeles,* plate 6.

44. Oneonta Park Account, Huntington Land and Improvement Company Ledger Book 1; Seymour Bisbee's Map of "Oneonta Park and Vicinity South Pasadena, Cal."; Indenture between the Huntington Land and Improvement Company and O. C. Conley, December 13, 1912, all in Huntington Land Company Files.

45. Map of the Townsite of Owensmouth; "Detailed Outline Reservation and Restriction Governing Sales of Acreage Near the New Town of Owensmouth," February 8, 1912, both in Whitley Papers.

46. Santa Monica Land and Water Corporate Records; Map of "Huntington Palisades 'on Santa Monica Bay'" (July 1927); Williams Engineering Company's Estimate to Complete Improvements at the Huntington Palisades (December 27, 1926); "Tract No. 6753. Restrictions. Huntington Palisades," all in Santa Monica Land and Water Company Files.

47. Charles H. Cheney to Edgar F. Conant, October 8, 1928, Palos Verdes Homes Association Files. This letter is worth quoting at length. "The type of protective restrictions and the high class scheme of layout which we have provided tends to guide and automatically regulate the class of citizens who are settling here. The restrictions prohibit occupation of land by Negroes or Asiatics. The minimum cost of house restrictions tends to group the people of more or less like income together as far as it is reasonable and advisable to do so."

48. Olmsted's description of the layout is revealing for greater Los Angeles as well as for Palos Verdes Estates. "In laying out the local streets . . . the controlling consideration has not been merely to cut up the land into the maximum number of lots of standard sizes with street frontage, but to select all the best sites for houses, having regard first to the views and the excellence of the final result rather than merely to the ease with which ordinary commonplace dwellings could be packed in . . . Accessibility is essential and is provided at Palos Verdes Estates, but if the principal thing a man is asking for is accessibility at a minimum cost for street work and lot improvement he had better pick any one of a hundred thousand lots on the flat plains, all just alike, utterly without views or individuality." Frederick Law Olmsted to Charles H. Cheney, undated, Palos Verdes Homes Association Files. See also, Frederick Law Olmsted, "Palos Verdes Estates," *Landscape Architecture,* 17 (July 1927), passim; Map of Palos Verdes Estates and "Tract 6882. Protective Restrictions Palos Verdes Estates, Los Angeles California," both in Palos Verdes Homes Association Files.

49. Harwood Hewitt, "A Plea for Distinctive Architecture in Southern California," Allied Architects Association of Los Angeles, *Bulletin,* 1, 5 (March 1, 1925); see also,

Los Angeles Chamber of Commerce, *Members Annual [1921]*, pp. 23ff.; Franklin Walker, *A Literary History of Southern California* (Berkeley and Los Angeles, 1950), chap. v.

50. "Types of Architecture Approved for Palos Verdes Estates," *Bulletin of the Palos Verdes Art Jury* (May 1925), Palos Verdes Homes Association Files; The Bungalowcraft Company, *Homes of the Moment,* 3d ed. (Los Angeles, 1931); G. H. Edgell, *The American Architecture of To-day* (New York, 1928), pp. 87–100.

51. "California Architecture" (1929), and Palos Verdes Art Jury Minutes, November 21, December 4, 1922, both in Palos Verdes Homes Association Files; Los Angeles Suburban Homes Company Minutes, May 3, 1910. Whitley Papers; The Bungalowcraft Company, *New Spanish Bungalows,* 6th ed. (Los Angeles, 1930), passim.

52. "California Architecture" (1929); Palos Verdes Art Jury Minutes, April 27, 1923, Palos Verdes Homes Association Files; Rex D. Weston, *Weston's Double Bungalows* (Los Angeles, 1924), passim; Edgell, *American Architecture,* pp. 101–109; McWilliams, *Southern California Country,* pp. 354–362.

53. Donald J. Witmer, "Wherein Styles Differ," Allied Architects Association of Los Angeles, *Bulletin,* 1, 12 (October 21, 1925).

54. Hewitt, "A Plea for a Distinctive Architecture in Southern California." The protest of Charles Gibbs Adams—"Our Architectural Tragedy," *California Southland,* 103: 28 (July 1928)—is even more graphic: "There are countless Colonial houses all banked with Palms where there should be only boxwood edgings and hollyhocks and Poplar trees. There are fake Italian Villas with the front yards all messed up with miniature Japanese gardens. There are Spanish houses profaned with variegated shrubs, such as Golden Privet, and shiny stylish bushes clipped into formal balls and cones and pyramids, where should be only graceful olives and peppers, figs and oranges, Jasmines and Tuberoses, Century plants and Scarlet Aloes ... There are Swiss Chalets, fitting only for cool mountain sides, in our lowest hollows with straight cement paths from street to door, and tropical plantings about them, oranges and fan palms in the majority." See also, "Types of Architecture Approved for Palos Verdes Estates"; The Bungalowcraft Company, *New Spanish Homes;* The Bungalowcraft Company, *Homes of the Moment.*

55. Esther McCoy, *Five California Architects* (New York, 1960), passim.

56. Carl Condit, *The Rise of the Skyscraper* (Chicago, 1962), chap. iii.

57. Other than downtown Los Angeles itself, the best sources for commercial architecture are the photograph collections of the Title Insurance and Trust Company and the Security-First National Bank, both in Los Angeles.

58. William E. Smythe, "Significance of Southern California," *Out West,* 32: 287ff (April 1910).

59. Clarence A. Dykstra, "Congestion de Luxe—Do We Want It?" *Pacific Outlook,* 40: 226ff (June 1927).

60. G. Gordon Whitnall Articles, Los Angeles City Planning Department Scrapbook.

CHAPTER 8: THE FAILURE OF THE ELECTRIC RAILWAYS

1. Board of Public Utilities of the City of Los Angeles, "Report No. 1. Valuation of Street and Interurban Railway Lines in the City of Los Angeles, January 8, 1914," California Railroad Commission, *Archives,* Application 894; "In the Matter of the Application of the Los Angeles Railway Corporation ... for Authority to ... Issue Stocks and Bonds," California Railroad Commission, *Archives,* Application 894, Reporter's Transcript, pp. 128–129; *Fourth Annual Report of the Board of Public Utilities of the City of Los Angeles [1912–1913]*, chart 20; *Fifth Annual Report of the Board of Public*

Utilities of the City of Los Angeles [*1913–1914*], 92ff; Lewis, "Street Railway Development," II, 151–154.

2. *California Outlook,* 11: 3–4 (August 26, 1911); Los Angeles Board of Public Utilities Minutes, March 27, 1912; Los Angeles *Examiner,* August 22, 1911; Reed, "Public Utility Corporations," pp. 646–655.

3. Los Angeles *Examiner,* November 17, 1911; see also, California Railroad Commission, *Archives,* Case 1602, Reporter's Transcript, pp. 128ff; *First Annual Report of the Board of Public Utilities of the City of Los Angeles* [*1909–1910*], pp. 128–136.

4. Board of Public Utilities, "Valuation of Street and Interurban Railway Lines"; Blon J. Arnold, "The Transportation Problem of Los Angeles," *California Outlook,* Supplement, 11: 9 (November 4, 1911).

5. California Railroad Commission, *Archives,* Application 894, Reporter's Transcript, pp. 60–84; Mason, *Street Railway in Massachusetts,* chap. ii; Delos F. Wilcox, *Analysis of the Electric Railway Problem. Report to the Federal Electric Railways Commission with Summary and Recommendation* (New York, 1921), pp. 644–657.

6. Jackson A. Graves to I. W. Hellman, March 16, 1910, Graves Papers; John R. Haynes, "Address to the City Club of Los Angeles, January 16, 1909," John R. Haynes Papers, Government and Public Affairs Reading Room, University of California Library, Los Angeles; W. C. Faulkauser to P. A. Sinsheimer, September 21, 1914, California Railroad Commission, *Archives,* Application 894. See also, Haines Reed to John R. Haynes, May 1, 1912, Haynes Papers; Paul Shoup to Meyer Lissner, July 21, 1912, Meyer Lissner Papers, Stanford University Library, Stanford, California; Records of the 1912 Board of Freeholders' Franchise Committee, Haynes Papers.

7. Their decisions were subject to appeal as discriminatory or confiscatory, but the burden of proof was placed on the corporations. See *First Annual Report of the Board of Public Utilities of the City of Los Angeles* [*1909–1910*], pp. 6–8; Carl I. Wheat et al., *Public Utility Regulation by the California Railroad Commission* (San Francisco, 1927), passim.

8. *First Annual Report of the Board of Public Utilities of the City of Los Angeles* [*1909–1910*], pp. 122–125; Arnold, "Transportation Problem"; on the political activities of the railways, see Chap. 10 below.

9. Board of Public Utilities, "Valuation of Street and Interurban Railway Lines"; the Correspondence of White, Weld and Company and Robert C. Gillis, Gillis Papers. For a general survey, see George W. Hilton and John F. Due, *The Electric Interurban Railways in America* (Stanford, Calif., 1960), chap. vii.

10. "It was considered a fairly well established transportation maxim that railroad passenger traffic (steam, electric and street railway taken together) in a given territory should show an annual increase equal to the square of the increase in population. This means that if in a given time the population of a territory doubled, the railway passenger traffic serving that territory, assuming reasonably good service, should have multiplied by four." Richard Sachse to the California Railroad Commission, October 7, 1921, in Railroad Commission of the State of California Engineering Department, *Application 5806. Report on Financial, Operating and Service Conditions of Pacific Electric Railway Company* (San Francisco, 1921), pp. 12–13, Los Angeles Department of Public Utilities Files. It should be noted however, that not everyone was unaware of the automobile. "The day is here when the smallest tradesman, builder, skilled mechanic, can own an automobile ECONOMICALLY," the *Examiner* announced in 1914. "And the ownership of a car, far from being an extravagance is an actual economy. It saves time and makes money during the week. It gives healthfulness to the entire family on Sunday. It is a healthful, useful pleasure that discourages pleasures that are harmful." Los Angeles *Examiner,* January 15, 1914.

11. J. A. Graves to I. W. Hellman, November 6, 1914, Graves Papers; Paul Shoup to Robert C. Gillis, May 28, 1915, Gillis Papers; Los Angeles Chamber of Commerce Minutes, December 9, 1914; *Sixth Annual Report of Public Utilities of the City of Los Ange-*

les [1914–1915], pp. 99–102; "In the Matter of the Application of the Los Angeles Railway Corporation for an Investigation of its Service and Financial Conditions . . .," California Railroad Commission, *Archives,* Application 4238, Reporter's Transcript, pp. 34–36; E. L. Lewis, "The Rise and Decline of the Jitney in Its Birthplace," *Electric Railway Journal,* 46: 500–502 (September 11, 1915); *ibid.,* 45: 76–77 (January 2, 1915); 45: 83 (January 9, 1915); 45: 156 (January 16, 1915); 45: 1,094 (June 5, 1915).

12. California Railroad Commission Engineering Department, *Application 4238. Report on Service, Operating and Financial Conditions of the Los Angeles Railway Corporation. Part I. Service, Operation and Financial* (Los Angeles, 1919), pp. 17–18, Department of Public Utilities Files; Railroad Commission, *Application 5806. Report,* pp. 63–64; Paul Shoup to Chas. T. Connell, July 13, 1918, Haynes Papers; Paul Shoup to All Employees of the Pacific Electric, June 5, 1918, Gillis Papers; "In the Matter of the Application of the Pacific Electric . . . to Increase Rates . . . ," California Railroad Commission, *Archives,* Application 3791, Reporter's Transcript, pp. 15–39, 211–221.

13. Railroad Commission, *Application 4238. Report,* p. 15; Railroad Commission, *Application 5806. Report,* p. 60; Lester S. Ready, J. O. Marsh, and Richard Sachse, *Joint Report on Street Railway Survey, City of Los Angeles* (Los Angeles, 1925), pp. 101, 171, Los Angeles Department of Public Utilities Files. Railroad Commission of the State of California, *Case No. 4002. Report on the Local Public Transportation Requirements of Los Angeles* (Los Angeles, 1935), pp. 74, 82, Los Angeles Department of Public Utilities Files.

14. Railroad Commission, *Application 4238. Report,* p. 15; Railroad Commission, *Application 5806. Report,* pp. 60, 92; Ready et al., *Joint Report,* p. 136.

15. California Railroad Commission, *Archives,* Application 3791, Reporter's Transcript, pp. 211ff.; Richard Sachse to California Railroad Commission, October 7, 1921, in Railroad Commission, *Application 5806. Report,* pp. 17, 27; Railroad Commission, *Application 5806. Report,* pp. 11, 12, 231–256; *Decisions of the Railroad Commission of the State of California,* 16: 7ff (1918), Decision No. 5731.

16. Richard Sachse to California Railroad Commission, November 10, 1919, Railroad Commission, *Application 4238. Report,* p. 9; California Railroad Commission, *Archives,* Application 4238, Reporter's Transcript, pp. 57–77; *Decisions of the Railroad Commission of the State of California,* XIX (1921), Decision 9029, pp. 980ff; Railroad Commission, *Application 4238. Report,* pp. 1–2, 152–158.

17. California Railroad Commission, *Archives,* Application 4238, Reporter's Transcript, p. 41; Railroad Commission, *Application 5806. Report,* pp. 121ff; Ready et al., *Joint Report,* pp. 297ff; Paul Shoup to Robert C. Gillis, December 17, 24, 1915, Gillis Papers.

18. John R. Haynes, "Testimony to Committee of the Illinois Legislature . . . January 15, 1926"; Los Angeles Railway Corporation to Committee on Franchises of the Honorable Board of Freeholders, City of Los Angeles, October 16, 1923, Haynes Papers; Railroad Commission, *Application 4238. Report,* pp. 33–36; Ready et al., *Joint Report,* pp. 272ff; Ray L. Chesebro et al., *Charter of the City of Los Angeles Annotated. As Adopted January 22, 1925 [and] Amended May 15, 1933* (Los Angeles, 1933), pp. 19–24.

19. "In the Matter of the Application of Pacific Electric Railway Company . . . to Increase Rates," California Railroad Commission, *Archives,* Application 5806, Reporter's Transcript, pp. 749ff, 905ff; Railroad Commission, *Application 5806. Report,* pp. 200–208; D. W. Pontius to Honorable Board of Commissioners City of Santa Monica, February 8, 1923, Gillis Papers; Los Angeles Board of Public Utilities Minutes, August 30, September 13, 15, 1927.

20. Edward Hungerford, "California and Her Tractions—Part II," *Electric Railway Journal,* 56: 490–491 (September 11, 1920). See also, Richard Sachse to California Railroad Commission, October 7, 1921, p. 12; Los Angeles *Examiner,* January 15, 1914; Kelker, de Leuw & Company, *Rapid Transit Plan for Los Angeles,* p. 36; Lewis,

"Street Railway Development," II, 126–128; "In the Matter of the Application of the Pacific Electric Railway Company . . . to Increase Passenger Rates . . . ," California Railroad Commission, *Archives,* Application 13460, Reporter's Transcript, I, 116–117.

21. Lewis, "Street Railway Development," II, 164–166, 292–297; Ready et al., *Joint Report,* pp. 83ff; *Los Angeles Realtor,* 1: 5 (September 1922); *ibid.,* 3: 5 (October 1923); *Decisions of the Railroad Commission of the State of California,* 19: 980ff (1921), Decision No. 9029; *Electric Railway Journal,* 54: 251 (August 2, 1919); *ibid.,* 55: 663 (March 27, 1920).

22. California Railroad Commission, *Archives,* Application 5806, Reporter's Transcript, p. 334; see also, *Decisions of the Railroad Commission of the State of California,* 20: 1087ff (1921), Decision 9928; 22: 235ff (1923), Decision No. 10930.

23. Railroad Commission, *Case No. 4002. Report,* pp. 74, 82; Ready et al., *Joint Report,* pp. 101, 171.

24. Ready et al., *Joint Report,* pp. 101, 136, 171; Railroad Commission, *Case No. 4002. Report,* p. 185.

25. On their motorbus operations, see D. W. Pontius and G. J. Kuhrts to Board of Public Utilities of the City of Los Angeles, May 2, 1923, in Lewis, "Street Railway Development," II, 142–143; Ready et al., *Joint Report,* pp. 212–271; Railroad Commission, *Case No. 4002. Report,* p. 78. See also, D. W. Pontius to Louis Evans, November 15, 1926, to Robert C. Gillis, February 12, 1927, Gillis Papers; Los Angeles Board of Public Utilities Minutes, December 30, 1926, January 11, 18, February 8, March 15, 1927.

26. Ready et al., *Joint Report,* pp. 30–39.

27. *Ibid.,* pp. 49–356.

28. *Ibid.,* pp. 369–430.

29. *Ibid.,* pp. 137–138, 297–300; Railroad Commission, *Case No. 4002. Report,* pp. 160–162.

30. California Railroad Commission, *Archives,* Application 5806, Reporter's Transcript, p. 327; Ready et al., *Joint Report,* pp. 77–78.

31. See the draft of the contract in W. B. Matthews to John R. Haynes, October 1, 1925, Haynes Papers.

32. Delos F. Wilcox, *Preliminary Report on Local Transportation Policy Submitted to the City Council of the City of Los Angeles* (April 28, 1927).

33. Los Angeles Board of Public Utilities Minutes, May 17, 24, 1927; Los Angeles City, *Records,* vol. 181, June 15, 1927; *Electric Railway Journal,* 69: 851, 877 (May 14, 1927); *ibid.,* 69: 925 (May 21, 1927); *ibid.,* 70: 31 (January 2, 1928).

34. California Railroad Commission, *Archives,* Application 13460, Reporter's Transcript, I, 135–136, II, 262–263; California Railroad Commission, *Archives,* Application 5806, Reporter's Transcript, p. 319.

35. Los Angeles *Examiner,* May 17, October 21, December 9, 10, 20, 27, 28, 1906, January 9, 16, 1907; *Street Railway Journal,* 29: 85 (January 12, 1907); *ibid.,* 29: 307 (February 16, 1907); *Electric Railway Journal,* 25: 165 (January 22, 1910).

36. *Ibid.,* 61: 899 (May 26, 1923); *ibid.,* 62: 75 (July 14, 1923); *ibid.,* 62: 872 (November 17, 1923); *ibid.,* 63: 84 (January 12, 1924); Spencer Crump, *Ride the Red Cars: How Trolleys Helped Build Southern California* (Los Angeles, 1962), pp. 149–152.

37. Municipal League of Los Angeles, *Bulletin,* 1: 4 (January 1906); *ibid.,* 2: 7 (January 1907); *Fifth Annual Report of the Board of Public Utilities of the City of Los Angeles* [*1913-1914*], pp. 115–118; *Electric Railway Journal,* 41: 705 (April 19, 1913); *ibid.,* 41: 903 (May 17, 1913); *ibid.,* 43: 1,138 (May 23, 1914); *ibid.,* 68: 317–318 (August 21, 1926); "Agreement between Southern Pacific Railroad Company . . . and Los Angeles & Salt Lake Railroad Company, July 18th, 1917," in possession of Mr. James Gibson, California Public Utilities Department, San Francisco.

38. Kelker, de Leuw & Company, *Rapid Transit Plan for Los Angeles,* pp. 1–16, 163–182.

39. A. F. Southwick, "Minority Report," S. A. Jubb et al., "Report on Rapid Transit to the Board of Directors, Los Angeles City Club," *Los Angeles City Club Bulletin*, 8: 10–12 (January 30, 1926), Haynes Papers. See also, Board of City Planning Commissioners, *Conference on the Rapid Transit Question* (January 21, 1930), pp. 5–9, 40–41; Board of City Planning Commissioners, *Second Conference on Mass Transportation* (May 16, 1930), pp. 5–6; Baker, *Rapid Transit Plan for Los Angeles*, p. 48.

40. Jubb et al., "Report on Rapid Transit," p. 9.

41. Dykstra, "Congestion de Luxe"; see also, City Planning Commissioners, *Conference on the Rapid Transit Question*, pp. 36–37; City Planning Commissioners, *Second Conference on Mass Transportation*, pp. 15–19.

42. Railroad Commission, *Case No. 4002*, chart following p. 66, pp. 72, 74, 82.

43. *Ibid.*, chart following p. 66, pp. 72, 184–185; Ready et al., *Joint Report*, p. 136.

44. A. G. Mott, "Memorandum on Effect of Various Passenger Fare Schedules on Pacific Electric Railway System," California Railroad Commission, *Archives*, Application 13460.

45. California Railroad Commission, *Archives*, Case 1602, Reporter's Transcript, pp. 128ff; California Railroad Commission, *Archives*, Application 5806, Reporter's Transcript, pp. 241, 879–880.

46. Ready et al., *Joint Report*, pp. 95ff, 308ff, 433ff; Joe R. Ong, "A Report on Some of the Problems of Operation of the Los Angeles Railway, July 31, 1923," in possession of Mr. John Curtis, Los Angeles Metropolitan Transit Authority, Los Angeles.

47. Baker, *Rapid Transit System for Los Angeles*, p. 37–d. See also, California Railroad Commission, *Archives*, Application 5806, Reporter's Transcript, p. 593; *Second Annual Report of the Board of Public Utilities of the City of Los Angeles [1910–1911]*, pp. 122–124; Los Angeles *Examiner*, May 27, 1912; Bert L. Glogston, "Subdivider: Keystone of Real Estate Business," *Los Angeles Realtor*, 3: 9 (July 1924).

48. California Railroad Commission, *Archives*, Application 13323, Reporter's Transcript, pp. 2–3.

49. *Decisions of the Railroad Commission of the State of California*, 31: 383ff (1928), Decision No. 19521.

50. Railroad Commission, *Case No. 4002. Report*, chart following p. 66, pp. 82, 184.

51. California Railroad Commission, *Archives*, Application 13460, Reporter's Transcript, VII, 1,063ff; see also, *ibid.*, II, 223–224.

52. *Decisions of the Railroad Commission of the State of California*, 26: 454ff (1928), Decision No. 19566; California Railroad Commission, *Archives*, Application 5806, Reporter's Transcript, pp. 821–822.

53. Railroad Commission, *Case No. 4002. Report*, pp. 72, 74, 185.

54. Arthur C. Jenkins, "Preliminary Report on Engineering and Economic Analysis of Operations, Facilities, Organization and Financial Status of Pacific Electric Railway Company, Los Angeles, California" (July 15, 1948), Los Angeles Department of Public Utilities Files.

55. Railroad Commission, *Case No. 4002. Report*, pp. 10–12, chart facing p. 66, pp. 72, 74, 84.

56. *Ibid.*, chart facing p. 66, pp. 72, 184, 185.

57. *Decisions of the Railroad Commission of the State of California*, 22: 244 (1923), Decision No. 10930.

58. California Railroad Commission, *Archives*, Application 13460, Reporter's Transcript, VII, 1,133; Railroad Commission, *Case No. 4002. Report*, pp. 262–263; *Decisions of the Railroad Commission of the State of California*, 26: 454ff (1928), Decision No. 19566; Hilton and Due, *Electric Interurban Railways*, chap. viii.

59. Railroad Commission of the State of California, *Application No. 21656. Report on Engineering Survey of Pacific Electric Railway Company* (Los Angeles, 1928), X, 2, California Public Utilities Commission Files, San Francisco; Railroad Commission of the State of California, *Report on Financial, Operating and Service Conditions of the Pacific Elec-*

tric Railway (Los Angeles, 1928), X, possession of Mr. Lawrence Veysey, Madison, Wis.

60. Los Angeles Board of Public Utilities Minutes, March 16, 1922, May 7, 1929; Los Angeles Chamber of Commerce Minutes, June 6, 1929.

CHAPTER 9: THE QUEST FOR COMMUNITY

1. Graves, *California Memories*, p. 100; see also, Marshall Stimson, "Memorandum to Harvard College," Marshall Stimson Papers, Henry E. Huntington Library, San Marino, Calif.

2. Salvator, *Los Angeles in the Sunny Seventies*, pp. 129–130; Truman, *Semi-Tropical California*, p. 21.

3. Isaac W. Lord to [?], March 24, 1876, Lord Letterbook, p. 142, Lord Papers; see also, Chap. 4, above.

4. On nineteenth-century American urban communities in general, see Oscar Handlin, "The Social System," *Daedelus* (Winter 1961), pp. 11–30.

5. See Thompson and West, *Los Angeles*, pp. 121–125; Chap. 2, above.

6. Issac W. Lord Letterbook, p. 50, Lord Papers; see also, Los Angeles *Evening Express*, February 16, 1886.

7. Los Angeles *Evening Express*, July 7, 1876, March 4, 1880, February 2, 1886; Los Angeles *Herald*, April 9, 1882; Charles Loring Brace, *The New West: or California in 1867–1868* (New York, 1869), pp. 277–280.

8. See, for example, T. S. Kenderdine, *A California Tramp . . . Life on the Plains and in the Golden State Thirty Years Ago* (Newton, Pa., 1888), pp. 197–198; T. S. Kenderdine, *California Revisited, 1857–1897* (Newtown, Pa., 1898), p. 161.

9. Graves, *Seventy Years*, pp. 437–438; Graves, *California Memories*, pp. 5, 6, 100.

10. Smith, *Adobe Days*, p. 107; see also, L. J. Rose, Jr., *L. J. Rose of Sunny Slope 1827–1899. California Pioneer, Fruit Grower, Wine Maker, Horse Breeder* (San Marino, Calif., 1959), foreword.

11. "President More's Address," *Historical Society of Southern California, Los Angeles, 1887* (San Francisco, 1888), pp. 11–13; *Annual Report of the Los Angeles County Pioneers of Southern California for the Year 1909–1910*, p. 6.

12. Bruce Bliven, "Los Angeles: The City That Is Bacchanalian—In a Nice Way," *The New Republic*, 51: 198 (July 13, 1927).

13. Los Angeles *Examiner*, March 3, 1912; see also, Luther, *The Boosters*, pp. 9–10, 34–35.

14. Los Angeles *Examiner*, March 23, 1914.

15. Los Angeles *Times*, July 11, 1909. See also, *Pacific Municipalities*, 27: 417–418 (August 1913).

16. Los Angeles *Examiner*, May 29, 1913; see also, *ibid.*, December 13, 1908; Los Angeles Suburban Homes Company Minutes, May 12, 1910, Whitley Papers; Leo B. Lesperance to Wendell M. Bishop, December 20, 1924, Leo B. Lesperance Papers, Special Collections Division, University of California Library, Los Angeles.

17. Kilner, *Arthur Letts*, p. 100, illustration facing p. 107. Abbot Kinney, the developer of Venice, Calif., made an even more memorable remark when he said that "In this country . . . the people can have what they talk." Los Angeles *Examiner*, May 30, 1913.

18. Willard Huntington Wright, "Los Angeles—The Chemically Pure," Burton Rascoe and Graff Conklin, eds., *The Smart Set Anthology* (New York, 1934), pp. 90–102.

19. *Out West*, 5: 208–209 (March 4, 1913); see also, Erik Linklater, *Juan in America* (New York, 1931), p. 392.

20. Los Angeles *Examiner*, February 28, 1913; see also, Los Angeles City, *Ordinances Scrapbook*, no. 9610, vol. 15, p. 104, no. 65355, vol. 79, p. 93, no. 19000, vol. 25, p. 97,

no. 38456, vol. 46, pp. 128–129, no. 38070, vol. 46, p. 16, no. 36674, vol. 44, p. 121, no. 20640, vol. 27, pp. 17–18, and no. 37699, vol. 45, pp. 114–115, City Hall, Los Angeles; Los Angeles Board of Playground and Recreation Commissioners Minutes, December 1, 1917, October 7, 1920; Gilman M. Ostrander, *The Prohibition Movement in California, 1848-1933* (Berkeley and Los Angeles, 1957), pp. 131–132, 139–140.

21. Dana W. Bartlett, *The Better City: A Sociological Study of a Modern American City* (Los Angeles, 1907), chaps. i–vi, ix–xii.

22. *Report of the Housing Commission of the City of Los Angeles [1909-1910]*, p. 26; Los Angeles *Examiner*, June 5, 1909.

23. See, for example, Willard, *Los Angeles Chamber of Commerce*, pp. 10–11.

24. *Fifteenth Census: 1930. Population, IV*, pp. 199–202; Chap. 6, above.

25. Los Angeles Chamber of Commerce, *Small Farm Home; Cahuenga Suburban*, April 1895; Los Angeles *Examiner*, July 10, 1910; *Pacific Outlook*, 9: 5 (July 16, 1910).

26. See, for example, Willard, *Los Angeles Chamber of Commerce*, pp. 102–104.

27. George Burlingame, "How Religious is the City of Los Angeles?" Los Angeles *Times*, August 28, 1927, quoted in Carl Douglas Wells, "A Changing Social Institution in an Urban Environment: A Study of the Changing Behavior Patterns of the Disciples of Christ in Los Angeles" (University of Southern California Doctoral Dissertation, 1931), p. 5. See also, Jan and Cora Gordon, *Star-Dust in Hollywood* (London, 1931), p. 36.

28. Wells, "Disciples of Christ in Los Angeles," p. 145; see also, *ibid.*, chaps. ii, iii, iv.

29. *Ibid.*, pp. 25–26; see also, H. Paul Douglas, *The Church in the Changing City* (New York, 1927), pp. 373ff.

30. J. F. Sartori to Edward A. Dickson, undated, Edward A. Dickson Papers, Special Collections Division, University of California Library, Los Angeles; the correspondence of the Hill Street Association and Robert C. Gillis; Los Angeles *Ledger* (published by the Greater Pico Street Association), Gillis Papers.

31. *Articles of Incorporation and By-Laws of the Huntington Palisades Property Owners Corporation Ltd.*, Gillis Papers; *Articles of Incorporation and By-Laws of Palos Verdes Homes Association*, Palos Verdes Homes Association Files; see also, McClenahan, *Changing Urban Neighborhood*, pp, 216–218.

32. McClenahan, *Changing Urban Neighborhood*, p. 57; *ibid.*, pp. 35, 47, 84; Hollywood *Citizen*, December 29, 1916; Douglas, "Real Estate Business in Los Angeles."

33. McClenahan, *Changing Urban Neighborhood*, p. 57; *ibid.*, pp. 64–65, 68–69.

34. October 22, 1905, September 24, 1906, Mrs. Ernest T. Emery's Diary.

35. McClenahan, *Changing Urban Neighborhood*, pp. 24, 61, 71, 78.

36. C. H. Parsons, quoted in *The Golden West: A Magazine of Progress*, 1: 7 (September 1, 1919); see also, Los Angeles *Times*, February 23, 1909; Los Angeles *Examiner*, December 26, 1909, March 18, 1911; Buford E. Pierce, *Illustrated Annual: Federation of State Societies of Southern California 1914* (Los Angeles, 1914), passim; McWilliams, *Southern California Country*, pp. 165–171.

37. Parsons, quoted in *The Golden West;* see also, Florence C. Parsons, "Story of the Federation of State Societies," *The Golden West: A Magazine of Progress*, 1: 7 (May 15, 1919). The magazine later became the "Official Organ of the Federation of State Societies," The purposes of the state societies were described in the Michigan group's constitution as follows: "To promote interest in the mother State, to aid in extending acquaintances among her people whether residents here or merely visitors in this place; to broaden each other's knowledge and information about local conditions whereby all may be benefited; and to arouse and strengthen the interest of visitors and intending settlers in all that pertains to the growth of the community and generally to promote the social welfare and common good of its members." Los Angeles *Examiner*, December 26, 1909.

38. McWilliams, *Southern California Country*, pp. 165–171.

39. Nathaniel West, *The Day of the Locust* (New York, 1939), pp. 224–225.

40. Meyer Lissner to Mark Sullivan, January 8, 1920, Lissner Papers; see also, Los Angeles *Examiner*, August 28, 1905.

41. Nancy Mavitz, *Sister Aimee* (Garden City, N.Y., 1931); H. T. Dohrman, *California Cult: The Story of "Mankind United"* (Boston, 1958); McWilliams, *Southern California Country*, chaps. xiii–xiv; Braden, *Spirits in Rebellion*, passim.

42. Jan and Cora Gordon, *Star-Dust in Hollywood*, p. 36. "In a land of optimism," they also wrote, "you cannot associate with people who break your heart; in a land where all social positions are fluid one must be prepared to reject those who fall behind in the money race, and to accept rejections philosophically from those who leave us behind . . . therefore a certain cold-bloodedness in acquaintanceship must be cultivated almost in self-defense." *Ibid.*, p. 24.

43. *Fifteenth Census: 1930. Population, Volume III, Part 1*, pp. 266–267; *Eleventh Census: 1890. Population, I*, p. 451; see also, Charlotta A. Bass, *Forty Years: Memoirs from the Pages of a Newspaper* (Los Angeles, 1960), p. 21, Pauline V. Young, *The Pilgrims of Russian-Town* (Chicago, 1934), chap. i.

44. Tuck, *Not with the Fist*, p. 88; see also, *ibid.*, 65–67; "Reports of the Immigration Commission," vol. 25, pt. III, pp. 125–163, 357–358, 470–471; *Annual Reports of the Commissioner General of Immigration to the Secretary of Labor [1911]*, pp. 38–43, *[1912]*, pp. 92–96, *[1913]*, pp. 64–70, *[1914]*, pp. 62–67, *[1915]*, pp. 82–87; Young, *Pilgrims of Russian-Town*, chap. i. Gamio, *Mexican Immigrant*, passim; Richards, "Negro's Migration to Los Angeles," pp. 42–49.

45. "Reports of the Immigration Commission, vol. 25, pt. I, pp. 223–248, pt. III, pp. 454–460; *Fifteenth Census: 1930. Population, IV*, pp. 199–202; John R. Haynes to Roy L. Garis, August 29, 1929, Haynes Papers; Ichihashi, *Japanese in the United States*, chaps. vii–xi; Bond, "The Negro in Los Angeles," pp. 150–151; Young, *Pilgrims of Russian-Town*, chap. ii.

46. Kit King Louis, "A Study of American-Born and American-Reared Chinese in Los Angeles" (University of Southern California Masters Thesis, 1931), p. 80; J. McFarline Ervin, "The Participation of the Negro in the Community Life of Los Angeles" (University of Southern California Masters Thesis, 1927), pp. 45–72; Barton S. Scruggs, *A Man in Our Community: The Biography of L. G. Robinson of Los Angeles* (Gardena, Calif., 1937), passim.

47. Commission of Immigration and Housing of California, *A Survey Made in Los Angeles City* (San Francisco, ca. 1910), p. 23; "Report of the Immigration Commission," vol. 25, pt. I, pp. 223–248, 361–362.

48. Kanichi Kawasaki, "The Japanese Community of East San Pedro, Terminal Island, California" (University of Southern California Masters Thesis, 1931), p. 50 (combined from her remarks); see also, Young, *Pilgrims of Russian-Town*, chap. ii; Richards, "Negro's Migration to Southern California," pp. 35–37, 47, 218.

49. Louis, "American-Born and American-Reared Chinese," p. 114; Bond, "Negro in Los Angeles," pp. 76–77; Bogardus, *Mexican in the United States*, p. 79; Bass, *Forty Years*, pp. 95–113.

50. Santa Monica *Weekly Interpreter*, April 26, 1922, Gillis Papers; see also, McClenahan, *Changing Urban Neighborhood*, pp. 216–218; Chap. 7, above.

51. Clara G. Smith, "The Development of the Mexican People in the Community of Watts" (University of Southern California Masters Thesis, 1933), passim; also Uono, "Japanese Residences in the City of Los Angeles," pp. 124ff; Bond, "The Negro in Los Angeles," pp. 68ff; *Fifteenth Census: 1930. Population. Volume VI*, pp. 156–160, 181–189.

52. *California Eagle*, September 18, 1915, December 8, 1917; Bass, *Forty Years*, pp. 21, 50–52; Los Angeles Board of Playground and Recreation Commissioners Minutes, September 10, 1925, Department of Parks and Playgrounds, City Hall, Los Angeles; Los Angeles City, *Petitions* (1931), No. 1636.

53. Louis, "American-Born and American-Reared Chinese," p. 103; *California Eagle*, September 24, 1914, September 13, 1919, April 29, 1922; Graaf, "Negro Migration to Los Angeles," chap. ii; Bass, *Forty Years*, pp. 13–14, 39–40; Tuck, *Not with the Fist*, pp. 197–207.

54. John R. Haynes to Roy L. Garis, August 29, 1929, Haynes Papers; *El Heraldo de Mexico*, January 7, 1920; *La Opinion*, April 2, 1927; Bogardus, *Mexican in the United States*, pp. 76–77.

55. *California Eagle*, April 24, May 1, August 22, 1914, September 9, 1916, April 28, 1917, April 21, May 12, 1923; Bass, *Forty Years*, passim; Committee on Immigration and Naturalization, House of Representatives, *Hearings. Japanese Immigration* (Washington, 1921), Part 3, pp. 924, 927; McWilliams, *Prejudice*, pp. 92–96.

56. Bogardus, *Mexican in the United States*, pp. 76–78; Committee on Immigration and Naturalization, *Japanese Immigration*, p. 934; Bass, *Forty Years*, pp. 39–42; Young, *Pilgrims of Russian-Town*, chap. ii.

57. Committee on Immigration and Naturalization, *Japanese Immigration*, p. 924; Tuck, *Not with the Fist*, pp. 152–164; McWilliams, *Prejudice*, pp. 77–78; Fumiko Fukuoha, "Mutual Life and Aid Among the Japanese in Southern California with Special Reference to Los Angeles" (University of Southern California Masters Thesis, 1937), p. 87; *California Eagle*, April 5, 1914; Bass, *Forty Years*, pp. 16–26.

58. Gamio, *Mexican Immigrant*, p. 27; Bogardus, *Mexican in the United States*, pp. 37–40; McWilliams, *Prejudice*, pp. 83–92; Louis, "American-Born and American-Reared Chinese," pp. 81, 89; *California Eagle*, April 13, 1928; Graaf, "Negro Migration to Los Angeles," chap. ii.

59. Young, *Pilgrims of Russian-Town*, pp. 124–125; see also, Smith, "Mexican People in the Community of Watts," p. 59; Louis, "American-Born and American-Reared Chinese," pp. 30, 43; Richards, "Negro's Migration to Southern California," p. 136.

60. Some of the observations made then have a chilling immediacy now. "They feel that they are Negroes and that as Negroes they will never get anywhere," remarked one white man. "They face an insecure and hopeless future. They don't have any social mooring. They are cut off from all the things that control people. No jobs to live up to, no home to aspire to and protect, no social agencies to guide them." "The Negro church in Los Angeles has certainly followed its original purpose," a Negro man noted. "The mission of the church is soul saving. Well, they do their work too well; they are so busy saving souls for Christ that the community around them is going to the devil." Bond, "The Negro in Los Angeles," pp. 150–151, 214.

61. Young, *Pilgrims of Russian-Town*, p. 227; see also, Bogardus, *Mexican in the United States*, pp. 24–32; Tuck, *Not with the Fist*, pp. 106–121; Committee on Naturalization and Immigration, *Japanese Immigration*, pp. 965–996; McWilliams, *Prejudice*, pp. 96–105; Richards, "Negro's Migration to Southern California," p. 128; Bond, "Negro in Los Angeles," p. 214.

62. Bogardus, *Mexican in the United States*, pp. 85, 97; Tuck, *Not with the Fist*, pp. 204–205; *California Eagle*, May 1, 1914, January 23, 1915, April 28, 1917; see also, Gamio, *Mexican Immigrant*, p. 154; Bond, "Negro in Los Angeles," pp. 150–151.

63. Robert Ezra Park, "Education and the Cultural Crisis," *American Journal of Sociology*, 48 (May 1943), reprinted in Robert Ezra Park, *Race and Culture* (Glencoe, Ill., 1950), p. 323.

64. George M. Day, "Races and Cultural Oases," *Sociology and Social Research*, 18: 328, 335–339 (March–April 1934).

65. The reader may well wonder why nothing has been said about education in Los Angeles here. The only answer is that the public schools received remarkably little attention before 1930. Certainly there were no crises comparable to the recent offensive of the radical right. The available materials (including the Board of Education Minutes) yield no simple explanation, and the entire subject probably requires separate study. It might begin with P. W. Search, Superintendent of Schools, *Los An-*

geles City Schools. Report of Conditions with Recommendations (Los Angeles, 1895) and Walter A. Jessup and Albert Shiels, *Report of the Advisory Committee to the Board of Education of the City of Los Angeles . . .* (Los Angeles, 1916).

CHAPTER 10: THE POLITICS OF PROGRESSIVISM

1. William Rich Hutton, *Glances at California 1847–1853. Diaries and Letters* (San Marino, Calif., 1942), pp. 14, 21; Shirley C. Bystrom, "Los Angeles, 1846–1860" (University of California at Berkeley Masters Thesis, 1951), passim.

2. Los Angeles *Herald,* March 12, 18, 1889; see also, Chaps. 2, 5, above.

3. Los Angeles *Evening Express,* December 16, 1876, March 10, 1877, January 2, 1886; Los Angeles *Herald,* December 31, 1882, July 31, 1888.

4. Los Angeles *Herald,* June 8, 1888; Los Angeles *Evening Express,* January 11, 18, 21, 1901; Los Angeles *Times,* February 11, 12, 1902; see also, Chap. 5, above.

5. George Mowry, *The California Progressives* (Berkeley and Los Angeles, 1951), chap. i.

6. Los Angeles *Times,* November 23, 1902; Los Angeles *Herald,* November 24, 26, December 8, 1891; Los Angeles *Times,* January 16, 1902, July 28, August 4, 6, 1903; C. T. H. Palmer's Memorandum of October 31, 1892, Porphyry Paving Company Records, Special Collections Division, University of California Library, Los Angeles.

7. Los Angeles *Herald,* May 17, 1889; Los Angeles *Evening Express,* May 12, 1897, January 18, 1901; Los Angeles *Examiner,* June 17, 1904. Similar situations existed regarding newspapers and official advertising (Los Angeles *Herald,* November 26, 1889, February 11, 1897) and banks and public funds (Los Angeles *Herald,* May 7, 28, 1889, January 19, February 11, 21, March 7, 11, 25, April 29, 1890).

8. "Message of the Mayor, 1887," *Los Angeles Municipal Reports;* Los Angeles *Herald,* March 6, June 8, August 28, 1888; Los Angeles *Evening Express,* July 14, September 22, 1897.

9. Los Angeles *Evening Express,* June 4, 1894; see also, *ibid.,* July 1, 1895; Los Angeles *Herald,* April 10, 1888; Los Angeles *Examiner,* December 1, 2, 9, 1903.

10. Los Angeles *Herald,* August 4, 18, 28, September 16, October 4, 7, November 16, 20, 24, 26, 30, 1890; Los Angeles *Evening Express,* March 1, 13, 20, September 15, 1899; Los Angeles *Examiner,* March 9, 1905; Ostrander, *Prohibition Movement in California,* pp. 67–69.

11. John R. Haynes to Thomas H. Reed, June 20, 1911, Haynes Papers; Charles D. Willard, "Old and New Politics," *California Outlook,* 12: 11–12 (February 17, 1912).

12. Los Angeles *Evening Express,* November 21, 1876; Los Angeles *Daily News,* November 9, 1869; Los Angeles *Semi-Weekly News,* November 17, 1868; Los Angeles *Evening Express,* November 8, 10, 21, 23, 1876.

13. Los Angeles *Evening Express,* December 7, 1880, November 28, December 4, 1900; Los Angeles *Herald,* November 28, 30, 1887, February 19, 20, 1889, November 30, December 2, 1890.

14. Los Angeles *Evening Express,* November 25, 29, 1876, November 25, 29, 1888, October 11, 18, 1898.

15. *Ibid.,* May 12, 1873, November 24, 1877; Los Angeles *Daily News,* November 27, 1872.

16. Los Angeles *Daily News,* November 25, 1869; Los Angeles *Evening Express,* February 5, 1874, October 5, November 24, 1877, February 9, 14, March 4, 1878; Los Angeles *Herald,* February 17, 1876.

17. Los Angeles *Evening Express,* November 25, 1876, November 30, 1877, December 3, 1878; Los Angeles *Herald,* November 30, 1877; Meyer Lissner's untitled typescript address, Lissner Papers; Mowry, *California Progressives,* chap. i.

18. Los Angeles *Star,* December 18, 1877; *ibid.,* December 4, 1870; Los Angeles *Daily News,* December 5, 1871; Los Angeles *Evening Express,* December 5, 1871.

19. Los Angeles *Evening Express,* November 13, November 29, 1878; Los Angeles *Star,* April 24, 1873.

20. *Charter of the City of Los Angeles 1889–1917,* passim; Los Angeles *Herald,* March 18, April 25, May 6, June 16, August 24, October 21, 1888.

21. Charles D. Willard to Samuel Willard, September 12, 1896, Willard Papers; Los Angeles *Herald,* August 22, 29, 1890; Los Angeles *Evening Express,* September 8, 21, 22, 1896; Editor, "What the 'Cranks' Have Done: Beginnings of the Movement for a Better City Government," *Pacific Outlook,* II, 20—II, 26 (May 18–June 29, 1907).

22. Charles D. Willard to Samuel Willard, January 23, 1897, Willard Papers. See also, Los Angeles *Evening Express,* June 16, 17, July 9, August 17, 20, October 24, November 12, 1898. For the previous attempt to revise the charter, see *ibid.,* June 13, August 18, September 10, November 23, 1894.

23. Charles D. Willard to Samuel Willard, May 11, 1889, Willard Papers. "Give me an out and out scoundrel every time," he added, "I know him; the other fellows are always showing up when you don't expect to see them."

24. Meyer Lissner, "Reform in Los Angeles. Retrospective-Prospective," an address reprinted in Los Angeles *Herald,* April 11, 1909, Lissner Papers; see also, Los Angeles *Examiner,* October 29, 1904.

25. Oscar Handlin, *The Uprooted* (Boston, 1951), chap. viii; Walton Bean, *Boss Ruef's San Francisco* (Berkeley and Los Angeles, 1952), passim.

26. Lissner, "Reform in Los Angeles"; see also, John R. Haynes to William H. Davis, March 10, 1906, Haynes Papers.

27. Russ Avery et al., "Report to the Non-Partisan Campaign Committee, 1906," Haynes Papers; Lissner, "Reform in Los Angeles"; Direct Legislation Committee of the Voters League of Los Angeles, "Direct Legislation or Majority Rule through the Initiative and Referendum," Haynes Papers.

28. Reynold E. Blight, "Municipal Government 50 Years from Now," *California Outlook,* 11: 11–12 (October 21, 1911); see also, Reynold Blight to Meyer Lissner, September 26, 1911, Lissner Papers; H. A. Mason, "Suggestions to Charter Makers," *Pacific Outlook,* 6: 70–76 (March 1902).

29. John R. Haynes to Thomas H. Reed, June 20, 1911, Haynes Papers; W. P. D. Bliss et al., "Statement of Union Reform League of Los Angeles to the Board of Freeholders of 1900"; Municipal League of Los Angeles, "Statement on Direct Legislation in the Los Angeles City Charter, November, 1902," Haynes Papers; Los Angeles *Evening Express,* October 2, 17, 1900; Los Angeles *Times,* December 2, 1902; *Charter of the City of Los Angeles 1889–1917,* pp. 134–151.

30. For a discussion of municipal ownership, see Chap. 11, below.

31. John R. Haynes, "The Widening Sphere of Municipal Activities" (November 24, 1915), Haynes Papers. See also, Los Angeles *Times,* December 2, 1902; *Charter of the City of Los Angeles 1889–1917,* pp. 184–194.

32. Meyer Lissner to Los Angeles *Herald,* 1910, Lissner Papers. For a concise statement of the regular Republican position, see A. P. Fleming to Meyer Lissner, February 28, 1908, Lissner Papers.

33. Lee C. Gates to Executive Committee of the Non-Partisan Campaign Committee, ca. 1906; Avery, "Report," Haynes Papers; Meyer Lissner to Kendrick C. Babcock, February 19, 1908; Lissner, "Reform in Los Angeles," Lissner Papers; Los Angeles *Examiner,* April 18, May 7, October 12, 13, 1905, July 3, 6, 10, December 6, 1906. See also, Albert Howard Clodius, "The Quest for Good Government in Los Angeles 1890–1910" (Claremont Graduate School Doctoral Dissertation, 1953), chap. iii.

34. Stimson, *Labor Movement in Los Angeles,* p. 323.

35. Charles D. Willard to Samuel Hiestand, November 25, 1909, to Sarah Willard, November 12, 1909, Willard Papers; see also, Los Angeles *Examiner,* January, February, March 1909; Los Angeles *Times,* January, February, March 1909; Francis J. Heney to E. W. Scripps, February 11, 1909; Meyer Lissner to Francisco J. Heney, February 2, 1909, Lissner Papers; "How Mayor Harper Was Forced Out of Office," *Pacific Outlook,* 6: 1ff (April 10, 1919); Clodius, "Quest for Good Government," chap. iv.

36. Stimson, *Labor Movement in Los Angeles,* pp. 324–325, 341–343; Alexander Irvine, *Revolution in Los Angeles* (1911), passim.

37. Charles D. Willard to Sarah Hiestand, November 2, 1911, Willard Papers; see also, B. W. Bartels to Meyer Lissner, November 16, 1911, Lissner Papers; Los Angeles *Examiner,* October 24, 30, November 1, 1911; Stimson, *Labor Movement in Los Angeles,* pp. 362–364.

38. Los Angeles *Examiner,* November 1, 3, 4, 1911; Municipal League of Los Angeles, *Statement of the Facts Relative to the Present City Campaign . . . November 18th, 1911,* passim; *California Outlook,* 11: 2–3 (November 11, 1911).

39. Los Angeles *Examiner,* December 6, 7, 14, 1911; Stimson, *Labor Movement in Los Angeles,* pp. 400–406.

40. John J. Hamilton to Meyer Lissner, October 8, 1912, Lissner Papers; see also, Los Angeles *Examiner,* January 2, 1912; T. P. Kelso to Meyer Lissner, December 5, 1912, and John J. Hamilton to Meyer Lissner, September 27, 1912, Lissner Papers.

41. Los Angeles *Examiner,* June 8, 9, 10, 12, 1910, June 15, 16, 21, 1911, June 9, 10, 24, 25, 1912, January 21, 22, 23, 1913; Ostrander, *Prohibition Movement in California,* pp. 139–140; Stimson, *Labor Movement in Los Angeles,* pp. 242–243; Charles D. Willard, "Is Meyer Lissner a Boss?" *Pacific Outlook,* quoted in Clodius, "Quest for Good Government," p. 492.

42. Blight, "Municipal Government"; see also, John R. Haynes, "The Proposed Charter as Related to Municipal Efficiency," ca. 1912, Haynes Papers; Meyer Lissner in E. T. Earl, July 31, 1911, Lissner Papers.

43. John J. Hamilton, "Dividing and Delegating Responsibility," *California Outlook,* 12: 10–11 (May 18, 1912); Fred C. Wheeler, quoted *ibid.,* 13: 12–13 (August 3, 1912); E. A. Walcott to John R. Haynes, ca. 1912, Haynes Papers; Meyer Lissner, "Address to the City Club, March 5, 1913," Lissner Papers.

44. Meyer Lissner, "Statement to the Charter Revision Commission," Haynes Papers; see also, Los Angeles *Examiner,* March 22, April 4, 1912; Charter Revision Commission Files, Haynes Papers. For previous efforts to amend the charter, see Los Angeles *Examiner,* July 28, 31, 1907, February 5, 12, 1908, February 16, 1910, March 2, 1911.

45. Board of Freeholders, "Statement to the People of Los Angeles" (1912), Haynes Papers.

46. J. B. Irvine to John R. Haynes, June 4, 1912, and C. S. Lamb, C. T. Herbert, E. R. Perry to Charter Revision Commission, 1912, both in Haynes Papers; Los Angeles *Examiner,* November 22, 1912; Los Angeles *Times,* December 4, 1912.

47. Meyer Lissner et al. to E. R. Earl, March 29, 1913, and William A. White to George Perkins, June 5, 1913, both in Lissner Papers; Los Angeles *Examiner,* March 31, April 3, 5, 10, 11, 26, May 8, 28, June 5, 1913; Marshall Stimson et al., "Why We Went into the 'Municipal Conference of 1913,'" *California Outlook,* 14 (April 5, 1913).

48. Meyer Lissner to Clinton R. Woodruff, April 8, 1916, Lissner Papers; Municipal League of Los Angeles, *Bulletin,* 11 (August 30, 1917), and 12 (July 5, 1918); Clodius, "Quest for Good Government," pp. 538–543.

49. William Bonelli Memorandum, Haynes Papers.

50. John T. Morgan, "Our American Mayors: VIII. Mayor George E. Cryer of Los Angeles," *National Municipal Review,* 17: 27 (January 1928); Los Angeles *Times,* May 30, June 2, 1915; Los Angeles *Examiner,* May 24, 26, June 2, 1919; Clodius,

"Quest for Good Government," pp. 543–552; James Clifford Findley, "The Economic Boom of the 'Twenties in Los Angeles" (Claremont Graduate School Doctoral Dissertation, 1958), pp. 43–44.

51. Los Angeles *Examiner,* May 25, 26, June 1, 7, 8, 1911; Los Angeles *Times,* May 4, June 3, 7, 8, 1911; Morgan, "Mayor George E. Cryer," p. 30.

52. John R. Haynes to Rudolph Spreckels, February 8, 1923, to G. G. Young, April 20, 1923, to Kent Parrott, April 26, 1913, Haynes Papers; Los Angeles *Times,* May 23, 1923; see also, Edward Layton, "The Better America Federation: A Case Study of Superpatriotism," *Pacific Historical Review,* 30: 137–147 (May 1961); Chap. 11, below.

53. John R. Haynes to Harland G. Palmer et al., February 26, 1925; Haynes to Evan Lewis, May 28, 1925; George E. Cryer to John J. Hamilton, April 19, 1925; John J. Hamilton to John R. Haynes, May 11, 1925; and J. H. Ryckman, "The Issue of the Campaign," all in Haynes Papers.

54. Los Angeles *Times,* March 27, April 23, May 2, 1925; Los Angeles *Examiner,* April 14, May 2, 4, 7, 1925; William G. Bonelli Memorandum, Haynes Papers.

55. For the progressive attempts at piecemeal revision, see Meyer Lissner, "Address Before the City Club of Los Angeles, March 5, 1913," Lissner Papers; Fred C. Wheeler, "Eight Proposed Charter Amendments," *California Outlook,* 14: 12ff (February 15, 1913); "Proportional Representation in Cities. A Joint Discussion by George H. Dunlop and J. J. Hamilton of a Los Angeles Charter Proposal," *ibid.,* 14: 11ff (February 8, 1913); "Special Committee Appointed by City Club to Study Various Provisions— Recommendations For and Against," *ibid.,* 14: 11ff (March 22, 1913); "Proposed Charter Amendments to be Voted on March 24, 25, 1913," Haynes Papers; Los Angeles *Examiner,* December 6, 8, 9, 1912, February 6, 19, March 13, 24, 25, 1913.

56. George H. Dunlop, "Charter Making Again," *California Outlook,* 19: 104–105 (September 1915); "Proposed Amendments to the Charter of the City of Los Angeles to be Submitted Dec. 31, 1914," Lissner Papers; Los Angeles *Examiner,* June 29, July 4, 20, August 5, 1915; Los Angeles *Times,* August 20, 1915.

57. John R. Haynes, "The Proposed New City Charter for Los Angeles" (1916); Citizens New Charter Committee, "The New Charter or the Old" (1916), Haynes Papers; Municipal League of Los Angeles, *Bulletin. Light on Your City's Affairs,* 7: 3–4 (April 25, 1916); Los Angeles *Times,* February 4, 1916.

58. Los Angeles Board of Public Service Commissioners Minutes, May 23, 1916; Meyer Lissner, "Address before the Women's City Club" (June 21, 1916), Lissner Papers; Los Angeles *Times,* March 26, May 12, 14, 16, June 4, 14, 1916; Los Angeles City, *Records,* vol. 104, June 10, 1916, pp. 546–547.

59. Municipal League of Los Angeles, *Bulletin. Light on Your City's Affairs,* 10: 1–7 (October 13, 1916); *ibid.,* 12: passim (October 24, 1918); *Statutes of California . . . Forty-Second Legislature . . . 1917* (Sacramento, 1917), pp. 1,686–1,695; *Statutes of California . . . Forty-Fourth Legislature . . . 1921* (Sacramento, 1921), pp. 1,802–1,820.

60. John R. Haynes to G. G. Young, April 20, 1923, Haynes Papers; Los Angeles *Times,* February 1, April 19, 1923.

61. Clarence A. Dykstra, "The Pending Los Angeles Charter," *National Municipal Review,* 13: 151 (March 1924).

62. "We have tried," one Freeholder explained, "to get into the public life of Los Angeles representative citizens who, as a matter of course, in smaller towns, give part-time to the public." Los Angeles *Times,* December 27, 1923; Los Angeles Board of Freeholders Minutes, passim; Board of Public Service Commissioners to Board of Freeholders, August 20, 1923; Board of Public Works to Board of Freeholders, 1923; Greater Harbor Committee of Two Hundred to Board of Freeholders, November 16, 1923; Municipal League of Los Angeles to Board of Freeholders, September 4, 1923; E. F. Scattergood, "Suggestions as to Charter," Haynes Papers; Los Angeles *Times,* July 5, 12, December 2, 1923, April 27, 28, 29, 30, May 1, 2, 3, 1924.

63. Clarence A. Dykstra, "Los Angeles Returns to the Ward System," *National Municipal Review,* 14: 210–212 (May 1925).

64. Los Angeles *Herald,* January 13, 1891; Los Angeles *Examiner,* November 19, 1905, January 5, February 7, 12, May 18, 1906; Meyer Lissner to M. N. Baker, February 2, 1916, Lissner Papers; George H. Dunlop, "City and County Consolidation," *California Outlook,* 16: 12 (March 21, 1914), and 16: 11 (April 11, 1914); Winston W. Crouch and Beatrice Dinerman, *Southern California Metropolis: A Study in Development of Government for a Metropolitan Area* (Berkeley and Los Angeles, 1964), pp. 182–183.

65. Los Angeles *Evening Express,* October 4, 5, December 2, 1895, March 19, 21, 23, 1896; Los Angeles *Examiner,* May 29, 30, June 13, 1906; Board of Economic Survey, *Port of Los Angeles,* Exhibit 1, pp. 1–16; Los Angeles Board of Water Commissioners Minutes, August 29, 1906, February 18, 1907, December 28, 1908; Crouch and Dinerman, *Southern California Metropolis,* pp. 56–58, 152–153, 200–201, 415.

66. "Report of the Municipal Annexation Commission to the City Council of Los Angeles, November 11, 1913," Lissner Papers; Los Angeles *Examiner,* November 16, 1913; Los Angeles Chamber of Commerce Minutes, March 31, 1915; Robert C. Gillis to Arthur H. Fleming, September 6, 1915, to Mrs. Percy W. Rairden, February 6, 1916, Gillis Papers; Crouch and Dinerman, *Southern California Metropolis,* pp. 154–158, 415.

67. Los Angeles Board of Water and Power Commissioners Minutes, November 20, 1925; George W. Bemis and Nancy Basche, *Los Angeles County as an Agency of Municipal Government* (Los Angeles, 1946), pp. 14–15; Luke Mader Smith, "Relations between the Territorial Structuring and the Local Government of a Metropolitan Suburb: The Sunland-Tujunga Valley, Los Angeles" (Harvard University Doctoral Dissertation, 1948), passim; Crouch and Dinerman, *Southern California Metropolis,* pp. 158–164, 181–205, 415.

CHAPTER 11: THE MUNICIPAL OWNERSHIP MOVEMENT

1. *First Annual Report of the Board of Public Utilities of the City of Los Angeles [1909–1910],* pp. 59–60, 68–69; see also, Chap. 5, 6, above.

2. Los Angeles *Socialist,* 1902–1909, passim. A Public Ownership party actually appeared in the early 1900's. Los Angeles *Examiner,* February 22, 1906.

3. *California Municipalities,* 6: 5–7 (August 1899); see also, *Second Annual Report of the Board of Public Utilities of the City of Los Angeles [1910–1911],* pp. 111–114; Chap. 5, 6, above.

4. William J. Carr, "Does Municipal Ownership Pay," *Pacific Municipalities,* 37: 142–144 (March 1907); see also, Los Angeles *Evening Express,* October 12, 13, December 4–9, 1894.

5. Los Angeles *Evening Express,* June 2, July 3, 1899, June 11, August 6, 1900; Richard E. Northmore to J. Gregg Layne, March 4, 1929, Miscellaneous Manuscripts, Special Collections, University of California Library, Los Angeles; *Fiftieth Annual Report of the Board of Public Utilities and Transportation City of Los Angeles [1958–1959],* p. 59.

6. Los Angeles City, *Records,* April 3, 17, 1905, vol. 70, pp. 282–283, 329; Los Angeles *Examiner,* March 8, 13–20, 1905.

7. Los Angeles City, *Records,* April 24, 1905, vol. 70, p. 347; Los Angeles *Examiner,* April 24, 1905.

8. Los Angeles City, *Records,* January 7, 28, 1907, vol. 73, pp. 220–221, 273–276.

9. Los Angeles *Examiner,* January 30, 1907; California Railroad Commission, *Archives,* Applications 1830 and 1853, Reporter's Transcript, pp. 90–91.

10. California Railroad Commission, *Archives,* Applications 1830 and 1853, Reporter's Transcript, pp. 2,526ff; *Fiftieth Annual Report of the Board of Public Utilities and Transportation City of Los Angeles [1958–1959],* pp. 17, 23, 24.

11. *First Annual Report of the Board of Public Utilities of the City of Los Angeles* [*1909–1910*], pp. 5–8; *Pacific Outlook*, 7: 1–2 (October 13, 1909).

12. John R. Haynes to William B. Munro, August 23, 1923; John R. Haynes, "Municipal Ownership"; John R. Haynes, "Public Ownership," all in Haynes Papers.

13. John R. Haynes to William B. Munro, August 23, 1923, Haynes Papers; Los Angeles City, *Archives*, vol. 585, p. 51; *Pacific Municipalities*, 10: 82–87 (April 1904).

14. Municipal League of Los Angeles, *Municipal Affairs*, 2: 7–8 (July 1907); see also, W. P. D. Bliss et al., "Memorial from the Union Reform League of Los Angeles," Haynes Papers.

15. W. F. Durand et al., "Preliminary Report of Consulting Board of Engineers of the Bureau of Los Angeles Aqueduct Power to the Board of Public Works," *First Annual Report of the Bureau of Los Angeles Aqueduct Power* [*1910*], Appendixes E, J. See also, Nelson S. Van Valen, "Power Politics: The Struggle for Municipal Ownership of Electric Utilities in Los Angeles, 1905–1937" (Claremont Graduate School Doctoral Dissertation, 1964), pp. 8–9.

16. *Journal of Electricity, Power and Gas*, 13: 10ff (January 1903); Frederick Hall Fowler, *Hydroelectric Power Systems of California and Their Extensions into Oregon and Nevada* (Washington, 1923), pp. 529–533, 541ff; Carol Green Wilson, *California Yankee: William R. Staats—Business Pioneer* (Claremont, Calif., 1946), pp. 46–55; B. C. Forbes, *Men Who Are Making the West* (New York, 1923), pp. 50–75.

17. Los Angeles Board of Public Service Commissioners Minutes, April 18, 25, May 16, 1911; *Fourteenth Annual Report of the Board of Public Service Commissioners of the City of Los Angeles* [*1915*], pp. 55–56; Van Valen, "Power Politics," pp. 22ff.

18. Los Angeles Board of Public Service Commissioners Minutes, December 31, 1912, January 3, 14, 28, 1913; Los Angeles *Examiner*, October 14, 1910, January 29, 1911.

19. H. Z. Osborne, "Report to the Los Angeles Board of Freeholders," Los Angeles Chamber of Commerce Minutes, August 28, 1912.

20. John R. Haynes Memorandum (concerning the criticisms of the municipal ownership provision), Haynes Papers.

21. Proceedings of the Board of Freeholders of 1923, passim, Lissner Papers.

22. W. B. Cline, John B. Miller, and G. C. Ward to George Williams, ca. 1913, and Municipal League of Los Angeles to Theodore Roosevelt, Jr., March 19, 1913, both in Haynes Papers; Southern California Edison Company Statement, April 9, 1913, Southern California Edison Company Files, Los Angeles *Examiner*, April 5, 9, 16, 1913; Van Valen, "Power Politics," pp. 53ff.

23. Albert Lee Stephens Statement, ca. 1913, Haynes Papers.

24. Los Angeles Chamber of Commerce Minutes, October 8, 1913, March 18, April 15, 22, 1914; R. H. Ballard, "The Truth about the Power Bonds," Southern California Edison Company Files; Los Angeles *Examiner*, March 3, May 1–9, 1914; *Electrical World*, 63: 1,026–1,027 (May 9, 1914); Van Valen, "Power Politics," pp. 56ff.

25. Los Angeles Board of Public Service Commissioners Minutes, April 21, 28, May 9, 13, 1916; "Statement of Negotiations with the Power Companies . . . April 30th, 1917," Department of Water and Power Files; Los Angeles *Times*, April 20, 23, 29, 1916; Van Valen, "Power Politics," pp. 96ff.

26. Committee on Municipal Ownership, City Club of Los Angeles, *Report on Government Ownership of Public Utility Service Undertakings* (Los Angeles, 1917), passim.

27. Lloyd H. Marvin, "Report to the Efficiency Commission of the City of Los Angeles, March 15, 1916," Common Council Files, City Hall, Los Angeles; *Fiftieth Annual Report of the Board of Public Utilities and Transportation City of Los Angeles* [*1958–1959*], pp. 36–37.

28. Los Angeles City, *Records*, February 8, 1915, vol. 99, pp. 331–332, March 10, 1915, vol. 99, p. 555, April 30, 1915, vol. 100, p. 308, May 14, 1915, vol. 100, p. 415,

June 8, 1915, vol. 100, p. 587; *Seventh Annual Report of the Board of Public Utilities of the City of Los Angeles [1915–1916]*, p. 102.

29. Los Angeles City, *Records,* March 28, 1916, vol. 103, p. 694; Los Angeles, *Petitions,* Nos. 495, 496, Volume 884 (1915).

30. *Seventh Annual Report of the Board of Public Utilities of the City of Los Angeles [1915–1916]*, pp. 102–107; Los Angeles City, *Records,* March 29, 1916, vol. 103, pp. 715–716; Los Angeles City, *Petitions,* No. 1037, Volume 889 (1916).

31. Los Angeles City, *Petitions,* Nos. 1505, 1567, Volume 894 (1916); Los Angeles City, *Records,* May 10, 1916, vol. 104, p. 255; Los Angeles Board of Public Utilities Minutes, April 11, 1916; Los Angeles Chamber of Commerce Minutes, May 10, 1916; Los Angeles *Examiner,* June 4, 1916.

32. Los Angeles City, *Records,* June 10, 1916, vol. 104, p. 543; Los Angeles *Examiner,* May 31, June 5, 6, 1916; *Seventh Annual Report of the Board of Public Utilities of the City of Los Angeles [1915–1916]*, p. 107.

33. The new company would purchase Pacific Telephone with stock and Home Telephone with bonds so that the Bell system would retain control over the enterprise. *Eighth Annual Report of the Board of Public Utilities of the City of Los Angeles [1916–1917]*, pp. 76–109; *Fiftieth Annual Report of the Board of Public Utilities and Transportation City of Los Angeles [1958–1959]*, pp. 40–41.

34. *Annual Report of the Southern California Edison Company [1916]*, p. 6; *Annual Report of the Southern California Edison Company [1917]*, pp. 10–11; *Sixteenth Annual Report of the Board of Public Service Commissioners of the City of Los Angeles [1917]*, pp. 42–45; W. F. Durand to John W. Kemp, January 3, 1917, Haynes Papers; "Statement of Negotiations with the Power Companies . . . April 30th, 1917."

35. *Decisions of the Railroad Commission of the State of California,* Decision 2960, VIII (1915); see also, Los Angeles Board of Public Service Commissioners Minutes, November 29, December 19, 1916; Los Angeles *Times,* January 7, 1917; Van Valen, "Power Politics," pp. 130ff.

36. John R. Haynes to F. T. Woodman, December 5, 1917, Haynes Papers; see also, Los Angeles Board of Public Service Commissioners Minutes, May 13, 26, 1919; *Eighteenth Annual Report of the Board of Public Service Commissioners of the City of Los Angeles [1919]*, pp. 50–53; Federal Trade Commission, "Hearing on Public Utility Corporations," United States Congress, *Senate Documents,* 70 Congress, 1 Session, Number 92, pp. 71a, 388–389.

37. Department of Public Service of the City of Los Angeles, *Public Service,* 3 (June 1919), passim.

38. Los Angeles Chamber of Commerce Minutes, November 20, 1910; see also, W. F. Durand, "Address to the City Club of Los Angeles, January 13, 1917," Haynes Papers. Not all businessmen agreed, however; see J. D. Smith to L. H. Valentine, February 8, 1917, Haynes Papers.

39. Los Angeles Board of Public Service Commissioners Minutes, April 24, 1922; John R. Haynes Memorandum, Haynes Papers; Van Valen, "Power Politics," pp. 143ff.

40. W. T. Bishop to Board of Directors of the Los Angeles Chamber of Commerce, December 14, 1920, Los Angeles Chamber of Commerce Files.

41. Los Angeles Board of Public Service Commissioners Minutes, June 12, 1923; *Annual Report of the Southern California Edison Company [1923]*, pp. 24–25; Kleinsorge, *Boulder Canyon Project,* pp. 89–92, 113–116.

42. Department of Public Service of the City of Los Angeles, "Municipal Hydro-Electric Power System" (December 1921); William Mulholland et al., "Summary of Statement . . . Covering Financial Requirements for Development . . . in Water and Power Supply and Distribution," Department of Water and Power Files; Los Angeles *Times,* May 24, 25, 29, June 3, 7, 1923; Van Valen, "Power Politics," pp. 168ff.

43. Frank G. Tyrrell, "The Los Angeles Experiment in Municipal Power" (April 7, 1924); see also, W. H. Fischer et al., "Public Ownership in Los Angeles," both in Southern California Edison Company Files.

44. John B. Miller quoted in Van Valen, "Power Politics," p. 333; see also, John B. Miller, "The Hydro-Electric Power Situation in the West" (December 7, 1925), Haynes Papers.

45. John R. Haynes to W. T. Bishop, ca. 1924, Haynes Papers; Mayor's Power and Water Committee, "Facts Are Better than 'Gas' Vote 'Yes,'" Haynes Papers; Van Valen, "Power Politics," pp. 191ff.

46. John R. Haynes to W. T. Bishop, ca. 1924, E. F. Scattergood to John R. Haynes, July 2, 1924, and John R. Haynes Memorandum, all in Haynes Papers; Los Angeles Chamber of Commerce Minutes, April 17, May 6, 1923; *Twenty-Third Annual Report of the Board of Public Service Commissioners of the City of Los Angeles [1924]*, pp. 31–33.

47. John R. Haynes to W. T. Bishop, undated, Haynes Papers.

48. Shirley Ward, "An Open Letter to H. H. Merrick, President, Greater Los Angeles Association," June 4, 1924, Los Angeles Chamber of Commerce Files.

49. E. F. Scattergood to John R. Haynes, July 2, 1924, and Citizens' Power Bond Committee, "Vote 'Yes' on Power Bonds," both in Haynes Papers; Los Angeles Board of Public Service Commissioners Minutes, March 21, 1924; *Twenty-Fourth Annual Report of the Board of Public Service Commissioners of the City of Los Angeles [1925]*, pp. 34–35; Van Valen, "Power Politics," pp. 203–210.

50. Lester S. Ready and H. G. Butler, "Report on Power Problems of the City of Los Angeles," Los Angeles Chamber of Commerce Files; *Annual Report of the Southern California Edison Company [1929]*, p. 18; Los Angeles Department of Water and Power, "System Planning," passim, Department of Water and Power Files.

51. John R. Haynes to Rudolph Spreckels, February 8, 1923, to G. G. Young, April 20, 1923, to Harlan Palmer et al., February 26, 1925, Haynes Papers; see also, Chap. 10, above.

52. Van Valen, "Power Politics," pp. 252ff; see also, Ostrom, *Water and Politics*, pp. 67–68.

53. Van Valen, "Power Politics, pp. 258ff; see also, Ostrom, *Water and Politics*, pp. 68–69.

54. Municipal League of Los Angeles, *Bulletin. Light on Your City's Affairs*, 8 (May 20, 1931); Van Valen, "Power Politics," pp. 264ff.

55. "Report of the Water and Power Committee . . . August 22, 1932"; John C. Porter Radio Talk, April 18, 1935, Haynes Papers; Van Valen, "Power Politics," pp. 271ff, Ostrom, *Water and Politics*, pp. 69–70.

56. Van Valen, "Power Politics," pp. 280ff; Ostrom, *Water and Politics*, pp. 70–71.

57. Van Valen, "Power Politics," p. 316; *ibid.*, pp. 297ff; Ostrom, *Water and Politics*, pp. 70–71.

58. Los Angeles City, *Minutes*, September 25, 1936, vol. 260, pp. 358ff, October 26, 1936, vol. 260, pp. 808ff; Van Valen, "Power Politics," pp. 315ff.

59. Los Angeles Department of Water and Power, "Highlights of Proposed Settlement with Los Angeles Gas and Electric Corporation, Southern California Gas Company, Southern Counties Gas Company," pp. 4–5, Municipal Reference Library, City Hall, Los Angeles; Municipal League of Los Angeles to Fellow Citizens, January 28, 1935, Los Angeles *Examiner*, September 27, 1934; Los Angeles *Chronicle*, April 1, 1935, Haynes Papers; Los Angeles City, *Petitions*, No. 3427, Volume 3048 (1936); *Annual Report of the Board of Public Utilities and Transportation City of Los Angeles [1958–1959]*, pp. 23, 24.

60. Los Angeles *Examiner*, May 31, 1916; Municipal League of Los Angeles, *Bulletin. Light on Your City's Affairs*, 7 (November 1, 1929).

61. Municipal League of Los Angeles, *Bulletin. Light on Your City's Affairs*, 4 (December 31, 1926); Los Angeles *Times*, February 22, 1927. See also, Chap. 8, above.

CHAPTER 12: CITY AND REGIONAL PLANNING

1. Los Angeles *Examiner,* June 15, 1910; Municipal League of Los Angeles, *Bulletin* (March 1914), passim; *ibid.* (April 1914), pp. 15–16.

2. Albert Lee Stephens, "The Significance of the New Laws Relative to Zoning and Set-Back Lines," *Pacific Outlook,* 32: 129–136 (March 1918); J. R. Douglas, "City Planning and the Protection of Private Property through Zoning," *ibid.,* 31: 117–122 (April 1917).

3. John W. Mitchell, "Art, Architecture and Art Commissions," *California Outlook,* 13: 15 (March 23, 1912); Meyer Lissner to J. H. Adams, July 13, 1911, Lissner Papers.

4. Charles Mulford Robinson, "The City Beautiful," Los Angeles Municipal Art Commission, *Report . . . to the Mayor, the City Council and Board of Public Works* (Los Angeles, 1909).

5. See Chaps. 7, 9, above.

6. "In determining what constitutes a 'nuisance,' " the courts held, "the question is whether the nuisance will or does produce such a condition of things as in the judgment of reasonable men is naturally productive of actual physical discomfort to persons of ordinary sensibility and ordinary tastes and habits." See Henry Campbell Black, *Black's Law Dictionary,* 3d ed. (St. Paul, 1933), pp. 1,263–1,264. The essential phrase here is "actual physical discomfort." On this basis, Los Angeles forced the removal of such businesses as gas works and glue factories from residential neighborhoods. See Los Angeles *Evening Express,* December 12, 13, 1892; Los Angeles *Examiner,* November 16, December 5, 7, 1904. The municipality had no such authority over the location of ordinary businesses, however.

7. Los Angeles City Planning Commission Minutes, July 7, 1920; Los Angeles City Planning Department Ordinance Book, Ordinance 399906, City Planning Department Files; G. Gordon Whitnall, "Tracing the Development of Planning in Los Angeles," *Annual Report. Department of City Planning. Los Angeles [1929–1930],* pp. 38–47.

8. Los Angeles City Planning Commission Minutes, January 10, 1922; *ibid.,* July 23, 1920, February 8, July 1, 12, 1921, January 10, 1922.

9. G. Gordon Whitnall, "The Development of Regional Planning and Subdivision Control," *Pacific Outlook,* 37: 419ff (November 1923); see also, Hugh Pomeroy, "How Regional Planning is Beneficial to Cities," *ibid.,* 11: 432ff (November 1926); R. F. McClellan Statement, "Interlocking Specifications for the Regional Plan of Los Angeles County," City Planning Department Files.

10. Los Angeles County Regional Planning Commission, untitled pamphlet, January 1, 1929, p. 3; G. Gordon Whitnall, "A Declaration of Interdependence," "Regional Planning Conference" (January 21, 1922), City Planning Department Files.

11. Municipal League of Los Angeles, *Bulletin* (April 1914); Walter M. Danburg, "Commission on Master Plan," *Annual Report. Department of City Planning. Los Angeles [1929–1930],* p. 26; Charles H. Cheney, "City Planning," *Pacific Outlook,* 29: 260–267 (June 1915); Charles H. Cheney, "How California Cities Can Profit by Active City Planning," *ibid.,* 28: 31–35 (January 1914).

12. G. Gordon Whitnall, "Highlights from the International Conference on City Planning," *Pacific Outlook,* 11: 53ff (February 1926); George A. Damon, "Relation of the Motor Bus to Other Methods of Transportation," *Proceedings of the Sixteenth National Conference on City Planning, Los Angeles, California, April 7–10, 1924* (Baltimore, 1924), pp. 79–90; John E. Lathrop, "City Planning for all the People," *California Outlook,* 16: 8ff (April 25, 1914); Charles K. Mohler, "Public Utility Regulation by Los Angeles," *The Annals of the American Academy of Political and Social Sciences,* 53: 108ff (May 1914).

13. Los Angeles City Planning Commission Minutes, April 30, 1923; C. H. Richards, "Highways," "Regional Planning Conference."

14. Los Angeles City Planning Commission Minutes, July 30, 1925; G. Gordon

Whitnall, "Relation of Downtown Commercial Districts to Outlying Business Districts," *Pacific Municipalities*, 13: 127–132 (March 1928), George A. Damon, "Inter and Intra Urban Transit and Traffic as a Regional Planning Problem," *Proceedings of the Fifteenth National Conference on City Planning, Baltimore, Md., April 30, May 1–2, 1923* (Baltimore, 1923), pp. 45–54.

15. Los Angeles City Planning Commission Minutes, January 10, 1922; *Annual Reports of the Traffic Commission of the City and County of Los Angeles [1925–1930]*.

16. Olmsted, Bartholemew and Cheney, *Major Traffic Street Plan*, passim; Los Angeles City Planning Commission Minutes, December 22, 1922, July 3, 1923.

17. Los Angeles Regional Planning Commission Minutes, September 18, 1929, Regional Planning Department Files; see also, Regional Planning Commission County of Los Angeles, *A Comprehensive Report on the Regional Plan of Highways. Section 2 E San Gabriel Valley* (Los Angeles, 1929), passim; Regional Planning Commission County of Los Angeles, *A Comprehensive Report of the Regional Plan of Highways. Section 4 Long Beach-Redondo Area* (Los Angeles, 1931), passim; *Regional Planning Commission County of Los Angeles, Report of a Highway Traffic Survey in the County of Los Angeles* (Los Angeles, 1934), pp. 7–12.

18. Olmsted, Bartholemew and Cheney, *Major Traffic Street Plan*, pp. 18–19.

19. Hugh Pomeroy, "Regional Planning in Practice," *First Annual Report of Los Angeles County Regional Planning Commission [1924]*, p. 6, Regional Planning Department Files.

20. Office of the County Surveyor, *The Official Subdividers Guide* (Los Angeles, ca. 1927), p. 34; J. R. Prince, "Subdivisions," "Regional Planning Conference"; Joseph H. L'Hommedieu, "The Laying Out of Subdivisions," *Pacific Outlook*, 29: 612–617 (December 1915).

21. County Surveyor, *Subdividers Guide*, pp. 29, 31, 68, 69; "Interlocking Specifications for the Regional Plan"; *Annual Report. Department of City Planning. Los Angeles. [1929–1930]*, pp. 49–54.

22. County Surveyor, *Subdividers Guide*, pp. 33, 69, 70; "Interlocking Specifications for the Regional Plan"; J. A. Mellen, "Report on Lot Sizes" (April 1929), Regional Planning Department Files.

23. Los Angeles City Planning Commission Minutes, September 29, 1920, December 27, 1921, August 30, 1923, October 23, 1929; *Annual Report. Department of City Planning. Los Angeles [1929–1930]*, pp. 49–54.

24. Ray E. Nimmo, "Accomplishing the Segregation of Industries," *California Outlook*, 15: 8–9 (September 6, 1913). For an early proposal to zone manufacturing, see the statement of Mayor Workman in the Los Angeles *Herald*, December 17, 1888. For the disadvantages of the initial zoning arrangements, see the Los Angeles *Times*, July 24, 1909; J. B. Irvine to the Mayor of Los Angeles, September 14, 1909, to J. H. Lapham, January 29, 1910, Haynes Papers; Los Angeles *Examiner*, September 14, 1909; Huber E. Smutz, "Zoning in Los Angeles," *Annual Report. Department of City Planning. Los Angeles [1929–1930]*, pp. 58–65.

25. Stephens, "New Laws Relative to Zoning," pp. 129–136; Charles H. Cheney, "Zoning in Practice," *Proceedings of the Eleventh National Conference on City Planning, Niagara Falls and Buffalo, May 26–28, 1919* (Boston, 1920), pp. 162–185; Perry Thomas, "Zoning," *Annual Report. Department of City Planning. Los Angeles [1929–1930]*, pp. 21–22.

26. George Lee Miller and Francis Miller *v.* Board of Public Works of the City of Los Angeles, 195 Cal. 477, Transcript on Appeal, Statement of Respondents, pp. 97–99, County Law Library, Los Angeles; Ex Parte Quong Wo, 161 Cal. 220; Hadacheck *v.* Sebastian 36. U.S. 143; In re Montgomery, 163 Cal. 457; Brown *v.* City of Los Angeles, 183 Cal. 783; Jefferson M. Hardin, "The Present Status of Zoning in the Law," *Pacific Outlook*, 13: 235ff (July 1928).

27. Harry H. Culver, "A Realtor's Viewpoint on Zoning," *Zoning in the United States. The Annals of the American Academy of Political and Social Sciences*, 155: 207–212

(March 1931); see also, William B. Munro, "A Danger Spot in the Zoning Movement," ibid., pp. 202–206.

28. Huber Earl Smutz, "The Department of City Planning of the City of Los Angeles" (September 1935), in possession of Mr. Smutz, Department of City Planning, Los Angeles; Los Angeles City Planning Commission Minutes, August 6, 1925; Los Angeles City Planning Commission, *Archives*, Petition 3,147, Reporter's Transcript, pp. 4,048, 6,180, 6,181, 8,064, 8,065, City Planning Department Files.

29. Municipal League of Los Angeles, *Bulletin. Light on Your City's Affairs*, 2: 11 (May 1925); see also, *National Municipal Review*, 13: 318 (May 1924).

30. Los Angeles County Regional Planning Commission, "Guide to Los Angeles County Zoning Ordinances" (August 1929), Regional Planning Department Files; Los Angeles City Planning Commission Minutes, October 15, 1920, January 14, 1921; Ordinance No. 42,666 (New Series); Huber Earl Smutz, "City Planning Impressions," p. 3 (June 5, 1930), City Planning Department Files.

31. Los Angeles City Planning Commission Minutes, November 3, 1922; Regional Planning Commission, untitled pamphlet, January 1, 1929, p. 25; Miller *v.* Board of Public Works, Statement of Respondents, pp. 97–99; in re Montgomery, 163 Cal. 457, Transcript on Appeal, Respondents Brief, pp. 60–61, County Law Library, Los Angeles; Douglas, "Protection of Private Property through Zoning," pp. 120–121; *The Los Angeles Zoning Atlas* (Los Angeles, 1930), passim.

32. Huber Earl Smutz, "Zoning Facts," 6 (June 15, 1929); see also, Carl Bush, "Zoning: Its Possibilities, Purposes and Difficulties," *Los Angeles Realtor*, 7: 12 (May 1928), 7: 24 (June 1928).

33. G. Gordon Whitnall, "Supply and Demand in Zoning," *Pacific Outlook*, 12: 107–109 (March 1927); Huber Earl Smutz, "Report on Percentage of City in Various Zones" (May 8, 1934), City Planning Department Files. Pasadena, Glendale, Burbank, Whittier, Monrovia, Inglewood, and West Hollywood were also overzoned for commercial use. See Regional Planning Commission, *Regional Plan of Highways. Section 2 E*, p. 63.

34. Los Angeles City Planning Commission Minutes, July 28, 1926; Los Angeles City Planning Commission, *Archives*, Petition 3,147, Reporter's Transcript, pp. 6,187–6,188; Huber Earl Smutz, "Zoning Facts," 4 (March 15, 1929).

35. Los Angeles City Planning Commission Minutes, August 27, 1925; G. Gordon Whitnall, "History of Zoning," C. J. Williamson, "Mechanics of Zoning," Munro, "Danger Spot," *Zoning in America*, pp. 1–14, 108–122, 202–206.

36. John Delafons, *Land-Use Controls in the United States* (Joint Center for Urban Studies of the Massachusetts Institute of Technology and Harvard University, 1962), passim. Less important as restrictions on land-use in Los Angeles were height (and bulk) limits and setback lines. Los Angeles City Planning Commission Minutes, December 27, 1920, October 20, 1923, January 13, 1926; Los Angeles *Examiner*, December 17, 19, 1910; G. Gordon Whitnall, "Address to the Municipal League," September 13, 1930, City Planning Department Files. All in all, these restrictions encouraged dispersal and decentralization without seriously inhibiting private development.

37. Los Angeles City Planning Commission Minutes, August 27, 1925.

38. Griffith J. Griffith, *Parks, Boulevards and Playgrounds* (Los Angeles, 1910), passim; Los Angeles Chamber of Commerce Minutes, January 4, 1923.

39. Los Angeles City Planning Commission Minutes, November 19, 1923; *ibid.*, November 26, 1922; Charles H. Cheney, "A Park System for a Metropolitan County," *California Southland*, 31: 10 (July 1922).

40. Frederick Law Olmsted, "The Distribution of Metropolitan Parks," Los Angeles City Planning Commission Minutes, volume IV, 993–1,006.

41. Los Angeles *Herald*, June 2, 9, 16, 1891; Los Angeles *Evening Express*, January

19, 26, 1892; Guinn, *Los Angeles,* I, chap. 1; Newmark, *Sixty Years,* pp. 349, 548; Griffith, *Parks, Boulevards and Playgrounds,* passim.

42. Los Angeles Chamber of Commerce Minutes, January 4, 1923; Robinson, *The City Beautiful,* passim; *Pacific Outlook,* 8: 7ff (May 5, 1910); Pomeroy, "Regional Planning in Practice," pp. 11–13.

43. Los Angeles City Planning Commission Minutes, April 15, 1926; this was the principle on which the Palos Verdes Estate project was based (Olmsted, "Palos Verdes Estates").

44. Los Angeles Board of Playground and Recreation Commissioners Minutes, February 21, May 15, June 7, 1923; Los Angeles City Planning Commission Minutes, April 2, 9, June 11, 1923; Los Angeles Chamber of Commerce Minutes, January 24, 1929.

45. Los Angeles Board of Playground and Recreation Commissioners Minutes, November 24, 1926, April 28, 1927, January 12, May 18, 1929; Los Angeles City Planning Commission, March 18, 1926; Los Angeles *Times,* May 19, 1909, February 22, June 4, 11, July 8, 16, 1924.

46. *Annual Report. Department of Playground and Recreation. Los Angeles [1929-1930],* pp. 20–21; *Annual Report. Department of Parks. Los Angeles [1925-1926],* pp. 17–18. 7 per cent had been acquired by district financing, 7 per cent by departmental transfers, 21 per cent by general funds, and the remainder by donation.

47. J. M. Paige, "Parks and Pleasure Boulevards," "Regional Planning Conference"; J. B. Lippincott, "Parks and Parkways Here and Elsewhere," *California Outlook,* 10: 11ff (June 3, 1911).

48. Cheney, "Park System for a Metropolitan County," p. 11; Robinson, *The City Beautiful,* p. 25; Paige, "Parks and Pleasure Boulevards"; *California Outlook,* Supplement, 9 (November 18, 1911), passim.

49. Los Angeles *Times,* December 21, 1923; Los Angeles *Examiner,* March 2, 1924; *Los Angeles Realtor,* 2: 12 (July 1923); Los Angeles City, *Petitions,* No. 6683, Volume 1431 (1923); Findley, "Boom of the 'Twenties in Los Angeles," pp. 220ff.

50. Los Angeles City Planning Commission Minutes, October 27, 1924; Los Angeles *Examiner,* October 28, 30, 31, November 7, 1924.

51. Los Angeles *Examiner,* April 14, 1926; *ibid.,* March 26, April 6, 8, 11, 25, 27, 1926; Los Angeles City, *Records,* February 5, 1925, vol. 165, p. 62, March 15, 1926, vol. 166, p. 126, April 1, 1926, vol. 167, p. 7, May 6, 1926, vol. 168, p. 64; Los Angeles City Planning Commission Minutes, April 17, August 28, 1925, July 2, 1926; J. F. Sartori to Edward A. Dickson, ca. 1925; James R. Martin to Edward A. Dickson, March 23, 1926; W. A. Faris to Edward A. Dickson, ca. 1926, Dickson Papers; Municipal League of Los Angeles, *Bulletin. Light on Your City's Affairs,* 2: 10–11 (May 1925).

52. Los Angeles City, *Records,* March 23, 1926, vol. 166, pp. 538–539; Los Angeles City, *Petitions,* No. 1823, Volume 2001 (1927); Los Angeles *Examiner,* March 24, 26, 1926; Ralph Hancock, *Fabulous Boulevard* (New York, 1949), pp. 149–164.

53. Ironically, of the few parkways in Los Angeles now, most—San Vicente Boulevard, for example—are located along the routes of abandoned railway lines.

54. John Galen Howard, "The Significance of the Civic Center," *California Outlook,* 12: 12–13 (May 25, 1912); *Pacific Outlook,* 9: 6ff (November 19, 1910); Allied Architects Association of Los Angeles *Bulletin,* II, 1 (November 1, 1925).

55. William Mulholland and G. Gordon Whitnall, "Report of the Civic Center Committee," Los Angeles City, *Petitions,* No. 1420, Volume 1066 (1919); Los Angeles *Times,* February 28, March 28, 30, April 16, 20, May 9, June 20, 27, 1919; Nina Lauretta Jermain, "The History of the Los Angeles Civic Center" (University of Southern California Masters Thesis, 1934), p. 15.

56. "Report of the City Planning Associations on our New City Hall and Administration Center" (1922), Municipal Reference Library, City Hall, Los Angeles; Los

Angeles City, *Records*, June 18, 1920, vol. 118, p. 437, October 16, 1922, vol. 131, p. 519; Los Angeles *Times*, June 7, 1923; Jermain, "Los Angeles Civic Center," p. 20.

57. "Administrative Center for Los Angeles," *California Southland*, 41 (May 1923); Wilbur D. Cook, "The Los Angeles Administrative Center Problem," *The Architect and Engineer* (October 1923), pp. 70–72; Los Angeles City, *Records*, February 19, 1922, vol. 134, p. 195; Jermain, "Los Angeles Civic Center," pp. 31–35.

58. "Report of the Allied Architects Association of Los Angeles on an Administrative Center for the County of Los Angeles and the City of Los Angeles, December 31, 1924," passim, City Planning Department Files; Los Angeles City, *Records*, November 22, 1924, vol. 152, p. 64; Gardner W. Gregg, "Los Angeles' Bold Plans for a Civic Center," *National Municipal Review*, 14: 406–409 (July 1925).

59. Los Angeles City, *Records*, January 29, 1925, vol. 153, p. 196; Cook and Hall to the City Council of Los Angeles, January 28, 1925, Municipal Reference Library, City Hall, Los Angeles; "Administrative Civic Center Plans," Municipal League of Los Angeles, *Bulletin. Light on Your City's Affairs*, 2: 10ff (January 20, 1925).

60. Los Angeles City, *Records*, February 5, 9, 1925, vol. 153, pp. 398, 474, November 12, 1925, vol. 162, pp. 109–110; Los Angeles City, *Petitions*, No. 8585, Volume 1590 (1924), No. 7010, Volume 1737 (1925); Los Angeles City Planning Commission Minutes, March 3, 1925, June 17, 1926; Allied Architects Association of Los Angeles, *Bulletin*, II, 1 (November 1, 1925); Jermain, "Los Angeles Civic Center," p. 36.

61. Los Angeles City, *Records*, November 18, 1927, vol. 187, pp. 624–645, November 28, 1927, vol. 188, p. 13, December 5, 1924, vol. 188, pp. 235–238; Los Angeles City, *Petitions*, No. 10559 (1927), reprinted as Hugh Pomeroy, "Los Angeles Civic Center Street Plan," *Community Builder*, 1: 18–25 (January 1928); Jermain, "Los Angeles Civic Center," pp. 37–40.

62. Robinson, *The City Beautiful*.

CONCLUSION: "THE SIMPLE LIFE"

1. *Eberle Economic Service*, 9: 5 (January 11, 1932); 9: 4 (January 25, 1932); 9: 49 (March 28, 1932).

2. Even residents of Los Angeles occasionally acknowledged the difficulties involved. "Can we, by spending more than a million annually, add appreciably to the total wealth or the total population of the United States?" the Municipal League, explaining its opposition to the county's promotional activities, asked in 1928. "Is it not, therefore, essentially an unfriendly act to entice away the men and millions which, mayhap, are more sorely needed in other less favored parts of the country? . . . Has not the country heard ad nauseum of snow-capped mountain peaks with sweetly scented citrus groves nestling between their comely feet, or the salubrious zephyrs and sylph-like sirens of sunny Southern California, where work is play and night is day and day is desire personified? . . . Is there not a great loss in the uprooting which accompanies our present policy? The social, political and economic ills of Los Angeles show all too clearly that families may not be broken with impunity, that one's place in his community, when fixed by honorable ancestry, is too precious to be bartered away lightly for climatic comfort or possible added wealth." Municipal League of Los Angeles Minutes, June 8, 1928, Haynes Papers.

3. Citizens Transportation Survey Commission, *Report on Traffic and Transportation Survey* (Berkeley, 1940), passim.

4. Automobile Club of Southern California, *Traffic Survey. Los Angeles Metropolitan Area Nineteen Hundred Thirty-Seven* (Los Angeles, 1937), pp. 5, 9, 21. Whereupon the traffic engineers proposed the creation of motorways—highways with exceptionally wide rights of way and completely separated grades—which, known as freeways, would later dissect greater Los Angeles.

5. Day, "Races and Cultural Oases," p. 328. Not surprisingly, then, Los Angeles was incapable of coping with the thousands of impoverished farmers who fled from the Dust Bowl, drove across the desert and over the mountains, and arrived in southern California during the depression. John Steinbeck, *The Grapes of Wrath* (New York, 1939).

6. Municipal League of Los Angeles, *Bulletin. Light on Your City's Affairs,* 8 (March 15, 1931), passim; Stanley Rogers, "The Attempted Recall of the Mayor of Los Angeles," *National Municipal Review,* 21: 416–419 (July 1932).

7. Ernest C. Steele's Diary, 1928, Henry E. Huntington Library, San Marino, Calif.

INDEX

Los Angeles Railway Corporation (Cont.) 167; costs and income, 167–168, 170–172, 178–182, 184; and Depression, 183, 185; and private enterprise, 229; and city planners, 250

Los Angeles Rangers, 35

Los Angeles River, 99, 138

Los Angeles *Southern News,* 17

Los Angeles *Star,* 15, 17, 27, 52, 66

Los Angeles Suburban Homes Company, 96, 104–105, 155, 223

Los Angeles Telephone Company, 41, 237

Los Angeles Terminal Railway, 111

Los Angeles *Times,* 61, 243; on harbor, 62, 113; on water supply, 95; on industry, 120; on unions, 131; on electric railways, 176; on boosterism, 190; dynamiting of, 214; on municipal electricity, 219–220, 236, 239–242, 244; on charter reforms, 221

Los Angeles *Tribune,* 217, 236

Los Angeles Water Company, 35, 95–96, 205–206, 229

Louisiana, 66

Lumber, 109, 117, 119, 132

McKee, H. S., 108

McKinley, William, 114

McLachlan, James, 112

McPherson, Aimee Semple, 197

Maine, 64, 65

Major Traffic Street Plan, 251

"Mankind United," 197

Manufacturers, 63–64, 131, 153–154, 228

Manufacturing, 120–121, 122, 124, 127–129, 133, 199

Marion, 104–105

Markey, Morris, 3

Marshall, Tex., 48

Mason, Richard B., 12

Masonic lodges, 187

Massachusetts, 64

Mayor, 28; on water supply, 38–39, 96, 97; and railways, 87; and municipalization of harbor, 117; political power of, 205, 208–209, 218; election of, 212–213; reform control of, 215; and charter reforms, 221–222; on municipal ownership of gas, 231; power of appointment, 232, 242; and municipal electricity fight, 242–243; and civic center, 262

Mediterranean architecture, 157, 159, 161

Memphis, El Paso and Pacific Railroad, 45, 46, 48, 50

Merchants, 20, 52–53, 64, 178, 206, 228

Merchants and Manufacturers Association, 98, 129–131, 222, 236

Methodist congregation, 187

Metropolis, 2; Los Angeles as southern, 67, 134; creation of, 77–79, 81, 83–84, 105, 107; area encompassed by, 142, 188, 228; dispersion and decentralization of, 161, 163, 252; fragmentation of, 164, 185, 194, 202–204; comprehensive transportation plan for, 177–178; population changes of, 188–189, 191–192; political changes of, 205, 245; planners' goals for, 247–248, 250, 260, 262, 265, 271–272; and zoning regulations, 257, 261; and vision of community, 273, 275, 276

Metropolitan district, 1, 133, 143

Metropolitan Water District of Southern California, 102, 144, 272

Mexicans, 189; in pueblo society, 24–27; as immigrants, 64, 75–77; as nonwhites, 81, 82n, 83; as unskilled labor, 131; residences of, 138, 146–147; segregation of, 187–188, 198, 200, 274; discrimination of, 201; voluntary associations of, 202; disintegration of, 203

Mexico, 7–9, 10

Michigan, 81

Middle Atlantic states, 186

Middle class, 189. *See also* Americans, middle-class, native-white

Midwest states, 65, 72–73, 134, 189–190, 208

"Mighty I Am," 197

Migration, 15, 64–70, 72, 74, 76

Military brigades, 187

Miller, John B., 234

Milwaukee, Wisc., 133, 143

Miners, 64

Minneapolis, Minn., 123, 124, 143

Minnesota, 65

Missions, 5–7

Missouri, 15, 64

Mobility, 146, 185, 195

Mojave, 60

Mono Basin, 99

Montebello, 127

Monterey, 12

Morse, Ephraim W., 59, 61, 62

Motion picture industry, 74–75, 125, 127, 132, 154

Motor bus, 169–170

Mulholland, William, 97–98, 101

Municipal Annexation Commission, 223

Municipal authority: responsibilities of, 28–29, 34, 41; and voluntary associations, 36; and water supply, 36, 38–39, 96–97, 153; and land development, 39, 248, 253, 255; and harbor, 114–115, 117–118; and transportation, 169–171, 185; changes in, 205, 208, 211, 215–216, 275; and private enterprise, 217–218; and park sites, 258,

Municipal authority (Cont.)
260; responsiveness of, 276. *See also various boards, bureaus, commissions, departments;* Common council; Mayor
Municipal Conference, 216–217
Municipal Gas League, 231–232
Municipal government, *see* Municipal authority
Municipal Improvement Districts, 94
Municipal League, 222; on water supply, 98; on municipal ownership, 229, 233, 236; and city planning, 249–250; on zoning, 255, 262
Municipal Light and Power Defense League, 242
Municipal ownership, 218; of public utilities, 2, 212, 229, 245; of water supply, 96–97, 174; of port, 114–115, 117–118; of transit system, 172–175, 178; of harbor, 174; reformers and, 214–217; of electricity, 219–220, 233–237; and progressivism, 233, 275; accomplishments in, 245–246. *See also* Electricity; Gas; Harbor; Highways; Railroads; Railways; Telephone; Water supply
Municipal Ownership Committee, 231
Municipal Reform Association, 210
Municipal Taxpayers League, 239
Municipal Terminal Railway, 118
Mushet, W. C., 214–215

Naples, Italy, 75
National Bank of California in Los Angeles, 86
National City, 60
National Ranch, 58, 59
National War Labor Board, 167
Nationalist party, 229
Nationality organizations, 36, 194, 202
Nebraska, 65, 69, 73, 74, 81
Negroes, 9, 83, 189; migration to southern California, 75, 77; as unskilled labor, 131; and restrictive deeds, 145–146, 195; segregation of, 147, 198, 200, 274; occupational distribution of, 199; discrimination against, 200–201; voluntary associations of, 202; disintegration of community, 203. *See also* Colored minority; Nonwhites
Neighborhood organizations, 195, 218
Nevada, 46
Neve, Felipe de, 6–7
New England, 65, 186, 189
New Orleans, 64, 70, 75
New York, N.Y., 18, 219; and migrants, 64–66; economic opportunity of, 70; population of, 78–82; area and density of, 143; housing of, 146; Lower Manhattan,

148; and municipal transit system, 174, 178; and zoning, 254
Newmark, Harris, 52–53
Newspapers, 19, 61; on cattle, 15, 17; on fire control, 26, 35; on religion, 27; on water supply, 38–39, 95, 98; on railroads, 52, 54; on San Diego, 52, 62; on immigration, 63, 66, 68, 69, 70; on harbor, 110, 113, 118; on industry, 120; on unions, 131; on traffic congestion, 151; on automobile ownership, 164; on electric railways, 176; and boosterism, 190; as community contact, 198; on racial segregation, 200; of minority groups, 202; on party loyalty, 207; on political bosses, 213; on mayoralty election, 214; and reform movement, 217–218; on municipal electricity, 219–220, 236, 239–242, 244; on municipal ownership of utilities, 245
Nickerson, Thomas E., 58–60
Nogales, Ariz., 58
Non-Partisan City Central Committee, 212
Nonpartisan politics: in municipal government, 205, 212, 220, 275; reformers and, 209–210; in elections, 213, 215; and charter, 216; and municipal ownership of utilities, 233, 245
Nonwhites, 82, 83, 199, 201. *See also* Chinese; Colored minority; Japanese; Mexicans; Negroes; Orientals

Oakland, 133, 143
Occupations: changes in, 2, 23; of early immigrants, 64; of cities, 69, 72; distribution of, in selected cities, 122, 124, 133; distribution of, between Negro and other male, 199
Odd Fellow lodges, 187
Ohio, 64, 66, 81
Oil, 131, 132. *See also* Petroleum industry
Oklahoma, 81
Olden, William R., 53
Olmsted, Frederick Law, Jr., 157, 258
Omaha, Nebr., 70
Oneonta Park, 154, 155
Open shop, 130, 131
Oregon, 65, 66
Orientals, 145–146, 195, 200. *See also* Chinese; Japanese
Otis, Harrison Gray, 130, 131
Owens River project, 97–98
Owens Valley Aqueduct, 99, 105, 213, 220, 223, 233–234
Owensmouth, 104–105, 155

Pacific Electric Railway Company, 89, 91
Pacific Electric Railway Corporation, 92, 104, 118, 154, 229; and industry, 148,

Protestants, 27, 35

Public authority, 24; and highway construction, 92, 94, 105; and central business district, 148; and electric railways, 165, 177, 178; and private enterprise, 206, 209, 212, 217–218; and political machine, 207; and suburban development, 247. *See also* Municipal authority

Public health, 29, 258

Public order, 26, 34–35, 205–206, 220

Public ownership, *see* Municipal ownership

Public services, 208–209, 228, 260, 271

Public utilities, 2; and private enterprise, 41–42, 229; and urban expansion, 103–104, 142–144; for industry, 131–132, 150–151; and decentralization, 153; and municipal authority, 205–206, 212; and politics, 207–208, 233; public ownership of, 212, 229, 234–235; and Boulder Dam, 240. *See also* Electricity; Gas; Harbor; Highways; Railways; Telephone; Water supply

Pueblos, 6–7, 10, 20–21, 23–27, 258

Radicalism, 2, 218, 229

Railroads, 1; transcontinental, 43–46, 48, 52, 58–59, 61–62; maps of, 47, 57; bond issues for, 53–55; and immigrants, 64–67, 69–70; and trade, 120; and industry, 131, 150–151; rail yards for, 138; and politics, 206–207

Railway system, electric: and urban expansion, 85–86, 105, 143, 147, 164, 185; maps of, 88, 93, 173; and residential dispersal, 151; failure of, 151, 153, 161, 250, 274; and fragmentation, 164, 275; franchises for, 166, 169; and competition, 166–167, 170; municipalization of, 172, 174–175, 177–178, 185, 212, 245–246; and Depression, 183, 185; and neighborhood associations, 195; and municipal authority, 205–206; private ownership of, 229; and city planning, 250; rejection of, 276. *See also* Interurban railways

Railways, cable, 40, 86–87

Railways, horse-drawn, 40–42, 142

Rancheros, 8–9, 13–14, 16

Ranchers, 16–17, 53, 69–70

Ranches, 18, 19

Ranchos, 8, 10, 12–14, 17–18

Rapid transit system, *see* Railway system, electric

Real estate, 63; taxes for education, 34; and subdividers, 41–42; speculation and population growth, 67, 74, 121; subdivision and urban expansion, 85–86, 89, 97, 102–104; and road costs, 92; values, and location of harbor, 113; speculation and electric railway system, 185; values, and neighborhood associations, 195; progres-

sive position on, 235; and zoning, 254, 255; values, and rezoning Wilshire Boulevard, 261–262. *See also* Land; Subdivision; Suburbs; Urban development; Urban expansion

Realty Board, 98, 236, 254

Recall, 212–213, 243

Reconstruction Finance Corporation, 102, 243–244

Red River Valley, Canada, 66

Redondo Beach, 109, 110

Referendum, 212, 240, 262

Reformers, 1, 2; on electric railways, 165–166; and defeat of political machine, 209–213; accomplishments of, 215; decline of, 216–218, 221; and political consensus, 220; for integrated metropolis, 228; for municipal ownership of utilities, 231, 232–233, 235, 239, 245; for planning, 248, 249. *See also* Progressives

Regional planning, 247–248. *See also* City planning

Regional Planning Commission, 249, 251, 252–253, 265

Regional Planning Conference, 249

Regional Planning Department, 249

Religion, 27, 35–36, 41, 197. *See also* Buddhist shrines; Catholic Church; Churches; Jews; Protestants

Religious congregations, 98, 105, 192, 201–203

Republican party, 187, 207–210, 212, 214–217

Residences: dispersal of, 1, 143–147, 151, 154, 161, 178, 273; Los Angeles as community of, 108, 123; separation from business, 138, 253; and creation of garden suburb, 157; and electric railways, 165; segregation in, 200; and residential-income classification, 255, 257, 261. *See also* Suburbs

Restrictive deeds, 145–147, 194–195, 200, 248

Roadways and streets, 25; and municipal authority, 29, 34, 206; from private to public responsibility, 92–95; and neighborhood associations, 195; and traffic congestion, 250–251; and subdivisions, 252. *See also* Highways; Transportation

Roberts, Marshall O., 48

Robinson, Charles Mulford, 265

Rochester, N.Y., 123, 124

Rocky Mountain states, 64

Roosevelt, Theodore, 98, 211

Rose, Harry, 217

Rosecrans, William S., 44–48

Rubber companies, 123, 129, 132

Rural tradition, 188–191, 198, 273, 276

Russian immigrants, 75, 198